Walk
of
Fame
Directory

A Walking Guide

Directory, Guide and Map

copyright 1993
Michael H. Kwas
The Hollywood Chamber of Commerce
under license authorized by
Curtis Management Group Indianapolis, IN 46202 USA
Marketing and Distribution by
Exposure Unlimited   Grandville, MI

Hollywood Walk of Fame Directory is available at
special discounts for bulk purchases for fund
raising or educational purposes. For details,
contact the Marketing Department.

Typesetting and Publication by
The Hollywood Connection

Marketing and Distribution by
Exposure Unlimited
3087 - 30th Street
Grandville, MI 49418

Library of Congress Card Number 93-61359
ISBN 0-9637955-0-3

Book Design by Author
All photographs from the collection of
Sharon and Michael H. Kwas

Trademark Information:
Hollywood, Walk of Fame, Hollywood Sign and
Hollywood Chamber of Commerce are all copyrighted
trademarks of the Hollywood Chamber of Commerce,
under license authorized by Curtis Management
Group, Indianapolis, IN 46202 USA

Manufactured in The United States of America
First U.S. Edition October 1993

10 9 8 7 6 5 4 3 2 1

90000

9 780963 795502

Dedicated to...

This premiere edition is dedicated to my three daughters,

Tristine, Tracy and Jessica

for their faith and understanding.

Acknowledgments

My Wife Sharon: For her consistent faith, support and priceless assistance, along with the comment, "I don't think you'll ever finish this, and you probably don't really want to." (Because it's really a never-ending hobby.)

Jack R. Harper: Owner of Heritage Record Shop, Grand Rapids, MI, who provided invaluable assistance with the Recording category, providing from memory, most artists and their recordings. Jack also opened his private collection of biographical books providing many of the birth dates.

Rosa Kim: My personal "Hollywood Connection". A Hollywood native (yes, there actually are a few) for her continued interest, support and valuable input on research and interview sources, but more importantly for a valued friendship.

Jessica Kwas: Maps and illustrations.

Ralph Edwards for his This is Your Life Classics televised on AMC which provides treasured memories to all fans of movies and television.

Ruth Harper: For proofreading and critiquing with a sharp eye and keen observations, and the grammatical suggestions which I humbly accept with gratitude.

Marvin Stern, of Birns & Sawyer, whose company provided excellent reference information.

Dick Sheehan: Of Hollywood National Studios, for historical information.

George Turner: Of the American Society of Cinematographers, for information about movie studios past and present.

Jean Hulst, of <u>Complete Exteriors</u> for the typing with diligence, patience, speed, accuracy and interpretating my handwriting.

Complete Exteriors, of Wyoming, MI, for the use of the equipment for Jean to do her job so well.

Frances Howard Goldwyn Hollywood Regional Library: for the otherwise unavailable books about Hollywood and Hollywood's people.

American Movie Classics: the cable television channel for providing many hours of classic movies with introductions by Bob Dorian along with credits, and their <u>Reflections on the Silver Screen</u> interviews with Dr. Richard Brown.

Our gratitude goes to the <u>*Hollywood Chamber of Commerce,*</u> especially *Ana Martinez-Holler*, Director of Public Relations, for endorsing this book and our participation in preparing and publishing it.

Mistakes, we've made a few,
but then again, too few to mention.
We each accept full responsibility,
then blame each other.

Special Thanks

A very special thank you to
the Orchid Suites Hotel
(a Hollywood Chamber of Commerce member)

In addition to their reasonable rates for excellent
service, their location is convenient and safe making it
a perfect starting point for any walking tour of
Hollywood.

The owner, Joseph Blum, manager Ijaz Kahn and their
entire staff have proven to be reliable, courteous,
honest, helpful and most of all friendly.

Located at 1753 Orchid, less than a city block directly
behind Mann's Chinese Theater and the Walk of Fame.
The Orchid Suites Hotel has served as my 1993
headquarters while researching the first edition of the
Walk of Fame Directory, *A Walking Guide* and other
Hollywood guides and publications.

To be honored with a star in the Hollywood's Walk of Fame, the world's most famous sidewalk, is a tribute as coveted and sought after as any of the entertainment industry's equally prestigious awards -- including the Oscar, Emmy, Grammy, Golden Mike or Tony. And, because it recognizes a life-long contribution of both public and peer appreciation, it is an honor uniquely in a class to itself, a permanent monument of the past, as well as the present.

Envisioned in 1958 as a lasting tribute to the personalities who helped make Hollywood the most famous city in the world, the Walk continues today as a superior asset to the community, perpetuating the aura that has made the name "Hollywood" synonymous with glamour, and remains one of the city's most widely seen tourist attractions.

Administered by the Hollywood Chamber of Commerce, the Walk of Fame was designated, in 1978, as a Cultural/Historic Landmark by the City of Los Angeles and has become a major component of the Hollywood Historic Trust. Through the efforts of the Trust, a continuing, self-financing program maintains the quality of honorees and the historic lure that is Hollywood.

Johnny Grant, Chairman of the Walk of Fame and Honorary Mayor of Hollywood, hopes you enjoy the memories your favorite stars have brought you the next time you visit the Walk of Fame. It is a permanent testimony to our community's dedication to maintaining the glamour the world recognizes as distinctly belonging to Hollywood.

Hollywood Chamber of Commerce

7000 Hollywood Boulevard   Suite 1   Hollywood, California 90028

Contents

People reading the names on the Walk of Fame

HOLLYWOOD'S WALK OF FAME

People reading the names on the Walk of Fame

Introduction

Hollywood is a city of prestige, fame and illusion.

While prestige and fame are, at best, temporary, the illusion is never-ending. Sometimes a name may be remembered far longer than an accomplishment and sometimes vice versa. Strange as it may seem, today's Hollywood residents are mostly unaware of the historical surroundings they encounter each day.

In fact, Historic Hollywood is disappearing at an alarming rate. Understandably, building codes and earthquake conditions make razing and new construction economically the most logical choice when compared to restoration or renovation. Therefore, the tragedy of vanishing 'landmarks,' difficult as it may be to watch, must be understood. With a revitalization plan in place since 1979, all salvageable structures are being preserved as well as today's building requirements allow.

As we look around, not much is immediately recognizable to remind us of the people or places which made Hollywood the Entertainment Capital of the World. Even the most ardent of movie fans will not easily identify most locations of important happenings. Some buildings, however, will seem immediately familiar as they have been seen in countless movies and television shows.

The Walk of Fame was created as one of the ways to refresh our memories and help keep alive the images of people we have seen or heard of in the past who have helped create the magical Hollywood we all want to remember.

The concept of the Walk of Fame was to offer a never-fading method to honor personalities for their accomplishments as well as a permanent, no cost way for tourists to enjoy their Hollywood visit and take a journey into Hollywood history.

The persons immortalized in this world-famous sidewalk have received an extreme honor, for as fleeting as fame is, it is important to the personalities as well as the public to preserve some of history's special moments in entertainment.

Every visitor has some movie interest. These interests may be the movies themselves, movie stars or things done behind the scenes. Whatever your personal interest may be, you will find every aspect of the entertainment industry represented.

The Walk of Fame encompasses the beginning of the industry through today, will grow into the future, and will always have an interest to each and every visitor.

It is common belief that the idea for Hollywood's Walk of Fame was conceived by Harry Sugarman who headed the then newly-formed Hollywood Improvement Association. The HIA established the Hollywood Assessment District to assess proposed Walk of Fame fronting businesses $85.00 per running foot. This created a fund just over $1 million for the sidewalk, trees and lighting. His idea was actually an extended concept of the courtyard collection of footprints at the original Grauman's Chinese Theater (Now Mann's Chinese Theater located at 6925 Hollywood Boulevard, Block 05). The idea was to create a permanent tribute to these famous people while improving on the quality and appearance of the rough footprints in concrete.

In 1956, the City Council approved using 3' X 3' squares of black terrazzo, and inset a star of contrasting pink terrazzo, outlined in bronze with the recipient's name and an emblem representing the earned category also in bronze. This project would include both sides of Hollywood Boulevard from Gower on the East to Sycamore on the West and both sides of Vine Street from Sunset on the South to Yucca on the North. (In 1993, the West boundary was extended to LaBrea. See map on page XX.) The original cost was estimated at approximately one million dollars. Official groundbreaking ceremonies were held February 9, 1960.

Several months earlier, September, 1958, in a special mass ceremony, the first eight Stars were dedicated. They were Preston Foster, Joanne Woodward, Ernest Torrence, Olive Borden, Edward Sedgwick, Louise Fazenda, Ronald Coleman and Burt Lancaster. Construction was completed in sixteen months with 1558 Stars dedicated.

Administered by the Hollywood Chamber of Commerce and the Hollywood Historic Trust, the Walk of Fame was designated in 1978, as a Cultural/Historic Landmark by the City of Los Angeles. Through the efforts of the Hollywood Historic Trust, a continuing, self-financing program maintains the quality of honorees and the historic lure that is Hollywood.

As Hollywood visitors travel this renowned sidewalk, they cannot possibly realize the number of hopefuls who have walked these same steps while seeking their opportunity to achieve fame in the entertainment industry. The dream of success including seeing their name embedded in this Walk has been a driving force for many.

Recently, Tom Hanks recalled his daily journey along the Walk of Fame prior to being in the business and during his early television days. He would read the names and recollect the achievements of each as he made his trek. As he lived only a few blocks off Hollywood Boulevard, this was a convenient pastime and reinforced his belief that he, too, could achieve this recognition. Faith and determination along with hard work made his dream possible. In June of 1992, he celebrated the dedication of his Star located near the Hollywood Roosevelt Hotel.

Garry Marshall introducing Tom Hanks at his Walk of Fame Star dedication ceremony on June 30, 1992.

Tom Hanks is not alone in this lonely walk, nor is this a recent way to help realize one's dreams. Since the first few Stars were implanted, hopefuls and those active, yet not discovered, made this same journey. Movie, television, music, theater and even radio personalities all dream of the day their name might be forever visible to the Hollywood visitor for recognition of their accomplishments. Almost as important to them is the fact that their name will then be seen by

others wishing to become famous, will serve as evidence that it is a possibility, and encourage them to continue the seemingly hopeless struggle to become "someone" in Hollywood.

This Directory has been designed as a *Walking Guide* to direct you to a favorite personality's Star location or to provide, in an uncomplicated format, other information about a celebrity honored with a Walk of Fame Star.

While studying the Walk of Fame, either looking down at the sidewalk while walking or reading lists in this book in the comfort of your home, motel or coffee shop, a few names will be immediately recognized as well as their claim to fame. Some names will be dragged out of the recesses of our memories; some accomplishments will totally evade recall and some names will seem unknown; and sometimes the reason for a Star being dedicated is unclear. Over two years of research has uncovered most of these mysteries, yet several names or accomplishments remain unclear. However, as our research is constant, subsequent volumes will update existing information as well as provide new additions.

The Walk of Fame is an amazing tribute to the pioneers and greats in the entertainment industry. In addition to the never ending reminder of things great (and near great), this is also a major tourist attraction. The tourist (you) is the primary purpose in the creation, maintainence and on-going additions to the **Hollywood Walk of Fame**. Yet, until now, there has been no easy way to examine and understand this fascinating attraction. We will explain its creation, purpose and meaning to you as we progress through this guide.

In addition to showing location, category and achievement, many other details which may be unknown even to a devoted fan are listed in the Alphabetical Section. Information such as:

Date of birth
Real Name
Place of birth
Date of death
Cause of death
Place buried
Best remembered performance
Famous relatives
Number of stars earned
Occupation within category
Date and number of dedication
Miscellaneous notes

are included to help you discover who some of these people are and why they became a part of Hollywood's history.

Included in this book, you will find photos that illustrate the Walk of Fame in all its glory as well as its shame. Even though this is a memorial and a representation of Hollywood to the public, it has been terribly abused and seemingly forgotten at times. Pieces of some stars have been broken just by use and shoddily repaired or neglected, some have had letters or symbols chopped out and stolen and some have even been improperly built and installed.

The daily cleaning requirement is often neglected by some of the lazy or uncaring shop owners. Many others diligently perform the early morning ritual of sweeping and washing the sidewalk prior to opening for business. Some even polish the brass letters and scrape away the gum and food spills.

Early morning cleaning ritual in front of the Masonic Temple on Hollywood Boulevard.

Bela Lugosi's Star, after a typical day's use as a sidewalk.

Please, in your journey along the Walk of Fame, be respectful, not only to the maintenance factor, but to the memories contained in each of these 3 X 3 squares. ☆

How to Use This Book

Memories. . .

Millions of memories are captured in this unusual and most famous of all walkways. People who have molded entertainment and the ways in which we are entertained are immortalized forever here.

As a visitor to Hollywood, you can see and touch memorials to these people. Unfortunately, why they became famous is sometimes difficult to remember. In fact, some names aren't even familiar.

This Directory has been developed and is designed to make all of the above a little easier.

Included you will find:

Who is this?
What did they do?
When/where were they born?
When/how did they die?
Where are they buried?
Who are they related to?
What is their real name?
What category made them famous?
Where is their Star located?
How many Stars do they have?

How many Stars are there?
How did it all begin?
How is a Star earned?
Who maintains it?
When were they honored?

All this and more is included, when available, for all of the dedicated Stars on the Walk of Fame.

The Chapters in this book have been developed with careful consideration. The author has no idea where you will be as you read this, therefore, the various sorting of compiled data will simplify any type of search you may wish. Whether you are actually walking the Boulevard, sitting in the comfort of your home or motel room, or in an airplane on your way to L.A., our intent is to make your "visit" painless, uncomplicated and fun.

Obviously, this Walk of Fame is a permanent monument to these creators of entertainment. But, it is much more. The concept, creation and people here deserve more than just walking by reading their names.

The purpose of this book is twofold.

First, as *a Walking Guide* to help you locate a particular Star location or to explain who or why some Stars are here. Second, as a permanent souvenir of your visit to Hollywood and your walk along the Walk of Fame. You can read this book again and again to relive this visit for years to come.

Chapter 9 is a sequential list with a starting point at the LaBrea Gateway. As we proceed following the map (in chapter 8), every Star, including undedicated blank stars, is listed in order as we follow the suggested route starting on the north side of Hollywood Boulevard heading east from LaBrea.

As an example, to find {36/64} the Block Information Section will tell us that Block 36 is on the south side of Hollywood Boulevard, and to find Star 64, we will travel west from McCadden Place toward Highland Avenue and count 64 Stars. Also provided will be the address and name of the business located nearest to this Star. In this case the address is 6776 and near McDonald's. Using this example, we have just located Marilyn Monroe's Star.

Chapter 10 is an alphabetical (by last name) list which includes a "fingernail sketch" paragraph to help identify those names not immediately recognizable. Detailed explanations precede this list. This is also the Index.

We are confident that the years of research and the data manipulation used to create these sorted listings will make any name or location easy to find.

For cross-referencing ease, detailed maps have been included in Chapter 8. Each Block is numbered for quick reference of {Block/Star}. This will give you an idea from where-you-are to where-you-want-to-go.

This Directory has been designed to be "user friendly." We have left "plenty of room" in white space and in the margins for your personal notes to be written. This is just one more way to help make your trek along Hollywood Boulevard and Vine Street more enjoyable and convenient.

You will probably like to pick up another copy of this Directory to keep clean as it makes a great souvenir. Keep one near your television for a movie reference guide.

Also consider The Walk of Fame Directory, A Walking Guide as gifts for friends and relatives back home. It will be used, valued and remembered far longer than the typical T-shirt, ashtray or keychain. They will appreciate it more and think of you every time they read through it. ✩

A common Hollywood Boulevard sight. A movie being made. This one is in front of the Guiness Museum of World Record.

Dedication

A Walk of Fame Star is a permanent reminder of accomplishments earned by the individual. Stars are selected primarily by their fans. This is not an award that can just be purchased by someone wanting to see his or her name in the sidewalk.

However, there is a cost of placing a star upon selection; at this writing it is $5000.00. This amount includes the cost of removing the blank Star which is presently at the location, making a new Star with the category emblem and name of the recipient, publicity and news releases, the cost of city security, barricades, dignitaries and the formal ceremony.

Nomination for a celebrity to receive a star can be made by anyone using a nomination form available from the Hollywood Chamber of Commerce at 7000 Hollywood Boulevard. This is usually done by a fan club, fan, family members or friends who can finance the procedure. Nominations are accepted by the Hollywood Chamber of Commerce during the scheduled 60-day nomination period announced each year to Hollywood's entertainment trade publications and print and broadcast media. Nomination of an individual or

group must be approved by the *Walk of Fame Committee*. Approval sometimes requires several annual nominations before a nominee is selected to receive a Star. The fifteen to twenty most qualified artists nominated are eligible for a Star to be installed in the Walk during the subsequent year. Those not selected for the current year are requested to resubmit for the following nomination period.

As mentioned, nomination and financing is not enough. The nominated person must also qualify by meeting the following criteria:

1. Professional achievement
2. Longevity of five years or more
3. Contribution to the community
4. Guarantee to personally attend the dedication ceremony (posthumous awards require a five year waiting period).

After nomination approval and ability to meet these requirements, the celebrity's application must go before a nomination committee headed by Johnny Grant, Chairman. The committee members' identities are naturally kept confidential as they would otherwise be bombarded with letters and other communications in an attempt to persuade them to select a favored person. After the Walk of Fame Committee has made its selections, the Chamber's Board of Directors also vote to approve the Star and then for a final vote, the names are submitted to the City of Los Angeles' Board of Public Works Department.

Although approximately two stars per month are dedicated, there are far more nominations that can receive awards. This should explain why, when you notice a name conspicuously missing from this list that you are sure is deserving of one, or if you see a name that you believe is not deserving or seems unknown, it is not an oversight. Maybe at the time of selection the person deserving was up against stiff competition of several other deserving people and was passed up by a slim margin, or the date for the dedication ceremony could not be mutually agreed upon. (see #4 above) The seemingly unknown (to you) may be highly regarded by others and receive a higher vote. There are also quite a few industry people who achieve their success "behind the scenes," and their names may not be recognized. It is an entirely fair procedure although the Stars in the sidewalk sometimes lead us to believe otherwise.

As *Chairman of the Walk of Fame, Johnny Grant* has often been asked about the possibility of running out of blank Stars for new dedications. This has been unlikely for quite some time, and as of August 1, 1993, there are still 569 blank

Stars scattered along the 3-plus miles of the terrazzo sidewalk.

However, as part of a $4.4 million Hollywood Boulevard Improvement Program, the Walk of Fame will be expanded from the present west ending block of Sycamore Avenue to LaBrea Avenue. To be known as the LaBrea Gateway, the new beginning of the walkway will contain 148 new Stars, a combination of 29 dedicated as well as 119 blank Stars. This makes 688 blank Stars and with an average addition of 2 newly dedicated Stars replacing these blanks per month. This means there are enough to last until the year 2021. At this writing, construction has begun and the old sidewalk has been torn out. The new section of the Walk of Fame will include new street surface and landscaping to match the existing section.

North side of Hollywood Boulevard, near the Screen Actors Guild, old walk being torn up for new Walk of Fame extension.

Additional modifications to the Walk of Fame include: addition of palm trees, new lighting, street furniture, and an information kiosk all as part of the

Hollywood Boulevard District Urban Design Plan. This project will make Hollywood Boulevard an attractive tourist destination increasing it's beauty and accessibility.

A special mass dedication ceremony will launch the new walkway with 29 well deserving celebrities being honored. These celebrities are Pearl Bailey, The Beatles, Irving Berlin, Lloyd Bridges, Sam Cook, The Dead End Kids, Frances Dee, George Fisher, John Garfield, Dan Haggerty, Signe Hasso, Jerry Herman, Pedro Infante, Katy Jurado, Clevon Little, Frankie Lymon, Mako, Spanky McFarland, Thelonious Monk, Terry Moore, Paul Newman, The Nicholas Brothers, Sidney Poitier, Jon Provost, Mamie Van Doren, Vera-Ellen, Richard Webb, Stevie Wonder and Efrem Zimbalist, Jr. The location of these Stars cannot be included at this time due to publication deadlines, but these as well as subsequent dedications will be included in June 1994 edition of *The Walk of Fame Directory*.

In 1960, a similar but smaller mass dedication was held when the Walk of Fame was first introduced. The first eight honorees were: Olive Bordon, Ronald Coleman, Louise Fazenda, Preston Foster, Burt Lancaster, Edward Sedgwick, Ernest Torrence and Joanne Woodward.

These ceremonies are planned months in advance to coincide with the celebrity's schedule, as one of the requirements is to be present at the dedication. This is one sure way to see at least one celebrity white in Hollywood. Many times at these ceremonies, you will get to see other personalities such as producers, writers or directors whom you would not otherwise recognize even if you did see them on the streets or in the restaurants of Hollywood. The crowd also usually includes several other imediately recognizable movie or television stars who are friends of the nominee.

And of course, the television cameras and crews for several popular shows will be there allowing you the added pleasure of possibly appearing on television yourself. The shows routinely covering these dedications include Entertainment Tonight, Current Affair and all the local and national network news shows. These shows are usually aired the day following the dedication ceremony. You may wish to set your VCR in advance or call a friend back home (taking into account any time change that may be involved) to capture another Hollywood moment. Please try to ask a Chamber of Commerce representative for the actual air date.

During the school year, you may even get to see the fantastic Hollywood High School marching band as they play "Hooray for Hollywood."

Overall, these ceremonies are well worth the time spent waiting and watching.

*To find out if there will be a ceremony during your visit to Hollywood, contact the **Hollywood Chamber of Commerce** for dates, times and addresses. They are located at 7000 Hollywood Boulevard, in the Roosevelt Hotel, on the southwest corner at Orange (Block 38). The telephone number is **213-469-8311**.* ☆

Johnny Grant, George Kennedy and Bill Welch at the
October 17, 1991 dedication ceremony of George Kennedy's
Walk of Fame Star.

Johnny Grant, George Kennedy and Bill Welch at the
October 17, 1991 dedication ceremony of George Kennedy's
Walk of Fame Star.

Kim Basinger's Walk of Fame Star four hours before
dedication ceremony.

July 8, 1992, at the dedication ceremony of Kim Basinger's
Walk of-Fame Star. (Kim is in the white dress)
This eventwas also used by Paramount to promote the
opening of the movie *Cool World*.

4

Categories

There are five categories in which the dedicated Stars can be earned. They are:

☆ Live Theater
☆ Motion Pictures
☆ Radio
☆ Recording
☆ Television

On the following pages are listed the most popular and most often mentioned professions within these five categories for the personalities immortalized on the **Hollywood Walk of Fame**, and brought to life in this *Walk of Fame Directory, A Walking Guide.*

Radio

Actor
Actress
Announcer
Author
Bandleader
Comedian
Comedienne
Commentator
Composer
Conductor
Director
Disc Jockey
Evangelist
Gossip Reporter
Host
Humorist
Interviewer
Lyricist
Master of Ceremonies
Musical Satirist
Narrator
Newscaster
Orchestra Leader
Producer
Singer
Sportscaster
Ventriloquist
Writer

Live Theater

Actor
Actress
Comedian
Dancer
Entertainer
Producer
Director

Record

Actor
Arranger
Bandleader
Comedian
Composer
Conductor
Gospel Singer
Musician
Opera Singer
Orchestra Leader
Organist
Pianist
Singer
Songwriter

Television

Actor
Actress
Animator
Announcer
Author
Bandleader
Basketball Player
Columnist
Comedian
Comedienne
Commentator
Composer
Conductor
Dancer
Executive
Host
Hostess
Impressionist
Interviewer
Musician
Narrator
Newscaster
Orchestra Leader
Panelist
Personality
Pianist
Producer
Singer
Sportscaster
Ventriloquist
Writer

Motion Picture

Acting Teacher
Actor
Actress
Animated Character
Announcer
Author
Cameraman
Cartoonist
Censor
Cinematographer
Columnist
Comedian
Comedienne
Composer
Costume Designer
Dancer
Director
Executive
Exhibitor
Inventor
Lyricist
Magician
Make Up Artist
Mogul
Narrator
Pioneer
Producer
Screenwriter
Singer
Special Effects
Stuntman
Theater Owner
Vaudeville Performer
Writer

13

Some of the different things you may notice about the Stars on the Walk of Fame
as you walk along Hollywood Boulevard or Vine Street.

Celeste Holm's emblem has been chisled out and stolen.

Maurice Diller's Star, spelled Mautitz Stiller

Star covered prior to a dedication ceremony.

Sidewalk raised and patched after earthquake.

Robert Shaw's emblem has been installed crooked.

Betty Compson's Star area, broken and "repaired".

Multiple Stars

Having a Star on the Walk of Fame is an extreme honor and once in a lifetime would be something to be proud of forever. However, some Walk of Famers have earned more than one Star.

The following lists show the multiple recipients in alphabetical order with their category, number of Stars *and their locations*. Some have earned more than one Star in the same category. As an example, in the Motion Picture category one may have been recognized as an Actor and later became a Director. In the Recording category one may have begun as a Singer and developed into a Songwriter or Composer.

Most multiple Stars have been awarded in different categories. Occasionally a person's accomplishment or character may have evolved from Radio to Television as an example.

More often the honoree has multiple talents and may have been well known and deserving as a Singer as well as an Actor.

The following abbreviations have been used in these lists:

> MP = Motion Pictures
>
> TV = Television
>
> RA = Radio
>
> RE = Recording
>
> LT = Live Theater

This information has never before been offered. The age of computers and database management has made the manipulation of input data simple, convenient, and as you can see, fun. We hope you enjoy this type of *new* information. ☆

Two Stars

Ben Alexander	MP	31/55	Rory Calhoun	MP	04/57
	TV	13/19		TV	17/28
Fred Allen	RA	08/43	Judy Canova	MP	06/37
	TV	04/21		RA	07/04
Steve Allen	RA	26/62	Leo Carrillo	MP	27/61
	TV	17/74		TV	26/26
Don Ameche	RA	15/41	Jack Carson	RA	14/38
	TV	20/76		TV	25/26
Eve Arden	RA	15/16	Ilka Chase	MP	14/36
	TV	35/25		TV	07/48
Desi Arnaz	MP	15/21	Nat "King" Cole	RE	09/48
	TV	23/10		TV	18/58
Lew Ayres	MP	14/01	Ronald Colman	MP	06/66
	RA	17/57		TV	27/42
Jack Bailey	RA	17/98	Broderick Crawford	MP	05/58
	TV	13/49		TV	36/20
Lucille Ball	MP	31/57	Bob Crosby	RA	15/32
	TV	21/15		TV	23/05
Lynn Bari	MP	21/25	Xavier Cugat	RE	27/13
	TV	15/25		TV	25/50
Lionel Barrymore	MP	17/51	Robert Cummings	MP	09/46
	RA	27/83		TV	17/78
William Bendix	RA	24/36	Cass Daley	RA	35/19
	TV	18/25		TV	15/53
Milton Berle	RA	07/18	Bette Davis	MP	18/60
	TV	18/07		TV	18/50
Charles Bickford	MP	36/72	Joan Davis	MP	26/32
	TV	24/71		RA	17/89
Ray Bolger	MP	36/54	Dennis Day	RA	38/86
	TV	37/48		TV	33/116
Pat Boone	RE	27/56	Doris Day	MP	08/17
	TV	23/30		RE	23/44
Bill Boyd	MP	16/65	Yvonne DeCarlo	MP	21/39
	RA	20/94		TV	08/39
Charles Boyer	MP	28/14	Cecil B. DeMille	MP	16/51
	TV	28/10		RA	22/61
Eddie Bracken	RA	27/88	Andy Devine	RA	23/14
	TV	07/50		TV	29/24
George Brent	MP	16/16	Walt Disney	MP	04/06
	TV	24/76		TV	08/05
Fanny Brice	MP	13/43	Melvyn Douglas	MP	13/31
	RA	25/80		TV	10/63
Vanessa Brown	MP	27/37	Paul Douglas	MP	24/25
	TV	32/47		TV	06/15
Bob Burns	MP	27/01	James Dunn	MP	11/17
	RA	27/37		TV	38/20
Spring Byington	MP	12/33	Jimmy Durante	MP	11/17
	TV	18/51		RA	24/23

Two Stars

Ralph Edwards	RA	21/29		Gabby Hayes	RA	13/25
	TV	23/20			TV	17/61
Faye Emerson	MP	12/03		Helen Hayes	MP	23/15
	TV	09/02			RA	11/23
Dale Evans	RA	33/104		Louis Hayward	MP	25/58
	TV	16/62			TV	24/12
Geraldine Farrar	MP	24/73		Van Heflin	MP	15/46
	RE	16/15			TV	20/62
Charles Farrell	MP	04/17		Horace Heidt	RA	27/55
	TV	27/30			TV	33/90
Frank Fay	MP	23/50		Paul Henreid	MP	29/26
	RA	17/13			TV	17/65
W.C. Fields	MP	38/10		Jean Hersholt	MP	12/45
	RA	15/39			RA	08/57
Eddie Fisher	RE	18/41		Alfred Hitchcock	MP	32/14
	TV	17/47			TV	04/49
Barry Fitzgerald	MP	23/06		Celeste Holm	MP	25/54
	TV	04/66			TV	06/11
Errol Flynn	MP	34/09		Miriam Hopkins	MP	16/05
	TV	38/18			TV	06/11
Nina Foch	MP	28/36		Lena Horne	MP	23/49
	TV	04/41			RE	23/01
Red Foley	RE	18/63		Warren Hull	RA	23/35
	TV	28/06			TV	20/48
Arlene Francis	RA	31/51		Kim Hunter	MP	27/34
	TV	16/67			TV	16/24
Betty Furness	MP	26/54		Boris Karloff	MP	16/63
	TV	09/20			TV	34/25
Ed Garner	RA	33/20		Buster Keaton	MP	10/27
	TV	34/43			TV	18/56
Judy Garland	MP	16/25		Arthur Kennedy	MP	09/14
	RE	36/50			TV	24/65
Dave Garroway	RA	14/44		Otto Kruger	MP	16/66
	TV	23/27			TV	15/13
Jackie Gleason	RE	18/55		Kay Kyser	RA	27/12
	TV	28/15			RE	17/106
Jon Hall	MP	17/56		Frankie Laine	RE	14/04
	TV	05/07			TV	27/73
Ann Harding	MP	19/17		Dorothy Lamour	MP	28/48
	TV	37/60			RA	22/55
Sir Cedric Hardwicke	MP	19/01		Frances Langford	MP	25/72
	TV	33/44			RA	26/44
Phil Harris	RA	09/62		Angela Lansbury	MP	10/19
	RE	32/19			TV	26/36
Rex Harrison	MP	37/78		Mario Lanza	MP	06/25
	TV	30/20			RE	16/89
June Havoc	MP	33/66		Jerry Lewis	MP	06/33
	TV	13/45			TV	22/03

Two Stars

Liberace	RE	12/05	Garry Moore	RA	17/73
	TV	08/13		TV	24/08
Art Linkletter	RA	25/01	Frank Morgan	MP	17/96
	RA	14/22		RA	33/03
Harold Lloyd	MP	26/08	Edward R. Murrow	RA	18/01
	MP	37/65		TV	31/29
Gene Lockhart	MP	15/52	Harriet Nelson	TV	06/41
	TV	09/12		RA	23/16
June Lockhart	MP	15/27	Ozzie Nelson	TV	11/23
	TV	29/18		RA	23/16
Edmund Lowe	MP	14/30	John Nesbitt	MP	16/28
	TV	10/59		RA	22/41
Ida Lupino	MP	06/07	David Niven	MP	30/24
	TV	17/53		TV	27/49
Diana Lynn	MP	27/52	Edmond O'Brien	MP	16/48
	TV	29/06		TV	12/11
Jeanette MacDonald	MP	20/02	Margaret O'Brien	MP	33/52
	RE	24/53		TV	24/46
Guy Madison	RA	05/15	Pat O'Brien	MP	26/52
	TV	15/02		TV	22/63
Hal March	RA	25/22	Donald O'Connor	MP	24/02
	TV	32/55		TV	04/31
Mary Martin	RA	10/47	Louella O. Parsons	MP	31/31
	RE	25/42		RA	28/05
Groucho Marx	RA	06/45	John Payne	MP	20/54
	TV	16/68		TV	09/06
Raymond Massey	MP	16/39	Harold Peary	RA	27/70
	TV	35/15		TV	16/37
Mercedes McCambridge	MP	17/71	Vincent Price	MP	19/23
	TV	18/35		TV	12/39
Joel McCrea	MP	05/70	George Raft	MP	22/05
	RA	18/39		TV	25/52
Hattie McDaniel	MP	16/35	Ella Raines	MP	04/45
	RA	05/27		TV	33/42
James Melton	RA	28/13	Martha Raye	MP	18/26
	RE	18/30		TV	11/29
Ethel Merman	MP	38/78	Gene Raymond	MP	04/62
	RE	16/70		TV	17/101
Ray Milland	MP	27/36	Irene Rich	MP	18/62
	TV	24/45		RA	22/07
Thomas Mitchell	MP	27/84	Will Rogers	MP	13/63
	TV	21/05		RA	33/54
Vaughn Monroe	RA	16/98	Cesar Romero	MP	10/35
	RE	24/97		TV	16/31
Robert Montgomery	MP	31/65	Ann Rutherford	MP	37/42
	TV	27/57		TV	15/10

Two Stars ● Three Stars

Eva Marie Saint	MP	33/76
	MP	36/14
George Sanders	MP	24/38
	TV	04/58
Penny Singleton	MP	11/27
	RA	06/01
Red Skelton	RA	07/34
	TV	34/01
Kate Smith	RA	35/31
	RE	20/10
Ann Sothern	MP	24/78
	TV	24/39
Barry Sullivan	MP	22/23
	TV	25/88
Gloria Swanson	MP	36/30
	TV	15/58
Kent Taylor	MP	27/81
	TV	37/26
Lowell Thomas	MP	13/18
	RA	17/15
Arturo Toscanini	RA	28/53
	RE	08/27
Lurene Tuttle	RA	17/11
	TV	04/55
Vera Vague	MP	17/70
	RA	27/67
Sarah Vaughan	RE	17/59
	RE	37/45
Jack Webb	RA	38/70
	TV	23/41
Lawrence Welk	RE	10/37
	TV	27/09
Orson Welles	MP	24/93
	RA	33/16
Paul Whiteman	RA	27/06
	RE	20/04
Walter Winchell	RA	35/27
	TV	27/74
Teresa Wright	MP	24/09
	TV	13/57
Jane Wyman	MP	10/51
	TV	24/67
Loretta Young	MP	21/17
	TV	20/50
Roland Young	MP	12/13
	TV	15/37

Bud Abbott	MO	12/21
	RA	35/01
	TV	21/26
Jack Benny	MO	19/03
	RA	11/10
	TV	15/08
Edgar Bergen	MO	27/24
	RA	26/51
	TV	33/29
George Burns	LT	19/38
	MO	12/66
	TV	17/21
Eddie Cantor	MO	18/120
	RA	27/30
	TV	02/04
Perry Como	RA	02/99
	RE	30/09
	TV	15/14
Lou Costello	MO	16/61
	RA	21/76
	TV	08/41
Bing Crosby	MO	12/22
	RA	27/22
	RE	27/54
Nelson Eddy	MO	35/43
	RA	17/23
	RE	12/69
Douglas Fairbanks Jr	MO	13/28
	RA	20/17
	TV	29/44
Tennessee Ernie Ford	RA	09/96
	RE	22/104
	TV	36/44
Jane Froman	RA	03/52
	RE	05/28
	TV	12/77
Arthur Godfrey	RA	03/49
	RE	18/62
	TV	11/90
Dick Haymes	RA	06/27
	RA	26/12
	RE	02/55
Al Jolson	MO	18/74
	RA	21/28
	RE	02/81
Spike Jones	RA	08/61
	RE	10/86
	TV	22/30

Three Stars

Danny Kaye	MP	31/05
	RA	05/86
	RE	22/46
Sammy Kaye	RA	26/03
	RE	27/26
	TV	33/37
Guy Lombardo	RA	29/18
	RE	19/33
	TV	34/32
Dean Martin	MP	32/17
	RE	12/33
	TV	29/60
Conrad Nagel	MP	01/42
	RA	02/38
	TV	02/19
Dick Powell	MP	25/44
	RA	10/44
	TV	28/07
Basil Rathbone	MP	31/25
	RA	13/19
	TV	25/39
Roy Rogers	MP	02/31
	RA	01/56
	TV	09/66
Mickey Rooney	MP	02/77
	RA	15/10
	TV	31/33
Charles Ruggles	MP	08/26
	RA	34/40
	TV	09/47
Dinah Shore	RA	01/69
	RE	25/56
	TV	22/94
Frank Sinatra	MP	09/99
	RE	12/64
	TV	17/59
Jo Stafford	RA	01/02
	RE	12/50
	TV	08/33
Gale Storm	RA	09/03
	RE	11/28
	TV	05/68
Fred Waring	RA	18/22
	RE	13/03
	TV	01/90

Marie Wilson	MP	30/57
	RA	35/54
	TV	27/28
Ed Wynn	MP	11/66
	RA	35/06
	TV	16/45
Robert Young	MP	25/03
	RA	09/70
	TV	14/14

Four Stars

Bob Hope	MP	31/35
	RA	05/36
	TV	21/40
	LT	28/28
Tony Martin	MP	12/59
	RA	02/09
	RE	35/12
	TV	01/43

Five Stars

Gene Autry	LT	23/23
	MP	18/112
	RA	17/33
	RE	15/26
	TV	29/36

 Trivia Counts

Just for the record, as general trivia-type information, the following miscellaneous counts about the Walk of Fame Stars are included, to be found *nowhere* else.

As of August 31, 1993, the numbers of male and female personalities commemorated in the sidewalk are 1112 and 518 respectively.

Many of the Walk of Fame Stars represent the efforts and talents of other than individuals. These are listed as Groups. For our purposes a group is any two or more people working together to entertain us. Some examples would be a pair of Radio disc jockeys, a ventriliquist and his dummy, a husband and wife team, a sports team, musical groups, songwriters or illustrators. There are 29 such Stars at this publication date.

Animals have not gone unremembered either. However, only three have been selected for a Star to date, yet each is very deserving. All three just happen to be dogs, and all have made major contributions to entertainment and saving or reviving their studio. They are:

Lassie	30/04
Rin-Tin-Tin	27/41
Strongheart	17/43

Animated characters are also immortalized. As you read the following names, and picture these characters you may remember something special and realize why these four were selected.

Bugs Bunny	04/56
Mickey Mouse	65/32
Snow White	37/85
Woody Woodpecker	38/50

Trivia Counts

The number of Stars in each of the five categories is:

Live Theater	17
Motion Pictures	930
Radio	226
Recording	297
Television	442

The number of people having one or more dedicated Stars are:

One	1468
Two	165
Three	34
Four	2
Five	1

The most-watched television event of all time (at its time) was the launching and flight of Apollo VII. This is remembered in a big way, even for Hollywood. Although not represented with a Walk of Fame Star, the astronauts Edwin E. Aldrin, Michael Collins and Neil A. Armstrong have been immortalized in a circle on each of the four corners of the most famous intersection in the world, Hollywood and Vine.

The corner of Hollywood and Vine Walk of Fame intersects at each of the four corners with a circle dedicated to the Apollo VII flight and astronauts.

More fun and interesting counts and comparisons can be found in our soon-to-be-released companion book
Fun with the Walk of Fame

 Block Info

The following pages contain simple and easy-to-read and use identification information about each of the 39 blocks on the Hollywood Walk of Fame.

There are several reasons you may wish to refer to these pages. However, the most common uses will be to locate a specific Star using our unique Locator Numbers. The designation {06/47} for example is located on Block 06, which is on the North side of Hollywood Boulevard. Star 47 would be the forty-seventh Star from the corner at Orchid going east toward Highland.

The second use will be to identify where you are at any time while you are on the Walk of Fame. Occasionally you may become temporarily "lost" and want to reorient yourself in order to find another location. ☆

Block 01 is on the East side of LaBrea.
Going North from Marshfield to Hollywood.
There are total Stars with blank.

Block 02 is on the North side of Hollywood Boulevard.
Going East from LaBrea to El Cerrito.
There are total Stars with blank.

Block 03 is on the North side of Hollywood Boulevard.
Going North from El Cerrito to Sycamore.
There are total Stars with blank.

Block 04 is on the North side of Hollywood Boulevard.
Going East from Sycamore to Orange.
There are 70 total Stars with 17 blank.

Block 05 is on the North side of Hollywood Boulevard.
Going East from Orange to Orchid.
There are 73 total Stars with 03 blank.

Block 06 is on the North side of Hollywood Boulevard.
Going East from Orchid to Highland.
There are 70 total Stars with 12 blank.

Block 07 is on the North side of Hollywood Boulevard.
Going East from Highland to McCadden.
There are 54 total Stars with 11 blank.

Block 08 is on the North side of Hollywood Boulevard.
Going East from McCadden to Las Palmas.
There are 57 total Stars with 17 blank.

Block 09 is on the North side of Hollywood Boulevard.
Going East from Las Palmas to Cherokee.
There are 63 total Stars with 14 blank.

Block 10 is on the North side of Hollywood Boulevard.
Going East from Cherokee to Whitley.
There are 63 total Stars with 25 blank.

Block 11 is on the North side of Hollywood Boulevard.
Going East from Whitley to Hudson.
There are 58 total Stars with 20 blank.

Block 12 is on the North side of Hollywood Boulevard.
Going East from Hudson to Wilcox.
There are 45 total Stars with 21 blank.

Block 13 is on the North side of Hollywood Boulevard.
Going East from Wilcox to Cahuenga.
There are 64 total Stars with 25 blank.

Block 14 is on the North side of Hollywood Boulevard.
Going East from Cahuenga to Ivar.
There are 59 total Stars with 22 blank.

Block 15 is on the North side of Hollywood Boulevard.
Going East from Ivar to Vine.
There are 64 total Stars with 01 blank.

Block 16 is on the West side of Vine Street.
Going North from Hollywood to Yucca.
There are 116 total Stars with 01 blank.

Block 17 is on the East side of Vine Street.
Going South from Yucca to Hollywood.
There are 113 total Stars with 02 blank.

Block 18 is on the North side of Hollywood Boulevard.
Going East from Vine to Argyle.
There are 65 total Stars with none blank.

Block 19 is on the North side of Hollywood Boulevard.
Going East from Argyle to Vista Del Mar.
There are 27 total Stars with 11 blank.

Block 20 is on the North side of Hollywood Boulevard.
Going East from Vista Del Mar to Gower.
There are 98 total Stars with 45 blank.

Block 21 is on the South side of Hollywood Boulevard.
Going West from Gower to El Centro.
There are 63 total Stars with 26 blank.

Block 22 is on the South side of Hollywood Boulevard.
Going West from El Centro to Argyle.
There are 65 total Stars with 28 blank.

Block 23 is on the South side of Hollywood Boulevard.
Going West from Argyle to Vine.
There are 64 total Stars with none blank.

Block 24 is on the East side of Vine Street.
Going South from Hollywood to Selma.
There are 99 total Stars with 01 blank.

Block 25 is on the East side of Vine Street.
Going South from Selma to Sunset.
There are 94 total Stars with 14 blank.

Block 26 is on the West side of Vine Street.
Going North from Sunset to Selma.
There are 98 total Stars with 29 blank.

Block 27 is on the West side of Vine Street.
Going North from Selma to Hollywood.
There are 97 total Stars with none blank.

Block 28 is on the South side of Hollywood Boulevard.
Going West from Vine to Ivar.
There are 64 total Stars with none blank.

Block 29 is on the South side of Hollywood Boulevard.
Going West from Ivar to Cosmo.
There are 26 total Stars with 11 blank.

Block 30 is on the South side of Hollywood Boulevard.
Going West from Cosmo to Cahuenga.
There are 27 total Stars with 07 blank.

Block 31 is on the South side of Hollywood Boulevard.
Going West from Cahuenga to Wilcox.
There are 65 total Stars with 26 blank.

Block 32 is on the South side of Hollywood Boulevard.
Going West from Wilcox to Hudson.
There are 64 total Stars with 27 blank.

Block 33 is on the South side of Hollywood Boulevard.
Going West from Hudson to Cherokee.
There are 122 total Stars with 52 blank.

Block 34 is on the South side of Hollywood Boulevard.
Going West from Cherokee to Las Palmas.
There are 49 total Stars with 19 blank.

Block 35 is on the South side of Hollywood Boulevard.
Going West from Las Palmas to McCadden.
There are 36 total Stars with 11 blank.

Block 36 is on the South side of Hollywood Boulevard.
Going West from McCadden to Highland.
There are 77 total Stars with 33 blank.

Block 37 is on the South side of Hollywood Boulevard.
Going West from Highland to Orange.
There are 123 total Stars with 22 blank.

Block 38 is on the South side of Hollywood Boulevard.
Going West from Orange to Sycamore.
There are 89 total Stars with 14 blank.

Block 39 is on the South side of Hollywood Boulevard.
Going WQest from Sycamore to LaBrea.
There are total Stars with blank.

Maps

The following maps were re-designed at the last minute, as the new LaBrea Gateway had to be included. The Walk of Fame extension had just begun and was under construction in June of 1993 during our last visit.

This *Walking Guide* was initially developed prior to this addition and our original map was hastily corrected. The Block Information Chapter has also been updated.

Our Number Identification has been changed also. However, as mentioned earlier, the age of computers makes this fairly easy and mostly uncomplicated.

The original Block One is now Block Four, and Blocks 01, 02, and 03 are not detailed, although outlined.

Block One is the island cutoff as you would travel North on LaBrea arriving at Hollywood Boulevard.

We then walk on the North side of Hollywood heading East. This is the flow of our Block and Star Identification Numbers.

The Star Numbers are in sequence beginning with 01 from the starting corner heading in the direction indicated in Block Information Chapter. These directions are East on the North side of Hollywood, West on the South side of Hollywood, South on the East side of Vine and North on the West side of Vine.

At any time, walking the Boulevard or reading the *Walk of Fame Directory*, you can look up any personality's Star, read the numbers and locate it on these maps. Regardless of where you may be, the process of finding the location of any Block in relation to where you are is as easy as turning this page and looking at the map. ☆

Hollywood Highlights

Listed below are some additional places of interest you will encounter as you follow our _Walking Guide_ while walking along the Walk of Fame. Some places you may want to visit, others are great photo ops, and others will not appeal to you at all.

These are mentioned as they all have generated many questions from friends, relatives and tourists over the several years spent researching Hollywood.

Enjoy your Walk.

Brown Derby	1628	24	
C.C. Brown	7007	04	
Cannell Productions	7083	03	
Capitol Records	1750	17	
Chinese Theater	6925	05	
Doolittle Theater	1615	27	
El Capitan	6838	37	
Egyptian	6712	35	
First National Building	6777	07	
Frederick's	6608	33	
Galaxy	7021	04	
Guiness Museum	6764	36	
Janes House	6541	11	
Musso & Frank Grill	6667	09	
Pacific Theater	6433	13	
Palace	1735	16	
Pantages	6233	18	
Plaza Hotel	1637	27	
Roosevelt Hotel	7000	38	
This Is Your Life Display	7000	38	
Screen Actors Guild	7065	03	
Snow White	6769	07	

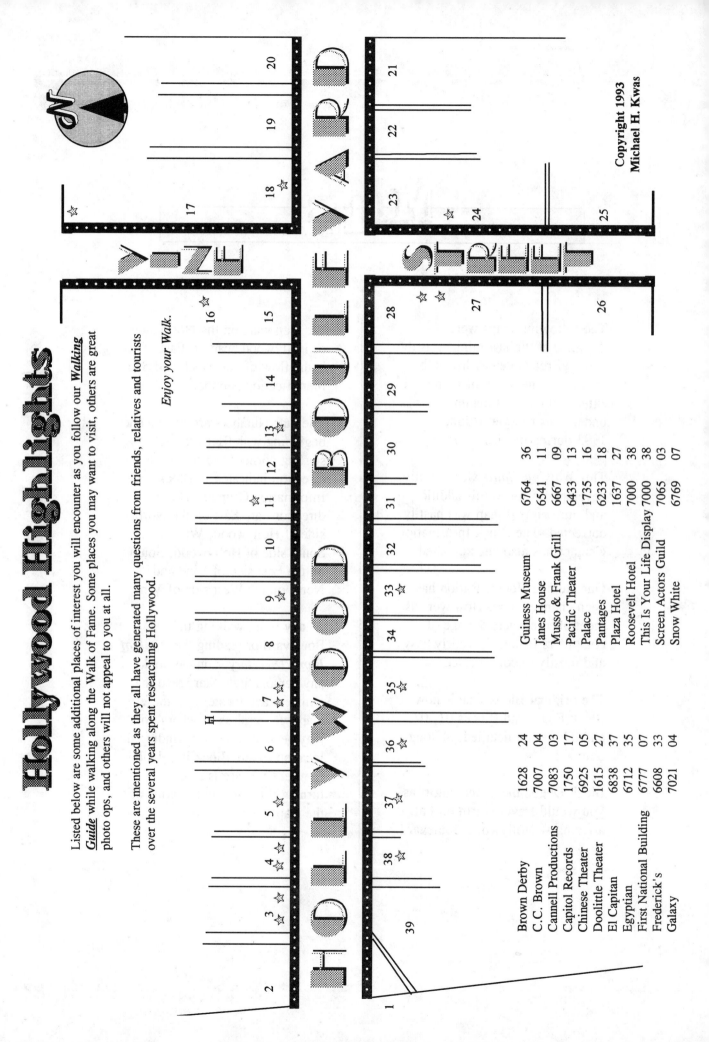

Walk of Fame Directory
Map and Block Info

HOLLYWOOD

Block	From	To
01	LaBrea	Hollywood
02	LaBrea	El Cerrito
03	ElCerrito	Sycamore
04	Sycamore	Orange
05	Orange	Orchid
06	Orchid	Highland
07	Highland	McCadden
08	McCadden	Las Palmas
09	Las Palmas	Cherokee
10	Cherokee	Whitley
11	Whitley	Hudson
12	Hudson	Wilcox

Block	From	To
13	Wilcox	Cahunga
14	Cahuenga	Ivar
15	Ivar	Vine
16	Hollywood	Yucca
17	Yucca	Hollywood
18	Vine	Argyle
19	Argyle	Vista Del Mar
20	Vista Del Mar	Gower
21	Gower	El Cerrito
22	El Cerrito	Argyle
23	Argyle	Vine
24	Hollywood	Selma

Block	From	To
25	Selma	Sunset
26	Sunset	Selma
27	Selma	Hollywood
28	Vine	Ivar
29	Ivar	Cosmo
30	Cosmo	Cahuenga
31	Cahuenga	Wilcox
32	Wilcox	Hudson
33	Hudson	Cherokee
34	Cherokee	Las Palmas
35	Las Palmas	McCadden
36	McCadden	Highland
37	Highland	Orange
38	Orange	Sycamore
39	Sycamore	Labrea

Hollywood Boulevard

Street names on map: LA BREA, EL CERRITO, SYCAMORE, ORANGE, ORCHID, HIGHLAND, McCADDEN, LAS PALMAS, CHEROKEE, WHITLEY, HUDSON, WILCOX, CAHUENGA, IVAR, YUCCA, VISTA DEL MAR, ARGYLE, GOWER, VINE, STREET, SUNSET BOULEVARD, MANSFIELD

Caution

Please be careful showing this Directory to friends, relatives and associates. Lending this book out is even more dangerous!

Everyone wants one; you may lose your only copy.

One sure fire-method to protect your valuable ***First Edition of the Hollywood Walk of Fame Directory*** is to purchase several copies as souvenirs and gifts.

Please return to the store where you got this issue and be prepared when you get home. ☆

Michael H. Kwas

Sequential

Let's Start!

Hollywood Boulevard! The magical street we have ALL heard of. Most of us have also wondered about the history and excitement that has happened along this mystical strip of road and sidewalk.

Yes. Most of what you have imagined happening here probably has happened at one time or another. Big stars, Big business deals, Big crimes, Big romances, Big cars, Big moments, Big money and much more.

This Guide and Directory is designed to begin at the new LaBrea Gateway, even though at this writing it is under construction and incomplete. So we will skip Blocks 01, 02, 03 and begin on Block 04 in front of Hollywood Galaxy. Be prepared for a little surprise when you get to the intersection of Hollywood and Vine. Most everyone visiting the Greater Los Angeles Area has stood on this corner, and certainly every Hollywood hopeful has looked up at the street sign and stepped off the curb here. Without a doubt, 98% of all these visitors have looked around in a 360 degree circle and said "So what's the big deal? This looks like a street corner found in any mid-sized city." And they would be correct. Looking at this intersection, this street or this city will immediately show you nothing. That's why we're here. To guide you along Hollywood Boulevard and explain what you are seeing. History and stories are everywhere. More detailed information can be found in our other book entitled *"Hollywood, A Historical Overview."*

The businesses located on these four corners have considerable turnover despite the fact that it is probably one of the most desirable locations in the United States to attract the tourism dollar. We will list the stores and businesses on the Boulevard in sequential order as of this writing.

Ready?

  Set?

    Go!

Details

✦✦✦✦✦✦✦✦✦✦✦✦✦✦✦✦✦✦✦✦✦✦✦✦✦✦✦✦✦✦✦✦✦✦✦

The blocks on Hollywood Boulevard are detailed first. The North side of the street from LaBrea to Gower is on the left side of the page heading East.

The right side of the page is the approximate corresponding South side of Hollywood Boulevard traveling West.

Vine Street is illustrated out of sequence, beginning at the end of Hollywood Boulevard at Gower (page 60), to make reading of double-sided maps a little easier.

This begins at Hollywood and Vine (page 61) on the northwest corner going North on Block 16 to Yucca, crossing West and then South on Blocks 17, 24 and 25. Cross West and head North on 26 and 27 back to Hollywood Boulevard.

North side going East

L
a
B
r
e
a

Hollywood Boulevard

G
o
w
e
r

South side going West

Yucca Street

East side
going North

West side
Going South

Sunset Boulevard

This page is provided for your convenience to take personal notes as you travel the Walk of Fame. You will discover many new names and accomplishments.

Hollywood Boulevard

by Michael H. Kwas

{Blocks 1,2 & 3}
Going East
From LaBrea to Sycamore

{Block 39}
Going West
From Sycamore to LaBrea

7051
The Beatles   RE
Sam Cooke   RE

7055
Thelonious Monk   RE

7057
Mamie Van Doren   MP

7059
Richard Webb   TV

7065   Screen Actors Guild
Lloyd Bridges   TV
John Garfield   MP
Katy Jurado   MP
Sidney Poitier   MP

7083   Stephen J. Cannell Productions
Pedro Infante   RE
Frankie Lymon   RE
The Nicholas Brothers   MP
Vera-Ellen   MP

7095
Irving Berlin   RE
Jerry Herman   LT
Mako   MP
Spanky McFarland   MP
Efrem Zimbalist, Jr.   TV

7060
Paul Newman   MP
Stevie Wonder   RE

7070
Dan Haggerty   TV

7072
George Fisher   RA

7076
Terry Moore   MP

7080
Pearl Bailey   RE
Frances Dee   MP
Signe Hasso   MP
The Dead End Kids   MP
Clevon Little   MP
John Provost   TV

Hollywood Boule

Welcome to the Walk of Fame, this area is known as the LaBrea Gateway. These are the 29 people mentioned in the Dedication Chapter. These Blocks and Stars were under construction at our last visit to the Walk of Fame and had not yet been assigned exact positions. By the time you read this these Stars should be in place.

Enjoy your Walk

u

by Michael H. Kwas

David Brian	35	☆
Blank	34	☆
Claire Windsor	33	☆
Blank	32	☆
Donald O'Connor	31	☆
Blank	30	☆
Ricardo Montalban	29	☆
Bob Hope	28	☆
Nancy Kelly	27	☆
Blank	26	☆
Bill Thompson	25	☆
Edward James Olmos	24	☆
Fay Bainter	23	☆
Paula Abdul	22	☆
Fred Allen	21	☆
Kim Basinger	20	☆
Mae Busch	19	☆
DeForest Kelley	18	☆
Charles Farrell	17	☆
Blank	16	☆
Kitty Kallen	15	☆
Mary Tyler Moore	14	☆
Alan Curtis	13	☆
Blank	12	☆
Jimmy Boyd	11	☆
Blank	10	☆
Noah Beery, Jr.	09	☆
Gloria Estefan	08	☆
Vilma Banky	07	☆
Blank	06	☆
Walt Disney	05	☆
Blank	04	☆
Richard Boleslawski	03	☆
Blank	02	☆
Jimmy Dodd	01	☆

4

Hollywood Boulevard

☆	*Roosevelt Hotel Parking*		*7024*
☆	61	Patti LaBelle	
☆	62	Placido Domingo	
☆	63	Blank	
☆	64	Charles Butterworth	
☆	*Andrea's Pizza*		*7038*
☆	65	Blank	
☆	66	James Gleason	
☆	67	Blank	
☆	68	Kathleen Williams	
☆	69	Blank	
☆	*Hollywood Liquor Store*		*7040*
☆	70	Jack Webb	
☆	71	Blank	
☆	72	Dick Jones	
☆	73	Blank	
☆	74	Ernst Lubitsch	
☆	*Souvenir Stop*		*7042*
☆	75	Blank	
☆	76	Elmo Lincoln	
☆	77	Blank	
☆	78	Ethel Merman	
☆	*International Love Boutique*		*7046*
☆	79	Blank	
☆	80	Lon Chaney	
☆	81	Blank	
☆	*Souvenir Boulevard*		*7046 W*
☆	82	Adele Jergens	
☆	83	Samuel Z. Arkoff	
☆	84	George Marshall	
☆	85	Blank	
☆	86	Dennis Day	
☆	87	Blank	
☆	88	Ann B. Davis	
☆	89	Blank	

38

{Block 04}
Going East
from Sycamore to Orange

{Block 39}
Going West
from Sycamore to LaBrea

Sycamore   **Sycamore**

3   **39**

Welcome to Hollywood and the Walk of Fame. Please read this <u>Walking Guide</u> thoroughly to enjoy your trek through entertainment history. There is much to see and learn here. This <u>Directory</u> has been developed to make your time here easy and fun.

by Michael H. Kwas

{Block 05}
Going East
From Orange to Orchid

Orange

4

7001	Hollywood Souvenirs	
Ethel Barrymore	70
Houdini	69
Wallace Beery	68
Mike Douglas	67
Barry Fitzgerald	66

7003	Haagen Dazs	
Barbara Eden	65
Roger Wagner	64
Phyllis Diller	63
Gene Raymond	62

7005	Hollywood Momentos	
Gene Nelson	61
Robert Stack	60
Diahann Carroll	59
George Sanders	58

7007	C.C. Brown Ice Cream	
Rory Calhoun	57
Bugs Bunny	56

7009	Fame and Fortune	
Lurene Tuttle	55
Blank	54
Lloyd Bacon	53
David Janssen	52

7013	Shelly's Cafe	
Lilli Palmer	51
Roger Corman	50
Alfred Hitchcock	49
Blank	48
Mitch Miller	47

7021	Hollywood Galaxy	
Blank	46
Ella Raines	45
Dick Van Dyke	44
Stan Laurel	43
Blank	42
Nina Foch	41
Blank	40
Regis Toomey	39
Blank	38
Lewis Milestone	37
Blank	36

Hollywood Boulevard

Roosevelt Hotel		7000
15	John Chambers	
16	Lily Pons	
17	Walter Lantz	
18	Errol Flynn	
19	Natalie Wood	
20	James Dunn	
21	The Everly Brothers	
22	Jo Van Fleet	
23	Gene Autry	
24	William Haines	
25	Cybil Shepherd	
26	Fred Niblo	
27	Angie Dickinson	
28	Sid Caesar	
29	Lionel Hampton	
30	Louis Armstrong	
31	Dudley Moore	
32	Mary Margaret McBride	
33	Mariette Hartley	
34	Anne Shirley	
35	Norman Jewison	
36	Joyce Compton	
37	Lalo Schifrin	
38	Douglas Fairbanks	
39	The Four Step Brothers	
40	Ann Sheridan	
41	Tony Danza	

38

Roosevelt Hotel Parking		7024
42	George Schlatter	
43	Mary Hart	
44	Engelbert Humperdinck	
45	Tichi Wilkerson-Kassel	
46	Joan Rivers	
47	Jaclyn Smith	
48	Chuck Norris	
49	Louis Gossett, Jr.	
50	Woody Woodpecker	
51	Keye Luke	
52	Levar Burton	
53	Vivian Vance	
54	The Original Fifth Dimension	
55	Liza Minelli	
56	Dean Stockwell	
57	Donna Summer	
58	Tom Hanks	
59	Brock Peters	
60	Fritz Freleng	

N

by Michael H. Kwas

{Block 05}
Going East
From Orange to Orchid

6925	*Mann's Chinese Theater*	
Billy Crystal		40
Basil Rathbone		39
John Green		38
Harry Langdon		37
Barbra Streisand		36
Charles McGraw		35
James Garner		34
Alan Young		33
Mickey Mouse		32
Lupe Velez		31
Michael Jackson		30
Lefty Frizzell		29
Army Archerd		28
Hattie McDaniel		27
Glen Campbell		26

6927	*Mann's Chinese Parking*	
Dorothy McGuire		25
Bruce Lee		24
John Charles Thomas		23
Casey Kasem		22
Lois Wilson		21
Tito Puente		20
Claire Trevor		19
Herb Alpert		18
Ward Bond		17
Blank		16
Guy Madison		15
Blank		14
Gail Russell		13
Blank		12
Gloria De Haven		11
Jerry Weintraub		10
Glenn Ford		09
The Carpenters		08
Jon Hall		07
Paul Williams		06

6935	*Casablanca Tours*	
Larry Semon		05
Lou Rawls		04
Robert Young		03
Lee Majors		02
Pola Negri		01

Hollywood Boulevard

Pro Electronics		6920
102	Peter Lawford	
103	Dionne Warwick	
104	Tennessee Ernie Ford	
105	Aretha Franklin	
106	James Cruze	

Hollywood Center		6922
107	The Harlem Globetrotters	
108	Eugene Ormandy	
109	Max Factor	
110	Eleanor Boardman	
111	Billy Barty	
112	Alice Faye	
113	Bill Cosby	
114	Carole Lombard	
115	Bette Midler	
116	George E. Stone	
117	Mickey Gilley	
118	Richard Denning	
119	Dennis Weaver	
120	Ethel Clayton	
121	Stan Chambers	
122	Elton Britt	
123	Chad Everett	

37

{Block 38}
Going West
From Orange to Sycamore

Orange

Roosevelt Hotel		7000
01	The Mills Brothers	
02	Guy Mitchell	
03	Arthur Cohn	
04	Pauline Frederick	
05	Jack Valenti	
06	Julie London	
07	Stephen J. Cannell	
08	Maureen O'Hara	
09	Ed McMahon	
10	W.C. Fields	
11	Hugh M. Hefner	
12	John Drew Barrymore	
13	Julio Iglesias	
14	Irving Thalberg	

38

5

by Michael H. Kwas

6845   *Starline Tour & Gift*

Bob Thomas	08	☆
Ida Lupino	07	☆
Gig Young	06	☆
Robert Rossen	05	☆
James Mason	04	☆
Sammy Kaye	03	☆
Bee Gees	02	☆
Penny Singleton	01	☆

6

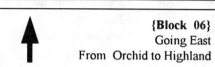

{Block 06}
Going East
From Orchid to Highland

Orchid

5

6925   *Mann's Chinese Theater*

Leonard Goldberg	73	☆
Ellen Drew	72	☆
Joan Collins	71	☆
Joel McCrea	70	☆
Earl Holliman	69	☆
Greta Garbo	68	☆
Olivia Newton-John	67	☆
Edgar Kennedy	66	☆
Julie Andrews	65	☆
Judy Holliday	64	☆
Billy Graham	63	☆
Beniamino Gigli	62	☆
Wayne Newton	61	☆
Buster Crabbe	60	☆
John Travolta	59	☆
Broderick Crawford	58	☆
Robin Williams	57	☆
Dinah Shore	56	☆
Charles Bronson	55	☆
Danny Thomas	54	☆
William Shatner	53	☆
William Dieterle	52	☆
Tom Selleck	51	☆
Creighton Hale	50	☆
Leon Shamroy	49	☆
Glenn Miller	48	☆
Johnny Grant	47	☆
Zsa Zsa Gabor	46	☆
Richard D. Zanuck	45	☆
Dick Powell	44	☆
Elton John	43	☆
Marion Martin	42	☆
Chill Wills	41	

Hollywood Boulevard

37

Masonic Temple   **6840**

062	Shirley Booth
063	Rod Serling
064	Clifton Webb
065	Harold Lloyd
066	Jane Russell
067	Paul Anka
068	Fred Thomson
069	Mahalia Jackson
070	Morey Amsterdam

Hollywood Tourist & Gifts   **6904**

071	Little Richard
072	Francis Lederer
073	Marlo Thomas
074	Marguerite De La Motte
075	Debbie Allen
076	Bruno Walter

Juice Master   **6906**

077	Burgess Merideth
078	Rex Harrison
079	Blank

Hollywood Emporium   **6908**

080	Dane Clark
081	Blake Edwards
082	Gregory LaCava
083	Cubby Broccoli
084	Phillips Holmes

Harley Davidson Shop   **6912**

085	Snow White
086	Jean Harlow
087	Tom Cruise

Hamburger Hamlet   **6914**

088	Phillips Lord
089	Roy Clark
090	Irving Reis
091	Clayton (Lone Ranger) Moore
092	Ann Miller
093	Charles Fries
094	Dinah Shore
095	Bobby Vinton
096	Veronica Lake
097	Richard & Robert Sherman

Gulliver's Travel   **6916**

098	Jeffery Hunter
099	Gary Collins
100	Sonny Burke
101	Ray Rennahan

by Michael H. Kwas

{Block 06}
Going East
From Orchid to Highland

{Block 37}
Going West
From Highland to Orange

6819   Hollywood Tours & Gifts

Leon Errol	49
Henry O'Neill	48
Ted Husing	47
Blank	46
Grocho Marx	45
Blank	44
Amelita Galli-Curci	43
Blank	42
Harriet Nelson	41
Blank	40
Frances Drake	39
Blank	38
Judy Canova	37
Blank	36
Mabel Normand	35
Billy Daniels	34
Jerry Lewis	33
Peter Frampton	32
Anita Louise	31
Blank	30
Y. Frank Freeman	29

6821   Hollywood Hamburger

Blank	28
Jules C. Stein	27
Henry Mancini	26
Mario Lanza	25
Blank	24
Bill Stern	23
Blank	22
Frank Parker	21
Blank	20
Anthony Perkins	19
Rex Allen	18
Taylor Holmes	17

6841   Pose With Stars

Sons of the Pioneers	16
Paul Douglas	15

6841   Budget-Rent-A-Car

Stuart Hamblen	14
Paul Lucas	13
Dick Haymes	12
Celeste Holm	11
Robert W. Morgan	10
Al Litchman	09

Hollywood Boulevard

Rock Star 2000   6816

23	Blank
24	Irving Cummings
25	Blank
26	Kent Taylor
27	Blank
28	Jane Powell
29	Blank

Starline Tours & Gifts   6822

30	Spike Jones
31	Blank
32	Erich Von Stroheim
33	Blank
34	Alolph Menjou
35	Blank
36	Bill Hay

El Capitan Building   6834

37	Blank
38	Louise Glaum
39	Blank
40	Buck Jones

Rocket Hollywood   6834

41	Annette Funicello
42	Ann Rutherford
43	The Andrews Sister
44	Jose Iturbi
45	Sarah Vaughn
46	Danny Kaye
47	Steve McQueen
48	Ray Bolger

El Capitan Theater   6838

49	Linda Evans
50	Victor Moore
51	Garry Marshall
52	Pee Wee Hunt
53	Burt Reynolds
54	Jan Sterling
55	Ron Howard
56	Pearl White

Masonic Temple   6840

57	Chuck Connors
58	George Gobel
59	Blank
60	Ann Harding
61	A.C. Lyles

6

37

by Michael H. Kwas

6773 Hollywood Fantasy Tours

Vivien Leigh	16
Ray Charles	15

6777 Hollywood First National

Elvis Presley	14
Bill Burrud	13
Kirsten Flagstad	12
Anna Lee	11
Andrew L. Stone	10
Blank	09
Bessie Love	08
Blank	07
Jascha Heifetz	06
Blank	05
Judy Canova	04
Brian Beirne	03
Lanny Ross	02
Blank	01

7

{Block 07}
Going East
From Highland to McCadden

Highland

6

6801	*Vacant*
Monty Hall	70
Olive Borden	69
Ernest Torrence	68
Joanne Woodward	67
Jeannie Cooper	66
Ronald Colman	65
Cliff Robertson	64
Edward Sedgwick	63
John Beradino	62
Preston Foster	61
Beverly Garland	60
Burt Lancaster	59
Telly Savalas	58
Louise Fazenda	57
Tony Curtis	56
Milburn Stone	55
Bobbie Vernon	54
William Primrose	53
J. Peverell Marley	52
Edgar Bergen	51
Alice Calhoun	50

Hollywood Boulevard

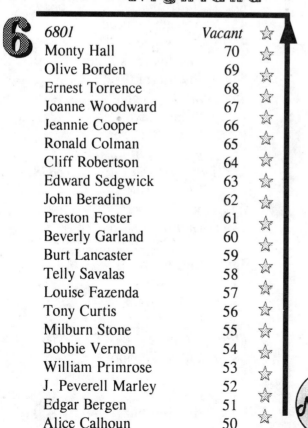

by Michael H. Kwas

McDonald's		6776
65	Arsenio Hall	
66	Edward Arnold	

Ripley's Museum		6780
67	Blank	
68	Victor Mature	
69	Blank	
70	Dorothy Kilgallen	
71	Blank	
72	Charles Bickford	
73	Blank	
74	Joseph Schildkraut	
75	Blank	
76	Lou Costello	
77	Blank	

36

Block {37}
Going West
From Highland to Orange

Highland

Souvenirs of Hollywood		6800
01	Art Laboe	
02	Evelyn Rudie	
03	Blank	
04	Richard Widmark	
05	Blank	
06	Buddy Clark	
07	Blank	
08	Elia Kazan	

37

Crazy Gideon's		6804
09	Blank	
10	Spade Cooley	
11	Blank	
12	Don De Fore	

Vacant		6810 & 08
13	Blank	
14	Woody Herman	
15	Blank	
16	Bill Goodwin	
17	Blank	
18	Claudette Colbert	
19	Blank	

Greco's Pizza		6814
20	Joni James	
21	Blank	
22	Spencer Tracy	

7

6751	Vacant Store
Bing Crosby	54
Charles Chaplin	53
Ken Maynard	52
Hanna Barbara	51
Eddie Bracken	50

6753	Vacant
Jill Ireland	49
Ilka Chase	48
Joel Grey	47
Richard Arlen	46

6755	Vacant
Dennis James	45
Richard Barthelmess	44
Blank	43
Joseph Schenck	42

6757	Vacant
Blank	41
Fran Allison	40
Lee Strasberg	39

6759	This is Hollywood
Ingrid Bergman	38
Blank	37
Katherine MacDonald	36
Blank	35
Red Skelton	34
Blank	33
Robert Merrill	32
Blank	31
Eddie Cantor	30
Blank	29

6765	Runkel's Jewlers
Marie Wilson	28
Chick Hern	27
Sammy Kaye	26

6767 Hollywood Wax Museum	
Roseanne Arnold	25
Edgar Bergen	24
Rafael Mendez	23
Bing Crosby	22
Lindsay Wagner	21

6769 Snow White Coffee Shop	
Al Christie	20
Blank	19

6771 Hollywood Leather & Gift	
Milton Berle	18
B.B. King	17

by Michael H. Kwas

Sports Emporium	6740
23 Jim Healy	
24 Jack Douglas	
25 Tim Conway	
26 Bud Abbott	
27 Blank	
28 Al Jolson	
29 Rev. James Cleveland	

36

Hollywood Passage	6752
30 Gloria Swanson	
31 Blank	
32 Harold Russell	
33 Blank	

International Kitchen	6752
34 Jack Oakie	
35 Blank	
36 Frank Albertson	

The Dome	6760
37 Blank	
38 Fred Astaire	
39 The Ritz Brothers	
40 Bob Hope	
41 Blank	
42 Andy Clyde	
43 Blank	
44 Patti Page	
45 Blank	
46 Henry Koster	

Guiness World of Records	6764
47 Blank	
48 Olivia de Havilland	
49 Blank	
50 Judy Garland	
51 Arnold Schwarzenegger	
52 Kay Frances	
53 Blank	
54 Ray Bolger	

Camera & Photo	6776
55 Blank	
56 Elsie Janis	
57 Blank	

McDonald's	6776
58 Feodor Chalipan	
59 Blank	
60 Ginger Rogers	
61 Blank	
62 Blank	
63 Stefanie Powers	
64 Marilyn Monroe	

8

6721	Vacant
Harry Belafonte	33
Oscar Micheaux	32
Ernest Truex	31
6723	*GiGi Boutique*
Blank	30
Aileen Pringle	29
The Spinners	28
Arturo Toscinini	27
Philip Dunne	26
6727	*Artesian Patio*
Owen Moore	25
Blank	24
Thomas H. Ince	23
Ritchie Valens	22
Ann Blyth	21
Blank	20
Carleton Young	19
Blank	18
6735	*Hollywood T-Shirts*
Doris Day	17
Blank	16
Jane Darwell	15
6739	*Capitol Rock*
Blank	14
Liberace	13
Sidney Sheldon	12
6743	*B.Dalton Book Store*
Anne Baxter	11
Harold Robbins	10
King Vidor	09
Shari Lewis	08
Dick Powell	07
Rod McKuen	06
Walt Disney	05
Gary Owens	04
Betty White	03
Allen Ludden	02
Tyrone Power	01

{Block 08}
Going East
From McCadden to Las Palmas

McCadden

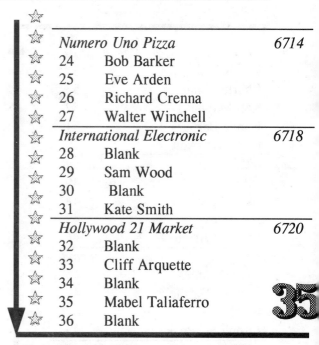

Hollywood Boulevard

Numero Uno Pizza	6714
24 Bob Barker	
25 Eve Arden	
26 Richard Crenna	
27 Walter Winchell	
International Electronic	6718
28 Blank	
29 Sam Wood	
30 Blank	
31 Kate Smith	
Hollywood 21 Market	6720
32 Blank	
33 Cliff Arquette	
34 Blank	
35 Mabel Taliaferro	
36 Blank	

35

{Block 36}
Going West
From McCadden to Highland

McCadden

Scientology Building	6724
01 Blank	
02 Norman Kerry	
03 Blank	
04 Eddy Howard	
05 Blank	
06 Anita Stewart	
07 Blank	
08 Nelson Riddle	
09 Blank	
Parking lot	6730
10 Oscar Levant	
11 Blank	
12 Gilbert Roland	
13 Blank	
14 Eva Marie Saint	
15 Blank	
16 Ruby Keeler	
17 Blank	
18 George M. Cohan	
19 Blank	
20 Broderick Crawford	
21 Blank	
22 Ella Fitzgerald	

36

by Michael H. Kwas

6689	Sub City
Ruth Warwick	04
Blank	03
Faye Emerson	02
Blank	01

9

{Block 09}
Going East
From Las Palmas to Cherokee

8

Las Palmas

6701	Best Mini-Mart
Jean Hersholt	57
Blank	56
Mary Astor	55
Blank	54
Roscoe Arbuckle	53
Blank	52
Mary Livingston	51
6705	Two Guys from Italy
Blank	50
Nils Asther	49
Blank	48
Madeline Carroll	47
6709	American Leather Shop
Blank	46
George Reeves	45
Blank	44
6711	Harry's Boutique
Fred Allen	43
Blank	42
6715	Outpost Building
Ken Niles	41
Blank	40
Yvonne DeCarlo	39
6717	Olympic Hamburger
Blank	38
Dr. Frank C. Baxter	37
6719	Hollywood Natural Foods
Blank	36
Barton McLane	35
Dorothy Dandridge	34

Hollywood Boulevard

National Stereo	6672
39 Gracie Allen	
40 Blank	
41 Ruth Roman	
Explosion	6674
42 Blank	
43 Ed Gardner	
44 Blank	
45 Laraine Day	
46 Blank	
47 Charles Vidor	
48 Blank	
49 Vincente Minnelli	

34

{Block 35}
Going West
From Las Palmas to McCadden

Las Palmas

L.A. Tattoo	6700
01 Thomas A. Edison	
02 Blank	
03 Frank Morgan	
04 Blank	
Hollywood Beauty	6702
05 Eugene Pallette	
06 Blank	
07 Morris Stoloff	
David & Emillo Shoes	6704
08 Blank	
09 Zino Francescatti	
10 Blank	
Vacant (burned out)	6706
11 Ford Bond	
12 Blank	
13 Ken Carpenter	
14 Bernadette Peters	
15 Raymond Massey	
Egyptian Theater	6712
16 Dolly Parton	
17 Douglas Fairbanks, Jr.	
18 Scatman Crothers	
19 Cass Daley	
20 Diana Ross	
21 Mack Sennett	
22 Sylvester Stallone	
23 Yehudi Menuhin	

35

by Michael H. Kwas

9

6667	*Musso and Frank Grill*
Peter Donald	42
Mark (Moviola) Serruier	41
Freddie Bartholomew	40
William Demarest	39
Harrison Ford	38
Quinn Martin	37
Gene Autry	36
Buck Owens	35
John Barrymore	34
Aaron Spelling	33
Frank Lloyd	32
6669	*Asia Imports*
Andy Williams	31
Patsy Kelly	30
Jerry Dunphy	29
6673	*Star Deli*
Licia Albanese	28
Ted Knight	27
6671	*Studio 2*
Flora Finch	26
Glen A. Larson	25
6675	*Vogue Theater*
Tommy Dorsey	24
Vin Scully	23
Ferlin Husky	22
George Peppard	21
Betty Furness	20
Robert Guillame	19
6679	*Los Burritos*
Guy Lombardo	18
The Monkees	17
Mary Carlisle	16
Blank	15
6681	*Dynamite Boutique*
Arthur Kennedy	14
George Takei	13
Gene Lockhart	12
6683	*Lazer Shoes*
Gene Roddenberry	11
Harry James	10
Blank	09
Myrna Loy	08
6687	*Me & Me*
Blank	07
John Payne	06
Blank	05

Hollywood Boulevard

34

Hurricane		*6650*
01	Red Skelton	
02	Norm Crosby	
03	Jack Benny	
04	Blank	
05	Smilin' Ed McConnell	
06	Blank	
Hollywood BBQ		*6652*
07	Bessie Barriscale	
08	Blank	
Combo's Pizza		*6654*
09	Errol Flynn	
10	Blank	
Ritz Theater		*6656*
11	Debbie Reynolds	
12	Blank	
13	Raymond Burr	
14	Blank	
15	Eartha Kitt	
In-Step Shoes		*6658*
16	Paul Robeson	
17	Marsha Hunt	
18	Blank	
Rock Center		*6660*
19	Rhonda Fleming	
20	Blank	
21	James Wallington	
Supply Sergeant		*6664*
22	Blank	
23	Hans Conried	
24	Blank	
25	Boris Karloff	
26	Blank	
27	Esther Ralston	
28	Blank	
Vacant Store		*6666*
29	Michael Ansara	
30	Kenny Rogers	
31	Marty Robbins	
32	Crosby, Stills & Nash	
33	Guy Lombardo	
34	Blank	
Vacant Store		*6670*
35	Jean Parker	
36	Blank	
37	William Lundigan	
38	George Burns	

by Michael H. Kwas

6631	Hollywood Book City	
Jerry Lee Lewis		10
Perry Como		09
6633	Fame of Hollywood	
Jim Henson		08
H.C. Potter		07
Blank		06
Dustin Farnum		05
Anatole Litvak		04
Nichelle Nichols		03
Mark Stevens		02
Blank		01

10

{Block 10}
Going East
From Cherokee to Whitley

Cherokee

6655-F5	Souvenir Shop	
Leonard Nimoy		63
Phil Harris		62
Blank		61
Dean Martin		60
6655-5	Camp Hollywood	
Blank		59
Antonio Moreno		58
Blank		57
6655-4	Star Search	
Alan Hale, Jr.		56
Blank		55
6655-3	USA Jeans Factory	
Dorothy Sebastian		54
Iron Eyes Cody		53
Fritz Kreisler		52
6655-A	Nicole	
Blank		51
Reginald Denny		50
Blank		49
Nat "King" Cole		48
6663	Hollywood Stars	
Blank		47
Robert Cummings		46
Blank		45
6665	Top Western	
Douglas Fairbanks, Jr.		44
Harry Ackerman		43

Hollywood Boulevard

Venetzia		6630-A
090	Horace Heidt	
091	Blank	
092	Charley Chase	
Z Rock		6630-B
093	Blank	
094	Sonny James	
City Life Sports		6630-C
095	Blank	
096	Roddy McDowall	
097	Blank	
European Menswear		6630-D
098	Vaughn De Leath	
099	Blank	
100	Neil Hamilton	
Hollywood Gift Connection		6638
101	Blank	
102	Norma Shearer	
103	Blank	
International Fashion		6638 1/2
104	Dale Evans	
105	Blank	
J.C. Amber		6640
106	Billy Eckstine	
107	Blank	
108	Schumann-Heink	
109	Blank	
110	Michael Curtiz	
Larry Edmunds Book Store		6644
111	Blank	
112	Gene Autry	
113	Blank	
114	Athur Lake	
Jambi-3 Jewelry		6646 3/4
115	Blank	
Hollywood Cherokee Building		6646
116	Dennis Day	
117	Blank	
Hurricane		6648
118	Cathy Downs	
119	Blank	
120	Eddie Cantor	
121	James Caan	
122	George Arliss	

33

{Block 34}
Going West
From Cherokee to Las Palmas

by Michael H. Kwas

Cherokee

6609	Gift Island	
Vincent Lopez	49	☆
Blank	48	☆
Mary Martin	47	☆
6611 1/2	JeTaime Boutique	☆
Blank	46	☆
Kitty Carlisle	45	☆
Blank	44	☆
James Whitmore	43	☆
Blank	42	☆
6613	700 Market	☆
Mildred Dunnock	41	☆
Blank	40	☆
6613 1/2	L.A. Roxx	☆
Hugh O'Brian	39	☆
Blank	38	☆
Lawrence Welk	37	☆
6615	China King	☆
Blank	36	☆
Ceasar Romero	35	☆
Norman Lear	34	☆
6617	Hollywood Fashion Place	☆
Billie Burke	33	☆
Blank	32	☆
Wallace Reid	31	☆
6619	Hollywood Styles	☆
Blank	30	☆
Peter Lorre	29	☆
Blank	28	☆
6621	Stairway Fashion	☆
Buster Keaton	27	☆
Blank	26	☆
J.M. Kerrigan	25	☆
6621-A	Legends Autographs	☆
Blank	24	☆
6623	Mona Lisa Tops	☆
Drew Pearson	23	☆
Blank	22	☆
Margaret Whiting	21	☆
Blank	20	☆
Angela Lansbury	19	☆
6331	Hollywood Book City	☆
Blank	18	☆
Enrico Caruso	17	☆
Blank	16	☆
Art Carney	15	☆
Jimi Hendrix	14	☆
Fred Zinnemann	13	☆
John Ritter	12	☆
Tex Ritter	11	

Hollywood Boulevard

Frederick's of Hollywood		6608
51	Robert Fuller	
52	Margaret O'Brien	
53	Dyan Cannon	
54	Will Rogers	
55	Fleetwood Mac	
56	Jack Palance	
57	Ken Minyard & Bob Arthur	
58	Ford Sterling	
Hollywood Magic Shop		6614
59	Eva Gabor	
60	Frank Capra	
61	Blank	
Burned out building		6612
62	Arthur Godfrey	
63	Blank	
64	Fats Domino	
65	Blank	
Burned out building		6618
66	June Havoc	
67	Blank	
68	Little Jack Little	
Burned out building		6620
69	Blank	
70	Albert Dekker	
71	Blank	
72	Gilda Gray	
73	Blank	
Galaxy DeLuxe Burger		6622
74	Al Jolson	
The Gallery		6624
75	Blank	
76	Eva Marie Saint	
77	Blank	
78	Otto Preminger	
79	Blank	
80	Janis Paige	
81	Blank	
Wig Outfitters		6626
82	Walter Huston	
83	Rip Taylor	
84	Gordon Jenkins	
85	Blank	
Asian Collection		6628
86	Alice Terry	
87	Blank	
88	Renata Tebaldi	
89	Blank	

N

by Michael H. Kwas

33

6555	Legends of Hollywood	
Smothers Brothers	18	☆
James Dunn	17	☆
Jack Klugman	16	☆
John Cromwell	15	☆
Gene Barry	14	☆
Ozzie Nelson	13	☆
6559	Bontoc Gifts	
Blank	12	☆
David Butler	11	☆
Blank	10	☆
6561	Hollywood Stars	
Toby Wing	09	☆
Blank	08	☆
6565	Cash It Here	
Ruth Etting	07	☆
Blank	06	☆
Danny Kaye	05	☆
Blank	04	☆
Clem McCarthy	03	☆
Blank	02	☆
Peggy King	01	☆

11

↑

{Block 11}
Going East
From Whitley to Hudson

10

Whitley

6601	Station Market	
Melvyn Douglas	63	☆
Blank	62	☆
George Fitzmaurice	61	☆
Blank	60	☆
Edmund Lowe	59	☆
Blank	58	☆
Marie Wilson	57	☆
Blank	56	☆
6605	U.T.B. Building	
Victor Jory	55	☆
Blank	54	☆
6607	Vacant Store	
Bonita Granville	53	☆
Blank	52	☆
Jane Wyman	51	☆
Blank	50	☆

Hollywood Boulevard

by Michael H. Kwas

Enterprise Shoes		6548
11	Blank	
12	Evelyn Brent	
Chalame		6550
13	Blank	
14	Leslie Howard	
15	Blank	
Prestige Jewelry		6554
16	Orson Welles	
17	Blank	
Hollywood Jewelry Exchange		6556
18	ZaSu Pitts	
19	Blank	
20	Ed Gardner	
21	Blank	
Body Image		6558
22	Fred Waring	
23	Blank	
24	Tay Garnett	
Fame Fashion Chest		6560
25	Blank	
26	Frachot Tone	
Hollywood Toys		6562
27	Blank	
28	Olga Petrova	
29	Pee Wee Herman	
30	James Melton	
31	Blank	
32	David Torrence	
33	Blank	
34	Sidney Franklin	
35	Blank	
J.J. Newberry		6602
36	H.B. Warner	
37	Blank	
38	Van Johnson	
39	Blank	
40	Joseph Szigeti	
41	Blank	
42	Ella Raines	
43	Blank	
44	Sir Cedric Hardwicke	
45	Blank	
46	Burton Holmes	
47	Blank	
Frederick's of Hollywood		6608
48	Peggy Ann Garner	
49	Tom Jones	
50	Annette Kellerman	

33

6531	*Timing Collection*	☆
Phyllis Thaxter	58	☆
John Derek	57	☆
Blank	56	☆
6533	*Vacant Store*	☆
Clyde Cook	55	☆
Blank	54	☆
Morton Gould	53	☆
6535	*Jean Machine*	☆
Blank	52	☆
Sol Lesser	51	☆
Blank	50	☆
Duke Ellington	49	☆
Blank	48	☆
David W. Griffith	47	☆
6541	*Janes House*	☆
Blank	46	☆
Johnny Weissmuller	45	☆
Maureen O'Sullivan	44	☆
William Fox	43	☆
Blank	42	☆
Viola Dana	41	☆
Jose Feliciano	40	☆
Jose Ferrer	39	☆
Leslie Neilson	38	☆
Bob Burns	37	☆
Bill Conti	36	☆
Bob Hope	35	☆
Nancy Wilson	34	☆
Mickey Rooney	33	☆
Blank	32	☆
Jack Warner	31	☆
6547	*Outfitters Wigs*	☆
Blank	30	☆
Martha Raye	29	☆
Blank	28	☆
Penny Singleton	27	☆
6551	*Bruce Fashion*	☆
Blank	26	☆
Basil Rathbone	25	☆
Blank	24	☆
Helen Hayes	23	☆
Blank	22	☆
6553	*London Connection*	☆
John Forsythe	21	☆
Blank	20	☆
Reed Hadley	19	☆

Hollywood Boulevard

by Michael H. Kwas

☆	*Blaxx Clothing*	6524
☆ 42	Blank	
☆ 43	Glenda Farrell	
☆ 44	Blank	
☆ 45	Lewis Stone	
☆	*Lisa Boutique*	6528
☆ 46	Blank	
☆ 47	Vanessa Brown	
☆ 48	Blank	
☆	*Georgio's Pizza*	6530
☆ 49	John Boles	
☆ 50	Blank	
☆ 51	Alan Hale	
☆	*Jewelry Magic*	6536
☆ 52	Blank	
☆ 53	Freddy Martin	
☆ 54	Blank	
☆	*Ziganne*	6538
☆ 55	Hal March	
☆ 56	Blank	
☆ 57	MacDonald Carey	
☆	*Greg Ward Levi*	6540
☆ 58	Jay Silverheels	
☆ 59	Frank Sinatra	
☆ 60	Sammy Cahn	
☆ 61	Louise Dresser	
☆ 62	Blank	
☆ 63	Isaac Stern	
☆ 64	Blank	

32

{Block 33}
Going East
From Hudson to Cherokee

Hudson

☆	*Consumer's Discount*	6542
☆ 01	Blank	
☆ 02	Monty Woolley	
☆ 03	Blank	
☆ 04	Ralph Bellamy	
☆ 05	Blank	
☆ 06	Andre Kostelanetz	
☆ 07	Blank	
☆ 08	Patric Knowles	
☆ 09	Blank	
☆ 10	John M. Stahl	

33

6507	*LA Roxx*	☆
Blank	34	☆
Spring Byington	33	☆
Blank	32	☆
Art Baker	31	☆
Blank	30	☆
6511	*Hollywood High Fashion Shoes*	☆
John Sturges	29	☆
Blank	28	☆
6513	*Burned out store*	☆
Clara Kimball Young	27	☆
Blank	26	☆
Rochester	25	☆
6515	*Tony's Sports*	☆
Blank	24	☆
John Howard	23	☆
Blank	22	☆
6517	*Los Burritos*	☆
Madge Bellamy	21	☆
Blank	20	☆
6519	*Kalypso Gifts*	☆
Leatrice Joy	19	☆
Blank	18	☆
Dean Martin	17	☆
Blank	16	☆
Harry Von Zell	15	☆
6523	*Maya Shoes*	☆
Blank	14	☆
Roland Young	13	☆
Blank	12	☆
Edmond O'Brien	11	☆
Blank	10	☆
Meriam C. Cooper	09	☆
6527	*Steve's Gifts*	☆
Blank	08	☆
Betty Grable	07	☆
Blank	06	☆
6529	*Hollywood Bargain*	☆
Liberace	05	☆
Blank	04	☆
Faye Emerson	03	☆
Blank	02	☆
Alfred Green	01	☆

Hollywood Boulevard

Dr. M. Grosberg		6502
07	James Cagney	
08	Blank	
Eddie's Starburger		6504
09	Don Alvarado	
10	Blank	
11	Agnes Ayres	
Misha Impex		6506
12	Blank	
13	Alfred Hitchcock	
14	Blank	
Fox Theater		6508
15	Florian Zabach	
16	Joe Williams	
17	Gale Robbins	
18	Count Basie	
19	Phil Harris	
20	Blank	
Roma Fashions		6510
21	George Burns	
22	Blank	
23	Nelson Eddy	
24	Blank	
25	David Rose	
26	Blank	
27	Marlin Hurt	
Combo's Pizza		6516
28	Blank	
29	Maurice Costello	
30	Blank	
New World Jewerly		6518
31	Louis Weber	
32	Blank	
33	Gene Autry	
Star Electronics		6520
34	Blank	
35	Walter Lang	
36	Blank	
Newberry School of Beauty		6522
37	Gloria Grahame	
38	Blank	
39	E. Power Biggs	
40	Blank	
41	Hobart Bosworth	

32

{Block 12}
Going East
From Hudson to Wilcox

N

by Michael H. Kwas

Hudson

13

6433	Pacific Theater	
Melissa Gilbert		22
Bob Hawk		21
Hal Mohr		20
Ben Alexander		19
Lowell Thomas		18
Jesse Lasky		17
Carol Burnett		16
Paul Muni		15
6435	By George, For Men	
Cloris Leachman		14
Jack Haley		13
6439	Schtromberg Jewlers	
Jim Nabors		12
Harry Warner		11
Blank		10
Eddie Albert		09
6443	Fast Break Shoes	
Blank		08
Barbara Whiting		07
Blank		06
6445	Best Tomy #21	
Louis Jordan		05
Blank		04
Carlton E. Morse		03
Blank		02
Yma Sumac		01

{Block 13}
Going East
From Wilcox to Cahuenga

12

6501	Burned out store	
Jean Hersholt		45
Blank		44
Julia Faye		43
Blank		42
Walter Brennen		41
Ann Margret		40
Vincent Price		39
Blank		38
6505	Tony's Shoes	
Jimmy Dorsey		37
Blank		36
Les Brown		35

Hollywood Boulevard

WILCOX

Hollywood Discount Center		6426
42	Blank	
43	Clyde McCoy	
44	Blank	
45	Ed Wynn	
46	Blank	
47	George O'Hanlon	
48	Blank	
Power Sports		6430
49	Mitzi Green	
50	Blank	
51	Arlene Francis	
Pickway Shoes		6434
52	Blank	
53	John Hart	
54	Ernest Gold	
55	Ben Alexander	
56	Blank	
Playmates		6440
57	Lucille Ball	
58	Cantinflas	
59	Tony Martin	
60	Chicago	
61	Lou Costello	
62	Richard Pryor	
63	Irene Dunne	
64	Blank	
65	Robert Montgomery	

31

{Block 32}
Going West
From Wilcox to Hudson

WILCOX

Nikki's		6500
01	Dale Robertson	
02	Blank	
03	Jack Lescoulie	
04	Blank	
05	Josephine Hull	
06	Edith Head	

32

N

by Michael H. Kwas

13

31

6405	Greco's Pizza
Teresa Wright	57
Blank	56
Graham McNamee	55
6411	Ness Shoes
Blank	54
Bennett Cerf	53
Blank	52
6411-A	Hollywood Boots
Slim Summerville	51
Blank	50
Jack Bailey	49
Blank	48
Meredith Willson	47
Blank	46
June Havoc	45
6415	Diamalaye
Blank	44
Fanny Brice	43
Blank	42
Snub Pollard	41
6417	Donner's Donuts
Blank	40
Bert Lytell	39
6419	Haunted Studio
Blank	38
Sammy Kaye	37
6421	Four M Shoes
Blank	36
Carl Reiner	35
Blank	34
Fred MacMurray	33
6423	Ben's Smoke Shop
Blank	32
Melvyn Douglas	31
6425	Pacific Hollywood Building
Blank	30
Edgar Bergen	29
6427	13th District
Blank	28
Edward Everett Horton	27
Blank	26
Gabby Hayes	25
6429	Yaba's Imports
Blank	24
Jennifer Jones	23

Hollywood Boulevard

The Spot		6402
06	Blank	
07	Charles Walters	
08	Blank	
Black & White		6402 1/2
09	John Reed King	
Hollywood Building		6404
10	Blank	
11	Beatrice Lillie	
Fox Cosmetics		6406
12	Blank	
13	Georgia Gibbs	
Christian Science Reading		6408
14	Blank	
15	Ginny Simms	
16	Blank	
17	Alma Rubens	
F.W. Woolworth		6410
18	Blank	
19	Cecil Brown	
20	Blank	
21	Edwin F. Goldman	
22	Blank	
23	Tex Williams	
24	Blank	
25	Lewis J. Selznick	
26	Blank	
27	Walter Pidgeon	
28	Blank	
29	Edward R. Murrow	
30	Blank	
Hollywood Discount Center		6418
31	Louella O. Parsons	
32	Andy Griffith	
33	Robert Donat	
Hilla of Hollywood		6420
34	Blank	
35	Helen Traubel	
Hollywood Mini-Mall		6422
36	Blank	
37	Richard Brooks	
38	Blank	
Mr. Burke's Shoes		6424
39	Adela St. John	
40	Blank	
41	Wesley Ruggles	

N

by Michael H. Kwas

6371	Antenna of Hollywood	☆
Jimmy Jam & Terry Lewis	29	☆
Victor Young	28	☆
Blank	27	☆
Erroll Garner	26	☆
Blank	25	☆
Harry Carey, Jr.	24	☆
Blank	23	☆
Art Linkletter	22	☆
6377	**Beeper Store**	☆
Blank	21	☆
Nathan Milstein	20	☆
6379	**Vacant store**	☆
Blank	19	☆
Sid Grauman	18	☆
Blank	17	☆
6385	**Security Pacific Bank**	☆
Anna Magnani	16	☆
Alan Freed	15	☆
Abbe Lane	14	☆
Blank	13	☆
Mel Blanc	12	☆
Tony Orlando	11	☆
Gail Davis	10	☆
Vikki Carr	09	☆
Don Murray	08	☆
Forrest Tucker	07	☆
Wally Cox	06	☆
Blank	05	☆
Frankie Lane	04	☆
Blank	03	☆
Dorothy Gish	02	☆
Lew Ayres	01	☆

Hollywood Boulevard

☆	Under Construction	6370
☆	01 Blank	
☆	02 Anne Bancroft	
☆	03 Blank	
☆	04 Lassie	
☆	05 Robert Goulet	
☆	06 Robert Z. Leonard	
☆	07 Blank	
☆	08 Jack Benny	
☆	09 Rich Little	
☆	**Burned out building**	**6378**
☆	10 Mickey Rooney	
☆	11 George Putnam	
☆	12 Ronald Reagan	
☆	13 Mark Goodson	
☆	**Demain**	**6376**
☆	14 Perry Como	
☆	15 Blank	
☆	16 Laura La Plante	
☆	17 Blank	
☆	18 George Cukor	
☆	**No Problem**	**6380**
☆	19 Blank	
☆	20 Rex Harrison	
☆	21 Blank	
☆	**Shanti's Vegetatarian**	**6382**
☆	22 Joseph Cotten	
☆	23 Pat Buttram	
☆	**Popeye Chicken**	**6384**
☆	24 David Nivin	
☆	25 Dick Whittinghill	
☆	26 Gene Autry	
☆	27 Jerry Fairbanks	

14

13

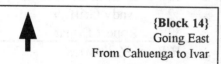
{Block 14}
Going East
From Cahuenga to Ivar

Cahuenga

{Block 31}
Going West
From Cahuenga to Wilcox

30

Cahuenga   **31**

6401	Community Check Cashing	☆
Josef von Sternberg	64	☆
Will Rogers	63	☆
Blank	62	☆
Johnny Maddox	61	☆
Blank	60	☆
6403	**Hollywood Pants**	☆
Del Moore	59	☆
Blank	58	☆

☆	Pizza Deli	6400
☆	01 Claude Raines	
☆	02 Hank Williams	
☆	03 Marlene Dietrich	
☆	**Georgio Cassini**	**6400 1/2**
☆	04 Blank	
☆	05 Robert Ripley	

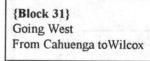

by Michael H. Kwas

Hollywood Boulevard

{Block15 }
Going East
From Ivar to Vine

{Block 29}
Going West
From Ivar to Cosmo

Ivar

Ivar

6349	*Hollywood Book & Poster*	☆
Blank	59	☆
Onslow Stevens	58	☆
Blank	57	☆
Zachary Scott	56	☆
Blank	55	☆
Fay Wray	54	☆
6351	*Hardy Shoes*	☆
Blank	53	☆
Gypsy Rose Lee	52	☆
Blank	51	☆
Billie Dove	50	☆
Blank	49	☆
Geraldine Fitzgerald	48	☆
Blank	47	☆
6357	*Star Fashion*	☆
Charles Ray	46	☆
Blank	45	☆
Dave Garroway	44	☆
Walter Matthau	43	☆
Jack Lemmon	42	☆
6359	*Vacant store*	☆
Blank	41	☆
Charles Ruggles	40	☆
6361	*Discoteca Hollywood*	☆
Chevy Chase	39	☆
Jack Carson	38	☆
Blank	37	☆
Ilka Chase	36	☆
6371	*Antenna of Hollywood*	☆
Blank	35	☆
William S. Hart	34	☆
Edward Asner	33	☆
Gut Lombardo	32	☆
Blank	31	☆
Edmund Lowe	30	

	Combo's Pizza	6350
☆ 01	Blank	
☆ 02	Bill Haley	
☆ 03	Blank	
☆ 04	Ramon Novarro	
☆ 05	Blank	
☆ 06	Diana Lynn	
☆	*Hollywood Eye Clinic*	6356
☆ 07	Blank	
☆ 08	Jane Wyatt	
☆ 09	Blank	
☆	*Glad's Discount Mini-Mall*	6358
☆ 10	Dorothy Phillips	
☆ 11	Blank	
☆ 12	Dave Willock	
☆ 13	George Kennedy	
☆ 14	Robert Young	
☆	*Africa Prinecess*	6360
☆ 15	Blank	
☆ 16	Mala Powers	
☆ 17	Blank	
☆	*Palmer Building*	6362
☆ 18	June Lockhart	
☆ 19	Bill Welsh	
☆	*Shaky Wigs*	6364
☆ 20	Phil Spitalny	
☆ 21	Blank	
☆ 22	Jack White	
☆	*Kassfy Sportswear*	6366
☆ 23	Blank	
☆ 24	Andy Devine	
☆ 25	Blank	
☆ 26	Paul Henreid	

29

{Block 30}
Going West
From Cosmo to Cahuenga

14

Cosmo

by Michael H. Kwas

6315	Cave Theater	
Jack Holt		38
Roland Young		37
Bill Cunningham		36
Mike Gore		35
6317	Hollywood Tattoo	
Dick Lane		34
Marjorie Lord		33
6319	Sandy Burger	
Bob Crosby		32
Peggy Lee		31
6321	Vine Theater	
Laurence Olivier		30
Sophie Tucker		29
Ann Dvorak		28
June Lockhart		27
Rusty Hamer		26
Lynn Bari		25
6325	Dr. Pachman Optometrist	
Gordon Macrae		24
Frank Lovejoy		23
Lawrence Tibbett		22
6327	Chicken Delight	
Desi Arnaz		21
Rosemary Clooney		20
Henry King		19
C. Aubrey Smith		18
6329	Fantasy T-Shirts	
Grace Kelly		17
Eve Arden		16
Kenny Baker		15
6331	Guaranty Building	
Dorothy Kirsten		14
Otto Kruger		13
Tony Martin		12
Blank		11
Ann Rutherford		10
Richard Carlson		09
Jetta Goudal		08
Paul Winchell		07
Ed Wynn		06
Jean Arthur		05
Jim Lowe		04
Charles Winninger		03
Guy Madison		02
Bud Abbott		01

Hollywood Boulevard

N

Hollywood Bazaar		6320
28	Douglas Fairbanks, Jr.	
29	Margaret Lindsay	
30	Mae Murray	
31	August Lumiere	
32	Tab Hunter	
33	Johnny Cash	
34	Humphrey Bogart	
35	William Frawley	
Vacant store		6324
36	Nina Foch	
37	William Farnum	
38	Sherry Jackson	
39	Ernest Borgnine	
Hollywood Cards		6328
40	Henry Morgan	
41	Marion Davies	
42	Wendell Corey	
43	Jayne Mansfield	
Tacosy Mariscos		6330
44	Henry Rowland	
45	Al Pearce	
Photo City		6332
46	Gene Austin	
47	Lillian Roth	
48	Dorothy Lamour	
Albert's Hosiery		6336
49	Kim Novak	
50	Darryl Zanuck	
51	Elizabeth Taylor	
52	Marjorie Rambeau	
53	Arturo Toscanini	
El Golfo De Fonseca		6338
54	Laurence Trimble	
55	Irene Hervey	
56	Stan Kenton	
57	Robert Wise	
58	Willian Collier	
Mr. Submarine		6340
59	Paul Gilbert	
60	Carlyle Blackwell	
61	Igor Stravinsky	
62	Gale Gordon	
63	Eleanor Parker	
64	Bela Lugosi	

28

by Michael H. Kwas

Neil A. Armstrong
Edwin E. Aldrin, Jr.
Michael Collins
7/20/69
APOLLO
XI

Neil A. Armstrong
Edwin E. Aldrin, Jr.
Michael Collins
7/20/69
APOLLO
XI

Your choice,
North (page 61)
or East

{Block 18 }
Going East
From Vine to Argyle

{Block 28 }
Going West
From Vine to Ivar

15   Vine   Vine   28

6301	vacant restaurant	☆
Marilyn Miller	64	☆
Carl Leammle	63	☆
Archie Mayo	62	☆
Don McNeill	61	☆
Carey Wilson	60	☆
Carmen Cavallaro	59	☆
Gloria Swanson	58	☆
Matt Moore	57	☆
Constance Binney	56	☆
George Montgomery	55	☆
Marie Wilson	54	☆
Cass Daley	53	☆
6305	Ventas	☆
Gene Lockhart	52	☆
George Sidney	51	☆
Ernie Kovacs	50	☆
6307	Last Moving Picture	☆
Mildred Harris	49	☆
Theda Bara	48	☆
6309	Hollywood Recovery Center	
Hillary Brooke	47	☆
Van Heflin	46	☆
Joan Blondell	45	☆
6311	Hollywood Wig	☆
Tennessee Ernie Ford	44	☆
Nelson Eddy	43	☆
6315	Cave Theater	☆
Al St. John	42	☆
Don Ameche	41	☆
Hedda Hopper	40	☆
W.C. Fields	39	☆

☆	New York Pizza Express	6302
☆	01 Constance Talmadge	
☆	02 Hank Mann	
☆	03 Fred Waring	
☆	04 Polly Moran	
☆	05 Louella Parsons	
☆	06 Red Foley	
☆	7 Tourist & Travel	6304
☆	07 Luise Rainer	
☆	08 Marguerite Clark	
☆	09 John Farrow	
☆	10 Charles Boyer	
☆	11 Frank Borzage	
☆	Exotic Hair & Nail	6306
☆	12 Ted Mack	
☆	13 James Melton	
☆	14 Charler Boyer	
☆	15 Jackie Gleason	
☆	Olympic Electronics	6310
☆	16 Nanette Fabray	
☆	17 Joan Bennett	
☆	18 Al Goodman	
☆	19 Basil Rathbone	
☆	Vacant store	6312
☆	20 Heather Angel	
☆	21 Helen Mack	
☆	22 Patty McCormack	
☆	23 King Baggott	
☆	DAV Tech Computers	6314
☆	24 Les Baxter	
☆	25 George Hicks	
☆	26 Rowland Lee	
☆	27 Nita Naldi	

Hollywood Boulevard

18

6245	*Frolic Room*
Gary Cooper	33
Randolph Scott	32
Sylvia Sidney	31
6247	*Ronnie's Donuts*
Phil Baker	30
June Knight	29
6249	*RTD Customer Service*
Hedy Lamarr	28
Connie Stevens	27
6251	*parking lot*
Martha Raye	26
William Bendix	25
Susan Hayward	24
Wayne King	23
Hugh Hubert	22
Sabu	21
Laura Hope Crews	20
6251	*Dos Burritos*
Dave O'Brien	19
Anthony Quinn	18
6253	*Equitible Building*
Robert Casadesus	17
Jack Albertson	16
Jerome Cowan	15
Howard Keel	14
Joi Lansing	13
Betty Hutton	12
Barry Nelson	11
Helen Twelvetrees	10
Helen Parrish	09
Allan Dwan	08
Milton Berle	07
Milton Sills	06
Ruth Chatterton	05
Billy Gilbert	04
Mike Wallace	03
Kirk Douglas	02
Edward R. Murrow	01
	Apollo

Hollywood Boulevard

23

parking lot		6274
31	Mitzi Gaynor	
32	Mel Ferrer	
33	Jo Stafford	
34	Constance Moore	
35	Warren Hull	
36	Ernest B. Schoedsach	
37	Grace Moore	
38	Stu Erwin	
39	Merle Oberon	
40	Arthur Treacher	
41	Lou Costello	
42	Richard Basehart	
43	Jack Webb	
44	Doris Day	
Original Coney Island		6282
45	Jean Muir	
46	Mary Pickford	
47	Marge Champion	
India Tandor		6284
48	Ben Bernie	
49	Lena Horne	
50	Frank Fay	
Metro Rail Field Office		6286
51	Janet Gaynor	
52	Paderewski	
53	Monte Blue	
Subway Sandwich Shop		6288
54	Katharine Hepburn	
55	Jim Davis	
56	Clifton Fadiman	
Holly Vine Shoppe		6290
57	Jonathan Winters	
58	Warner Baxter	
59	Tom Breneman	
60	Jessica Tandy	
61	Spike Jones	
62	Marguerite Chapman	
63	Gladys Swarthout	
64	Julius La Rosa	
	Apollo	

{Block 18 }
Going East
From Vine to Argyle

{Block 28 }
Going West
From Vine to Ivar

(or South to Block 24)

V i n e   **V i n e**

by Michael H. Kwas

6211	Capitol Records Annex	☆
Johnnie Ray	03	☆
Blank	02	☆
Sir Cedric Hardwicke	01	☆

19

↑   {Block 19 }
Going East
From Argyle to Vista Del Mar

18

A r g y l e

6225	vacant bank building	☆
Tod Browning	65	☆
Red Foley	64	☆
Irene Rich	63	☆
Eddy Arnold	62	☆
Bette Davis	61	☆
Quintin Reynolds	60	☆
Nat "King" Cole	59	☆
Anthony Mann	58	☆
Buster Keaton	57	☆
Jackie Gleason	56	☆
6231	vacant store	☆
Karl Malden	55	☆
Constance Collier	54	☆
Jane Froman	53	☆
6233	Pantages Theater	☆
Keith Carradine	xx	☆
Spring Byington	52	☆
Bette Davis	51	☆
Arthur Godfrey	50	☆
Joshua Logan	49	☆
Edward G. Robinson	48	☆
Kathleen Lockhart	47	☆
Sir Andrew Lloyd Webber	46	☆
Marshall Neilan	45	☆
James Nederlander	44	☆
Mitchell Leison	43	☆
Barry Manilow	42	☆
Eddie Fisher	41	☆
Carol Channing	40	☆
Joel McCrea	39	☆
Henry Winkler	38	☆
Lana Turner	37	☆
Edward Dmytryk	36	☆
6243	Ticketmaster	☆
Mercedes McCambridge	35	☆
Maurice Tourneur	34	☆

Hollywood Boulevard

West Coast Ensemble		6240
62	Blank	
63	Pat O'Brien	
64	Blank	
65	Nunnally Johnson	

{Block 23 }
Going West
From Argyle to Vine ↓

22

A r g y l e   **23**

☆	Stella Adler Theater		6250
☆	01	Lena Horne	
☆	02	Ona Munson	
☆	03	Arlene Harris	
☆	04	Constance Bennett	
☆	burned out store		6254
☆	05	Bob Crosby	
☆	06	Barry Fitzgerald	
☆	07	Everett Sloane	
☆	08	Everett Mitchell	
☆	09	Sammy Davis, Jr.	
☆	10	Desi Arnaz	
☆	vacant lot		6256
☆	11	Imogene Coca	
☆	12	Henry Wilcoxon	
☆	13	Fulton Lewis	
☆	14	Andy Devine	
☆	15	Helen Hayes	
☆	16	Ozzie & Harriet Nelson	
☆	17	Donald Woods	
☆	18	Ruth Roland	
☆	vacant lot		6262
☆	19	Thelma Todd	
☆	20	Ralph Edwards	
☆	21	Marian Anderson	
☆	22	Una Merkel	
☆	23	Carmen Miranda	
☆	parking lot		6274
☆	24	Peggy Knudsen	
☆	25	Ogden Nash	
☆	26	Charles Ruggles	
☆	27	Dave Garroway	
☆	28	Peggie Castle	
☆	29	Charles Coburn	
☆	30	Pat Boone	

by Michael H. Kwas

6161	Network Body Shop	☆
Blank	13	☆
Jan Murray	12	☆
Blank	11	☆
Kate Smith	10	☆
Blank	09	☆
Herbert Kalmus	08	☆
Blank	07	☆
House Peters	06	☆
Blank	05	☆
Paul Whiteman	04	☆
Blank	03	☆
Jeanette MacDonald	02	☆
Blank	01	☆

20

↑
{Block 20 }
Going East
From Vista Del Mar to Gower

19 Vista Del Mar

6207	parking lot	☆
Sam Warner	27	☆
Blank	26	☆
Henry B. Walthall	25	☆
Blank	24	☆
Vincent Price	23	☆
Philip Ahn	22	☆
George O'Brien	21	☆
Blank	20	☆
Pinky Lee	19	☆
Blank	18	☆
Ann Harding	17	☆
Blank	16	☆
6211	Capitol Records Annex	☆
Earl Godwin	15	☆
Blank	14	☆
Marie Prevost	13	☆
Blank	12	☆
Frank Faylen	11	☆
Blank	10	☆
Joseph L. Mankiewicz	09	☆
Blank	08	☆
Constance Cummings	07	☆
Carol Lawrence	06	☆
Alice Brady	05	☆
Blank	04	☆

Hollywood Boulevard

Network Body Shop		6150
19	Bud Collyer	
20	Blank	
Raji		*6160*
21	Ina Claire	
22	Blank	
23	Barry Sullivan	
24	Blank	
25	Yul Brynner	
26	Blank	
Hastings Hotel		*6162*
27	Gower Champion	
28	Blank	
29	Tommy Riggs & Betty Lou	
30	Blank	
31	Rudolph Valentino	
32	Blank	
33	Theodore Roberts	
34	Blank	
parking lot		*6200*
35	Jan Clayton	
36	Blank	
37	Leonard Bernstein	
38	Blank	
39	Gordon Hollingshead	
40	Blank	
41	John Nesbitt	
42	Blank	
43	Rochelle Hudson	
44	Tex Beneke	
45	Herbert Marshall	
46	Blank	
47	Jack Paar	
48	Blank	
49	Jean Negulesco	
50	Blank	
51	Gigi Perreau	
52	Blank	
53	Jean Renoir	
54	Blank	
55	Dorothy Lamour	
West Coast Ensemble 6240		
56	Loretta Swit	
57	William Seiter	
58	Celia Cruz	
59	John Carradine	
60	Robert Mitchum	
61	Cecil B. DeMille	

22

N ←

by Michael H. Kwas

6125		*Pep Boys*
Blank	57	
Virginia Valli	56	
Blank	55	
John Payne	54	
Smiley Burnette	53	
Gene Tierney	52	
6141		*Mid-Town Towing*
Blank	51	
Loretta Young	50	
Blank	49	
Warren Hull	48	
Blank	47	
Buddy Rogers	46	
Blank	45	
Raoul Walsh	44	
Blank	43	
W.S. Van Dyke	42	
Blank	41	
Lloyd Hamilton	40	
Blank	39	
Tallulah Bankhead	38	
Blank	37	
Bob Hope	36	
Blank	35	
6161		*Network Body Shop*
Hildegarde	34	
Blank	33	
J. Carrol Naish	32	
Blank	31	
Dan Duryea	30	
Blank	29	
Jane Froman	28	
Blank	27	
Stan Freberg	26	
Jester Hairston	25	
Jack Smith	24	
Blank	23	
Bill Williams	22	
Jay Thomas	21	
Gene Kelly	20	
Blank	19	
Louis Jourdan	18	
Blank	17	
Walter O'Keefe	16	
Blank	15	
Helen Ferguson	14	

Hollywood Boulevard

20

by Michael H. Kwas

Hollywood Psychic		*6128*
45	Jimmie Fidler	
46	Blank	
47	Raymond Knight	
48	Blank	
Henry Fonda Theater Offices		*6140*
49	Evelyn Knight	
50	Blank	
51	Bill Leyden	
52	Blank	
53	Don Cornell	
54	Blank	
55	Mona Barrie	
56	Blank	
57	Karl Dane	
58	Blank	
59	Eileen Heckart	
60	Blank	
61	Nazimova	
62	Blank	
63	Don Haggerty	

21

{Block 22 }
Going West
From El Centro to Argyle

El Centro

Network Body Shop		*6150*
01	Roy Del Ruth	
02	Blank	
03	Jerry Lewis	
04	Blank	
05	George Raft	
06	Blank	
07	Irene Rich	
08	Blank	
09	Art Mooney	
10	Blank	
11	Anna Q. Nilsson	
12	Blank	
13	Mary Boland	
14	Blank	
15	Jeanie MacPherson	
16	Blank	
17	Herbert Rawlinson	
18	Blank	

22

Gower

20

Gower →→

Hollywood Boulevard

6125	Pep Boys	
Benny Goodman	98	☆
Ray Briem	97	☆
Richard Thorpe	96	☆
Blank	95	☆
Bill Boyd	94	☆
Blank	93	☆
Marvin Miller	92	☆
Blank	91	☆
Ed Sullivan	90	☆
Blank	89	☆
Sonja Henie	88	☆
Blank	87	☆
Danny Kaye	86	☆
Blank	85	☆
William DeMille	84	☆
Blank	83	☆
John Hodiak	82	☆
Blank	81	☆
Johnny Mack Brown	80	☆
Blank	79	☆
George Meeker	78	☆
Blank	77	☆
Don Ameche	76	☆
Blank	75	☆
Sidney Lanfield	74	☆
Blank	73	☆
Genevieve Tobin	72	☆
Blank	71	☆
Thomas L. Tully	70	☆
Blank	69	☆
Gale Storm	68	☆
Blank	67	☆
John Conte	66	☆
Blank	65	☆
Jane Withers	64	☆
Blank	63	☆
Van Heflin	62	☆
Blank	61	☆
Pauline Starke	60	☆
Blank	59	☆
William Wellman	58	☆

Gower

21

Chevron Service Station		6100
01	Stanley Kramer	
02	Blank	
03	Gregory Peck	
04	Blank	
05	Thomas Mitchell	
06	Blank	
07	Allan Jones	
08	Jack Jones	
09	Audrey Meadows	
10	Blank	
11	Gregory Ratoff	
12	Blank	
13	Montgomery Clift	
14	Blank	
15	Lucille Ball	
16	Lee Remick	
17	Loretta Young	
18	Blank	
19	Will H. Hays	
20	Blank	
21	Sigmund Lubin	
22	Blank	
23	Anita Page	
24	Carmen Dragon	
25	Lynn Bari	
26	Blank	
27	Dick Haymes	
28	Blank	
29	Ralph Edwards	
30	Blank	
31	Rock Hudson	
32	Blank	
33	William N. Selig	
Doug's Sports Corner		6124
34	Blank	
35	Raymond Griffith	
36	Blank	
37	Edna Best	
38	Blank	
Henry Fonda Theater		6126
39	Yvonne DeCarlo	
40	John Raitt	
41	Art Lund	
42	Martha Scott	
43	Gracie Fields	
44	Blank	

by Michael H. Kwas

1719	*parking lot*
Barbara Britton	36
Hattie McDaniel	35
Victor Fleming	34
Charlie Murray	33
Mark Sandrich	32
Cesar Romero	31
James Dean	30
Verna Felton	29
John Nesbitt	28
1715	*Hair Vine*
John Bunny	27
Pee Wee King	26
Judy Garland	25
Kim Hunter	24
1713	*Dan Dee Shoe Repair*
John Lupton	23
Walter Catlett	22
Mauritz Stiller	21
Fred Clark	20
Glen Gray	19
1711	*vacant restaurant*
Robert Walker	18
Elena Verdugo	17
George Brent	16
Geraldine Farrar	15
Eddie Haywood	14
Rouben Mamoulian	13
Robert Sterling	12
Slim Whitman	11
John Bowers	10
George Eastman	09
Art Acord	08
Deborah Kerr	07
Robert Q. Lewis	06
Miriam Hopkins	05
George Stevens	04
Jessica Dragonette	03
Jo Stafford	02
Artie Shaw	01

Vine Street

Sun Palace Restaurant		*1718*
081	Al Jolson	
082	Lila Lee	
083	Bebe Daniels	
084	Delbert Mann	
085	Dorothy Malone	
086	Kay Starr	
087	Dave Brubeck	
Collectors Book Store		*1708*
088	Miriam Hopkins	
089	Joan Davis	
090	George Shearing	
091	Rosalind Russell	
092	Parkyakarkus	
093	Alfred Newman	
094	Mantovani	
095	Frazier Hunt	
096	Frank Morgan	
vacant store		*1706*
097	Betty Blythe	
098	Jack Bailey	
099	Perry Como	
Krisseli's Center		*1704*
100	Raymond Hatton	
101	Gene Raymond	
102	Teresa Brewer	
Hollywood & Vine Dentistry		*1702*
103	Helen Gahagan	
104	Howard Hawks	
Equitible Building		*1700*
105	Anna May Wong	
106	Kay Kyser	
107	Eleanor Steber	
108	Tom Mix	
109	Molly O'Day	
110	Frank Luther	
111	Joanne Dru	
112	Wendy Barrie	
113	James Stewart	

{Block 16 }
Going North
From Hollywood to Yucca

{Block 24}
Going South
From Hollywood to Selma

Hollywood   **Hollywood**   (or East to Argyle)

by Michael H. Kwas

1749	*parking lot*
Frankie Carle	78
Billy Wilder	77
Elliott Dexter	76
Betty Compson	75
Virginia Mayo	74
Margaret Sullavan	73
Barbara Stanwyck	72
Johnny Carson	71
Ethel Merman	70
Dinah Shore	69
Grocho Marx	68

1735	*Palace*
Arlene Francis	67
Otto Kruger	66
William Boyd	65
Artur Rubinstein	64
Boris Karloff	63
Dale Evans	62
Barbara Lawrence	61
Lottie Lehmann	60
Victor McLaglen	59
Jim Backus	58
Bobby Darin	57
Roy Rogers	56
William Wyler	55
Marie Dressler	54
Vic Damone	53
May McAvoy	52
Cecil B. DeMille	51

1719	*parking lot*
Nancy Carroll	50
Marie Doro	49
Edmond O'Brien	48
Carroll Baker	47
Pierre Monteux	46
Eddie Foy	45
Wendell Niles	44
Tony Martin	43
Conrad Nagel	42
Agnes Moorehead	41
Charles Christie	40
Raymond Massey	39
Thomas Meighan	38
Harold Peary	37

Vine Street

39	Jack Mulhall
40	Shelly Winters
41	Marian Nixon
42	Alex Templeton
43	Strongheart

parking lot	*1724*
44	Steve Cochran
45	Carter De Haven
46	Lauren Bacall
47	Eddie Fisher
48	Mary Miles Minter
49	Norman Z. McLeod
50	Ben Lyon
51	Lionel Barrymore
52	Robert Benchley
53	Ida Lupino
54	William Faversham
55	Dick Haymes
56	Jon Hall
57	Lew Ayres
58	Deanna Durbin
59	Sarah Vaughan
60	Blue Barron
61	George "Gabby" Hayes
62	Mr. & Mrs. Sidney Drew
63	Irish McCalla
64	Ella Mae Morse
65	Paul Henreid
66	Mark Robson
67	Hoagy Carmichael
68	George Pal
69	Rod Cameron
70	Vera Vague

Nick's Diner	*1722*
71	Mercedes McCambridge
72	Lillian Gish
73	Garry Moore
74	Steve Allen

Sun Palace Restaurant	*1718*
75	Beulah Bondi
76	Lauritz Melchior
77	Mickey Rooney
78	Robert Cummings
79	Donald Cook
80	Laird Cregar

by Michael H. Kwas

16   Yucca Street   17

1779	Capezio Dance	
Texas Guinan	116	☆
Tommy Tune	115	☆
John Huston	114	☆
Chuck Berry	113	☆
Richard Hayman	112	☆
Dom DeLuise	111	☆
1777	Vine Street Building	
Marlon Brando	110	
Janet Leigh	109	
Hoot Gibson	108	
June Haver	107	
Buddy Ebsen	106	
Meiklejohn	105	
John Daley	104	
William Beaudine	103	
Carole Landis	102	
1749	parking lot	
George Jessel	101	
Edmund Gwenn	100	
Harry Joe Brown	99	
Vaughn Monroe	98	
Jack Perrin	97	
John Gilbert	96	
Charles "Andy" Correll	95	
Earle Williams	94	
Freeman "Amos" Gosden	93	
Jan Peerce	92	
Rudolf Serkin	91	
Fred Waring	90	
Mario Lanza	89	
Gene Vincent	88	
Russ Morgan	87	
James Arness	86	
Ernest Tubb	85	
Stepin Fetchit	84	
Ray Anthony	83	
Blanche Sweet	82	
Virginia Field	81	
Carmel Meyers	80	
Sarah Bernhardt	79	

Vine Street

Xxxx		177X
01	Blank	
02	Jeff Chandler	
03	Billy Vera	
04	Eddie Cantor	
05	Duran Duran	
06	John Lennon	
07	Heinie Conklin	
parking lot		1770
08	Bob Seeger & Silver Bullet Band	
09	Tony Martin	
10	Buddy DeSylva	
11	Lurene Tuttle	
12	The Steve Miller Band	
13	Frank Fay	
Capitol Record Building		1750
14	Tina Turner	
15	Lowell Thomas	
16	Anne Murray	
17	Lee DeForest	
18	Natalie Cole	
19	Conrad Nagel	
20	Beverly Sills	
21	Vera Ralston	
22	Helen Reddy	
23	Joe Penner	
24	Bruce Humberstone	
25	Beverly Bayne	
26	Joan Crawford	
27	Clarence Brown	
28	Rory Calhoun	
29	Brian Aherne	
30	George Seaton	
31	Roy Rogers	
32	Donald Meek	
33	Ralph Staub	
34	Madge Evans	
35	Lloyd Nolan	
36	Charles Laughton	
37	Ken Murray	
38	Conrad Nagel	

N

by Michael H. Kwas

 **27** Hollywood   Hollywood **24**

1645	*Hollywood Vine Building*	
Rex Ingram	97	
Blanche Thebom	96	
Alistair Cooke	95	
Bronco Billy Anderson	94	
Greer Garson	93	
Red Buttons	92	
Maurice Chevalier	91	
William Holden	90	
Francis X. Bushman	89	
Eddie Bracken	88	
Katrina Paxinou	87	
Ben Turpin	86	
David Powell	85	
Thomas Mitchell	84	
Lionel Barrymore	83	
Rita Hayworth	82	
Kent Taylor	81	
Sessue Hayakawa	80	
Michele Morgan	79	
Mary Anderson	78	
Jane Froman	77	
Jerry Colona	76	
William Steinberg	75	
Walter Winchell	74	
Frankie Laine	73	
Joan Fontaine	72	
Dolores Costello	71	
1637	*Early World Restaurant*	
Harold Peary	70	
Nelson Eddy	69	
Sue Carol Ladd	68	
Vera Vague	67	
George Burns	66	
1637	*Plaza Hotel*	
Louis B. Mayer	65	
Frank Sinatra	64	
Cornel Wilde	63	
1635	*Futurama Furniture*	
Don Fedderson	62	
Leo Carrillo	61	
Linda Darnell	60	

Vine Street

Taft Building		1680
01	Maria Callas	
02	Donald O'Connor	
03	Gale Storm	
04	Vladimir Horowitz	
05	Joe E. Brown	
06	Duncan Renaldo	
07	Ted Weems	
08	Garry Moore	
09	Teresa Wright	
10	Michael O'Shea	
11	Jimmy Wakely	
12	Louis Hayward	
13	Arthur Spiegel	
14	Jack Pearl	
Jan's Hair Shop		1656
15	Morton Downey	
Wig Shop		1654
16	Jackie Coogan	
17	Hal Roach	
Jerimiha Comey Studio		1648
18	Paulette Goddard	
19	Vera Miles	
20	Audrey Hepburn	
21	Scott Forbes	
22	Al Hibbler	
23	Jimmy Durante	
24	Tom Brown	
25	Paul Douglas	
26	Blank	
27	Eric Linden	
Bernard Luggage		1642
28	Rosemary DeCamp	
29	John Ford	
30	Tom Moore	
31	Portland Hoffa	
Hollywood Import House		1638
32	Hanley Stafford	
33	Henry Hathaway	
34	Lee Tracy	
35	William Bendix	

1635	Futurama Furniture
Samuel Goldwyn	59
Floyd Gibbons	58
Robert Montgomery	57
Pat Boone	56
Horace Heidt	55

1627	parking lot
Sidney Blackmer	54
Howard Duff	53
Diana Lynn	52
Milton Cross	51
Jo Stafford	50
David Niven	49
Bobby Sherwood	48
Edna May Oliver	47
Melachrino	46
Ilona Massey	45
Dean Jagger	44
Gordon Jones	43
Ronald Colman	42
Rin-Tin-Tin	41
Pete Smith	40
Barbara Lamarr	39
Richard Cromwell	38
Vanessa Brown	37
Ray Milland	36

1615	Doolittle Theater
Marcus Loew	35
Kim Hunter	34
Dean Martin	33
Tom Conway	32
Adolph Zukor	31
Charlie Farrell	30
Ralph Morgan	29
Theodore Kosloff	28
Anne Francis	27
Shirley MacLaine	26
Elissa Landi	25
James A. Fitzpatrick	24
Bea Benaderet	23
Bing Crosby	22
Bud Abbott	21
Victor Schertzinger	20

1605	Molly Coney Island
John B. Kennedy	19
George Murphy	18

Vine Street

vacant store		1636
36	William Powell	
37	George Sanders	
Madame Rosinka		1634
38	Ann Sothern	
39	Ezra Stone	
40	Delmar L. Daves	
parking lot		1630
41	Fred Stone	
42	Akim Tamiroff	
43	Jane Greer	
44	Ray Milland	
45	Margaret O'Brien	
46	Charlie Ruggles	
47	Rudy Vallee	
48	Grantland Rice	
49	Joe Kirkwood, Jr.	
50	Emil Jannings	
51	Dolores del Rio	
52	Jeanette MacDonald	
53	Donald Crisp	
54	Tex McCrary	
55	Robert Edeson	
56	Barbara Hale	
57	Ted Malone	
58	Johnny Mercer	
Brown Derby ruins		1628
59	Charlton Heston	
60	Arthur Fiedler	
61	Arlene Dahl	
62	Alice Lake	
63	Lizabeth Scott	
64	Arthur Kennedy	
65	Roy Rogers	
66	Jane Wyman	
67	Estelle Taylor	
Juice Fountain		1616
68	Fredric March	
69	Robert Young	
parking lot		1614
70	Charles Bickford	
71	Leroy Anderson	
72	Geraldine Farrar	
73	Eugene O'Brien	
74	Norman Luboff	
75	George Brent	

24

27

N

by Michael H. Kwas

1605	Molly Coney Island	
Willard Waterman		17
Ezio Pinza		16
Susan Peters		15
Charlotte Greenwood		14
1601	parking lot	
Xavier Cugat		13
Kay Kyser		12
Cid Charisse		11
Renee Adoree		10
Lawrence Welk		09
Gisele MacKenzie		08
Henry Fonda		07
Paul Whiteman		06
Preston Sturges		05
Audie Murphy		04
Alan Ladd		03
Frank Crumit		02
Bob Burns		01

27

{Block 27 }
Going North
From Selma to Hollywood

Selma

26

1555	TAV	
Robert Shaw		98
George Carlin		97
Jules White		96
Max Steiner		95
Alec Guiness		94
Marie Windsor		93
Mary Brian		92
Lorne Greene		91
Arthur Godfrey		90
Blank		89
Warren William		88
Blank		87
1549	TAV Celebrity Center	
Farley Granger		86
Blank		85
Ruth Hussey		84

V i n e

S t r e e t

N

by Michael H. Kwas

Hollywood Collateral		1612
76	Adrienne Ames	
77	Ann Sothern	
78	Donna Reed	
Vine Street Bar & Grill		1610
79	Julia Sanderson	
80	Cary Grant	
81	Henri Rene	
82	Richard Dix	
83	Clark Gable	
84	John Ireland	
85	Mae Marsh	
vacant store		1606
86	Jimmy Durante	
87	Norman Taurog	
88	Leopold Stokowski	
D M V		1600
89	Dick Foran	
90	Webb Pierce	
91	Tim McCoy	
92	Orson Welles	
93	Fritz Lang	
94	Kathryn Grayson	
95	Tennessee Ernie Ford	
96	Vaughn Monroe	
97	Madge Kennedy	
98	Frank Sinatra	
99	Hugo Winterhalter	

24

{Block 25 }
Going South
From Selma to Sunset

Selma

25

parking lot		1560
01	Art Linkletter	
02	Ava Gardner	
03	Tommy Sands	
04	Dorothy Dalton	
05	Ruth Ashton Taylor	
06	Mervyn LeRoy	
07	Billie Holiday	
08	Mischa Elman	
09	The Three Stooges	
10	Chester Conklin	
11	Al Lohman & Roger Barkley	

1549	*TAV Celebrity Center*	
Blank	83	
Brian Donlevy	82	
Blank	81	
Colleen Moore	80	
Bill Keene	79	
Andrea King	78	
Jamie Farr	77	
Frederick Stock	76	
Joe Pasternak	75	
Virginia Cherrill	74	
Dick Van Patten	73	
Richard Rowland	72	
Michael Jackson	71	
Les Paul & Mary Ford	70	
Eleanor Powell	69	
Roy Acuff	68	
Shirley Jones	67	
1541	*TAV Celebrity Center*	
Ed Wynn	66	
Merv Griffin	65	
John Wayne	64	
Steve Lawrence & Eydie Gorme	63	
Steve Allen	62	
Mel Torme	61	
June Allyson	60	
Blank	59	
Paul Weston	58	
Blank	57	
Roger Williams	56	
Blank	55	
Betty Furness	54	
Blank	53	
Pat O'Brien	52	
Blank	51	
Perez Prado	50	
Blank	49	
Lina Basquette	48	
Blank	47	
Louis Lumiere	46	
1501	*West Sunset Offices*	
Blank	45	
Frances Langford	44	
Blank	43	
Marjorie Reynolds	42	
Blank	41	

26

by Michael H. Kwas

12	Bobby Driscoll
13	Charlie Tuna
14	Mae West
15	Rick Dees
16	Richard Wallace
17	Humberto Luna
18	Joan Leslie
19	Richard Farnsworth
20	Isabel Jewell
21	Hal Fishman
22	Hal March
23	Blank
24	Rod LaRocque
25	Blank
26	Jack Carson
27	Blank
28	Ester Williams
29	Blank
30	Tony Bennett
31	Blank
32	Jeannie Carson
33	Blank
34	Corinne Griffith
35	Blank
36	Helen Vinson
37	Blank
38	Kurt Kreuger
39	Blank
40	Jean Hagen
41	Marvin Gaye
42	Mary Martin
43	Larry Hagman
44	Dick Powell

25

Home Savings parking lot		*1550*
45	John Philip Sousa	
46	Evelyn Venable	
47	Yakima Canutt	
48	Jinx Falkenburg	
49	Janet Jackson	
50	Xavier Cugat	
51	Martin Sheen	
52	George Raft	
53	Bill Stout	
54	Celeste Holm	
55	The Lennon Sisters	
56	Jack Conway	

1501	*West Sunset Offices*			
John Ericson	40			
Blank	39		57	Klaus Landsberg
Jack Pickford	38		58	Louis Hayward
Blank	37		59	Dorothy Arzner
Angela Lansbury	36		60	William K. Howard
Blank	35		61	Michael Landon
Edith Storey	34		62	Shirley Temple
Blank	33		63	Blank
Joan Davis	32		64	Ricardo Cortez
Billy Dee Williams	31		65	Blank
Harry Carey	30		*Home Savings*	*1500*
Blank	29		66	Robert Taylor
Gale Storm	28		67	Blank
Blank	27		68	Clara Bow
Leo Carrillo	26		69	Blank
Blank	25		70	Don Wilson
Carl Smith	24		71	Blank
Loretta Lynn	23		72	Frances Langford
Keenan Wynn	22		73	Blank
Blank	21		74	Norma Talmadge
Major Bowes	20		75	Bob Keeshan Captain Kangaroo
Blank	19		76	Mack Swain
Belle Bennett	18		77	Fibber McGee & Molly
Blank	17		78	Joan Caulfield
Alice White	16		79	Smokey Robinson
Blank	15		80	Fanny Brice
Jackie Cooper	14		81	The Jacksons
Blank	13		82	Leo McCarey
Clint Walker	12		83	Dick Clark
Blank	11		84	B.P. Schulberg
Jack Benny	10		85	Beach Boys
Rick Nelson	09		86	Spike Jones
Harold Lloyd	08		87	Quincy Jones
Cliffie Stone	07		88	Barry Sullivan
Percy Faith	06		89	Neil Sedaka
Blank	05		90	Helene Costello
Binnie Barnes	04		91	George Fenneman
Johnny Mathis	03		92	Oliver Hardy
Anne Jeffreys	02		93	David Wolper
Edward Small	01		94	Franklin Pangborn

Vine Street

Sunset Boulevard

26   25

by Michael H. Kwas

Alphabetical/Index

The following alphabetical list is multi-functional. Two primary purposes have been combined to streamline your study time and actual use of this Guide.

The first purpose is to provide a complete list of the Walk of Famers in alphabetical order for ease of cross referencing with the sequential list and maps. Personalities with more than one Star (see chapter 5 for details) will have their complete biographical data included in the first listing. The second, third, etc. will list only the information that is different, such as {Block/Star}, Address, Near, Category and For.

The second purpose is to replace the usual type of Index found in other books. This will work the same way except each Index listing will be detailed with biographical information. This Index has been arranged alphabetically by last name, then first name and finally, category.

This book has been designed about and because of the Walk of Fame and a special **{Block/Star}** identification has been created and used rather than typical page numbers. The Block Number and information is located in a box in the 'intersections' in the Sequential Chapter (9), the Block Number is also in the margins on each page there. The Star Number is the actual count of all embedded Stars including blanks, from the beginning corner.

The storefront address and name of the business located there is included to make any search easier to complete rather than staring down at the sidewalk. The businesses on Hollywood Boulevard have considerable turnover, so even this most recent edition may at times be incorrect. However, every effort has been made to keep current with any changes.

The Block Information Section (Chapter 7), is also helpful, as it will tell you the intended direction of this walking tour as if taken from the beginning. When seeking any location, this Section will also tell you; *a)* which side of the street to look for, *b)* which direction to be headed, and *c)* the two cross streets you will be looking between. As an example, to find **{36/64}** the Block Information Section will tell you that Block 36 is on the South side of Hollywood Boulevard, and to find Star 64, we will travel west from McCadden Place towards Highland Avenue. Also provided will be the address and name of the business this Star is located nearest to. In this example, the address is 6776, on the South side of Hollywood Boulevard near McDonald's. Using this method, we have just located Marilyn Monroe's Star. ☆

EXPLANATIONS

Some of the information provided in this chapter may need some explanation to be easier understood. All of the information used in the following reports has been extracted from a single database which at times may make some results seem to read unnaturally.

All information is as accurate as possible at the time of publication using the sources indicated . As with Hollywood itself, information is sometimes incomplete and conflicting depending on who you talk to and when. The most accurate information was from the people themselves in the form of Ralph Edwards' *This Is Your Life, the Classics* televised on American Movie Clasics cable television channel, as well as *Reflections on the Silver Screen*, also on AMC.

Last name, first name: alphabetically in that order and secondly by category.

{Block Number / Star Number}: is used in reference to the specially designed maps (Chapter 8) and Block Info (Chapter 7) used in this *Walk of Fame Directory* and have no other official representation or association with other lists or maps available about Hollywood.

Address: the first line below the name and Block Identifier is the number of the business in front of which this Star is most closely located.

Street: is either Hollywood Boulevard or Vine Street.

(Side): is the side of the street this Star is on and is either North or South on Hollywood Boulevard, and East or West on Vine Street. (The one exception to Street and Side is Block 01, the New LaBrea Gateway.)

Near: indicates the *name* of the business using the address listed. As the face of Hollywood Boulevard changes on a fairly regular basis, this may not always be accurate.

Category: This is the actual symbol embedded in the Walk of Fame Star at this location representing the earned category of the five choices. This was researched *only* by walking the Walk.

As: Many of the personalities are deserving of recognition in more than one "occupation" within their earned category. For example, in the Motion Picture category, some may have been recognized as Actors as well as Writers, Producers or Directors. In Recording, they may be Singers as well as Writers, Musicians, Conductors, etc. Selected is the one field in which that person will be most readily recognized by the general public (you).

For: (best, or best remembered, performance this person is associated with) Many persons honored have been successful over a number of years and have many accomplishments worthy of mention. Therefore, the selection of their most remembered performance or character portrayal was in many cases difficult. The selection mentioned here is the one most likely to be remembered by the largest number of readers. When the list was large and well known, the author exercised personal preference as well as the input of friends and relatives. Note: the year indicated is the closest date found to be the beginning of the achievement.

Studio: This is not necessarily the studio mentioned for the performance in 'For:'. This is the studio this person is most often associated with.

Dedicated on: This is the date the dedication ceremony was held and has been derived directly from the list provided by the Hollywood Chamber of Commerce. When not mentioned, this Star was dedicated prior to the Chamber's official recordkeeping. Their numbering begins with 1725 on December 30, 1980, which is the Beach Boys Star.

Real Name: This was, and is difficult to determine. Various media sources as well as interviews with Hollywood residents have provided most of this background information. If the real name is found to be the same, there is no mention. If the real name is similar, any variation such as nicknames, middle names or Jr.s are indicated when known. 'Same or unknown' here means we have discovered no other name used by that person, and have no reason to believe the name has ever been changed or a stage name used. In some instances, even if there were a name change, it may have been kept private. In other cases, no record of a name change was found.

Born: These dates have been reported on television or radio interviews, newspaper or magazine articles, autobiographies or biography type books. Books about movies and studios also provided some of these dates. Many conflicting dates were found, especially in the years from 1890

most repeated date or most reliable and detailed reference was used.

Place Born: Same as above applies. In several instances the exact city was difficult to find and the major city is listed, mostly Chicago and New York. Where more difficulty was encountered, only the state is shown.

Died: Various newspapers and books have been used to collect these dates. In most cases, the year only is indicated, as accurate information in earlier years was rarely documented or extremely difficult to locate.

From: This indicates the most often reported cause of death from the sources previously mentioned.

Buried: When known, the City and State of burial is included. Actual cemetery names and locations are available by writing the author.

Related to: These are the names of famous relatives and how they are related. Not all relatives have been included as this section is still under research.

Awards: Also still under study, the awards such as Oscar, Emmy, Grammy, Golden Mike etc. are listed here.

Notes: (when used) indicate any miscellaneous information which seems more important than all of the other important information available for each personality. ☆

MOTION PICTURES • RADIO

TELEVISION   RECORDING

LIVE THEATRE

LATE ADDITIONS

A few names have been submitted for publication too late for full inclusion into lists and maps. These can be found at end of Zs, page 178.

72

Abbott, Bud...{27/21}
1615 Vine Street (West)
Near: Doolittle Theater
Category/As: Motion Pictures as Comedian
For: Buck Privates (1940) Universal
Real name: William Alexander Abbott
Born: October 2, ~~1974~~ in Asbury Park, NJ *1898*
Died: April 24, 1974 from cancer

Abbott, Bud...{15/01}
6331 Hollywood Boulevard (North)
Near: Guaranty Building
Category/As: Radio as Comedian
For: The Abbott & Costello Show (1944) NBC

Abbott, Bud...{36/26}
6740 Hollywood Boulevard (South)
Near: Sports Emporium
Category/As: Television as Comedian
For: The Abbott & Costello Show (1951)

Abdul, Paula...{04/22}
7021 Hollywood Boulevard (North)
Near: Hollywood Galaxy
Category/As: Recording as Singer
For: Nasty Boys
Dedicated on December 4, 1991
Real name: same or unknown

Ackerman, Harry...{09/43}
6665 Hollywood Boulevard (North)
Near: Top Western
Category/AS: Television as Producer.
For: Bewitched (1964)
Dedicated on June 26, 1985
Real name: same or unknown
Born: November 17, 1912 in NY
Died: 1991, from pulmonary failure
Related to Eleanor Donahue (spouse)

Acord, Art... {16/08}
1711 Vine Street (West)
Near: Vacant
Category: Motion Pictures as Actor
For: The Oregon Train (1923)
Real name: same or unknown
Born: 1892 in Stillwater, OK.
Died: 1931, from suicide and buried in Glendale, CA
Related to Louise Lorraine (spouse)

Acuff, Roy...{26/68}
1549 Vine Street (West)
Near: TAV Celeberity Center
Category: Recording as Singer
For: Wabash Cannonball
Born: September 15, 1903 in Maynardsville, TX
Died: 1992

Adoree, Renee...{27/10}
1601 Vine Street (West)
Near: Parking Lot
Category/As: Motion Pictures as Actress
For: The Big Parade (1925)
Real name: Jeanne de la Fonte
Born: September 30, 1898 in Lille, France
Died: 1933, from tuberculosis and buried in Hollywood, CA

Aherne, Brian...{17/29}
1750 Vine Street (East)
Near: Capitol Record Building
Category/As: Television as Actor
For: My Son, My Son (1940)
Real name: William Brian de lacy Aherne
Born: May 2, 1902 in Norton, England
Died: 1986, from heart failure
Related to Joan Fontaine (spouse)

Ahn, Philip...{19/22}
6207 Hollywood Boulevard (North)
Near: Parking Lot
Category/As: Motion Pictures as Actor
For: China Sky (1945)
Dedicated on November 14, 1984
Real name: same or unknown
Born: March 29, 1911 in Los Angeles, CA
Died: 1978, from lung cancer

Albanese, Licia...{09/28}
6673 Hollywood Boulevard (North)
Near: Star Deli
Category/As: Recording as Opera Singer
Real name: same or unknown
Born: July 22, 1913 in Italy.

Albert, Eddie...{13/09}
6439 Hollywood Boulevard (North)
Near: Schtromberg Jewlers
Category/As: Television as Actor
For: Green Acres (1965-1970)
Real name: Edward Albert Heimberger
Born: April 22, 1908 in Rock Island, IL

Albertson, Frank...{36/36}
6752 8A Hollywood Boulevard (South)
Near: International Kitchen
Category/As: Motion Pictures as Actor
For: Room Service (1938)
Born: February 2, 1909
Died: 1964, and buried in Culver City, CA

Albertson, Jack...{18/16}
Located at 6253 Hollywood Boulevard (North)
Near: Equitible Building Entrance
Category/As: Television as Actor
Best remembered for: Chico and the Man (1975) as Ed Brown
Born: June 16, 1910 in Lynn, MA
Died: 1981, from cancer and ashes scattered

Alexander, Ben...{31/55}
6434 Hollywood Boulevard (South)
Near: Picway Shoes
Category/As: Motion Pictures as Actor
For: All Quiet on the Westen Front (1930)
Real name: Nicholas Benton Alexander
Born: May 26, 1911
Died: 1969, from natural causes

Alexander, Ben...{13/19}
6433 Hollywood Boulevard (North)
Near: Pacific Theater
Category/As: Television as Actor
For: Dragnet (1952) NBC as Frank Smith

Allen, Debbie...{37/75}
6904 Hollywood Boulevard (South)
Near: Hollywood Tourist & Gifts
Category/As: Television as Actress
For: Fame (19__)
Dedicated on October 11, 1991
Real name: same or unknown
Born: Unknown in TX

Allen, Fred...{08/43}
6711 Hollywood Boulevard (North)
Near: Harry's Boutique
Category/As: Radio as Comedian
For: Town Hall Tonight (1939)
Real name: John Florence Sullivan
Born: May 31, 1894 in Cambridge, MA
Died: 1956 from heart attack and buried in Hawthorne, NY
Related to Portland Hoffa (spouse)

Allen, Fred...{04/21}
7021 Hollywood Boulevard (North)
Near: Hollywood Galaxy
Category: Television as Panelist
For: Fred Allen's Sketchbook (1954)

Allen, Gracie...{34/39}
6672 Hollywood Boulevard (North)
Near: Hollywood Hamburger
Category/As: Television as Actress
For: Burns & Allen Show (1950-1958)
Real name: Grace Ethel Cecil Rosale
Born: July 26, 1902
Died: 1964, from heart attack and buried in Glendale, CA
Related to George Burns (spouse)

Allen, Rex...{06/18}
6821 Hollywood Boulevard (North)
Near: Hollywood Hamburger
Category/As: Motion Pictures as Actor
For: Old Overland Trail (1953)
Real name: same or unknown
Born: December 31, 1922 in Wilcox, AZ

Allen, Steve...{26/62}
Located at 1541 Vine Street (West)
Near: TAV Celeberity Center
Category/As: Radio as Actor
For: The Steve Allen Show (1952)
Born: December 26, 1921 in New York, NY
Related to Jayne Meadows (spouse)

Allen, Steve...{17/74}
1722 Vine Street (East side)
Near: Nick's diner
Category/As: Television as Actor
For: The Tonight Show (1953) NBC

Allison, Fran...{07/40}
6757 Hollywood Boulevard (North)
Near: Vacant
Category/As: Television as Hostess.
For: Kukla, Fran & Ollie (1947-1957) NBC
Real name: same or unknown
Born: 1923 in IA
Died 1989, from blood disorder

Allyson, June...{26/60}
Located at 1541 Vine Street (West)
Near: TAV Celebrity Center
Category/As: Motion Pictures as Actress
For: The Glenn Miller Story (1954)
Real Name: Ella Geisman
Born: October 7, 1917 in New York, NY
Related to Dick Powell (spouse)

Alpert, Herb...{05/18}
Located at 6935 Hollywood Boulevard (North)
Near: Mann's Chinese Parking
Category/As: Recording as Musician
For: A Taste of Honey
Born: March 31, 1936

Alvarado, Don...{32/09}
Located at 6504 Hollywood Boulevard (South)
Near: Eddie's Starburger
Category/As: Motion Pictures as Actor
For: The Big Steal (1949)
Real name: Jose Page
Born: November 5, 1904
Died: 1967, from cancer

Ameche, Don...{15/41}
Located at 6315 Hollywood Boulevard (North)
Near: Cave Theater

Category/As: Radio as Actor
For: The Bickersons (1946) NBC
Real Name: Dominic Felix Amici
Born: May 31, 1908, in Kenosha, WI

Ameche, Don...{20/76}
6125 Hollywood Boulevard (North)
Near: Pep Boys
Category/As: Television as Actor
For: Coke Time with Eddie Fisher (1953)

Ames, Adrienne...{24/76}
1612 Vine Street (East)
Near: Hollywood Collaterial
Category/As: Motion Pictures as Actress
For: George White's Scandals (1934)
Real name: Adrienne McClure
Born: August 3, 1907 in Fort Worth, TX
Died: 1947, from cancer

Amsterdam, Morey...{37/70}
6840 Hollywood Boulevard (South)
Near: Masonic Temple
Category/As: Radio as Comedian
For: The Morey Amsterdam Show (1948) CBS
Real name: same or unknown
Born: December 14, 1914

Anderson, Bronco Billy...{27/94}
1645 Vine Street (West)
Near: Hollywood Vine Building
Category/As: Motion Pictures as Actor
For: The Bounty Killer (1967)
Real name: Max Aronson
Born: March 21, 1882
Died: 1971, and buried in Los Angeles, CA
Studio: Essany (Co-Founder)   Awards: Oscar

Anderson, Leroy...{24/71}
1614 Vine Street (East)
Near: Parking Lot
Category/As: Recording as Composer
For: The Typewriter song
Real name: same or unknown
Born: June 29, 1908 in MA.   Died: 1975

Anderson, Marion...{23/21}
6262 Hollywood Boulevard (South)
Near; Vacant Lot
Category/As: Recording as Opera Singer
Real name: Same or unknown
Born: February 17, 1902 in Philadelphia, PA

Anderson, Mary...{27/78}
1745 Vine Street (West)
Near: Hollywood Vine Building
Category/As: Motion Pictures as Actress
For: Gone With The Wind (1939)
Real name: same or unknown
Born: April 3, 1924

Andrews, Julie...{05/65}
6925 Hollywood Boulevard (North)
Near: Mann's Chinese Theater
Category/As: Motion Pictures as Actress
For: Mary Poppins (1964)
Real name: Julie Elizabeth Wells
Born: October 1, 1935 in Surrey, England
Awards: Oscar

Andrews Sisters, The...{37/43}
6834 Hollywood Boulevard (South)
Near: Rocket Hollywood
Category/As: Recording as Singers
Best remembered for: Rum & Coca Cola

Dedicated on October 1, 1987
Real names: LaVerne, Maxine and Patty Andrews
Born: 1913, 1916, 1918
Died: LaVerne, 1967 from cancer and buried in Glendale, CA

Angel, Heather...{28/20}
6312 Hollywood Boulevard (South)
Near: Vacant
Category/As: Motion Pictures as Actress
For: Berkeley Square (1933)
Real name: same or unknown
Born: February 9, 1909 in Great Britan
Died: 1986 and buried in Santa Barbara, CA.

Anka, Paul...{37/67}
Located at 6840 Hollywood Boulevard (South side)
Near: Masonic Temple
Category/As: Recording as Singer
Best remembered for: Diana
Dedicated on September 26, 1984
Born: July 30, 1941 in Ottawa, Canada.

Ansara, Michael...{34/29}
6666 Hollywood Boulevard (South)
Near: vacant
Category/As: Television as Actor
For: Broken Arrow (1956-1960) ABC
Real name: same or unknown
Born: April 15, 1922

Anthony, Ray...{16/83}
1749 Vine Street (West)
Near: parking lot
Category/As: Recording as Orchestra Leader
For: The Hokey Pokey
Real name: Raymond Antonini
Born: January 20, 1922 in PA.

Arbuckle, Roscoe...{08/53}
6701 Hollywood Boulevard (North)
Near: Best Mini-Mart
Category/As: Motion Pictures as Comedian
For: The Traveling Salesman (1921) as "Fatty"
Real name: Roscoe Conklin Arbuckle
Born: March 24, 1887 in South Center, AR
Died: 1933, from heart attack and ashes were scattered
Studio: Mack Sennett

Archerd, Army...{05/28}
6925 Hollywood Boulevard (North)
Near: Mann's Chinese Theater
Category/As: Television as Columnist
For: Daily Variety (19__)
Dedicated on June 27, 1984
Real name: same or unknown

Arden, Eve...{15/16}
6329 Hollywood Boulevard (North)
Near: Fantasy T-Shirts
Category/As: Radio as Actress.
For: Our Miss Brooks (1948) CBS
Real name: Eunice Quedens
Born: April 30, 1912 in Mill Valley, CA
Died: 1990, from cancer
Related to/as: spouse: Brooks West

Arden, Eve...{35/25}
6714 Hollywood Boulevard (South)
Near: Numero Uno Pizza
Category/As: Television as Actress
For: Our Miss Brooks (1952-1957)

Arkoff, Samuel Z.....{38/83}
7046 Hollywood Boulevard (South)
Near: X Building

Category/As: Motion Pictures as Producer
Dedicated on January 14, 1993

Arlen, Richard...{07/46}
6755 Hollywood Boulevard (North)
Near: Vacant
Category/As: Motion Pictures as Actor
For: The Four Feathers (1928)
Real name: Richard Cornelius Van Mattemore
Born: September 1, 1899 in Charlottesville, VA
Died: 1976, and buried in Culver City, CA

Arliss, George...{33/122}
6648 Hollywood Boulevard (South)
Near: Hurricane
Category/As: Motion Pictures as Actor
For: The House of Rothschild (1934)
Real name: George Augustus Andrews
Born: April 10, 1868 in London, England
Died: 1946, from bronchial trouble
Studio: Warner Brothers   Awards: Oscar
Related to Florence Montgomery (spouse)

Armstrong, Louis...{38/30}
7000 Hollywood Boulevard (South)
Near: Roosevelt Hotel
Category/As: Recording as Musician
For: Hello Dolly
Real name: Louis Daniel Armstrong
Born: July 4, 1900
Died: 1971, from heart ailment and buried in Flushing, NY

Arnaz, Desi...{15/21}
6327 Hollywood Boulevard (North)
Near: Chicken Delight
Category/As: Motion Pictures as Actor
For: The Long, Long Trailer (1954)
Real name: Desiderio Alberto Arnaz y de Acha III
Born: March 12, 1917 in Santiago, Cuba
Died: 1986, from lung cancer and ashes scattered
Related to Lucille Ball (spouse)

Arnaz, Desi...{23/10}
6254 Hollywood Boulevard (South)
Near: Burned Out
Category/As: Television as Actor
For: I Love Lucy (1951-1957) CBS

Arness, James...{16/86}
1749 Vine Street (West)
Near: Parking Lot
Category/As: Television as Actor
For: Gunsmoke (1955-1975) as Matt Dillon
Real name: James Aurness
Born: May 26, 1923 in Minneapolis, MN
Studio: CBS
Related to Peter Graves (brother)

Arnold, Eddy...{18/62}
6225 Hollywood Boulevard (North)
Near: Vacant
Category: Recording as Singer
For: Make The World Go Away
Real name: Richard Edward Arnold
Born: May 15, 1918 in Henderson, TN

Arnold, Edward...{36/66}
6776 Hollywood Boulevard (South)
Near: McDonald's
Category/As: Recording as Singer
For: Vairous
Real name: Guenther Edward Arnold Scheider
Born: February 18, 1890
Died: April 26, 1956, from cerebral hemorrhage
             and buried in Mission Hills, CA

Aronold, Roseanne...{07/25}
6767 Hollywood Boulevard (North)
Near: Hollywood Wax Museum
Category/As: Television as Comedienne
For: Roseanne (19__) as Roseanne CBS
Dedicated on September 25, 1992
Real name: Roseanne Barr

Arquette, Cliff...{35/33}
6720 Hollywood Boulevard (South)
Near: Hollywood 21 Market
Category/As: Radio as Actor
For: Fibber Mcgee & Molly (1935)
Born: December 28, 1905
Kied: 1974, from heart attack

Arthur, Jean...{15/05}
6331 Hollywood Boulevard (North)
Near: Guaranty Building
Category/As: Motion Pictures as Actress
For: Mr. Deeds Goes to Town (1936)
Real name: Gladys Georgianne Greene
Born: October 17, 1905 in New York, NY
Bied: 1991, from heart failure

Arzner, Dorothy...{25/59}
1550 Vine Street (East)
Near: Parking Lot
Category/As: Motion Pictures as Director
For: The Wild Party (1929)
Dedicated on January 24, 1986
Born: January 3, 1900 in San Francisco, CA
Died: 1979

Asner, Edward...{14/33}
6371 Hollywood Boulevard (North)
Near: Antenna of Hollywood
Category/As: Television as Actor
For: Mary Tylor Moore Show (19__) as Lou Grant
Dedicated on September 17, 1992
Studio: MTM

Astaire, Fred...{36/38}
6754 Hollywood Boulevard (South)
Near: The Dome
Category/As: Motion Pictures as Dancer
For: Easter Parade (1948)
Real name: Frederick Austerlitz
Born: May 10, 1899 in Omaha, NE
Died: 1987, from pneumonia and buried in Chatsworth, CA
Studio: RKO   Awards: Oscar

Asther, Nils...{08/49}
6705 Hollywood Boulevard (North)
Near: Stefano's Two Guys from Italy
Category/As: Motion Pictures as Actor
For: By Candlelight (1934)
Real name: same or unknown
Born: January 17, 1897 in Sweden
Died: 1981

Astor, Mary...{08/55}
6701 Hollywood Boulevard (North)
Near: Best Mini-Mart
Category/As: Motion Pictures as Actress
For: The Great Lie (1941)
Real name: Lucille Vasconcells Langhanke
Born: May 3, 1906 in Quincy, IL
Died: 1987, from emphysema
Awards: Oscar

Austin, Gene...{28/46}
6332 Hollywood Boulevard (South)
Near: Photo City
Category/As: Recording as Singer
For: My Blue Heaven

Real name: same or unknown
Born: June 24, 1900 Died: 1972 from cancer

Autry, Gene...{38/23}
7000 Hollywood Boulevard (South)
Near: Roosevelt Hol\tel
Category/As: Live Theater as Entertainer
For: Various arena performances
Dedicated on April 6, 1987
Real Name: Orvin Gene Autry
Born September 29, 1907 in Tioga, TX

Autry, Gene...{33/112}
6644 Hollywood Boulevard (South)
Near: Larry Edmonds Book Store
Category/As: Motion Pictures as Actor
For: Back in the Saddle (1941)

Autry, Gene...{32/33}
6518 Hollywood Boulevard (South)
Near: New World Jewelry
Category/As: Radio as Singer
For: Gene Autry's Melody Ranch (1940) CBS

Autry, Gene...{30/26}
6384 Hollywood Boulevard (South)
Near: Popeye Chicken
Category/As: Recording as Singer
For: Rudolph the Red-Nosed Reindeer

Autry, Gene...{09/36}
6667 Hollywood Boulevard (North)
Near: Musso & Frank Grill
Category/As: Television as Actor
For: The Gene Autry Show (1951-1954)

Ayres, Agnes...{32/11}
6504 Hollywood Boulevard (South)
Near: Eddie's Starburger
Category/As: Motion Pictures as Actress
For: The Sheik (1921)
Real name: Agnes Hinkle
Born: September 4, 1896   Died: 1940

Ayres, Lew...{14/01}
6385 Hollywood Boulevard (North)
Near: Security Pacific Bank
Category/As: Motion Pictures as Actor
For: all Quiet on the Western Front (1930)
Real name: Lewis Frederick Ayer III
Born: December 28, 1908 in Minneapolis, MN
Studio: MGM
Related to Ginger Rogers (spouse)

Ayres, Lew...{17/57}
1724 Vine Street (East)
Near: Parking Lot
Category/As: Radio as Actor

Bacall, Lauren...{17/46}
1724 Vine Street (East)
Near: Parking Lot
Category/As: Motion Pictures as Actress
For: How to Marry a Millionaire (1953)
Real name: Betty Jean Perske
Born: September 16, 1924 in New York, NY
Related to Humphrey Bogard, Jason Robards (spouses)

BOGART

Bacus, Jim...{16/58}
1735 Vine Street (West)
Near: Palace
Category/As: Television as Actor
For: Gilligan's Island (1964-1966) as Thurston Howell III
Real name: same or unknown
Born: February 25, 1913 in Cleveland, OH
Died: 1989, from Parkinson's disease and buried in Los Angeles, CA

Bacon, Lloyd...{04/53}
7009 Hollywood Boulevard (North)
Near: Fame & Fortune
Category/As: Motion Pictures as Director
For: 42nd Street (1933)
Born: January 16, 1890 in San Jose, CA
Died: 1955, from cerebral hemorrhage

Baggott, King...{28/23}
6312 Hollywood Boulevard (South)
Near: vacant store
Category/As: Motion Pictures as Actor
For: Dr. Jekyll & Mr. Hyde (1913)
Real name: same or unknown
Born: 1880   Died: 1948, from stroke

Bailey, Jack...{17/98}
1706 Vine Street (East)
Near: Vacant
Category/As: Radio as Announcer
For: The Adventures of Ozzie & Harriet (1944)
Born: September 15, 1907 in IA
Died: 1980

Bailey, Jack...{13/49}
6411 Hollywood Boulevard (North)
Near: Hollywood Boots
Category/As: Television as Host
For: Truth or Consequences (1954)

Bainter, Fay...{04/23}
7021 Hollywood Boulevard (North)
Near: Hollywood Galaxy
Category/As: Motion Pictures as Actress
For: Jezebel (1938)
Real name: same or unknown
Born: December 7, 1892   Died: 1968
Awards: Oscar

Baker, Art...{12/31}
6509 Hollywood Boulevard (North)
Near: LA Roxx
Category/As: Radio as Announcer
For: Hollywood in Person (1937) CBS
Real name: same or unknown
Born: 1898 in NY
Died: 1966, from heart attack

Baker, Carroll...{16/47}
1719 Vine Street (West)
Near: Parking Lot
Category: Motion Pictures as Actress
For: Giant (1955)
Real name: same or unknown
Born: May 28, 1931 in Johnstown, PA

Baker, Kenny...{15/15}
Located at 6329 Hollywood Boulevard (North side)
Near: Fantasy T-Shirts
Category/As: Radio as Singer
Best remembered for: The Jack Benny Program (1943)
Real Name: same or unknown
Born: September 30, 1912
Died: 1985, from heart attack and buried in Solvang, CA

Baker, Phil...{18/30}
6247 Hollywood Boulevard (North)
Near: Ronnie's Donuts
Category/As: Radio as Host
For: Take It or Leave It (1940) CBS
Born: August 24, 1898 in Philadelphia, PA
Died: 1963, from long illness

Ball, Lucille...{31/57}
6440 Hollywood Boulevard (South)
Near: Playmates
Category/As: Motion Pictures as Actress
For: Fancy Pants (1950)
Real name: Dianne Belmont
Born: August 6, 1911 in Wyandotte, MI
Died: 1989, from heart surgery and buried in Los Angeles, CA
Related to Desi Arnaz, Gary Morton (spouses)

Ball, Lucille...{21/15}
6100 Hollywood Boulevard (South)
Near: Chevron Gas Station
Category/As: Television as Comedienne
For: I Love Lucy (1951-1957)

Bancroft, Anne...{30/02}
6370 Hollywood Boulevard (South)
Near: Vacant Lot
Category/As: Television as Actress
Real name: Anna Maria Louisa Italiano
Born: September 17, 1932 in New York, NY

Bankhead, Tallulah...{20/38}
6141 Hollywood Boulevard (North)
Near: Mid-Town Towing
Category/As: Motion Pictures as Actress
For: Lifeboat (1944)
Real name: same or unknown
Born: January 31, 1902 in Huntsville, AL
Died: 1968, from double pneumonia
Studio: Paramount

Banky, Vilma...{04/07}
7021 Hollywood Boulevard (North)
Near: Hollywood Galaxy
Category/As: Motion Pictures as Actress
For: The Dark Angel (1925)
Real name: Vilma Lonchit
Born: January 9, 1903 in Budapest
Related to Rod LaRoque (spouse)

Bara, Theda...{15/48}
6307 Hollywood Boulevard (North)
Near: Last Moving Picture
Category/As: Motion Pictures as Actress.
Best remembered for: Romeo & Juliet (1916)
Real name: Theodosia Goodman
Born: July 20, 1890 in Cincinnati, OH
Died: 1988

Bari, Lynn...{21/25}
6100 Hollywood Boulevard (South)
Near: Chevron Gas Station
Category/As: Motion Picture as Actress
For: Always Goodbye (1938)
Real Name: Marjorie Schuyler Fisher
Born: December 18. 1915 in Roanoke, VA
Died: 1989, from long illness

Bari, Lynn...{15/25}
6323 Hollywood Boulevard (North)
Near: A AALL Hollywood Key
Category/As: Television as Actress
For: Detective's Wife (1950)

Barker, Bob...{35/24}
6714 Hollywood Boulevard (South)
Near: Numero Uno Pizza
Category/As: Television as Host
For: The Price is Right (1957) CBS

Barnes, Binnie...{26/04}
1501 Vine Street (West)
Near: Shopping Center
Category/As: Motion Pictures as Actress
For: The Trouble With Angels (1956)
Real name: Gitelle Enoyce Barnes
Born: March 25, 1905 in England.

Barrie, Mona...{21/55}
6140 Hollywood Boulevard (South)
Near: Henry Fonda Theater
Category/As: Motion Pictures as Actress
For: Never Give a Sucker an Even Break (1941)
Real name: Mona Smith
Born: December 18, 1909 in Australia

Barrie, Wendy...{17/112}
1700 Vine Street (East)
Near: Equitable Building
Category/As: Motion Pictures as Actress
For: The Hound of the Baskervilles (1939)
Real Name: Margaret Wendy Jenkins
Born: April 18, 1912 in England
Died: 1978, from long illness

Barriscale, Bessie...{34/07}
6652 Hollywood Boulevard (South)
Near: Hollywood BBQ
Category/As: Motion Pictures as Actress
For: Various silent films
Real name: same or unknown

Barron, Blue...{17/60}
1724 Vine Street (East)
Near: Parking Lot
Category/As: Recording as Musician
Real name: same or unknown

Barry, Gene...{11/14}
6555 Hollywood Boulevard (North)
Near: Legends of Hollywood
Category/As: Live Theater as Actor
For: Bat Masterson (1958)
Dedicated on May 5, 1988
Real name: same or unknown
Born: 1921

Barrymore, Ethel...{04/70}
7001 Hollywood Boulevard (North)
Near: Hollywood Souvenirs
Category/As: Motion Pictures as Actress
For: None But the Lonely Heart (1944)
Real name: Ethel Mae Blythe
Born: August 15, 1879 In Philadelphia, PA
Died: June 18, 1958, from heart condition and buried in Los Angeles, CA.
Awards: Oscar
Related to/ John Barrymore & Lionel Barrymore (brothers)

Barrymore, John...{09/34}
6667 Hollywood Boulevard (North)
Near: Musso & Frank Grill
Category/As: Motion Pictures as Actor
For: Dr. Jekyll & Mr. Hyde (1920)
Real name: John Sidney Blythe
Born: February 14, 1882 in Philadelphia, PA
Died: May 29, 1942, from cardiac condition and buried in Philadelphia, PA.
Related to Delores Costello (spouse), John Drew (son), Ethel (sister)

DOLORES?

Barrymore, John Drew...{38/12}
7000 Hollywood Boulevard (South)
Near: Roosevelt Hotel
Category/As: Motion Pictures as Actor
For: Kung Fu (1974)
Real Name: John Blythe Barrymore, Jr.
Born: June 4, 1932
Related to John Barrymore (father), Delores Costello (mother)

DOLORES?

Barrymore, Lionel...{17/51}
1724 Vine Street (East)
Near: Parking Lot
Category/As: Motion Pictures as Actor
For: A Free Soul (1931)
Real Name: Lionel Blythe
Born: April 28, 1878 in Philadelphia, PA
Died: 1954 from heart attack and buried in Los Angeles, CA
Awards: Oscar
Related to Ethel Barrymore (sister), John Barrymore (brother)

Barrymore, Lionel...{27/83}
1645 Vine Street (West)
Near: Hollywood Vine Building
Category/As: Radio as Actor

Barthelmess, Richard...{07/44}
6753 Hollywood Boulevard (North)
Near: Vacant
Category: Motion Pictures as Actor
For: The Enchanted Cottage (1945)
Real Name: same or unknown
Born: May 9, 1895 in New York, NY
Died: 1963, from cancer and buried in Hartsdale, NY

Bartholomew, Freddie...{09/40}
6667 Hollywood Boulevard (North)
Near: Musso & Frank Grill
Category/As: Motion Pictures as Actor
For: David Copperfield (1935) MGM
Real Name: Frederick Llwewellyn
Born: March 28, `1924 in London, England
Died: 1983, from emphysema

Barty, Billy...{37/111}
6922 Hollywood Boulevard (South)
Near: Hollywood Center.
Category/As: Television as Actor
Dedicated on July 1, 1981
Born: October 25, 1919

Basehart, Richard...{23/42}
6274 Hollywood Boulevard (South)
Near: Parking Lot
Category/As: Motion Pictures as Actor
For: Moby Dick (1956)
Real Name: same or unknown
Born: August 31, 1915 in OH.
Died: 1984, from stroke and buried in Los Angeles, CA

Basie, Count...{32/18}
6508 Hollywood Boulevard (South)
Near: Fox Theater (closed)
Category/As: Recording as Orchestra Leader
Real Name: William Basie
Born: August 21, 1904
Died: 1984, from cancer

Basinger, Kim...{04/20} *
7021 Hollywood Boulevard (North)
Near: Hollywood Galaxy
Category/As: Motion Pictures as Actress
For: Cool World (1992)
Dedicated on July 8, 1992
Related to Alec Baldwin (spouse)

Basquette, Lina...{26/48}
1541 Vine Street (West)
Near: TAV Celebrity Center
Category/As: Motion Pictures as Dancer
For: Juvenile Dancer (1916)
Real Name: Lina Baskette
Born: April 19, 1907

Baxter, Anne...{08/11}
6743 Hollywood Boulevard (North)
Near: B. Dalton Book Store
Category/As: Motion Pictures as Actress
For: All About Eve (1950)
Born: May 7, 1923 in Michigan City, IN
Died: 1985, from stroke
Awards: Oscar
Related to John Hodiak (spouse)

Baxter, Dr. Frank C....{08/37}
6717 Hollywood Boulevard (North)
Near: Olympic Hamburger
Category/As: Television as Host
For: Telephone Time (1957)
Died: 1982

Baxter, Les...{28/24}
6314 Hollywood Boulevard (South)
Near: DAV Tech Computers
Category/As: Recording as Composer
For: The Raven (1963)
Real name: same or unknown
Born: March 14, 1922 in Texas

Baxter, Warner...{23/58}
6290 Hollywood Boulevard (South)
Near: Holly Vine Shoppe
Category/As: Motion Pictures as Actor
For: Daddy Long Legs (1931)
Real name: same or unknown
Born: March 29, 1889 in Columbus, OH
Died: 1951, from pneumonia
Studio: Fox   Awards: Oscar

Bayne, Beverly...{17/25}
1750 Vine Street (East)
Near: Capitol Record Building
Category/As: Motion Pictures as Actress
For: Romeo & Juliet (1916)
Real name: Pearl Von Name
Born: November 11, 1894 in Minneapolis, MN
Died: 1982, from natural causes
Related to Francis X. Bushman (spouse)

Beach Boys...{25/85}
1500 vine Street (East)
Near: Home Savings
Category/As: Recording as Singers
For: Surfin' USA
Dedicated on December 30, 1980
Real names: Brian Wilson, Carl Wilson, Dennis Wilson,
          Mike Love, Al Jardine
Died: Dennis, 1983, from drowning

Beaudine, William...{16/103}
1777 Vine Street (West)
Near: Vine Street Building
Category/As: Motion Pictures as Director
For: Torchy Blane in Chinatwon (1939)   Chinatown?
Real name: same or unknown
Born: January 14, 1892 in NY
Bied: 1970

Bee Gees ...{06/02}
6845 Hollywood Boulevard (North)
Near: Starline Tours & Gifts

Category/As: Recording as Musicians
For: Staurday Night Fiver
Real name: Robin and Maurice Barry
Born: Barry, September 1, 1946, in England.

Beery, Wallace...{04/68}
7001 Hollywood Boulevard (North)
Near: Hollywood Souvenirs
Category/As: Motion Pictures as Actor
For: The Champ (1931)
Born: april 1, 1885
Died: 1949, from heart attack and buried in Glendale, CA
Awards: Oscar
Related to Gloria Swanson (spouse)

Beery, Jr., Noah...{04/09}
7021 Hollywood Boulevard (North)
Near: Hollywood Glaaxy
Category/As: Television as Actor
For: The Rockford Files (1974) NBC
Born: August 10, 1915 in New York, NY

Beirne, Brian...{07/03}
6777 Hollywood Boulevard (North)
Near: Hollywood First National Building
Category/As: Radio as Unknown
Dedicated on January 18, 1991
Real name: same or unknown

Belafonte, Harry...{08/33}
6721 Hollywood Boulevard (North)
Near: Vacant
Category/As: Recording as Singer
For: Dao-O
Real name: Harold George Belafonte, Jr.
Born: March 1, 1927 in Harlem, NY
Awards: Grammy, Emmy
Related to Shari Belafonte (daughter)

Bellamy, Madge...{12/21}
6517 Hollywood Boulevard (North)
Near: Los Burritos
Category/As: Motion Pictures as Actress
For: Lorna Doone (1922)
Real name: Margaret Philpott
Born: June 30, 1903 in Hillsboro, TX
Died: 1990, from heart failure

Bellamy, Ralph...{33/04}
6542 Hollywood Boulevard (South)
Near: Consumer's Discount
Category/As: Television as Actor
For: Ellery Queen, Master Detective (1940)
Real name: Ralph Rexford Bellamy
Born: June 17, 1904
Died: 1991, from respiratory infection
Awards: Oscar

Benaderet, Bea...{27/23}
1615 Vine Street (West)
Near: Doolittle Theater
Category/As: Television as Actress
For: Petticoat Junction (1963) as Kate Bradley
Born: April 4, 1906 in New York, NY.
Died: 1968, from cancer and burried in Burbank, CA
Studio: CBS

Benchley, Robert...{17/52}
1724 Vine Street (East)
Near: Parking lot
Category/As: Motion Pictures as Screenwriter
For: How to Sleep (1935) Award: Oscar
Real name: same or unknown
Born: September 15, 1889 in Worcester, MA
Died: 1945, from cerebral hemorrhage

Bendix, William...{24/35}
1638 Vine Street (East)
Near: Hollywood Import House
Category/As: Radio as Actor
For: The Life of Riley (1943) NBC as Chester A. Riley
Born: January 14, 1906 in New York, NY.
Died: December 14, 1964, from pnuemonia
and buried in Mission Hills, CA

Bendix, William...{18/25}
6251 Hollywood Boulevard (North)
Near: Parking Lot
Category/As: Television as Actor
Best remembered for: The Life of Riley (1953-1958)

Beneke, Tex...{22/44}
6200 Hollywood Boulevard (South)
Near: Parking Lot
Category/As: Recording as Singer
Dedicated on September 12, 1991
Real Name: same or unknown

Bennett, Belle...{26/18}
1501 Vine Street (West)
Near: Shopping Center
Category/As: Motion Pictures as Actress
For: Stella Dallas (1925)
Real name: same or unknown
Born: October 21, 1892 in MN
Died: 1932, from long illness

Bennett, Constance...{23/04}
6250 Hollywood Boulevard (South)
Near: Stella Adler Theater
Category/As: Motion Pictures as Actress
For: Topper (1938)
Real name: same or unknown
Born: October 22, 1904 in New York, NY
Died: 1965, from cerebral hemorrhage and buried in Arlington, VA
Related to Gilbert Roland (spouse), Joan Bennett (sister)

Bennett, Joan...{28/17}
6310 Hollywood Boulevard (South)
Near: Olympic Electronics
Category/As: Motion Pictures as Actress
For: Little Women (1938)
Real name: same or unknown
Born: February 27, 1910 in Palasades, NJ
Died: 1990, from cardiac arrest
Related to Constance Bennett (sister)

Bennett, Tony...25/30}
1560 Vine Street (East)
Near: Parking Lot
Category/As: Recording as Singer
For: I Left My Heart In San Francisco
Real Name: Anthonio Dominick Benedetto
Born: August 3, 1926
Awards: Grammy

Benny, Jack...{34/03}
6650 Hollywood Boulevard (South)
Near: Hurricane
Category/As: Motion Pictures as Comedian
For: Charlie's Aunt (1941)
Real name: Benjamin Kubelsky
Born: February 14, 1894 in Waukegan, IL
Died: 1974, from cancer and buried in Los Angeles, CA
Related to/as: spouse: Mary Livingstone

Benny, Jack...{26/10}
1501 Vine Street (West)
Near: Shopping Center
Category/As: Radio as Comedian
For: The Jack Benny Show (1944)

Benny, Jack...{30/08}
6370 Hollywood Boulevard (South)
Near: Vacant Lot
Category/As: Television as Actor
For: The Jack Benny Show (1950-1965)

Beradino, John...{06/62}
6801 Hollywood Boulevard (North)
Near: Vacant
Category/As: Television as Actor.
For: General Hospital (1953) as Dr. Steve Hardy _(3-95_
Dedicated on April 1, 1993

Bergen, Edgar...{07/24}
6767 Hollywood Boulevard (North)
Near: Hollywood Wax Museum
Category/As: Motion Pictures as Actor
For: I Remember Mama (1948)
Real name: Edgar John Bergren
Born: February 16, 1903
Died: 1978, from heart attack and buried in Inglewood, CA
Awards: Oscar

Bergen, Edgar...{06/51}
6801 Hollywood Boulevard (North)
Near: Vacant
Category/As: Radio as Ventriloquist
For: The Charlie McCarthy Show (1937)

Bergen, Edgar...{13/29}
6425 Hollywood Boulevard (North)
Near: Pacific Hollywood Building
Category/As: Television as Host
For: Do You Trust Your Wife? (1956)

Bergman, Ingrid...{07/38}
6759 Hollywood Boulevard (North)
Near: This is Hollywood
Category/As: Motion Pictures as Actress
Best remembered for: for Whom the Bell Tolls (1943)
Born: August 29, 1915 in Stockholm, Sweden
Died: August 29, 1982, from cancer
Awards: Oscar

Berle, Milton...{07/18}
6771 Hollywood Boulevard (North)
Near: Hollywood Leather & Gift
Category/As: Radio as Comedian
For: Stop Me If You've Heard This One (1939)
Real name: Milton Berlinger
Born: July 12, 1908 in New York, NY
Studio: NBC

Berle, Milton...{18/07}
6263 Hollywood Boulevard (North)
Near: Equitible Building
Category/As: Television as Comedian
For: The Texaco Star Theater (1948-1956)

Bernhardt, Sarah...{16/79}
Located at 1749 Vine Street (West side)
Near: Parking Lot
Category/As: Motion Pictures as Actress
Best remembered for: Queen Elizabeth (1912)
Real name: Henriette-Rosine Bernard
Born: October 25, 1844 in France
Died: 1923, from uremic poisioning

Bernie, Ben...{23/48}
6284 Hollywood Boulevard (South)
Near: India Tandor
Category/As: Radio as Bandleader
For: Sweet Georgia Brown
Real name: same or unknown

Born: May 30, 1891 in New York, NY
Died: 1943, from long illness

Bernstein, Leonard...{22/37}
6200 Hollywood Boulevard (South)
Near: parking Lot
Category/As: Recording as Conductor
For: West Side Story (1961)
Real name: same or unknown
Born: August 25, 1918 in Lawrence, MA
Died: 1990, from emphysema and buried in Brooklyn, NY

Berry, Chuck...{16/113}
1779 Vine Street (West)
Near: Capezio Dance
Category/As: Recording as Musician
For: Johnny B. Good
Dedicated on October 8, 1987
Real Name: Charles Edward Berry

Best, Edna...{21/37}
6124 Hollywood Boulevard (South)
Near: Doug's Sports Corner
Category/As: Motion Pictures as Actress
For: The Man Who Knew Too Much (1934)
Real name: same or unknown
Born: March 3, 1900 in England
Died: 1974
Related to Herbert Marshall (spouse)

Bickford, Charles...{36/72}
6780 Hollywood Boulevard (South)
Near: Ripley's Museum
Category/As: Motion Pictures as Actor
For: Johnny Belinda (1948)
Real name: Charles Ambrose Bickford
Born: January 1, 1889
Died: November 9, 1967, from emphysema

Bickford, Charles...{24/70}
1614 Vine Street (East)
Near: Parking Lot
Category/As: Television as Actor
For: The Virginian (1966)

Biggs, E. Power...{32/39}
6522 Hollywood Boulevard (South)
Near: Newberry School of Beauty
Category/As: Recording as Organist
Real Name: same or unknown
Born: March 29, 1906   Died: 1977

Binney, Constance...{15/56}
6301 Hollywood Boulevard (North)
Near: Vacant
Category/As: Motion Pictures as Actress
For: Various Paramount silent films
Real Name: same or unknown

Blackmer, Sidney...{27/54}
1627 Vine Street (West)
Near: Parking Lot
Category/As: Motion Pictures as Actor
For: The Count of Monte Cristo (1934)
Born: July 13, 1895 in Salisbury, NC.
Died: 1973, from cancer

Blackwell, Carlyle...{28/60}
6340 Hollywood Boulevard (South)
Near: (closed) Mr. Submarine
Category/As: Motion Pictures as Actor
For: Uncle Tom's Cabin (1909)
Real Name: same or unknown
Born: April 21, 1888   Died: 1955

Blanc, Mel...{14/12}
6385 Hollywood Boulevard (North)
Near: Security Pacific Bank
Category/As: Radio as Actor
For: Jack Benny Program (1940) as Monsieur Le Blanc
Real name: Melvin Jerome Blanc
Born: 1908 in San Francisco., CA
Died: 1989, from heart disease and buried in Hollywood, CA
Studio: Warner Brothers

Blondell, Joan...{15/45}
6309 Hollywood Boulevard (North)
Near: Hollywood Recovery Center
Category/As: Motion Pictures as Actress
For: Stage Struck (1936)
Real name: same or unknown
Born: August 30, 1909 in New York, NY
Died: 1979 from luekemia and buried in Glendale, CA
Related to Dick Powell (spouse)

Blue, Monte...{23/53}
6286 Hollywood Boulevard (South)
Near: Metro Rail Field Office
Category/As: Motion Pictures as Actor
For: The Marriage Circle (1924)
Real name: same or unknown
Born: January 11, 1890 in Indianapolis, IN
Died: 1963 from coronary attack and buried in Glendale, CA

Blyth, Ann...{08/21}
6727 Hollywood Boulevard (North)
Near: Artesian Patio
Category/As: Motion Pictures as Actress
For: Mildred Pierce (1945) MGM
Real name: Ann Marie Blyth
Born: August 16, 1928 in NY

Blythe, Betty...{17/97}
1706 Vine Street (East side)
Near: vacant
Catergory/As: Motion Pictures as Actress
For: The Queen of Sheeba (1921)
Real name: Elizabeth Blythe Slaughter
Born: September 1, 1893 in Los Angeles, CA   Died: 1972

Boardman, Eleanor...{37/110}
6922 Hollywood Boulevard (South)
Near: Hollywood Center
Category/As: Motion Pictures/Actress
For: The Crowd (1928) Goldwyn
Born: August 19, 1898 in Philadelphia, PA   Died: 1991
Related to King Vidor, Henri D'Addabie D'Arrasti (spouses)

Bogart, Humphrey...{28/34}
6320 Hollywood Boulevard (South side)
Near: Hollywood Bazaar
Category/As: Motion Pictures as Actor
For:The African Queen (1951)
Real name: Humphrey DeForest Bogart
Born: December 25, 1899 in New York, NY
Died: January 14, 1957 from esophagus cancer
        and buried in Glendale, CA

Boland, Mary...{22/13}
6150 Hollywood Boulevard (South)
Near: Network Body Shop
Category/As: Motion Pictures as Actress
For: Ruggles of Red Gap (1935)
Real name: same or unknown
Born: January 28, 1880 in Philadelphia, PA   Died: 1965

Boles, John...{32/49}
6530 Hollywood Boulevard (South)
Near: Georgio's Pizza
Category/As: Motion Pictures as Actor
For: Stella Dallas (1937)

Born: October 28, 1895
Died: February 27, 1969 from a heart attack
and buried in Los Angeles, CA

Boleslawski, Richard...{04/03}
7021 Hollywood Boulevard (North)
Near: Hollywood Galaxy
Category/As: Motion Pictures as Director
For: Les Miserables (1935) MGM
Real name: Rysard Srzedniki Boleslawsky
Born: February 4, 1889 in Warsaw, Poland
Died: 1937

Bolger, Ray...{36/54}
6764 Hollywood Boulevard (South)
Near: Guiness World Record Museum
Category/As: Motion Pictures as Actor
For: The Wizard of Oz (1930)
Real name: Raymond Wallace
Born: January 10, 1904
Died: 1987, from cancer and buried in Culver City, CA

Bolger, Ray...{37/48}
6834 Hollywood Boulevard (South)
Near: Rocket Hollywood
Category/As: Television as Actor
For: The Ray Bolger Show (1953)

Bond, Ford...{35/11}
6706 Hollywood Boulevard (South)
Near: burned out store
Category/As: Radio as Announcer
Real name: David Bond
Died: 1962

Bond, Ward..{05/17}
6935 Hollywood Boulevard (North)
Near: Chinese Theater Parking Lot
Category/As: Television as Actor
For: Wagon Train (1957)
Born: April 9, 1904
Died: 1960, from a heart attack

Bondi, Beulah...{17/75}
1718 Vine Street (East)
Near: Sun Palace Restaurant
Category/As: Motion Pictures as Actress
For: The Snake Pit (1948)
Real name: Beulah Bondy
Born: May 3, 1888 in Chicago, IL
Died: January 14, 1981 from pulmonary complications

Boone, Pat...{27/56}
1633 Vine Street (West)
Near: Plaza Building
Category/As: Recording as Singer
For: Love Letters in the Sand
Real name: Charles Eugene Boone
Born: June 1, 1934

Boone, Pat...{23/30}
6274 Hollywood Boulevard (South)
Near: parking lot
Category/As: Television as Singer
For: The Pat Boone Chevy Showroom (1957)

Booth, Shirley...{37/62}
6840 Hollywood Boulevard (South)
Near: Masonic Temple
Category/As: Motion Pictures as Actress
For: Come Back Little Sheba (1952)
Real name: Thelma Booth Ford
Born: August 30, 1898 in New York, NY
Related to Ed Gardner (spouse)

Borden, Olive...{06/69}
6801 Hollywood Boulevard (North)
Near: vacant office building
Category/As: Motion Pictures as Actress
For: Sinners in Love (1928)
Real name: Sybil Trinkle
Born: July 14, 1907 in Richmond, VA
Died: 1947, from stomach ailment and buried in Glendale, CA

Borgnine, Ernest...{28/39}
6324 Hollywood Boulevard (South)
Near: vacant building
Category/As: Motion Pictures as Actor
For: Marty (1955)
Real name: Ermes Effron Borgnino
Born: January 24, 1917 in Hamden, CT

Borzage, Frank...{28/11}
6304 Hollywood Boulevard (South)
Near: 7 Tourist and Travel
Category/As: Motion Pictures as Director
For: Seventh Heaven (1927) MGM
Born: April 23, 1893 in Salt Lake City, UT
Died: 1962, from cancer and buried in Glendale, CA

Bosworth, Hobart...{32/41}
6522 Hollywood Boulevard (South)
Near: Newberry School of Beauty
Category/As: Motion Pictures as Actor
For: The Big Parade (1925)
Born: August 10, 1865
Died: 1943, from pneumonia and buried in Glendale, CA

Bow, Clara...{25/68}
1500 Vine Street (East)
Near: parking lot
Category/As: Motion Pictures as Actress
For: My Lady of Whims (1925)
Real name: same or unknown
Born: August 15, 1905 in New York, NY
Died: 1965, from a heart attack and
buried in Glendale, CA
Related to Rex Bell (spouse)

Bowers, John...{16/10}
1711 Vine Street (West)
Near: vacant restaurant
Category/As: Motion Pictures as Actor
For: various silent films
Real name: same or unknown
Born: December 25, 1899 in Garrett, IN
Died: 1936, from drowning

Bowes, Major...{26/20}
1501 Vine Street (West)
Near: shopping center
Category/As: Radio as Host
For: Original Amateur Hour (1934) NBC
Real name: Major Edward Bowes
Born: 1874, in CA
Died: 1946, and buried in Ridgewood, NY

Boyd, Bill...{20/94}
6125 Hollywood Boulevard (North)
Near: Pep Boys
Category/As: Radio as Actor
For: Hopalong Cassidy (1941) CBS, as Hopalong
Real name: William Boyd
Born: June 5, 1898 in OH
Died: 1972, from Parkinson's disease

Boyd, Jimmy...{04/11}
7021 Hollywood Boulevard (North)
Near: Hollywood Galaxy
Category/As: Recording as Singer

r: I Saw Mommy Kissin' Santa Claus
rn: January 9, 1940

yd, William...{16/65}
35 Vine Street (West)
ar: Palace
tegory/As: Motion Pictures as Actor
r: Hopalong Cassidy Enters (1935) as Hopalong
te: (See Bill Boyd)

yer, Charles...{28/14}
06 Hollywood Boulevard (South)
ar: Exotic Hair and Nail
tegory/As; Motion Pictures as Actor
r: Algiers (1938)
al name: same or unknown
rn: August 28, 1897 in Figeac, France
ed: 1978, from suicide (overdose) and buried in Culver City, CA

yer, Charles...{28/10}
04 Hollywood Boulevard (South)
ar: 7 Tourist and Travel
tergry/As: Television as Actor
r: The Rouges (1964)

acken, Eddie...{27/88}
45 Vine Street (West)
ar: Hollywood Vine Building
tegory/As: Radio as Actor
al name: Edward Vincent Bracken
rn: February 7, 1915 in Astoria, NY

acken, Eddie...{07/50}
51 Hollywood Boulevard (North)
ar: vacant store
tegory/As: Television as Host
r: Masquerade Party (1957)

ady, Alice...{19/05}
11 Hollywood Boulevard (North)
ar: Capitol Records Annex
tegory/As: Motion Pictures as Actress
r: In Old Chicago (1938)
al name: same or unknown
rn: November 2, 1892 in NY
ed: October 28, 1939 from cancer

ando, Marlon...{16/110}
77 Vine Street (West)
ar: Vine Street Building
tegory/As: Motion Pictures as Actor
r: The Godfather (1972) as Don Vito Corleone Paramount
al name: Marlon Brando, Jr.
rn: April 3, 1925 in Omaha, NE

eneman, Tom...{23/59}
90 Hollywood Boulevard (South)
ar: Holly Vine Shoppe
tegory/As: Radio as MC
r: Breakfast in Hollywood (1942) ABC
al name: same or unknown
rn: 1902 Died: 1948

ennan, Walter...{12/41}
01 Hollywood Boulevard (North)
ar: burned out store
tegory/As: Motion Pictures as Actor
r: Kentucky (1938)
al name: same or unknown
rn: July 25, 1894 in Swampscott, MA
ed: 1974, from emphysema

ent, Evelyn...{33/12}
48 Hollywood Boulevard (South)
ar: Enterprise Shoes

Category/As: Motion Pictures as Actress
For: Underworld (1927) Warner Brothers
Real name: Mary Elizabeth Riggs
Born: October 20, 1899
Died: 1975, from a heart attack

Brent, George...{16/16}
1711 Vine Street (West)
Near: vacant restaurant
Category/As: Motion Pictures as Actor
For: The Spiral Staircase (1945)
Real Name: George Brent Nolan
Born: March 15, 1904 in Shannonbridge, Ireland
Died: May 26, 1979 from emphysema
Studio: Warner Brothers
Related to Ruth Chatterton, Ann Sheridan (spouses)

Brent, George...{24/75}
1614 Vine Street (East)
Near: parking lot
Category/As: Television as Actor
For: Wire Service (1956)

Brewer, Teresa...{17/102}
1704 Vine Street (East)
Near: Krisseli's Center
Category/As: Recording as Singer
For: Music, Music, Music
Real name: Theresa Breuer
Born: May 7, 1931 in Toledo, OH

Brian, David...{04/35}
7021 Hollywood Boulevard (North)
Near: Hollywood Galaxy
Category/As: Television as Actor
For: Mr. District Attorney (1954)
Born: August 5, 1914

Brian, Mary...{26/92}
1555 Vine Street (West)
Near: TAV Celebrity Center
Category/As: Motion Pictures as Actress
For: The Front Page (1931)
Real name: Louise Byrdie Dantzler
Born: February 17, 1908 in TX

Brice, Fanny...{13/43}
6415 Hollywood Boulevard (North)
Near: Diamalaye
Category/As: Motion Pictures as Comedianne
For: The Great Ziegfeld (1936)
Real name: Fannie Borach
Born: October 29, 1891 in New York, NY
Died: 1951, from cerebral hemorrhage and buried in Los Angeles, CA

Brice, Fanny...{25/80}
1500 Vine Street (East)
Near: Home Savings Bank
Category/As: Radio as Actress
For: The Baby Snooks Show (1939)

Briem, Ray...{20/97}
6125 Hollywood Boulevard (North)
Near: Pep Boys
Category: Radio
Dedicated on October 22, 1992
Real name: same or unknown

Britt, Elton...{37/122}
6922 Hollywood Boulevard (South)
Near: Hollywood Center
Category/As: Recording as Singer
For: There's a Star Spangeled Banner Waving Somewhere
Real Name: same or unknown
Born: June 17, 1917

Britton, Barbara...{16/36}
1719 Vine Street (West)
Near: parking lot
Category/As: Televison as Actress
For: Mr. & Mrs. North (1952) as Mrs. North
Real name: Barbara Brantingham Czukor
Born: September 26, 1920 in Long Beach, CA

Broccoli, Cubby...{37/83}
6908 Hollywood Boulevard (South)
Near Hollywood Emporium
Category/As: Motion Picture as Producer
For: James Bond films
Dedicated on January 16, 1990
Real name: Albert R. Broccoli

Bronson, Charles...{05/55}
6925 Hollywood Boulevard (North)
Near: Mann's Chinese Theater
Category/As: Motion Pictures as Actor
For: Death Wish (1974)
Real name: Charles Dennis Bunchinsky
Born: November 3, 1922 in PA
Related to Jill Ireland (spouse)

Brooke, Hillary...{15/47}
6309 Hollywood Boulevard (North)
Near: Hollywood Recovery Center
Category/As: Television as Actress
For: My Little Margie (1952) as Roberta
Real name: Beatrice Sophia Mathilda Peterson
Born: September 8, 1914 in Brooklyn, NY

Brooks, Richard...{31/37}
6422 Hollywood Boulevard (South)
Near: Hollywood Mini-Mall
Category/As: Motion Pictures as Director
For: Cat on a Hot Tin Roof (1956) MGM
Real name: same or unknown
Born: May 18, 1912 in Philadelphia, PA
Died: 1992, from heart failure
Related to Jean Simmons (spouse)

Brown, Cecil...{31/19}
6410 Hollywood Boulevard (South)
Near: F.W. Woolworth
Category/As: Radio as Newscaster
Real name: same or unknown

Brown, Clarence...{17/27}
1750 Vine Street (East)
Near: Capitol Record Building
Category/As: Motion Pictures as Director
For: Anna Karenina (1935) MGM
Born: May 10, 1890 in MA
Died: 1987, from kidney failure and buried in Glendale, CA

Brown, Harry Joe...{16/99}
1749 Vine Street (West)
Near: parking lot
Category/As: Motion Pictures as Producer
For: Captain Blood (1935) Fox
Real name: same or unknown
Born: September 22, 1890 in Pittsburg, PA
Died: 1972

Brown, Joe E. ...{24/05}
1680 Vine Street (East)
Near: Taft Building
Category/As: Motion Pictures as Actor
For: Some Like It Hot (1959)
Real name: same or unknown
Born: July 28, 1892 in OH
Died: 1973, from a long illness and buried in Glendale, CA

Brown, Johnny Mack...{20/80}
6125 Hollywood Boulevard (North)
Near: Pep Boys
Category/As: Motion Pictures as Actor
For: Billy the Kid (1930)
Real name: same or unknown
Born: September 1, 1904 in AL
Died: 1974, from cardiac condition and buried in Glendale, CA

Brown, Les...{12/35}
6505 Hollywood Boulevard (North)
Near: Tony's Shoes
Category/As: Recording as Conductor
For: The Band of Renown
Real name: Same or unknown
Born: March 14, 1912

Brown, Tom...{24/24}
1648 Vine Street (East)
Near: Jerimiha Comey Studio
Category/As: Motion Pictures as Actor
For: Judge Priest (1934)
Real name: Thomas E. Brown
Born: January 6, 1913 in New York, NY
Died: 1990, from cancer

Brown, Vanessa...{27/37}
1627 Vine Street (West)
Near: parking lot
Category/As: Motion Pictures as Actress
For: The Ghost and Mrs. Muir (1947)
Real name: Smylla Brind
Born: March 24, 1928 in Vienna, Austria

Brown, Vanessa...{32/47}
6528 Hollywood Boulevard (South)
Near: Lisa Boutique
Category/As: Television as Panelist
For: Leave It to the Girls (1949)

Browning, Tod...{18/65}
6225 Hollywood Boulevard (North)
Near: vacant store
Category/As: Motion Pictures as Director
For: Dracula (1930)
Real name: Charles Browning
Born: July 12, 1882 In Louisville, KY
Died: 1962, from cancer

Brubeck, Dave... {17/87}
1718 Vine Street (East)
Near: Sun Palace Restaurant
Category/As: Recording as Jazz Composer
Born: December 6, 1920 in Concord, CA

Brynner, Yul...{22/25}
6160 Hollywood Boulevard (South)
Near: Raji
Category/As: Motion Picture as Actor
For: The King and I (1956)
Real Name: Tuidje Khan
Born: July 12,1915 in Sakhalim, Russia
Died: 1985, from lung cancer

Bunny, Bugs...{04/56}
7007 Hollywood Boulevard (North)
Near: C.C. Brown Ice Cream
Category/As: Motion Pictures as Animated Character
For: Knighty Knight Bugs (19__)
Decicated on: December 21, 1985
Born: 1937 in Hollywood

Bunny, John... {16/27}
1715 Vine Street (West)
Near: Hair Vine

Category/As: Motion Picture as Actor
For: Vanity Fair (1911)
Real Name: same or Unknown
Born September,21 1863 in New York NY
Died: 1915, from Brights disease

Burke, Billie...{10/33}
6617 Hollywood Boulevard (North)
Near: Hollywood Fashion Place
Category/As: Motion Picture as Actress
For: The Wizard of Oz (1939)as Gilda, The Good Witch

Burke, Sonny...{37/100}
6916 Hollywood Boulevard (South)
Near: Gulliver's Travel
Category/As: Recording as Bandleader
Born: March 22, 1914

Burnett, Carol...{13/16}
6433 Hollywood Boulevard (North)
Near: Pacific Theater
Category/As: Television as Comedianne CBS
For: The Carol Burnett Show (1967)
Born: April 26, 1933 in San Antonio, TX

Burnette, Smiley...{20/53}
6425 Hollywood Boulevard (North)
Near: Pep Boys
Category/As: Motion Pictures as Actor
For: Frog Milhouse
Dedicated on May 22, (1986)
Real name: Lester Alvin Burnette
Born: March 18, 1911 in IL
Died: 1967, From lukema and Buried Los Angeles, CA

Burns, Bob... {27/01}
1501 Vine Street (West)
Near: Parking lot
Category/As: Motion Picture as Actor
For: Wells Fargo (1937)
Real name: Bob "Bozooka" Burns
Born: August 2, 1893 in AR
Died: 1956, and Buried in Glendale, Ca

Burns, Bob...{11/37}
6541 Hollywood Boulevard (South)
Near: Janes House
Category/As: Radio as Actor
For: The Arkansas Travler (1941) CBS

Burns, George...{34/38}
6670 Hollywood Boulevard (south)
Near: vacant
Category/As: Live Theater as Actor
Dedicated on November 8, 1984
Real name: Nathan Burnbaum
Born: January 20, 1896
Related to Gracie Allen (spouse)

Burns, George...{27/66}
1637 Vine Street (West)
Near: Early World Restaurant
Category/As: Motion Picture as Actor
For: Oh, God! (1977)

Burns, George...{32/21}
6510 Hollywood Boulevard (South)
Near: Roma Fashions
Category/As: Television as Actor
For: Burns and Allen Show (1950-1958) CBS

Burr, Raymond...{34/13}
6656 Hollywood Boulevard (South)
Near: Ritz Theater

Category/As: Television as Actor
For: Perry Mason (1957)   Award: Emmy
Real name: Raymond William Stacy Burr
Born: May 21, 1917 in New Westminster, B.C.
Died: September 12, 1993 from metastatic cancer

Burrud, Bill...{07/13}
6777 Hollywood Boulevard (North)
Near: Hollywood First National Building
Category/As: Television as Host
For: Animal World (1968)
Real name: same or unknown
Born: January 12, 1925 in Hollywood, CA
Died: 1990, from a heart attack

Burton, Levar...{38/52}
7024 Hollywood Boulevard (South)
Near: Roosevelt Hotel parking structure
Category/As: Television as Actor
For: Roots (19__)
Dedicated on November 15, 1990
Real name: same or unknown

Busch, Mae...{04/19}
7021 Hollywood Boulevard (North)
Near: Hollywood Galaxy
Category/As: Motion Pictures as Actress
For: Foolish Wives (1922)
Born: January 20, 1897 in Australia Died: 1946

Bushman, Francis X. ...{27/89}
1645 Vine Street (West)
Near: Hollywood Vine Building
Category/As: Motion Pictures as Actor
For: Romeo and Juliet (1916)
Real name: same or unknown
Born: January 12, 1883
Died: 1966, from a heart attack due to a fall and buried in Glendale, CA
Related to Beverly Bayne (spouse)

Butler, David...{11/11}
6559 Hollywood Boulevard (North}
Near: Bontoc Gifts
Category/As: Motion Pictures as Director
For: Road to Morrocco (1942) Fox
Real name: same or unknown
Born: December 17, 1894 in San Francisco, CA
Died: 1979, from heart failure

Butterworth, Charles...{38/64}
7024 Hollywood Boulevard (South)
Near: Roosevelt Hotel parking structure
Category/As: Motion Pictures as Actor
For: Bulldog Drummond (1934)
Born: July 25, 1895 Died: 1946, from auto accident

Buttons, Red...{27/92}
1645 Vine Street (West)
Near: Hollywood Vine Building
Category/As: Television as Actor
For: The Red Button Show (1952-1954) CBS
Real name: Aaron Chwatt
Born: February 5, 1919 in New York, NY

Buttram, Pat...{30/23}
6382 Hollywood Boulevard (South)
Near: Shanti's Vegitarian
Category/As: Television as Actor
For: Gene Autry Show (1940-1954)
Dedicated on August 18, 1988
Real name: same or unknown

Byington, Spring...{12/33}
6507 Hollywood Boulevard (North)
Near: LA Roxx
Category/As: Motion Pictures as Actress

For: You Can't Take It With You (1938)
Real name: same or unknown
Born: October 17, 1893 in Colorado Springs, Co Died: 1971

Byington, Spring...{18/52}
6233 Hollywood Boulevard (North)
Near: Pantages Theater
Category/As: Television as Actress
For: December Bride (1954) CBS

C

Caan, James...{33/121}
6648 Hollywood Boulevard (South)
Near: Hurricane
Category/As: Motion Pictures as Actor
For: The Godfather (1972)
Real name: James Cahn
Born: March 26, 1939

Caesar, Sid...{38/28}
7000 Hollywood Boulevard (South)
Near: Roosevelt Hotel
Category/As: Television as Comedian
For: Your Show of Shows (1949-1954) NBC
Born; September 8, 1922

Cagney, James...{32/07}
6502 Hollywood Boulevard (South)
Near: Dr. M. Grosberg
Category/As: Motion Pictures as Actor
For: The Public Enemy (1931)
Real name: James Francis Cagney, Jr.
Born: July 17, 1899 in New York, NY
Died: 1986, from diabetes and buried in Hawthorn, NY
Studio: Warner Brothers   Awards: Oscar

Cahn, Sammy...{32/60}
6540 Hollywood Boulevard (South)
Near: Greg Ward Levi
Category/As: Recording as Composer
For: Three Coins in the Fountain
Dedicated on February 2, 1990
Real name: Samuel Cohen
Born: 1913   Died: January 15, 1992

Calhoun, Alice...{06/50}
6801 Hollywood Boulevard (North)
Near: vacant office building
Category/As: Motion Pictures as Actress
Real name: same or unknown
Born: November 21, 1900 in Cleveland, Oh   Died: 1966

Calhoun, Rory...{04/57}
7007 Hollywood Boulevard (North)
Near: C.C. Brown Ice Cream
Category/As: Motion Pictures as Actor
For: The Hired Gun (1957)
Real name: Francis Timothy Durgin

Calhoun, Rory...{17/28}
1750 Vine Street (East)
Near: Capitol Record Building
Category/As: Television as Actor
For: The Texan (1958-1959) CBS

Callas, Maria...{24/01}
1680 Vine Street (East)
Near: Taft Building
Category/As: Recording as Opera Singer

Real name: Cecilia Maria Calogeropoulous
Born: December 3, 1923 in New York, NY
Died: 1977, from a heart attack

Cameron, Rod...{17/69}
1724 Vine Street (East)
Near: parking lot
Category/As: Television as Actor
For: City Detective (1953)
Real name: Nathan Cox
Born: December 7, 1910 in Calgary, Canada
Died: 1983, from a long illness

Campbell, Glen...{05/26}
6925 Hollywood Boulevard (North)
Near: Mann's Chinese Theater
Category/As: Recording as Singer
For: By the Time I Get to Phoenix
Born: April 22, 1936

Cannell, Stephen J. ...{38/07}
7000 Hollywood Boulevard (South)
Near: Roosevelt Hotel
Category/As: Television as Producer
For: The Rockford Files (1974)
Dedicated on January 14, 1986
Born: February 5, 1942

Cannon, Dyan...{33/53}
6608 Hollywood Boulevard (South)
Near: Frederick's of Hollywood
Category/As: Motion Pictures as Actress
For: Bob & Ted & Carol & Alice (1969)
Dedicated on June 22, 1983
Real name: Samile Diane Friesen
Born: January 4, 1939
Related to Cary Grant (spouse)

Canova, Judy...{06/37}
6819 Hollywood Boulevard (North)
Near: Hollywood Tours & Gifts
Category/As: Motion Pictures as Actress
For: Puddin' Head (1941)
Real name: Juliet Canova
Born: November 20, 1916 in Starke, FL
Died: August 5, 1983 from cancer and buried in Glendale, CA

Canova, Judy...{07/04}
6777 Hollywood Boulevard (North)
Near: Hollywood First National Building
Category/As: Radio as Singer
For: Judy Canova Show (1943) CBS

Cantinflas...{31/58}
6440 Hollywood Boulevard (South)
Near: Playmates
Category/As: Motion Pictures as Actor
For: Pepe (1960)
Real name: Mario Reyes
Born: August 12, 1911

Cantor, Eddie...{33/120}
6648 Hollywood Boulevard (South)
Near: Hurricane
Category/As: Motion Picture as Actor
For: Roman Scandals (1933)
Real name: Edward Israel Itzkowitz
Born: January 31, 1892 in New York, NY
Died: 1964, from a heart attack and buried in Los Angeles, CA

Cantor, Eddie...{07/30}
6763 Hollywood Boulevard (North)
Near: This Is Hollywood
Category: Radio
For: The Eddie Cantor Show (1931) NBC

tor, Eddie...{17/04}
'0 Vine Street (East)
ar: parking lot
egory/As: Television as Actor
: The Colgate Comedy Hour (1950) NBC

nutt, Yakima...{25/47}
·0 Vine Street (East)
ar: parking lot
egory/As: Motion Pictues as Stuntman
: Stuntman in numerous films
dicated on August 14, 1985
l name: Enos Edward Canutt
n: November 29, 1895 in Colfax, WA
d: 1986 from natural causes

ra, Frank...{33/60}
4 Hollywood Boulevard (South)
ar: Hollywood Magic Shop
egory/As: Motion Pictures as Director
: It's A Wonderful Life (1947)
n: May 18, 1897 in Palermo, Italy
d: 1991 from natural causes

ey, Harry...{26/30}
·1 Vine Street (West)
ar: shopping center
egory/As: Motion Pictures as Actor
: Mr. Smith Goes to Washington (1939) Universal
l name: Henry De Witt Carey II
n: January 16, 1878 in New York, NY
d: 1947 from coronary thrombosis

ey, Jr., Harry...{14/24}
'1 Hollywood Boulevard (North)
ar: Antenna of Hollywood
egory/As: Television as Actor
: Rio Grande (1950)
n: May 16, 1921 in CA

ey, MacDonald...{32/57}
·8 Hollywood Boulevard (South)
ar: Ziganne
egory/As: Television as Actor
·: Days of Our Lives (1965-)
l name: Edward MacDonald Carey
n: March 15, 1913 in Sioux City, IA

le, Frankie...{16/78}
·9 Vine Street (West)
ar: parking lot
egory/As: Recording as Composer
: Sunrise Serenade
l name: Francis Carlone
n: March 25, 1903

lin, George...{26/97}
·5 Vine Street (West)
ar: TAV
egory/As: Live Theater as Comedian
·: Seven Words You Can Never Use On Television
dicated on January 21, 1987
n: May 12, 1938 in Bronx, NY
ards: Grammy

lisle, Kitty...{10/45}
1 1/2 Hollywood Boulevard (North)
ar: Je Taime Boutique
egory/As: Motion Pictures as Actress
: A Night at the Opera (1935)
l name: Catherine Holzman
n: September 3, 1915 in New Orleans, LA

lisle, Mary...{09/16}
'9 Hollywood Boulevard (North)

Near: Los Burritos
Category/As: Motion Pictures as Actress
For: College Humor (1933)
Born: February 3, 1912 in Boston, MA

Carlson, Richard...{15/09}
6331 Hollywood Boulevard (North)
Near: Guaranty Building
Category/As: Television as Actor
For: I Led Three Lives (1953) as Herbert Philbrick
Born: April 29, 1912
Died: 1977 from cerebral hemorrhage

Carmichael, Hoagy...{17/67}
1724 Vine Street (East)
Near: parking lot
Category/As: Television as Actor
For: Laramie (1959-1962) NBC
Real name: Hoaglund Howard Carmichael
Born: November 22, 1899 in Bloomington, IN
Died: December 27, 1981 from a heart attack
Awards: Oscar

Carney, Art...{10/15}
6631 Hollywood Boulevard (North)
Near: Hollywood Book City
Category/As: Television as Actor
For: The Honeymooners (1955) as Ed Norton
Born: November 4, 1918 in Mount Vernon, NY
Studio: CBS   Awards: Oscar, Emmy

Carpenter, Ken...{35/13}
6706 Hollywood Boulevard (South)
Near: burned out store
Category/As: Radio as Announcer
For: Kraft Music Hall (1936)
Born: August 21, 1900

Carpenters, The...{05/08}
6535 Hollywood Boulevard (North)
Near: Chinese Theater parking lot
Category/As: Recording as Singers
For: Rainy Days and Mondays
Dedicated on October 12, 1983
Real names: Richard and Karen Carpenter
Born: Richard, October 15, 1945
Died: Karen, ~~1982~~ Feb 4 83

Carr, Vikki...{14/09}
6385 Hollywood Boulevard (North)
Near: Security Pacific Bank
Category/As: Recording as Singer
For: It Must Be Him
Dedicated on September 23, 1981
Real name: Florencia Bisenta de Casillas Martinez Cardona
Born: July 19, 1942 in El Paso, TX

Carradine, John...{22/59}
6240 Hollywood Boulevard (South)
Near: West Coast Ensemble
Category/As: Motion Pictures as Actor
For: The Grapes of Wrath (1940)
Real name: Richmond Reed Carradine
Born: February 5, 1906 in Greenwich Village, NY

Carradine, Keith...{18/XX}
6233 Hollywood Boulevard (North)
Near: Pantages Theater
Category/As: Live Theater
Dedicated on July 15, 1993

Carrillo, Leo...{27/61}
1635 Vine Street (West)
Near: Fururama Furniture
Category/As: Motion Pictures as Actor

For: The Gay Desperado (1936)
Born: August 6, 1880
Died: 1961 from cancer

Carrillo, Leo...{26/26}
1501 Vine Street (West)
Near: shopping center
Category/As: Television as Actor
For: The Cisco Kid (1951-1956) as Poincho
Studio: ZIV-TV

Carroll, Diahann...{04/59}
7005 Hollywood Boulevard (North)
Near: Hollywood Momentos
Category/As: Recording as Singer
Dedicated on April 3, 1990
Real name: Carol Diahann Johnson

Carroll, Madeleine...{08/47}
6705 Hollywood Boulevard (North)
Near: Stefano's Two Guys from Italy
Category/As: Motion Pictures as Actress
For: The Prisoner of Zenda (1937)
Real name: Marie Madeline Bernadette O'Carroll
Born: February 26, 1906 in West Bromwich, England
Died: 1987 from a long illness
Related to Sterling Hayden (spouse)

Carroll, Nancy...{16/50}
1719 Vine Street (West)
Near: Parking lot
Category/As: Motion Pictures as Actress
For: The Shopworn Angel (1929)
Real name: Ann Veronica LaHiff
Born: November 19, 1905 in New York, NY
Died: 1965 from natural causes

Carson, Jack...{14/38}
6361 Hollywood Boulevard (North)
Near: Discoteca Hollywood
Category/As: Radio as Actor
For: The Jack Carson Show (1943) NBC
Real name: John Elmer Carson
Born: October 27, 1910 in Carman, Canada
Died: January 2, 1963 from Cancer buried Glendale, CA

Carson, Jack...(25/26)
1560 Vine Street (East)
Near: Parking lot
Category/As: Television as Host
For: All Star Revue (1950)

Carson, Jeannie...{25/32}
1560 Vine Street (East)
Near: Parking lot
Category/As: Television as Actress
For: Hey, Jeanie! (1956)
Real name: Jean Shufflebottom
Born: May 28, 1929

Carson, Johnny...{16/71}
1749 Vine Street (West)
Near: Parking lot
Category/As: Television as Host
For: The Tonight Show (1962-1992) NBC
Real name: same or unknown
Born; October 23, 1925 in NE

Caruso, Enrico...{10/17}
6631 Hollywood Boulevard (North)
Near: Hollywood Book City
Caregory/As: Recording as Singer
For: First recorded opera singer
Real name: same or unknown
Born: February 25, 1873 in Italy

Died: 1921, from peritontis

Casadesus, Robert...{18/17}
6253 Hollywood Boulevard (North)
Near: Equitible Building Entrance
Category/As: Recording as Pianist
Real name: same or unknown

Cash, Johnny...{28/33}
6320 Hollywood Boulevard (South)
Near: Hollywood Bazaar
Category/As: Recording as Singer
For: I Walk the Line
Born: February 26, 1932

Castle, Peggie...{23/28}
6274 Hollywood Boulevard (South)
Near: Parking lot
Catergory/As: Television as Actress
For: The Lawman (1959)
Real name: same or unknown
Born: December 22, 1927 in VA
Died: 1973, from cirrhosis of the liver

Catlett, Walter...{16/22}
1713 Vine Street (West)
Near: Dan Dee Shoe Repair
Category/As: Motion Pictures as Actor
For: Bringing Up Baby (1938)
Real name: same or unknown
Born: February 4, 1889 in San Francisco, CA
Died: 1960, from stroke

Caulfield, Joan...{25/78}
1500 Vine Street (East)
Near: Home Savings
Category/As: Television as Actress
For: Sally (1957) as Sally Truesdale
Real name: Beatrice Joan Caulfield
Born: June 1, 1922 in NJ
Died: 1991, from cancer

Cavallaro, Carmen...{15/59}
6301 Hollywood Boulevard (North)
Near: vacant
Category/As: Recording as Pianist
For: Various movie soundtracks
Real name: same or unknown
Born: May 6, 1913 Died: 1941 from cancer

Cerf, Bennett...{13/53}
6411 Hollywood Boulevard (North)
Near: Ness Shoes
Category/As: Television as Panelist
For: What's My Line (1950)
Real name: same or unknown
Born: May 25, 1898 in NY
Died: 1971, from heart attack, ashes scattered

Chaliapin, Feodor...{36/58}
6776 Hollywood Boulevard (South)
Near: McDonald's
Category/As: Recording as Opera Singer
Real name: same or unkown
Born: February 11, 1873 in Kazan, Russia Died: 1938

Chambers, John...{38/15}
7000 Hollywood Boulevard (South)
Near Roosevelt Hotel
Category/As: Motion Pictures as Make-up Artist
For: Planet of the Apes (1969)

Chambers, Stan...{37/121}
6922 Hollywood Boulevard (South)
Near: Hollywood Center

egory/As: Television as Newscaster
: KTLA-TV Newcaster
licated on December 1, 1982
n: August 11, 1923

mpion, Gower...{22/27}
2 Hollywood Boulevard (South)
r: Hastings Hotel
egory/As: Television as Dancer
: The Marge and Gower Champion Show (1957) MGM
n: June 21, 1921 in Geneva IL
d: 1980, from Waldenstrom's disease
ated to Marge Champion (spouse)

mpion, Marge...{23/47}
2 Hollywood Boulevard (South)
r: Original Coney Island
egory/As: Television as Dancer
: Model for Snow White
l name: Marjorie Celeste Belcher
n: September 2, 1923 in Hollywood, CA
ated to Gower Champion (spouse)

ndler, Jeff...{17/02}
0 Vine Street (East)
r: Parking lot
egory/As: Motion Pictures as Actor
: Broken Arrow (1950)
l name: Ira Grossell
n; December 15, 1918 in Brooklyn, NY
d: 1961, from spinal surgery and buried in Los Angles, CA

ney, Lon...{38/80}
6 Hollywood Boulevard (South)
r: International Love Boutique
egory/As: Motion Pictures as Actor
: Phantom of the Opera (1925)
l name: Alonzo Chaney
n: April 1, 1883
d: August 26, 1930 from lung cancer and buried in Glendale,CA

nning, Carol...{18/40}
3 Hollywood Bouldevard (North)
r: Pantages Theater
egory/As: Television as Actress
n: January 31, 1925 in San Francisco, CA

plin, Charles...{07/53}
1 Hollywood Boulevard (North)
r: Vacant
egory/As: Motion Pictures as Actor
: The Great Dictator (1940)
l name: Sir Charles Spencer Chaplin
n: April 16, 1889 in London, England
d: 1977, from a blood clot
ards: Oscar
ated to Mildred Harris, Paulette Goddard, Oona Chaplin (spouses)

pman, Marguerite...{23/62}
0 Hollywood Boulevard (South)
r: Holly Vine Shoppe
egory/As: Television as Actress
: The Seven Year Itch (1955)
l name: same or unknown
n: March 9, 1920 in NY

risse Cyd...{27/11}
l Vine Street (West)
r: Parking lot
egory/As: Motion Picture as Actress
: Singing in the Rain (1952) MGM
l name: Tula Ellice Finklea
n: March 8, 1921 in Amirillo, TX
ated to Tony Martin (spouse)

Charles, Ray...{07/15}
6773 Hollywood Boulevard (North)
Near: Hollywood Fantasy Tours
Category/As: Recording as Singer
For: Georgia on My Mind
Dedicated on December 16, 1981
Real name: Ray Charles Robinson
Born: September 23, 1930 in Albany, GA

Chase, Charley...{33/92}
6630 Hollywood Boulevard (South)
Near: Venetzia
Category/As: Motion Pictures as Director
For: The Three Stooges
Real name: Charles Parrott
Born: October 20, 1893 in Baltimore, MD
Died: 1940, from heart attack and buried in Glendale, CA

Chase, Chevy...{14/39}
6361 Hollywood Boulevard (North)
Near: Discoteca Hollywood
Category/As: Motion Pictures as Actor
For: Fletch
Dedicated on September 23, 1993
Born October 8, 1943

Chase, Ilka...{14/36}
6361 Hollywood Boulevard (North)
Near: Discoteca Hollywood (North)
Category/As: Motion Pictures as Actress
For: Johnny Dark 1960
Real name: same or unknown
Born: April 8, 1903 in New York, NY
Died: 1978, from hemorrhage from fall

Chase, Ilka...{07/48}
Near: vacant
Category/As: Television as Host
For: Glamor Go Round (1950)

Chatterton, Ruth...{18/05}
6263 Hollywood Boulevard (North)
Near: Equitibible Building
Category/As: Motion Pictures as Actress
For: Madame X (1929) MGM
Real name: same or unknown
Born: December 24, 1893 in NY Died: 1961
Related to George Brent (spouse)

Cherrill, Virginia...{26/74}
1549 Vine Street (West)
Near: TAV Celeberity Center
Category/As: Motion Pictures as Actress
For: City Lights (1931)
Real name: same or unknown
Born: April 12, 1908 in Carthage, IL
Related to Cary Grant (spouse)

Chevalier, Maurice...{27/91}
1645 Vine Street (West)
Near: Hollywood Vine Building
Category/As: Motion Pictures as Actor
For: Gigi (1958)
Real name: same or unknown
Born: September 12, 1888 in Paris, France
Died: 1972, from a heart attack

Chicago...{31/60}
6440 Hollywood Boulevard (South)
Near: Playmates
Category/As: Recording as Singers
Dedicated on July 23, 1992

Christie, Al...{07/20}
6769 Hollywood Boulevard (North)
Near: Snow White Coffee Shop
Category/As: Motion Pictures as Producer

For: Charlie's Aunt (1925)
Real name: same or unknown
Born: November 24, 1886 in Canada Died: 1951
Studio: Christie Comedies

Christie, Charles...{16/40}
1719 Vine Street (West)
Near: parking lot
Category/As: Motion Pictures as Executive
For: Co-Founder of Christie Comedies Studio
Born: April 13, 1880 in Canada   Died: 1955

Claire, Ina...{22/21}
6160 Hollywood Boulevard (South)
Near: Raji
Category/As: Motion Picuures as Actress
For: Ninotchka (1939)
Real name: Ina Fagan
Born: October 15, 1892 in Washington, D.C.   Died: 1985
Related to John Gilbert (spouse)

Clark, Buddy...{37/06}
6800 Hollywood Boulevard (South)
Near: Souvenirs of Hollywood
Category/As: Recording as Singer
For: It Had to Be You
Real name: Samuel Goldberg
Born: July 26, 1912
Died: 1949, in an airplane crash and buried in Glendale, CA

Clark, Dane...{37/80}
6908 Hollywood Boulevard (South)
Near: Hollywood Emporium
Category/As: Television as Actor
For: Wire Service (1956)
Real name: Bernard Zanville
Born: February 18, 1913 in New York, NY
Related to Margo Yoder (spouse)

Clark, Dick...{25/83}
1500 Vine Street (East)
Near: Home Savings Bank
Category/As: Television as Host
For: American Bandstand (1957) ABC
Born: November 30, 1929 in Mount Vernon, NY

Clark, Fred...{16/20}
1713 Vine Street (West)
Near: Dan Dee Shoe Repair
Category/As: Television as Actor
For: Burns and Allen Show (1950-1958) as Harry Morton
Real name: Frederic Leonard Clark
Born: March 9, 1914 Died: 1968, from a liver ailment

Clark, Marguerite...{28/08}
6304 Hollywood Boulevard (South)
Near: 7 Tourist and Travel
Category/As: Motion Pictures as Actress
For: Mrs. Wiggs of the Cabbage Patch (1918)
Born: February 22, 1883
Died: September 25,1940 from pneumonia

Clark, Roy...{37/89}
6914 Hollywood Boulevard (South)
Near: Hamburger Hamlet
Category/As: Television as Musician
For: Hee Haw (19__)
Born: April 15, 1933

Clayton, Ethel...{37/120}
6922 Hollywood Boulevard (South)
Near: Hollywood Center
Category/As: Motion Pictures as Actress
For: Wings of YOuth (1925)
Real name: same or unknown
Born: 1884 Died: 1966

Clayton, Jan...{22/35}
6200 Hollywood Boulevard (South)
Near: parking lot
Category/As: Television as Actress
For: Lassie (1954) CBS
Real name: same or unknown
Born: August 26, 1917 in NM Died: 1983, from cancer

Cleveland, Rev. James...{36/29}
6740 Hollywood Boulevard (South)
Near: Sports Emporium
Category/As: Recording as Gospel Singer
Dedicated on August 14, 1981
Born: December 5, 1932 Died: 1991 from heart failure

Clift, Montgomery...{21/13}
6100 Hollywood Boulevard (South)
Near: Chevron Gas Station
Category/As: Motion Pictures as Actor
For: The Misfits (1960)
Real name: Edward Montgomery Clift
Born: October 17, 1920 in Omaha, NE
Died: 1966, from coronary disease and buried in Brooklyn, NY

Clooney, Rosemary...{15/20}
6327 Hollywood Boulevard (North)
Near: Chicken Delight
Category/As: Recording as Singer
For: Come ona My House
Real name: same or unknown
Born: May 23, 1928 in KY

Clyde, Andy..{36/42}
6758 Hollywood Boulevard (South)
Near: the Dome
Category/As: Motion Pictures as Actor
For: Abe Lincoln in Illinois (1940)
Real name: same or unknown
Born: March 23, 1891 Died: 1967 and buried in Glendale, CA

Coburn, Charles...{23/29}
6274 Hollywood Boulevard (South)
Near: parking lot
Category/As: Motion Pictures as Actor
For: Gentlemen Prefer Blondes (1953)
Real name: Charles Douville Coburn
Born: June 19, 1877 in Savannah, GA
Died: August 10, 1961 from a heart ailment

Coca, Imogene...{23/11}
6256 Hollywood Boulevard (South)
Near: vacant lot
Category/As: Television as Comedianne
For: Your Show of Shows (1949-1954) NBC
Real name: same or unknown
Born: November 18, 1908 in Philadelphia, PA

Cochran, Steve...{17/44}
1724 Vine Street (East)
Near: parking lot
Category/As: Television as Actor
For: The Best of Our Lives (1946)
Real name: Robert Alexander Cochran
Born: May 25, 1917 in Eureka, CA
Died: 1965, from edema of the lung

Cody, Iron Eyes...{09/53}
6655-3 Hollywood Boulevard (North)
Near: USA Jeans Factory
Category/As: Television as Actor
For: Westward Ho the Wagons (1956)
Dedicated on April 20, 1983
Real name: Little Eagle
Born: February 2, 1875 in Bacone, OK

Cohan, George M. ...{36/18}
6730 Hollywood Boulevard (South)
Near: parking lot
Category/As: Motion Pictures as Writer
For: Give My Regards to Broadway (1948)
Born: July 4, 1878
Died: 1942, from cancer and buried in Bronx, NY

Cohn, Arthur...{38/03}
7000 Hollywood Boulevard (South)
Near: Roosevelt Hotel
Category: Motion Pictures
Dedicated on November 17, 1992
Real name: same or unknown

Colbert, Claudette...{37/18}
6810 Hollywood Boulevard (South)
Near: vacant
Category/As: Motion Pictures as Actress
For: It Happened One Night (1934) Paramount
Real name: Lily Claudette Chauchoin
Born: September 13, 1905 in Paris, France

Cole, Nat "King"...{09/48}
6655-A Hollywood Boulevard (North)
Near: Nicole
Category/As: Recording as Singer
For: Unforgetable
Real name: Nathaniel Adam Coles
Born: March 17, 1919 in Montgomery, AL
Died: 1965, from lung cancer and buried in Glendale, CA

Cole, Nat "King"...{18/59}
6225 Hollywood Boulevard (North)
Near: vacant
Category/As: Television as Singer
For: The Nat "King" Cole Show (1957)

Cole, Natalie...{17/18}
1750 Vine Street (East)
Near: Capitol Record Bulding
Category/As: Recording as Singer
For: Unpredictable
Real name: Stephnie Natalie Cole
Born: February 6, 1949 in Los Angeles, CA

Collier, Constance... {18/54}
6231 Hollywood Boulevard (North)
Near: vacant
Category/As: Motion Pictures as Actress
For: Anna Karenia (1935)
Real name: Laura Constance Hardie
Born: January 22: 1878 in London, England Died: 1955

Collier, William...{28/58}
6338 Hollywood Boulevard (South)
Near: vacant
Category/As: Motion Pictures as Actor
For: Thanks for the Memory (1938)
Real Name: William Enoir
Born: November 6, 1866
Died: 1944, from pneumonia and buried in Glendale, CA

Collins, Gary...{37/99}
6916 Hollywood Boulevard (South)
Near: Gulliver's Travel
Category/As: Television as Host
For: Home Show (19__)
Dedicated on September 18, 1985
Born: April 30, 1938

Collins, Joan...{05/71}
6925 Hollywood Boulevard (North)
Near: Mann's Chinese Theater
Category/As: Television as Actress

For: Dynasty (1981) as Alexis Carrington   ABC
Dedicated on December 14, 1983
Real name: same or unknown
Born: May 23, 1933
Related to: Jackie Collons (sister)

Collyer, Bud...{22/19}
6150 Hollywood Boulevard (South)
Near: Network Body Shop
Category/As: Radio as Host
For: Break the Bank (1945)
Real name: Clayton Collyer
Born: 1908 in NY Died: 1969

Colman, Ronald...{06/65}
6801 Hollywood Bouldevard (North)
Near: vacant
Category/As: Motion Pictures as Actor
For: A Double Life (1947)
Born: February 9, 1891 Richmond, Surrey, England
Died: 1958, from lung cancer infection
Awards: Oscar
Related to: Benita Hume (Spouse)

Colman, Ronald...{27/42}
1627 Vine Street (West)
Near: parking lot
Category/As: Television as Actor
For: The Halls of Ivy (19__)

Colonna, Jerry...{27/76}
1645 Vine Street (West)
Near: Hollywood Vine Building
Category/As: Radio as Actor
For: The Bob Hope Show (1934)
Real name: Gerald Colonna
Born: September 17, 1904 Died: 1986 from kidney failure

Como, Perry...{17/99}
1706 Vine Street (East)
Near: vacant
Category/As: Radio as Host
For: Chesterfield Supper Club (1944)
Real name: Pierino Roland Como
Born: May 18, 1912

Como, Perry...{10/09}
6631 Hollywood Boulevaed (North)
Near: Hollywood Book Store
Category/As: Recording as Singer
For: 'Til The End of Time

Como, Perry...{30/14}
6376 Hollywood Boulevard (South)
Near: Demain
Category/As: Television as Singer
For: The Perry Como Show (1950)

Compson, Betty...{16/75}
1749 Vine Street (West)
Near: parking lot
Category/As: Motion Pictures as Actress
For: On With the Show (1930)
Born: March 18, 1897 in UT Died: April 19, 1974
Studio: Christie Comedies

Compton, Joyce...{38/36}
7000 Hollywood Boulevard (South)
Near: Roosevelt Hotel
Category/As: Motion Pictures as Actress
For: Dangerous Curves (1929)
Real name: Eleanor Hunt
Born: January 27, 1907

Conklin, Chester...{25/10}
1560 Vine Street (East)
Near: parking lot
Category/As: Motion Picture as Actor
For: Modern Times (1930)
Real name: Jules Cowles
Born: January 11, 1888 in Oskaloosa, IA Died: 1971

Conklin, Heinie...{17/07}
1770 Vine Street (East)
Near: parking lot
Category/As: Motion Pictures as Actor
For: Original Keystone Kop
Real name: Charles Conklin
Born: April 2, 1880 in CA Died: 1959

Conners, Chuck...{37/57}
6840 Hollywood Boulevard (South)
Near: Masonic Temple
Category/As: Television as Actor
For: The Rifleman (1957-1960) ABC
Dedicated on July 18, 1984
Real name: Kevin Joseph Connor
Born: April 10, 1921 Died: November 10, 1992

Conreid, Hans...{34/23}
6664 Hollywood Boulevard (South)
Near: Supply Sergeant
Category/As: Television as Actor
For; The Danny Thomas Show (1958)
Real name: Frank Foster Conreid
Born; April 15, 1917 Died: 1982, from heart ailment

Conte, John...{ 20/66}
6125 Hollywood Bouldvard (North)
Near: Pep Boys
Category/As: Radio as Host
For: Montavani Welcomes You (1958)
Real name: same or unknown

Conti, Bill...{11/36}
6541 Hollywood Boulevard (North)
Near: Janes House
Category/As: Motion Pictures as Composer
For: Rocky Theme (1976)
Dedicated on November 10, 1989
Real name: same or unknown

Conway, Jack...{25/56}
1550 Vine Street (East)
Near: parking lot
Category/As: Motion Picture as Director
For: Bringing Up Father (1927) MGM
Born: July 17, 1887 in Graceville, MN Died: 1951

Conway, Tim...{36/25}
6740 Hollywood Boulevard (South)
Near: Sports Emoprium
Category/As:Television as Comedian
For: Carol Burnett Show (1975)
Dedicated on February 21, 1989
Real name: same or unknown

Conway, Tom...{27/32}
1615 Vine Street (West)
Near: Doolittle Theater
Category/As: Television as Actor
For: Mystery Theater (1951-1954)
Real name: Thomas Sanders
Born: September 15, 1904 in Russia
Died: 1967, from liver ailment

Coogan, Jackie... {24/16}
1654 Vine Street (East)
Near: Wig Shop

Category/As: Motion Pictures as Actor
For: The Kid (1920)
Real name: John Leslie Coogan
Born: October 24, 1914 in Hollywood, CA
Died: 1984, from a heart ailment and buried in Culver City, CA

Cook, Clyde...{ 11/55}
6533 Hollywood Boulevard (North)
Near: vacant
Category/As: Motion Pictures as Actor
For: Wee Willie Winkle (1937)
Real name: same or unknown
Born: December 16, 1891 in Austrailia
Died: 1984, in his sleep

Cook, Donald...{17/79}
1718 Vine Street (East)
Near: Sun Palace Restrauant
Category/As: Motion Picture as Actor
For: Unfaithful (1931)
Born: September 26, 1901 in Portland, OR
Died: October 1, 1961 from a heart attack

Cooke, Alistair...{27/95}
1645 Vine Street (West)
Near: Hollywood Vine Building
Category/As: Television as Host
For:Masterpiece Theater (1969) PBS
Real name: Alfred Alistair Cooke
Born: November 20, 1908

Cooley, Spade...{37/10}
6804 Hollywood Boulevard (South)
Near: Crazy Gideon's
Category/As: Radio as Bandleader
Real Name: Donnell Clyde Cooley
Born: December 17, 1910 Died: 1969, from a heart attack

Cooper, Gary... {18/33}
6245 Hollywood Boulevard (North)
Near: Frolic Room
Category/As: Motion Pictures as Actor
For: Meet John Doe (1941) Paramount
Real name: Frank James Cooper
Born: May 7, 1901 in Helena, MT
Died: May 13, 1961 from cancer and buried in Southampton, NY

Cooper, Jackie...{26/14}
1501 Vine Street (West)
Near: Shopping Center
Category/As: Motion Pictures as Actor
For: The Champ (1931)
Real name: John Cooperman, Jr.
Born: September 15, 1921 in Los Angeles, CA

Cooper, Jeanne...{06/66}
6801 Hollywood Boulevard (North)
Near: vacant
Category: Television
Dedicated on August 20, 1993

Cooper, Merian C. ...{12/09}
6523 Hollywood Boulevard (North)
Near: Maya Shoes
Category/As: Motion Pictures as Producer
For: King Kong (1933) RKO
Born: October 24, 1893 in Jacksonville, FL
Died: 1973, from cancer

Corey, Wendell...{28/42}
6328 Hollywood Boulevard (South)
Near: Hollywood Card
Category/As: Television as Actor
For: Harbor Command (1957)
Born: March 20, 1914 in Dracut, MA
Died: November 8, 1968 from a liver ailment

Corman, Roger...{04/50}
7013 Hollywood Boulevard (North)
Near: Shelly's Cafe
Category/As: Motion Pictures as Producer
For: House of Usher (1960)
Dedicated on June 12, 1991
Born: 1926 in Los Angeles
Studio: American International

Cornell, Don...{21/53}
6140 Hollywood Boulevard (South)
Near: Henry Fonda Theater
Category/As: Recording as Singer
For: Smoke Dreams
Real name: Louis Varlaro
Born: April 21, 1919 in NY

Correll, Charles "Andy"...{16/95}
1749 Vine Street (West)
Near: parking lot
Category/As: Radio as Actor
For: Amos 'n' Andy (1926) CBS
Real name: Charles J. Correll
Born: February 1, 1890
Died: 1972, from a heart attack and buried in Culver City, CA

Cortez, Ricardo...{25/64}
1550 Vine Street (East)
Near: parking lot
Category/As: Motion Pictures as Actor
For: The Maltese Falcon (1931) as Sam Spade   Paramount
Real name: Jacob Krantz
Born: September 19, 1899   Died: 1977

Cosby, Bill...{37/113}
6922 Hollywood Boulevard (South)
Near: Hollywood Center
Category/As: Television as Actor
For: The Bill Cosby Show (1984) NBC
Born: July 12, 1938

Costello, Dolores...{27/71}   DELORES?
1645 Vine Street (West)
Near: Hollywood Vine Building
Category/As: Motion Pictures as Actress
For: The Magnificent Ambersons (1942)
Born: September 17, 1905 Died: 1979
Related to John Barrymore (spouse), John Drew Barrymore (son)

Costello, Helene...{25/90}
1500 Vine Street (East)
Near: Home Savings
Category/As: Motion Pictures as Actress
For: Lights of New York (1928)
Born: June 21, 1903 in New York, NY
Died: 1957, from a long illness

Costello, Lou...{31/61}
6440 Hollywood Boulevard (South)
Near: Playmates
Category/As: Motion Pictures as Comedian
For: Jack and the Beanstalk (1952) Universal
Real name: Louis Francis Cristillo
Born: March 6, 1906 in Patterson, NJ
Died: March 3, 1959 from a heart attack

Costello, Lou...{36/76}
6780 Hollywood Boulevard (South)
Near: Ripley's Museum
Category/As: Radio as Comedian
For: Who's on First?

Costello, Lou...{23/41}
6274 Hollywood Boulevard (South)

Near: parking lot
Category/As: Television as Actor
For: Abbott and Costello Show (1951)

Costello, Maurice...{32/29}
6516 Hollywood Boulevard (South)
Near: Combo's Pizza
Category/As: Motion Pictures as Actor
For: Camille (1927)
Real name: same or unknown
Born: February 2, 1877   Died: 1950, from a heart ailment

Cotten, Joseph...{30/22}
6382 Hollywood Boulevard (South)
Near: Shanti's Vegetarian
Category/As: Motion Pictures as Actor
For: Citizen Kane (1941)
Real name: Joseph Cheshire Cotten
Born: May 15, 1905 in Petersburg, VA

Cowan, Jerome...{18/15}
6253 Hollywood Boulevard (North)
Near: Equitible Building
Category/As: Television as Actor
For: The Tycoon (1964)
Real name: Jerome Palmer Cowan
Born: October 6, 1897 in New York, NY Died: 1972

Cox, Wally...{14/06}
6385 Hollywood Boulevard (North)
Near: Security Pacific Bank
Category/As: Television as Actor
For: Mr. Peepers (1952-1955) NBC
Real name: Wallace Maynard Cox
Born: December 6, 1924 in Detriot, MI
Died: 1973, from a heart attack

Crabbe, Buster...{05/60}
6925 Hollywood Boulevard (North)
Near: Mann's Chinese Theater
Category/As: Television as Actor
For: Captain Gallant (1954)
Real name: Clarence Linden Crabbe
Born: February 7, 1908 in Oakland, CA
Died: 1983, from a heart attack

Crawford, Broderick..{05/58}
6925 Hollywood Boulevard (North)
Near: Mann's Chinese Theater
Category/As: Motion Pictures as Actor
For: All the King's Men (1949)
Real name: William Broderick Crawford
Born: December 9, 1911 in Philadelphia, PA
Died: 1986, from a stroke
Awards: Oscar
Related to Kay Griffith, Joan Tabor (spouses)

Crawford, Broderick...{36/20}
6730 Hollywood Boulevard (South)
Near: parking lot
Category: Television as Actor
For: Highway Patrol (1955-1959)   Studio: ZIV-TV

Crawford, Joan...{17/26}
1750 Vine Street (East)
Near: Capitol Record Building
Category/As: Motion Pictures as Actress
For: What Ever Happened to Baby Jane? (1962)
Real name: Lucille Fay LeSueur
Born: March 23, 1906 in San Antonio, TX
Died: May 10, 1977 from cancer and buried in Hartsdale, NY
Studio: MGM Awards: Oscar
Related to Franchot Tone, Douglas Fairbanks, Jr., Alfred Steele (all spouses)
Albert

Cregar, Laird...{17/80}
1718 Vine Street (East)
Near: Sun Palace Restaurant
Category/As: Motion Pictures as Actor
For: The Lodger (1944)
Real name: Sameul Laird Cregar   *Samuel*
Born: July 28, 1916 in Philadelphia, PA
Died: 1944, from a heart attack and buried in Glendale, CA

Crenna, Richard...{35/26}
6714 Hollywood Boulevard (South)
Near: Numero Uno Pizza
Category/As: Motion Pictures as Actor
For: Wait Until Dark (1967)
Dedicated on May 23, 1988
Real name: same or unknown
Born: 1926

Crews, Laura Hope...{18/20}
6251 Hollywood Boulevard (North
Near: parking lot
Category/As: Motion Pictures as Actress
For: Gone With the Wind (1939)
Born: December 12, 1879 in San Francisco, Ca
Died: 1942 from a short illness

Crisp, Donald...{24/53}
1630 Vine Street (East)
Near: parking lot
Category/As: Motion Pictures as Actor
For: How Green Was My Valley (1941)
Real name: same or unknown
Born: July 27, 1880 in Abervelde, Pentshire
Died: 1974 from a stroke
Studio: Biograph Awards: Oscar

Cromwell, John...{11/15}
6555 Hollywood Boulevard (North)
Near: Legends of Hollywood
Category/As: Motion Pictures as Director
For: The Prisoner of Zenda (1937)
Real name: Elwood Cromwell
Born: December 23, 1888 in Toledo, OH
Died: 1979, from a heart attack

Cromwell, Richard...{27/38}
1627 Vine Street (West)
Near: parking lot
Category/As: Motion Pictures as Actor
For: Lives of a Bengal Lancer (1935)
Real name: Roy M. Radabaugh
Born: January 8, 1910 in Los Angeles, CA
Died: October 11, 1960
Related to Angela Lansbury (spouse)

Crosby, Bing...{27/22}
1615 Vine Street (West)
Near: Doolittle Theater
Category/As; Motion Pictures as Actor
 For: Holiday Inn (1942)
Real name: Harry Lillis Crosby
Born: May2,1901 in Tacoma, WA
Died: October 13, 1977 from a heart attack and buried in Culver City, CA
Studio: Universal Awards: Oscar *10/14/77 stroke*
Related to Bob Crosby (brother)

Crosby, Bing...{07/22}
6767 Hollywood Boulevard (North)
Near: Hollywood Wax Museum
Category/As: Radio as Singer
For: Kraft Music Hall (1935)

Crosby, Bing...{07/54}
6751 Hollywood Boulevard (North)
Near: vacant

Category/As: Recording as Singer
For: White Chtistmas

Crosby, Bob...{15/32}
6319 Hollywood Boulevard (North)
Near: Sandy Burger
Category/As: Radio as Orchestra leader
For: The Bob Crosby Show (1939) CBS
Born: August 23, 1913 in Spokane, WA
Related to Bing Crosby (brother)

Crosby, Bob...{23/05}
6254 Hollywood Boulevard (South)
Near: burned out store
Category/As: Television as Bandleader
For: The Bob Crosby Show (1958)

Crosby, Norm...{34/02}
6650 Hollywood Boulevard (South)
Near: Hurricane
Category/As: Television as Comedian
For: Liar's Club (1976)
Dedicated on February 24, 1982
Real name: same or unknown
Born: September 15, 1927

Crosby, Stills & Nash...{34/32}
6666 Hollywood Boulevard (South)
Near: vacant store
Category/As: Recording as Singers
For: Love the One You're With
Real names: David Crosby, Stephen Stills and Graham Nash

Cross, Milton...{27/51}
6727 Vine Street (West)
Near: parking lot
Category/As: Radio as Host
For: Metropolitan Opera Broadcasts (1931)
Born: April 16, 1897 in NY
Died: 1975, from a heart attack

Crothers, Scatman...{35/18}
6712 Hollywood Boulevard (South)
Near: Egyptian Theater
Category: Motion Pictures as Actor
For: One Flew Over the Cookoo's Nest (1975)
Dedicated on April 8, 1981
Real name: Benjamin Sherman Crothers
Born: May 23, 1910 Died: 1986, from lung cancer

Cruise, Tom...{37/87}
6912 Hollywood Boulevard (South)
Near: Harley Davidson Shop
Category/As: Motion Pictures as Actor
For: Top Gun (1986)
Dedicated on October 16, 1986
Real name: same or unknown
Born: July 3, 1962

Crumit, Frank...{27/02}
1601 Vine Street (West)
Near: parking lot
Category/As: Radio as Host
For: The Battle of the Sexes (1938)
Born: September 26, 1889 in Jackson, OH Died: 1943
Related to Julia Sanderson (spouse)

Cruz, Celia...{22/58}
6240 Hollywood Boulevard (South)
Near: West Coast Ensemble
Category: Recording
Dedicated on September 17, 1987
Real name: same or unknown

Cruze, James...{37/106}
6920 Hollywood Boulevard (South)

Near: Pro Electronics
Category/As: Motion Pictures as Director
For: Ruggles of Red Gap (1923)
Real name: Jens Cruz Bosen
Born: March 27, 1884 in Ogden, UT
Died: 1942, and buried in Hollywood, CA

Crystal, Billy...{05/40}
6925 Hollywood Boulevard (North)
Near: Mann's Chinese Theater
Category/As: Motion Pictures as Actor
For: When Harry Met Sally (1990)
Dedicated on June 4, 1991
Real name: same or unknown

Cugat, Xavier...{27/13}
1601 Vine Street (West)
Near: parking lot
Category/As: Recording as Bandleader
Born: January 1, 1900 in Spain
Died: 1990, from arterial sclerosis
Related to Charo (spouse)

Cugat, Xavier...{25/50}
1550 Vine Street (East)
Near: parking lot
Category/As: Television as Bandleader
For: The Xavier Cugat Show (1957)

Cukor, George...{30/18}
6376 Hollywood Boulevard (South)
Near: Demain
Category/As: Motion Pictures as Director
For: My Fair Lady (1964)
Born: July 7, 1899 in New York, NY
Died: 1983, from heart failure and buried in Glendale, CA
Studio: MGM   Awards: Oscar

Cummings, Constance..{19/07}
6211 Hollywood Boulevard (North)
Near: Capitol Record Annex
Category/As: Motion Pictures as Actress
For: Busman's Honeymoon (1940)
Real name: Constance Halverstadt
Born: May 15, 1910 in Seattle, WA

Cummings, Irving...{37/24}
6816 Hollywood Boulevard (South)
Near: Rock Star 2000
Category/As: Motion Pictures as Director
For: Curley Top (1935)
Real name: same or unknown
Born: October 9, 1888   Died: 1959, from a heart attack

Cummings, Robert...{09/46}
6663 Hollywood Boulevard (North)
Near: Hollywood Stars
Category/As: Motion Pictures as Actor
For: Dial M for Murder (1954)
Real name: Clarence Orville Cummings
Born: June 10, 1908 in Joplin, MO
Died: 1990, from Parkinson's disease
Studio: Universal

Cummings, Robert...{17/78}
1718 Vine Street (East)
Near: Sun Palace Restaurant
Category/As: Television as Actor
For: Love that Bob (1954-1959) NBC

Cunningham, Bill...{15/36}
6315 1/2 Hollywood Boulevard (North)
Near: Le Sex Shoppe
Category/As: Radio as Host
For: Meet the Boss (1952)

Real name: same or unknown

Curtis, Alan...{04/13}
7021 Hollywood Boulevard (North)
Near: Hollywood Galaxy
Category/As: Motion Pictures as Actor
For: Buck Privates (1940)
Real name: Harold Neberroth
Born: July 24, 1909   Died: 1953, from kidney operation

Curtis, Tony...{06/56}
6801 Hollywood Boulevard (North)
Near: vacant office building
Category/As: Motion Pictures as Actor
For: Some Like It Hot (1959)
Real name: Bernard Schwartz
Born: June 3, 1925 in New York, Ny
Studio: Universal
Related to Janet Leigh (spouse), Jamie Lee Curtis (daughter)

Curtiz, Michael...{33/110}
6640 Hollywood Boulevard (South)
Near: J.C. Amber
Category/As: Motion Picture as Director
For: Casablanca (1943)
Real name: Mihaly Kertesz
Born: December 24, 1888 in Budapest, Hungary
Died: 1962, from cancer and buried in Glendale, Ca
Studio: Warner Brothers   Awards: Oscar

D

Dahl, Arlene...{24/61}
1628 Vine Street (East)
Near: Brown Derby ruins
Category/As: Motion Pictures as Actress
For: My Wild Irish Rose (1947)
Real name: same or unknown
Born: August 11, 1924 in Minneapolis, MN

Daley, Cass...{35/19}
6712 Hollywood Boulevard (South)
Near: Egyptian Theater
Category/As: Radio as Comedianne
For: Maxwell House Coffee Time (1937)
Real name: Katherine Dailey
Born: July 17, 1915 in Philadelphia, PA
Died: March 23, 1974 from a neck pierce due to a fall

Daley, Cass...{15/53}
6301 Hollywood Boulevard (North)
Near: vacant
Category/As: Television as Comedianne
For: The Fleet's In (1942)

Dalton, Dorothy...{25/04}
1560 Vine Street (East)
Near: parking lot
Category/As: Motion Pictures as Actress
For: The Disciple (1915)
Born: May 4, 1894 in Chicago, IL   Died: 1972

Daly, John...{16/104}
1777 Vine Street (West)
Near: Vine Streeet Building
Category/As: Television as Host
For: What's My Line? (1950)   CBS
Real name: John Charles Daly
Born: February 20, 1914 in Johannesburg, South Africa

Damone, Vic...{16/53}
1735 Vine Street (West)
Near: Palace
Category/As: Recording as Singer
For: Kismet (1955)
Real name: Vito Farinola
Born: June 12, 1928 in Brooklyn, NY

Dana, Viola...{11/41}
6541 Hollywood Boulevard (North)
Near: Janes House
Category/As: Motion Pictures as Actress
For: Rosie O'Grady (1917)
Real name: Virginia Flugrath
Born: June 28, 1897 in Brooklyn, NY
Died: 1987, from heart failure

Dandridge, Dorothy...{08/34}
6719 Hollywood Boulevard (North)
Near: Hollywood Natural Food
Category/As: Motion Pictures as Actress
For: Porgy and Bess (1959)
Dedicated on January 18, 1984
Real name: same or unknown
Born: November 9, 1923 in Cleveland, OH
Died: 1965, from a drug overdose and buried in Glendale, CA

Dane, Karl...{21/57}
6140 Hollywood Boulevard (South)
Near: Henry Fonda Theater
Category/As: Motion Pictures as Actor
For: The Big Parade (1925)
Real name: Karl Dean
Born: October 12, 1886 in Denmark
Died: 1934, from suicide (gunshot)

Daniels, Bebe...{17/83}
1718 Vine Street (East)
Near: Sun Palace Restaurant
Category/As: Motion Pictures as Actress
For: The Affairs of Anatol (1921)
Real name: Phyllis Virginia Daniels
Born: January 13, 1901 in Dallas, TX
Died: March 16, 1971 from cerebral hemorrhage
and buried in Hollywood, CA
Related to Ben Lyon (spouse)

Daniels, Billy...{06/34}
6819 Hollywood Boulevard (North)
Near: Hollywood Tours and Gifts
Category/As: Recording as Singer
For: That Old Black Magic
Real name: William Daniels
Born: September 12, 1915 in Jacksonville, FL
Died: 1988, from stomach cancer

Danza, Tony...{38/41}
7000 Hollywood Boulevard (South)
Near: Roosevelt Hotel
Category/As: Television as Actor
For: Who's the Boss? (19__)
Dedicated on November 21, 1988
Real name: Anthony Ladanza

Darin, Bobby...{16/57}
1735 Vine Street (West)
Near: Palace
Category/As: Recording as Singer
For: Splish Splash
Dedicated on May 26, 1982
Real name: Robert Walden Cassotto
Born: May 14, 1936 in New York, NY
Died: 1973, from heart surgery and body donated to UCLA
Awards: Grammy
Related to Sandra Dee (spouse)

Darnell, Linda...{27/60}
1635 Vine Street (West)
Near: Futurama Furniture
Category/As: Motion Pictures as Actress
For: Forever Amber (1947) Fox
Real name: Monetta Eloise Darnell
Born: October 16, 1923 in Dallas, TX
Died: April 10, 1965 from burns due to fire
Related to J. Peverell Marley (spouse)

Darwell, Jane...{08/15}
6735 Hollywood Boulevard (North)
Near: Hollywood T-Shirts
Category/As: Motion Pictures as Actress
For: The Grapes of Wrath (1940) as Ma Joad
Real name: Patti Woodward
Born: October16, 1880 in Palmyro, MO
Died: 1967, from heart attack and buried in Glendale, CA
Studio: Jesse L. Lasky   Awards: Oscar

Daves, Delmer L. ...{24/40}
1634 Vine Street (East)
Near: Madame Rosinka
Category/As: Motion Pictures as Screenwriter
For: Dark Passage (1947) Warner Brothers
Real name: Delmer Lawrence Daves
Born: July 24, 1904 in San Francisco, Ca   Died: 1977

Davies, Marion...{28/41}
6328 Hollywood Boulevard (South)
Near: Hollywood Cards
Category/As: Motion Pictures as Actress
For: Show People (1928)
Real name: Marion Cecillia Douras
Born: January 3, 1897 in New York, NY
Died: 1961, from cancer and buried in Hollywood, CA

Davis, Ann B. ...{38/88}
7046 Hollywood Boulevard (South)
Near: Souvenir Boulevard
Category/As: Television as Actress
For: The Brady Bunch (1969) as Alice
Real name: same or unknown
Born: May 5, 1926

Davis, Bette...{18/61}
6225 Hollywood Boulevard (North)
Near: vacant
Category/As: Motion Pictures as Actress
For: What Ever Happened to Baby Jane? (1962)
Real name: Ruth Elizabeth Davis
Born: April 5, 1908 in Lowell, MA
Died: 1989, from cancer and buried in Los Angeles, CA
Awards: Oscar

Davis, Bette...{18/51}
6233 Hollywood Boulevard (North)
Near: Pantages Theater
Category/As: Televison as Actress
For: Hotel (1983)
Awards: Oscar

Davis, Gail...{ 14/10}
6385 Hollywood Boulevard (North)
Near: Security Pacific Bank
Category/As: Television as Actress
For: Annie Oakley (1953)
Real name: Betty Jeanne Grayson
Born: October 5, 1925

Davis, Jim...23/55
6288 Hollywood Boulevard (South)
Near: Subway Sandwich Shop
Category/As: Television as Actor
For: Dallas (1978)

Davis, Joan...(26/32)
1501 Vine Street (West)
Near: Shopping Center
Category/As: Motion Pictures as Actress
For: George White's Scandels (1945)
Real name: Madonna Davis
Born: June 29, 1907 in Minneapolis MN
Died: 1961, from a heart attack and buried Culver city, CA

Davis, Joan...{17/86}
1708 Vine Street (East)
Near: Collectors Book Store
Category/As: Radio as Actress
For: Leave It To Joan (1949) CBS

Davis, Jr., Sammy {23/09}
6254 Hollywood Boulevard (South)
Near: burned out store
Category/As: Recording as Singer
For: Candy Man
Real name: same or unknown
Born: December 8, 1925
Died: 1990, from throat cancer and buried Glendale, CA

Day, Dennis...{38/86}
7046 Hollywood Boulevard (South)
Near: Souvenir Biulevard
Category/As: Radio as Singer
For: The Jack Benny Show (1939)
Real name: Eugene Patrick McNulty
Born: May 21, 1921

Day, Dennis...{ 33/116}
6646 Hollywood Boulevard (South)
Category/As: Television as Actor
For: The Jack Benny Show (1950-1965)

Day, Doris...{08/17}
6735 Hollywood Boulevard (North)
Near: Hollywood T-Shirts
Category/As: Motion Pictures as Actress
For: The Pajama Game (1957)
Real name: Doris Von Kappelhoff
Born: April 3, 1924 in Cincinnati, Oh

Day, Doris...{23/44}
6274 Hollywood Boulevard (South)
Near: parking lot
Category/As: Recording as Singer
For: Que Sera Sera

Day, Laraine...{34/45}
6674 Hollywood Boulevard (South)
Near: Explosion
Category/As: Motion Pictures as Actress
For: Dr. Kildare (1939)
Real name: Laraine Johnson
Born: October 13, 1917 in Roosevelt, UT
Related to Leo Durocher

De Camp, Rosemary...{24/28}
1642 Vine Street (East)
Near: Bernard Luggage
Category/As: Television as Actress
For: Love That Bob (1954-1959) as Magaret McDonald NBC
Real name: same or unknown
Born: November 14, 1914 in Prescott, AZ

De Fore, Don...{37/12}
6804 Hollywood Boulevard (South)
Near: Crazy Gideon's
Category/As: Television as Actor
For: Hazel (1961)
Born: August 25, 1917

De Forest, Lee...{17/17}
1750 Vine Street (East)
Near: Capitol Record Building
Category/As: Motion Pictures as Inventor
For: Inventor of synchronized sound
Real name: Dr. Lee D. De Forest
Born: August 26, 1873 in Council Bluffs, IA   Died: 1961

De Haven, Carter...{17/45}
1724 Vine Street (East)
Near: parking lot
Category/As: Motion Pictures as Director
For: A Gentleman of Nerve (1916)
Real name: same or unknown
Born: 1887 in Chicago, IL   Died: 1977

De Haven, Gloria...{05/11}
6935 Hollywood Boulevard (North)
Near: Chinese Theater parking lot
Category/As: Motion Picture as Actress
For: Two Girls and a Sailor (1944)
Real name: Gloria Mildred De Haven
Born: July 23, 1924 in Los Angeles, CA
Studio: Metro
Related to John Payne (spouse)

de Havilland, Olivia...{36/48}
6764 Hollywood Boulevard (South)
Near: Guiness World of Records Museum
Category/As: Motion Pictures as Actress
For: Hush, Hush Sweet Charlotte (1964)
Real name: same or unknown
Born: July 1, 1916 in Tokyo, Japan
Studio: Warner Brothers Awards: Oscar

De La Motte, Marguerite...{37/74}
6904 Hollywood Boulevard (South)
Near: Hollywood Tourist & Gifts
Category/As: Motion Pictures as Actress
For: The Mark of Zorro (1920)
Real name: same or unknown
Born: June 22, 1902   Died: 1950

De Leath, Vaughn...{33/98}
6630-D Hollywood Boulevard (South)
Near: European Menswear
Category/As: Radio as Singer
For: The Firestone Hour (1939)
Born: September 26, 1896   Died: 1943, from a heart condition

De Sylva, Buddy...{17/10}
1770 Vine Street (East)
Near: parking lot
Category/As: Recording as Lyracist
Dedicated on June 4, 1992
Real name: B.G. De Sylva
Born: 1845   Died: 1950
Note: Paramount Studio's head of production

Dean, James...{16/30}
1715 Vine Street (West)
Near: Hair Vine Beauty Shop
Category/As: Motion Pictures as Actor
For: Rebel Without a Cause (1955), East of Eden (1955), Giant (1956)
Real name: James Byron Dean
Born: February 8, 1931 in Marion, IN
Died: September 30, 1955 from auto accident and buried in Faimont, IN
Studio: Warner Brothers

DeCarlo, Yvonne...{21/39}
6126 Hollywood Boulevard (South)
Near: Henry Fonda Theater
Category/As: Motion Pictures as Actress
For: The Ten Commandments (1956)
Real name: Peggy Yvonne Middleton

Born: September 1, 1922 in Vancouver, Canada
Studio: Universal

DeCarlo, Yvonne...{08/39}
6715 Hollywood Boulevard (North)
Near: Outpost building
Category/As: Television as Actress
For: The Munsters (1964) as Mortissa

Dees, Rick...{25/15}
1560 Vine Street (East)
Near: parking lot
Category/As: Radio as Disc Jockey
For: KIIS morning personality
Dedicated on September 17, 1984
Real name: same or unknown
Born: Greensboro, NC

Dekker, Albert...{33/70}
6620 Hollywood Boulevard (South)
Near: Burned out
Category/As: Television as Actor
For: Dr. Cyclops (1940)
Real name: same or unknown
Born: December 20, 1904   Died: 1968, from suicide

del Rio, Dolores...{24/51}
1630 Vine Street (East)
Near: parking lot
Category/As: Motion Pictures as Actress
For: Flying Down to Rio (1933) RKO
Real name: Lolita Dolores Martinez Asunsolo Lopez Negrette
Born: August 3, 1905 in Durango, Mexico
Died: 1983: from natural causes

Del Ruth, Roy...{22/01}
6150 Hollywood Boulevard (South)
Near: Network Body Shop
Category/As: Motion Pictures as Director
For: Meltese Falcon (1931)
Born: October 18, 1895 in Philadelphia, PA
Died: 1961, from heart attack

DeLuise, Dom...{16/111}
1779 Vine Street (West)
Near: Capezio Dance
Category/As: Motion Pictures as Actor
For: Smokey and the Bandit (1977)
Dedicated on May 6, 1985
Real name: same or unknown
Born: August 1, 1933 in Brooklyn, NY

Demarest, William...{09/39}
6667 Hollywood Boulevard (North)
Near: Musso and Frank Grill
Category/As: Motion Pictures as Actor
For: Hail the Conqueroring Hero (1943)
Real name: same or unknown
Born: February 27, 1892 in St. Paul, MN   Died: 1983

DeMille, Cecil B. ...{16/51}
1735 Vine Street (West)
Near: Palace
Category/As: Motion Pictures as Director
For: The Ten Commandments (1923)
Real Name: Cecil Blount De Mille
Born: August 12, 1881 in Ashfield, MA
Died: 1959, from heart disease and buried in Hollywood, CA
Studio, Lasky   Awards: Oscar
Related to William De Mille (brother)

DeMille, Cecil B. ...{22/61}
6240 Hollywood Boulevard (South)
Near: West Coast Ensemble
Category/As: Radio as Director

For: Lux Radio Theater (1936)

DeMille, William...{20/84}
6125 Hollywood Boulevard (North)
Near: Pep Boys
Category/As: Motion Pictures as Director
For: The Ragamuffin (1916)
Born: July 25, 1878 in Washington, D.C. Died: 1955
Related to Cecil B. DeMille (brother)

Denning, Richard...{37/118}
6922 Hollywood Boulevard (South)
Near: Hollywood Center
Category/As: Television as Actor
For: Hawaii Five-0 (1968) CBS
Real name: Louis A. Denninger
Born: March 27, 1914

Denny, Reginald...{09/50}
6655-A Hollywood Boulevard (North)
Near: Nicole
Category/As: Motion Pictures as Actor
For: The Secret Life of Walter Mitty (1947)
Real name: Reginald Leigh Daymore
Born: November 2, 1891 in England   Died: 1967 from a stroke

Derek, John...{11/57}
6531 Hollywood Boulevard (North)
Near: Timing Collection
Category/As: Television as Actor
For: Frontier Circus (19___) as Ben Travis
Real name: Derek Harris
Born: August 12, 1926 in Hollywood, CA
Studio: Columbia
Related to Bo Derek, Ursla Andress (spouses)

Devine, Andy...{23/14}
6256 Hollywood Boulevard (South)
Near: vacant lot
Category/As: Radio as Actor
Real name: Jeremiah Schwartz
Born: October 7, 1905 in Flagstaff, AZ
Died: 1977, from lukemia

Devine, Andy...{29/24}
6366 Hollywood Boulevard (South)
Near: Kassfy Sportswear
Category/As: Television as Actor
For: Wild Bill Hickok (1951) as "Jingles"

Dexter, Elliott...{16/76}
1749 Vine Street (West)
Near: parking lot
Category/As: Motion Pictures as Actor
For: Adam's Rib (1923)
Real name: same or unknown
Born: September 11, 1870 in Galveston, TX
Died: 1941, from a short illness

Dickinson, Angie...{38/27}
7000 Hollywood Boulevard (South)
Near: Roosevelt Hotel
Category/As: Television as Actress
For: Police Woman (1974) NBC
Dedicated on September 10, 1987
Real name: Angeline Brown
Born: 1931, in Kulm, ND
Related to Burt Bacharach

Dieterle, William...{05/52}
6925 Hollywood Boulevard (North)
Near: Mann's Chinese Theater
Category/As: Motion Pictures as Director
For: The Last Flight (1931)
Real name: Wilhelm Dieterle

Born: July 15, 1893 in Ludwigshafen, Germany   Died: 1972
Studio: Warner Brothers

Dietrich, Marlene...{31/03}
6400 Hollywood Boulevard (South)
Near: Pizza Deli
Category/As: Motion Pictures as Actress
For: Destry Rides Again (1939)
Real name: Maria Magdalene von Losch
Born: December 27, 1901 in Berlin, Germany
Died: May of 1992
Studio: Paramont

Diller, Phyllis...{04/63}
7003 Hollywood Boulevard (North)
Near: Haagen Dazs
Category/As: Television as Comedianne
For: The Beautiful Phyllis Diller Show (1968)
Real name: Phyllis Driver
Born: July 17, 1917

Disney, Walt...{04/05}
7021 Hollywood Boulevard (North)
Near: Hollywood Galaxy
Category/As: Motion Pictures as Executive
For: Creator of Mickey Mouse
Real name: Walter Elias Disney
Born: December 5, 1901 in Chicago, IL
Died: 1966, from ciculatory collapse and buried in Glendale, CA

Disney, Walt..{08/05}
6743 Hollywood Boulevard (North)
Near: B. Dalton Book Store
Category/As: Television as Host
For: Walt Disney (1954)

Dix, Richard...{24/82}
1610 Vine Street (East)
Near: Vine Street Bar and Grill
Category/As: Motion Pictures as Actor
For: The Whistler (1944)
Real name: Ernest Carlton Brimmer
Born: July 18, 1894 in St. Paul, MN
Died: September 20, 1949 from heart trouble and buried in Glendale, CA

Dmytryk, Edward...{18/36}
6233 Hollywood Boulevard (North)
Near: Pantages Theater
Category/As: Motion Pictures as Director
For: The Caine Mutiny (1954) RKO
Born: September 4, 1908 in Grand Forks, Canada

Dodd, Jimmie...{04/01}
7021 Hollywood Boulevard (North)
Near: Hollywood Galaxy
Category/As: Television as Host
For: Mickey Mouse Club (1955)
Real name: same or unknown
Born: March 29, 1910   Died: 1964

Domino, Fats...{33/64}
6612 Hollywood Boulevard (South)
Near: burned out
Category/As: Recording as Singer
For: Blueberry Hill
Real Name: Antonie Domino
Born: February 26, 1928

Donald, Peter...{09/42}
6667 Hollywood Boulevard (North)
Near: Musso and Frank Grill
Category/As: Television as Panelist
For: Pantomime Quiz (1953)
Real name: same or unknown
Born: 1918   Died: 1979

Donat, Robert...{31/33}
6418 Hollywood Boulevard (South)
Near: Hollywood Discount Center
Category/As: Motion Picture as Actor
For: Goodbye Mr. Chips
Born: March 18, 1905 in Manchester, Lancashire   Died: 1958
Awards: Oscar

Donlevy, Brian...{26/82}
1549 Vine Street (West)
Near: TAV Celeberity Center
Category/As: Television as Actor
For: Family Affair (19__)
Real name: Waldo Brian Donlevy
Born: February 9, 1901 in Ireland Died: 1972, from throat cancer

Doro, Marie...{16/49}
1719 Vine Street (West)
Near: parking lot
Category/As: Motion Pictures as Actress
For: Oliver Twist (1916)
Real name: Marie Stewart
Born: February 4, 1882 in Duncannon, PA   Died: 1956

Dorsey, Jimmy...{12/37}
6505 Hollywood Boulevard {North}
Near: Tony's Shoes
Category/As: Recording as Musician
Real name: James Dorsey
Born: February 29, 1904 in PA   Died: in 1957, from cancer

Dorsey, Tommy...{09/24}
6675 Hollywood Boulevard (North)
Near: Vogue Theater
Category/As: Recording as Bandleader
For: I'm Getting Sentimental Over You
Real name: same or unknown
Born: November 19, 1905 in PA
Died: 1956, from Choked in his sleep and buried in Valhalla, NY

Douglas, Jack...{36/24}
6740 Hollywood Boulevard (South)
Near: Sports Emporium
Category/As: Television as Narrator
For: Golden Voyage (19__)
Real name: same or unknown
Born: 1927

Douglas, Kirk...{18/02}
6263 Hollywood Boulevard (North)
Near: Equitible Building
Category/As: Motion Pictures as Actor
For: Spartacus (1960)
Real name: Issur Danielovitch
Born: December 9, 1916 in Amsterdam, NY
Related to Michael Douglas (son)

Douglas, Melvyn...{13/31}
6423 Hollywood Boulevard (North)
Near: Ben's Smoke Shop
Category/As: Motion Pictures as Actor
For: Mr. Blandings Builds His Dream House (19__)
Real name: Melvyn Hesselberg
Born: April 5, 1901 in Macon, GA
Died: 1981, from pneumonia
Awards: Oscar
Related to Helen Gahagan (spouse)

Douglas, Melvyn...{10/63}
6601 Hollywood Boulevard (North)
Near: Station Market
Category/As: Television as Actor
For: The Statesman (1969) as Ben Franklin
Awards: Emmy

Douglas, Mike...{04/67}
7001 Hollywood Boulevard (North)
Near: Hollywood Souvenirs
Category/As: Television as Host
For: The Mike Douglas Show (1962-1973)
Real name: Michael Delaney Dowd, Jr.
Born: August 11, 1933
Studio: Group W

Douglas, Paul...{24/25}
1648 Vine Street (East)
Near: Jerimiha Comey Studios
Category/As: Motion Pictures as Actor
For: The Mating Game (1959)
Real name: same or unknown
Born: November 4, 1907 in Philadelphia, PA
Died: 1959, from heart attack
Studio: Fox
Related to Jan Sterling, Virginia Field (spouse)

Douglas, Paul...{06/15}
6841 Hollywood Boulevard (North)
Near: Pose with Stars
Category/As: Television as Host
For: Adventure Theater (1956)

Dove, Billie...{14/50}
6351 Hollywood Boulevard (North)
Near: Hardy Shoes
Category/As: Motion Pictures as Actress
For: Polly of the Follies (1922)
Real name: Lillian Bohny
Born: May 14, 1900 in NY

Downey, Morton...{24/15}
1656 Vine Street (East)
Near: Jan's Hair Shop
Category/As: Radio as Singer
For: The Coke Club (1946) as Camel Minstrel Boy
Born: November 14, 1901 in CN   Died: 1985 From a stroke

Downs, Cathy...{33/118}
6648 Hollywood Boulevard (South)
Near: Hurricane
Category/As: Television as Actress
For: Joe Palooka (1946)
Real name: same or unknown
Born: March 3, 1924   Died: 1976

Dragon, Carmen...{21/24}
6100 Hollywood Boulevard (South)
Near: Chevron Gas Station
Category: Radio
Dedicated on September 7, 1989
Real name: same or unknown

Dragonette, Jessica...{16/03}
1711 Vine Street (West)
Near: vacant
Category/As: Radio as Singer
For: Saturday Night Serenade (1944)
Born: 1910, in Calcutta, India   Died: 1980
Studio: ABC

Drake, Frances...{06/39}
6819 Hollywood Boulevard (North)
Near: Hollywood Tours and Gifts
Category/As: Motion Pictures as Actress
For: Les Miserables (1935)
Real name: Frances Dean
Born: October 22, 1908 in New York, NY

Dresser, Louise...{32/61}
6540 Hollywood Boulevard (South)
Near: Greg Ward Levi

Category/As: Motion Pictures as Actress
For: State Fair (1933)
Real name: Louise Kerlin
Born: October 5 1887   Died: 1965, from intestinal obstruction

Dressler, Marie...{16/54}
1735 Vine Street (West)
Near: Palace
Category/As: Motion Pictures as Actress
For: Min and Bill (1930) MGM
Real name: Leila Marie Von Koerber
Born: November 9, 1869 in Coburg, Ontario
Died: 1934, from cancer and buried in Glendale, CA

Drew, Ellen...{05/72}
6925 Hollywood Boulevard (North)
Near: Mann's Chinese Theater
Category/As: Motion Pictures as Actress
For Christmas in July (1940)
Real name: Terry Ray
Born: November 23, 1915 in Kansas City, MO

Drew, Mr.and Mrs. Sidney...{17/62}
1724 Vine Street (East)
Near: parking lot
Category/As: Motion Pictures as Actors
For: Hypochondriacs (1917)
Real name: Sidney White, Lucile, McVey
Born: 1864, 1868 in New York, NY
Died: 1920, 1925

Driscoll, Bobby...{25/12}
1560 Vine Street (East)
Near: parking lot
Catergory/As: Motion Pictures as Actor
For: Treasure Island (1950)
Real Name: Robert, Driscoll
Born: May 3, 1937 in Cedar Rapids, IA
Died: March 30, 1968 from hardening of the arteries
Awards: Oscar

Dru, Joanne...{17/111}
1700 Vine Street (East)
Near: Equitible Building
Catergory/As: Television as Actress
For: Gustward Ho (1960) ABC
Real name: Joanne Letita la Coque
Born: January 31, 1923 in Logan, WV
Related to Dick Haymes, John Ireland (spouse)

Duff, Howard...{27/53}
1627 Vine Street (West)
Near: parking lot
Category/As: Television as Actor
For: Mr. Adams and Mrs. Eve (1957-1958) CBS
Born: November 24, 1917 in Bremerton, WA
Died: 1990, from a heart attack
Related to Ida Lupino (spouse)

Dunn, James...{11/17}
6555 Hollywood Boulevard (North)
Near: Legends Of Hollywood
Category/As: Motion Pictures as Actor
For: A Tree Grows in Brooklyn (1945)
Real name: James Howard Dunn
Born: November 2, 1901 in New York, NY   Died: November 3, 1967
Awards: Oscar

Dunn, James...{38/20}
7000 Hollywood Boulevard (South)
Near: Roosevelt Hotel
Category/As: Television as Actor
For: It's a Great Life (1954)

Dunne, Irene...{31/63}
6440 Hollywood Boulevard (South)
Near: Playmates
Category/As: Motion Pictures as Actress
For: Magnificent Obsession (1935)
Real name: Irene Marie Dunn
Born: December 20, 1898 in Louisville, KY
Died: 1990, from heart failer
Studio: RKO

Dunne, Philip...{08/26}
6723 Hollywood Boulevard (North)
Near: GiGi Boutique
Category/As: Motion Pictures as Screenwriter
For: The Robe (1953)
Real name: same or unknown
Born: 1908, in New York, NY
Studio: Fox

Dunnock, Mildred...{10/41}
6613 Hollywood Boulevard (North)
Near: 700 Market
Category/As: Motion Pictures as Actress
For: Death of a Salesman (1951)
Real name: same or unknown
Born: January 25, 1906 in Baltimore, MD   Died: 1991

Dunphy, Jerry...{09/29}
6669 Hollywood Boulevard (North)
Near: Asia Imports
Category/As: Television as Announcer
For: Eyewitness News (LA area)
Dedicated on May 9, 1984
Born: Milwaukee, Wi   Awards: Emmy, Golden Mike

Duran, Duran...{17/05}
1770 Vine Street (East)
Near: parking lot
Category/As: Recording as Singers
Dedicated on August 23, 1993

Durante, Jimmy...{24/86}
1606 Vine Street (East)
Near: vacant store
Category/As: Motion Pictures as Actor
For: The Man Who Came to Dinner (1941)
Real name: James F. Durante
Born: February 10, 1893
Died: 1980, from pneumonia and buried in Culver City, CA

Durante, Jimmy...{24/23}
1648 Vine Street (East)
Near: Jerimiha Comey Studio
Category/As: Radio as Comedian
For: Camel Caravan (1943) CBS

Durbin, Deanna...{17/58}
1724 Vine Street (East)
Near: parking lot
Category/As: Motion Pictures as Actress
For: It Started With Eve (1941)
Real name: Edna Mae Durbin
Born: December 4, 1921 in Winnipeg, Manatoba
Studio: Universal   Award: Oscar

Duryea, Dan...{20/30}
6161 Hollywood Boulevard (North)
Near: Network Body Shop
Category/As: Television as Actor
For: Peyton Place (1968)
Born: January 23, 1907 in White Plains, NY
Died: June 7, 1968 from cancer

Dvorak, Ann...{15/28}
6321 Hollywood Boulevard (Morth)

Near: Vine Theater
Category/As: Motion PIctures as Actress
For: Blind Alley (1939)
Real name: Ann McKim
Born: August 2, 1912 in NY   Died: 1979

Dwan, Allan...{18/08}
6263 Hollywood Boulevard (North)
Near: Equitible Building
Category/As: Motion Pictures as Director
For: Heidi (1937)
Born: April 3, 1885 in Toronto, Canada   Died: 1981
Studio: First National

Eastman, George...{16/09}
1711 Vine Street (West)
Near: vacant
Category/As: Motion Pictures as Inventor
For: Inventor of celluloid roll film
Born: July 13, 1854 in Waterville, NY Died: 1932, from suicide
Awards: Oscar

Ebsen, Buddy...{16/106}
1777 Vine Street (West)
Near: Vine Street Building
Category/As: Motion Picture as Actor
For: Breakfast at Tiffany's (1961)
Real name: Christian Rudolf Ebsen, Jr.
Born: April 2, 1908 in TX

Eckstine, Billy...33/106
6640 Hollywood Boulevard (South)
Near: J.C. Amber
Category/As: Recording as Singer
For: My Foolish Heart
Born: July 8, 1914   Died: March 7, 1993

Eddy, Nelson...{32/23}
6512 Hollywood Boulevard (South)
Near: Roma Fashions
Category/As: Radio as Singer
For: The Kraft Music Hall (1949) NBC
Born: June 29, 1901 in Providence, RI
Died: 1967, from a stroke and buried in Hollywood, CA

Eddy, Nelson...{27/69}
1637 Vine Street (West)
Near: Early World Restaurant
Category/As: Recording as Singer

Eddy, Nelson...{15/43}
6311 Hollywood Boulevard (North)
Near: Hollywood Wig
Category/As: Motion Pictures as Actor
For: Rose Marie (1936)

Eden, Barbara...{04/65}
7003 Hollywood Boulevard (North)
Near: Haagen Dazs
Caregory/As: Television as Actress
For: I Dream of Jeannie (19651969) NBC
Dedicated on November 17, 1988
Real name: Barbara Huffman
Born: 1934

Edeson, Robert...{24/55}
1630 Vine Street (East)
Near: parking lot

Category/As: Motion Pictures as Actor
For: various silent films
Real name: same or unknown
Born: January 23, 1868 in New Orleans, LA
Died: 1931, from hardening of the arteries

Edison, Thomas A. ...{35/01}
6700 Hollywood Boulevard (South)
Near: L.A. Tattoo
Category/As: Motion Pictures as Inventor
For: Inventing the motion picture camera
Born: February 11, 1847 in Orange, NJ   Died: 1931

Edwards, Blake...{37/81}
6908 Hollywood Boulevard (South)
Near: Hollywood Emporium
Category/As: Motion Pictures as Producer
For: The Pink Panther (1964)
Dedicated on April 3, 1991
Real name: William Blake Edwards
Born: 1922, in Tulsa, OK

Edwards, Ralph...{21/29}
6100 Hollywood Boulevard (South)
Near: Chevron Gas Station
Category/As: Radio as Host
For: This Is Your Life (1948)
Born: June 13, 1913 in CO

Edwards, Ralph...{23/20}
6262 Hollywood Boulevard (South)
Near: vacant lot
Category/As: Television as Host
For: This Is Your Life (1951)

Ellington, Duke...{11/49}
6535 Hollywood Boulevard (North)
Near: Jean Machine
Category/As: Recording as Orchestra Leader
For: Take the 'A' Train
Real name: Edward Kennedy Ellington
Born: April 29, 1899 in Washington, D.C.
Died: 1974, from lung cancer and buried in Bronx, NY

Elman, Mischa...{25/08}
1560 Vine Street (East)
Near: parking lot
Category/As: Recording as Violonist
Born: January, 20, 1891 in Russia   Died: 1967

Emerson, Faye...{12/03}
6529 Hollywood Boulevard (North)
Near: Hollywood Bargain
Category/As: Motion Pictures as Actress
For: Murder in the Big House (1942)
Real name: Faye Margaret Emerson
Born: July 8, 1917 in Elizabeth, LA
Died: March 9, 1893 from stomach cancer   1983
Related to Skitch Henderson (spouse)

Emerson, Faye...{09/02}
6689 Hollywood Boulevard (North)
Near: Sub City
Category/As: Television as Actress
For: Peter Gun (1958)   Gunn

Ericson, John...{26/40}
1501 Vine Street (West)
Near: West Sunset Offices
Category/As: Television As Actor
For: Police Story (1973-1977)
Real name: Joachim Meibes
Born: September 25, 1926 in Dusseldorf, Germany

Errol, Leon...{06/49}
6819 Hollywood Boulevard (North)

Near: Hollywood Tours and Gifts
Category/As: Motion Pictures As Actor
For: Mexican Spitfire (1940)
Real name: same or unknown
Born: July 3, 1881 in Australia   Died: 1952, from heart attack

Erwin, Stu...{23/38}
6274 Hollywood Boulevard (South)
Near: parking lot
Category/As: Television as Actor
For: The Trouble With Father (1950)
Born: February 14, 1902   Died: 1967, from a heart attack

Estefan, Gloria...{04/08}
7021 Hollywood Boulevard (North)
Near: Hollywood Galaxy
Category/As: Recording As Singer
Dedicated on February 3, 1993

Etting, Ruth...{11/07}
6565 Hollywood Boulevard (North)
Near: Cash It Here
Category/As: Motion Pictures As Actress
For: Roman Scandals (1933)
Real name: same or unknown
Born, November 23, 1896 in NV   Died: 1978

Evans, Dale...{33/104}
6638 1/2 Hollywood Boulevard (South)
Near: International Fashion
Category/As: Radio As Singer
For: The Roy Rogers Show (1946)
Real name: Frances Octavia Butts
Born: October 31, 1912 in Uvalde, TX
Related to Roy Rogers (spouse)

Evans, Dale...{16/62}
1735 Vine Street (West)
Near: Palace
Category/As: Television As Actress
For: The Roy Rogers Show (1946)   51-57

Evans, Linda...{37/49}
6838 Hollywood Boulevard (South)
Near: El Capitan
Category/As: Television As Actress
For: Dallas (1978)   (Minx 57/
Dedicated on August 20, 1987
Real name: Linda Evenstad

Evans, Madge...{17/34}
1750 Vine Street (East)
Near: Capitol Record Building
Category/As: Motion Pictures As Actress
For: Dinner at Eight (1933)
Real name: Margherita Evans
Born: July 1, 1909 in NY   Died: 1983, from cancer

Everett, Chad...{37/123}
6922 Hollywood Boulevard (South)
Near: Hollywood Center
Category/As: Television As Actor
For: Medical Center (1969)
Dedicated on November 13, 1986
Real name: Raymond Lee Cramton
Born: June 11, 1936

Everly Brothers, The...{38/21}
7000 Hollywood Boulevard (South)
Near: Roosevelt Hotel
Category/As: Recording As Singers
For: Bye Bye Love
Dedicated on October 2, 1986
Real Name: Don and Phil Everly
Born: Don, Feburary 1, 1937; Phil, January 1939

F

Fabray, Nanette...{28/16}
6922 Hollywood Boulevard (South)
Near: Olympic Electronics
Category/As: Television as Actress
For: The Happy Ending (1969)
Real name: Nanette Fabares
Born: October, 27 1920

Factor, Max...{37/109}
6922 Hollywood Boulevard (South)
Near: Hollywood Center
Category/As: Motion Pictures as Make-Up Artist
For: Actress' Make-Up Man
Real name: Max Faktor
Born: August 5, 1877 in Lodz, Poland   Died: 1938

Fadiman, Clifton...{23/56}
6288 Hollywood Boulevard (South)
Near: Subway Sandwich Shop
Category/As: Radio as Host
For: Information Please (1938)
Real name: same or unknown
Born: May 15, 1904

Fairbanks, Douglas...{38/38}
7000 Hollywood Boulevard (South)
Near: Roosevelt Hotel
Category/As: Motion Pictures as Actor
For: Robin Hood (1922)
Real name: Douglas Elton Ulman
Born: May 23,1883 in Denver, CO
Died: December 12, 1939 from a heart attack and buried in Hollywood CA
Studio: United Artist   Awards: Oscar
Related to Mary Pickford (spouse) Douglas Fairbainks, Jr. (son)

Fairbanks, Jr., Douglas...{28/28}
6320 Hollywood Boulevard (South)
Near: Hollywood Bazaar
Cctegory/As: Motion Pictures as Actor
For: The Prisoner of Zenda (1937)   OF MAN
Real name: Douglas Elton Ulma, Jr.
Born: December 9, 1909 in New York, NY
Related to Joan Crawford (Spouse) Douglas Fairbanks (Father)

Fairbanks, Jr., Douglas...{35/17}
6712 Hollywood Boulevard (South)
Near: Egyptian Theater
Category/As: Radio as Actor

Fairbanks, Jr., Douglas...{09/44}
6665 Hollywood Boulevard (North)
Near: Top Western
Category: Television as Actor
For: Fairbanks Presents

Fairbanks, Jerry...{30/27}
6384 Hollywood Boulevard (South)
Near: Popeye Chicken
Category/As: Motion Pictures as Cameraman
For: Speaking of Animals
Born: November 1, 1904

Faith, Percy...{26/06}
1501 Vine Street (West)
Near: Shopping Center
Category/As: Recording as Composer
For: Love Me or Leave Me
Real name: same or unknown
Born: April 7, 1908 in Toronto, Canada
Died: 1976, from cancer and buried in Los Angeles, CA

Falkenburg, Jinx...{25/48}
1550 Vine Street (East)
Near: parking lot
Category/As: Television as Host
For: Talk About a Lady (1946)
Real name: Eugenia Falkenburg
Born: January 21, 1919
Related to Tex McCrary (Spouse)

Farnsworth, Richard...{25/19}
1560 Vine Street (East)
Near: parking lot
Category: Motion Pictures

Farnum, Dustin...{10/05}
6633 Hollywood Boulevard (North)
Near: Fame of Hollywood Cafe
Category/As: Motion Pictures as Actor
For: The Squaw Man (1911)
Born: May 27, 1874   Died: 1929 from Kidney trouble
Note: First complete Hollywood movie

Farnum, William...{28/37}
6324 Hollywood Boulevard (South)
Category/As: Motion Pictures as Actor
For: The Spoilers (1914)
Born: July 4, 1876 Died: 1953 from cancer

Farr, Jamie...{26/77}
1549 Vine Street (West)
Near: TAV Celebrity Center
Category/As: Television as Actor
For: M.A.S.H. (1973) as Corporal Klinger
Dedicated on April 10, 1985
Real name: Jameel Farah
Born: July 1, 1934 in Toledo, OH

Farrar, Geraldine...{24/72}
1711 Vine Street (East)
Near: parking lot
Category/As: Motion Pictures as Actress
For: Camille (1915)
Born: February 28, 1882 in Melrose, MA   Died: March 11, 1967

Farrar, Geraldine...{16/15}
1711 Vine Street (West)
Near: vacant
Category/As: Recording as Singer

Farrell, Charles...{04/17}
7021 Hollywood Boulevard (North)
Near: Hollywood Galaxy
Category/As: Motion Pictures as Actor
For: Seventh Heaven (1927)
Born: August 9, 1901 Died: 1962
Related to Virginia Valli (spouse)

Farrell, Charlie...{27/30}
1615 Vine Street (West)
Near: Doolittle Theater
Category/As: Television as Actor
For: My Little Margie (1952) as Vernon Albright

Farrell, Glenda...{32/43}
Born: June, 19046524 Hollywood Boulevard (South)
Near: Blaxx Clothing
Category/As: Motion Pictures as Actress
For: Torchy Gets Her Man (1938)
Born: June 30, 1904   Died: May 1, 1971

Farrow, John...{28/09}
6304 Hollywood Boulevard (South)
Near: 7 Tourist and Travel
Category/As: Motion Pictures as Director

For: Around The World in 80 Days (1956)
Real name: John Villers Farrow
Born: February 10, 1904 in Sydney, Australia
Died: 1963, from a heart attack
Related to Maureen O'Sullivan (spouse) Mia Farrow (daughter)

Faversham, William...{17/54}
1724 Vine Street (East)
Near: parking lot
Category/As: Motion Pictures as Actor
For: The Sin That Was His (1921)
Real name: same or unknown
Born: February 12, 1868 in England   Died: 1940

Fay, Frank...{23/50}
6284 Hollywood Boulevard (South)
Near: India Tandor
Category/As: Motion Pictures as Actor
For: God's Gift to Women (1931)
Real name: same or unknown
Born: November 17, 1894 in Dublin, Ireland   Died: 1960
Related to Barbara Stanwyck (spouse)

Fay, Frank...{17/13}
1770 Vine Street (East)
Near: parking lot
Category/As: Radio as Comedian

Faye, Alice...{37/112}
6922 Hollywood Boulevard (South)
Near: Hollywood Center
Category/As: Motion Pictures as Actress
For: George White's Scandles (1934)
Real name: Ann Leppert
Born: May 5, 1912
Studio: Fox
Related to Tony Martin, Phil Harris (spouses)

Faye, Julia...{12/43}
6501 Hollywood Boulevard (North)
Near: burned out store
Category/As: Motion Pictures as Actress
For: The Ten commandments (1956)
Real name: same or unknown
Born: September 24, 1896 in VA   Died: 1966, from cancer

Faylen, Frank...{19/11}
6211 Hollywood Boulevard (North)
Near: Capital Records annex office
Category/As: Television as Actor
For: The Many Loves of Dobie Gillis (1959-1962) as Herbert T. Gillis
Real name: Frank Ruf
Born: December 8, 1901 in St. Louis MO
Died: 1958, from long illness and buried in Mission Hills, CA
Studio: CBS

Fazenda, Louise...{06/57}
6801 Hollywood Boulevard (North)
Near: vacant
Category/As: Motion Pictures as Actress
For: Cheaper to Marry (1925)
Real name: same or unknown
Born: June 17, 1889 in Lafayette, IN
Died: 1962, from cerebral hemmorhage
Studio: Mack Sennett
Related to Hal Wallis (spouse)

Fedderson, Don..{27/62}
1635 Vine Street (West)
Near: Futurama Furniture
Category/As: Television as Producer
For: My Three Sons (1959)   ABC

Feliciano, Jose...{11/40}
6541 Hollywood Boulevard (North)

Near: Janes House
Category/As: Recording as Singer
For: I Want to Wish You a Merry Christmas
Dedicated on December 1, 1987

Felton, Verna...{16/29}
1719 Vine Street (West)
Near: parking lot
Category/As: Television as Actress
For: Pete & Gladys (1960)
Real name: same or unknown
Born: July 29, 1890 in Salinas, CA
Died: 1966 from a stroke

Fenneman, George...{25/91}
1500 Vine Street (East)
Near: Home Savings
Category/As: Television as Announcer
For: You Bet Your Life (1950)
Dedicated on October 7, 1981
Born: November 10, 1919

Ferguson, Helen...{20/14}
6161 Hollywood Boulevard (North)
Near: Network Body Shop
Category/As: Motion Pictures as Actress
For: The Scarlet West (1925)
Real name: Same or unknown
Born: July 23, 1901 in IL

Ferrer, Jose...{11/39}
6541 Hollywood Boulevard (North)
Near: Janes House
Category/As: Motion Pictures as Actor
For: Cyrano de Bergerac (1950)
Real name: Jose Vincente Ferrer de Otero y Cintron
Born: January 8, 1912 in Santruce, Puerto Rico
Died: January, 1992, from a short illness
Awards: Oscar

Ferrer, Mel...{23/32}
6274 Hollywood Boulevard (South)
Near: Parking ot
Category/As: Motion Pictures as Director
For: Wait Until Dark (1967)
Real name: Melchoir Gaston Ferrer
Born: August 25, 1917 in Elberton NJ
Related to Audrey Hepburn (spouse)

Fetchit, Stepin...{16/84}
1749 Vine Street (West)
Near: Parking Lot
Category/As: Motion Pictures as Actor
For: In Old Kentucky (1927)
Real name: Lincoln Theodore Monroe Andrew Perry
Born: May 30, 1902 in Key West, FL
Died: 1985, from pneumonia

Fidler, Jimmie...{21/45}
6128 Hollywood Boulevard (South)
Near: Hollywood Psychic
Cateogry/As: Radio as Gossip Reporter.
For: Jimmie Fidler in Hollywood (1932)
Real name: Jimmy Fidler
Born: August 26, 1898   Died: 1988

Fiedler, Arthur...{24/60}
1628 Vine Street (East)
Near: Brown Derby ruins
Category/As: Recording as Conductor.
For: Conductor, Boston Pops
Real name: same or unknown
Born: December 17, 1894 in Boston, MA
Died: 1979, from heart failure and buried in West Roxbury, MA

Field, Virginia...{16/81}
1749 Vine Street (West)
Near: Parking Lot
Category/As: Television as Actress.
Real name: Margaret Cynthia Field
Born: November 4, 1917 in London, England
Died: 1992, from cancer
Related to Paul Douglas (spouse)

Fields, Gracie...{21/43}
6126 Hollywood Boulevard (South)
Near: Henry Fonda Theater
Category/As: Radio as comedienne.
For: Sing As We Go (1942) NBC
Real name: Grace Stansfield
Born: January 9, 1898 in Lancashire, England
Died: December 25, 1979

Fields, W.C....{38/10}
7000 Hollywood Boulevard (South)
Near: Cave Theater
Category/As: Motion Pictures as Actor
For: My Little Chickadee (1940)
Real name: William Claude Dukenfield
Born: February 10, 1879 in Philadelphia, PA
Died: 1946, from hemorrhage and buried in Glendale, CA

Fields, W.C. ...{15/39}
6315 Hollywood Boulevard)North)
Near: Cave Theater
Category/As: Radio as Comedian
For: Your Hit Parade (1938) NBC

Fifth Dimension, The Original...{38/54}
7024 Hollywood Boulevard (South)
Near: Roosevelt Hotel parking structure
Category/As: Recording as Singers
For: Up, Up and Away
Dedicated on August 9, 1991

Finch, Flora...{09/26}
6671 Hollywood Boulevard (North)
Near: Studio 2
Category/As: Motion Pictures as Comedienne
For: Bunny's Mistake (1911)
Real name: same or unknown
Born: February 11, 1869 in London, England
Died: 1940, from streptococcus

Fisher, Eddie...{18/41}
6233 Hollywood Boulevard (North)
Near: Pantages Theater
Category/As: Recording as Singer
For: Oh! My Papa
Real name: Edwin Fisher
Born: August 10, 1928
Related to Elizabeth Taylor, Connie Stevens and Debbie Reynolds (spouses)

Fisher, Eddie...{17/47}
1724 Vine Street (East)
Near: Parking Lot
Category/As: Television Host
For: Coke Time with Eddie Fisher (1953) NBC

Fishman, Hal...{25/21}
1560 Vine Street (East)
Near: parking lot
Category: Television
Dedicated on April 8, 1992
Real name: same or unknown

Fitzgerald, Barry...{23/06}
6254 Hollywood Boulevard (South)
Near: burned out
Category/As: Motion Pictures as Actor

For: Going My Way (1944)
Real name: William Joseph Shields
Born: March 10, 1888 in Dublin, Ireland
Died: January 4, 1961
Awards: Oscar

Fitzgerald, Barry...{04/66}
7001 Hollywood Boulevard (North)
Near: Hollywood Souvenirs
Category/As: Television as Actor

Fitzgerald, Ella...{36/22}
6730 Hollywood Boulevard (South)
Near: parking lot
Category/As: Recording as Singer
For: Billie
Real name: same or unknown
Born: April 25, 1918

Fitzgerald, Geraldine...{14/48}
6353 Hollywood Boulevard (North)
Near: entrance to 2nd level
Category/As: Television as Actress
For: Wuthering Heights (1939)
Real name: same or unknown
Born: November 24, 1914 in Ireland

Fitzmaurice, George...{10/61}
6601 Hollywood Boulevard (North)
Near: Station Market
Category/As: Motion Pictures as Director
For: The Dark Angel (1925)
Born: February 13, 1885 in Paris, France   Died: 1940

Fitzpatrick, James A....{27/24}
1615 Vine Street (West)
Near: Doolittle Theater
Category/As: Motion Pictures as Producer
For: Fitzpatrick Taveltalks (1925)
Born: February 26, 1902
Died: 1980, from stroke

Flagstad, Kirsten...{07/12}
6777 Hollywood Boulevard (North)
Near: Hollywood First National Building
Category: Recording
Real name: same or unknown
Born: July 12, 1895 in Norway   Died: 1962

Fleetwood Mac...{33/55}
6608 Hollywood Boulevard (South)
Near: Frederick's of Hollywood
Category/As: Recording as Singers
Real name: Mick Fleetwood, Stevie Nicks, Christine McVie,
          John McVie and Lindsay Buckingham

Fleming, Rhonda...{34/19}
6660 Hollywood Boulevard (South)
Near: Rock Center
Category/As: Motion Pictures as Actress
For: The Spiral Staircase (1945)
Real name: Marilyn Louis
Born: August 10, 1923 in Los Angeles, CA
Related to Ted Mann of Mann's Theaters (spouse)

Fleming, Victor...{16/34}
1719 Vine Street (West)
Near: parking lot
Category/As: Motion Pictures as Director
For: Gone With The Wind (1939)
Born: February 23, 1883 in Pasadena, CA
Died: 1949, from heart attack and buried in Hollywood, CA
Studio: MGM   Awards: Oscar

Flynn, Errol...{34/09}
6654 Hollywood Boulevard (South)
Near: Combo's Pizza
Category/As: Motion Pictures as Actor
For: The Adventures of Robin Hood (1938)
Real name: Errol Leslie Flynn
Born: June 20, 1909 in Tasmania, Australia
Died: October 14, 1959, from a heart attack and buried in Glendale, CA

Flynn, Errol...{38/18}
7000 Hollywood Boulevard (South)
Near: Roosevelt Hotel
Category: Television as Actor
For: The Charge of the Light Brigade (1936)

Foch, Nina...{28/36}
6324 Hollywood Boulevard (South)
Near: vacant
Category/As: Motion Pictures as Actress
For: An American in Paris (1951)
Real name: Nina Consuelo Maud Fock
Born: April 20, 1924

Foch, Nina...{04/41}
7021 Hollywood Boulevard (North)
Near: Hollywood Galaxy
Category/As: Television as Actress

Foley, Red...{18/64}
6225 Hollywood Boulevard (North)
Near: vacant
Category/As: Recording as Singer
For: Chattanooga Shoe Shine Boy
Real name: Clyde Julian
Born: June 17, 1910   Died: 1968, from pulmonary edema

Foley, Red...{28/06}
6302 Hollywood Boulevard (South)
Near: New York Pizza Express
Category/As: Television as Host
For: Ozark Mountain Jubilee (1954)

Fonda, Henry...{27/07}
1601 Vine Street (West)
Near: parking lot
Category/As: Motion Pictures as Actor
For: The Grapes of Wrath (1940)
Real name: Henry Jaynes Fonda
Born: May 16, 1905 in Grand Island, NE
Died: August 12, 1982, from heart failure
Awards: Oscar
Related to Magaret Sullivan (spouse), Jane Fonda (daughter), Peter Fonda (son)

Fontaine, Joan...{27/72}
1645 Vine Street (West)
Near: Hollywood Vine Building
Category/As: Motion Pictures as Actress
For: Jane Eyre (1944)
Real name: Joan de Havilland
Born: October 22, 1917 in Tokyo, Japan
Awards: Oscar
Related to Brian Anherne (spouse), Olivia de Havilland (sister)

Foran, Dick...{24/89}
1600 Vine Street (East)
Near: (closed)
Category/As: Television as Actor
Real name: John Nicholas Foran

Forbes, Scott...{24/21}
1650 Vine Street (East}
Near: closed store
Category/As: Television as Actor
For: The Adventures of Jim Bowie (1956)
Real name: same or unknown

Ford, Glenn...{05/09}
6935 Hollywood Boulevard (North)
Near: Mann's Chinese Parking
Category/As: Motion Pictures as Actor
For: The Blackboard Jungle (1955)
Real name: Gwyllyn Samuel Newton Ford
Born: May 1, 1916 in Quebec, Canada
Studio: Columbia

Ford, Harrison...{09/38}
6667 Hollywood Boulevard (North)
Near: Musso & Frank Grill
Category/As: Motion Pictures as Actor
For: Vanity Fair (1923)
Real name: same or unknown
Born: March 16, 1892 in MO   Died: 1957

Ford, John...{24/29}
1642 Vine Street (East)
Near: Bernard Luggage
Category/As: Motion Pictures as Director
For: The Grapes of Wrath (1940)
Real name: Sean Aloysius O'Feeney
Born: February 1, 1895 in Cape Elizabeth, ME
Died: 1973, from cancer and buried in Culver City, CA
Studio: Fox   Awards: Oscar

Ford, Tennessee Ernie...{24/95}
1600 Vine Street (East)
Near: D M V
Category/As: Radio as Singer
Real name: Ernest Jennings Ford
Born: February 13, 1919 in Bristol, TN
Died: 1991 from liver disease

Ford, Tennessee Ernie...{37/104}
6920 Hollywood Boulevard (South)
Near: Pro Electronics
Category/As: Recording as Singer
For: Sixteen Tons

Ford, Tennessee Ernie...{15/44}
6311 Hollywood Boulevard (North)
Near: Hollywood Wig
Category/As: Television as Singer
For: The Ford Show (1956)
Studio: NBC   Awards: Grammy

Forsythe, John...{11/21}
6553 Hollywood Boulevard (North)
Near: London Connection
Category/As: Television as Actor
For: Dynasty (1981) as Blake Carrington
Real name: John Freund
Born: January 29, 1918 in Penn's Grove, NJ

Foster, Preston...{06/61}
6801 Hollywood Boulevard (North)
Near: vacant
Category/As: Television as Actor
For: Waterfront (1954) as Captain John Herrick
Born: August 24, 1901 in NJ   Died: July 14, 1970

Fox, William...{11/43}
6541 Hollywood Boulevard (North)
Near: Janes House
Category/As: Motion Pictures as Executive
For: Founder of Fox Film Corp. (1915)
Real name: Wilhelm Friedman
Born: January 1, 1879 in Tulchva, Hungary   Died: 1952

Foy, Eddie...{16/45}
1719 Vine Street (West)
Near: parking lot
Category/As: Motion Pictures as a Vaudeville Performer

For: A Favorite Fool (1915)
Real name: Edward Fitzgerald
Born: March 9, 1856 in New York, NY   Died: 1928, from heart disease

Frampton, Peter...{06/32}
6819 Hollywood Boulevard (North)
Near: Hollywood Tours & Gifts
Category/As: Recording as Musician
For: Something's Happening
Real name: same or unknown
Born: April 22, 1950 in England

Francescatti, Zino...{35/09}
6704 Hollywood Boulevard (South)
Near: David & Emilio Shoes
Category/As: Recording as Violinist
Real name: Vituoso Francescatti
Born: August 9, 1905   Died: 1991

Francis, Anne...{27/27}
1615 Vine Street (West)
Near: Doolittle Theater
Category/As: Television as Actress
For: Dallas (1981) Arliss Cooper
Born: September 16, 1930 in Ossining, NY

Francis, Arlene...{31/51}
6430 Hollywood Boulevard (South)
Near: Power Sports
Category/As: Radio as Actress
For: Betty & Bob (1932) NBC
Real name: Arlene Francis Kazanjian
Born: October 20, 1912

Francis, Arlene...{16/67}
1735 Vine Street (West)
Near: Palace
Category/As: Television as Panelist
For: What's My Line? (1950)

Francis, Kay...{36/52}
6764 Hollywood Boulevard (South)
Category/As: Motion Pictures as Actress
For: Charlie's Aunt (1941)
Real name: Katherine Edwina Gibbs
Born: January 13, 1903 in Oklahoma City, OK   Died: 1968 from cancer

Franklin, Aretha...{37/105}
6920 Hollywood Boulevard (South)
Near: Pro Electronics
Category/As: Recording as Singer
For: Respect
Real name: same or unknown
Born: March 25, 1942

Franklin, Sidney...{33/34}
6562 Hollywood Boulevard (South)
Near: Hollywood Toys Inc.
Category/As: Motion Pictures as Director
For: Mrs. Miniver (1942)
Real name: same or unknown
Born: May 21, 1893 in San Francisco, CA   Died: 1972
Studio: First national

Frawley, William...{28/35}
6320 Hollywood Boulevard (South)
Near. Hollywood Bazaar
Category/As: Motion Pictures as Actor
For: Roxie Hart (1942)
Real name: same or unknown
Born: February 26, 1887
Died: 1966, from heart attack and buried in Mission Hills, CA

Freberg, Stan...{20/26}
6161 Hollywood Boulevard (North)

Near: Network Body Shop
Category/As: Recording as Comedian
Born: August 7, 1926 in Los Angeles, CA
Awards: Grammy

Frederick, Pauline...{38/04}
7000 Hollywood Boulevard (South)
Near: Roosevelt Hotel
Category/As: Motion Pictures as Actress
For: Madame X (1929)
Real name: Beatrice Libbey
Born: August 12, 1883   Died: 1938, from asthma

Freed, Alan...{14/15}
6385 Hollywood Boulevard (North)
Near: Security Pacific Bank
Category/As: Radio as Disc Jockey
For: Father of Rock and Roll
Real name: same or unknown

Freeman, Y. Frank...{06/29}
6819 Hollywood Boulevard (North)
Near: Hollywood Tours & Gifts
Category/As: Motion Pictures as Executive
For: VP of Paramount from 1938
Real name: Young Frank Freeman
Born: December 14, 1890 in GA   Died: 1969

Freleng, Friz...{38/60}
7024 Hollywood Boulevard (South)
Near: Roosevelt Hotel parking structure
Category: Motion Pictures
Real name: same or unknown

Fries, Charles...{37/93}
6914 Hollywood Boulevard (South)
Near: Hamburger Hamlet
Category/As: Television as Producer
For: Founder of Fries Entertainment
Real name: Charles W. Fries
Born: September 30, 1928
Note: Star relocated in front of this building, which he owns (rumored)

Frizzell, Lefty...{05/29}
6925 Hollywood Boulevard (North)
Near: Mann's Chinese Theater
Category/As: Recording as Singer
For: If You Got the Money, Honey
Real name: William Frizzell
Born: March 31, 1928   Died: 1975

Froman, Jane...{18/53}
6231 Hollywood Boulevard (North)
Near: vacant store
Category/As: Radio as Singer
For: The Intimate Revue (1934) NBC
Real Name: Ellen Jane Froman
Born: November 10, 1907   Died: 1980, from natural causes

Froman, Jane...{20/28}
6161 Hollywood Boulevard (North)
Near: Network Body Shop
Category/As: Recording as Singer
For: With a Song in My Heart

Froman, Jane...{27/77}
1645 Vine Street (West)
Near: Hollywood Vine Building
Category/As: Television as Singer
For: Jane Froman's USA Canteen (1952)

Fuller, Robert...{33/51}
6608 Hollywood Boulevard (South)
Near: Frederick's of Hollywood
Category/As: Television as Actor

Real name: Same or unknown
Born: July 29, 1934

Funicello, Annette...{37/41}
6834 Hollywood Boulevard (South)
Near: Rocket Hollywood
Category/As: Motion Pictures as Actress
For: Beach Blanket Bingo (19__)
Dedicated on September 14, 1993

Furness, Betty...{26/54}
1541 Vine Street (West)
Near: TAV Celebrity Center
Category/As: Motion Pictures as Actress
For: Magnificent Obsession (1935)
Born: January 3, 1916 in New York, NY

Furness, Betty...{09/20}
6675 Hollywood Boulevard (North)
Near: Vogue Theater
Category/As: Television as Actress
For: Today Show (1976) NBC
Real name: same or unknown

Gable, Clark...{24/83}
1610 Vine Street (East)
Near: Vine Street Bar & Grill
Category/As: Motion Pictures as Actor
For: Gone With The Wind (1939) as Rhett Butler
Real Name: William Clark Gable
Born: February 1, 1901 in Cadiz, OH
Died: November 16, 1960, from heart attack and buried in Glendale, CA
Awards: Oscar
Related to: Carole Lombard (spouse)

Gabor, Eva...{33/59}
6614 Hollywood Boulevard (South)
Near: Hollywood Magic Shop
Category/As: Television as Actress
For: Green Acres (1965-1970) CBS
Dedicated on October 23, 1984
Real name: same or unknown
Born: February 11, 1924
Related to Zsa Zsa Gabor (sister)

Gabor, Zsa Zsa...{05/46}
6925 Hollywood Boulevard (North)
Near: Mann's Chinese Theater
Category/As: Television as Actress
For: Touch of Evil (1959)
Real name: Sari Gabor
Born: February 6, 1920
Related to George Sanders (spouse) Eva Gabor (sister)

Gahagan, Helen...{17/103}
1702 Vine Street (East)
Near: H & V Dentistry
Category/As: Motion Pictures as Actress
For: She (1935)
Born: November 25, 1900 in NJ
Related to: Melvyn Douglas (spouse)
Note: This was her only movie

Galli-Curci, Amelita...{06/43}
6819 Hollywood Boulevard (North)
Near: Hollywood Tours & Gifts
Category/As: Recording as Opera Singer

Born: November 18, 1882 in Milan, Italy   Died: 1963

Garbo, Greta....{05/68}
6925 Hollywood Boulevard (North)
Near: Mann's Chinese Theater
Category/As: Motion Pictures as Actress
For: Camille (1936)
Real name: Greta Louisa Gustaffson
Born: September 18, 1905 in Stockholm, Sweden   Died: 1990
Studio: MGM

Gardner, Ava...{25/02}
1560 Vine Street (East)
Near: parking lot
Category/As: Motion Pictures as Actress
For: The Sun Also Rises (1957)
Real name: Ava Lavina Gardner
Born: December 24, 1922 in Grabtown, NC   Died: 1990, from pneumonia
Studio: MGM
Related to Mickey Rooney, Artie Shaw, Frank Sinatra (spouses)

Gardner, Ed...{33/20}
6556 Hollywood Boulevard (South)
Near: Hollywood Jewelry Exchange
Category/As: Radio as Actor
For: Duffy's Tavern (1939) as Archie
Real name: same or unknown
Born: 1901   Died: 1963
Related to Shirley Booth (spouse)

Gardner, Ed...{34/43}
6674 Hollywood Boulevard (South)
Near: Explosion
Category/As: Television as Actor
For: Duffy's Tavern (1948)

Garland, Beverly...{06/60}
6801 Hollywood Boulevard (North)
Near: vacant
Category/As: Television as Actress
For: My Three Sons (1966) as Barbara Harper
Dedicated on January 26, 1983
Real name: Beverly Lucy Fessenden
Born: October 17, 1926 in Santa Cruz, CA

Garland, Judy...{16/25}
1715 Vine Street (West)
Near: Hair Vine
Category/As: Motion Pictures as Actress
For: The Wizard of Oz (1939)
Real name: Frances Ethel Gumm
Born: June 10, 1922 in Grand Rapids, MI
Died: 1969, from drug overdose and buried in Hartsdale, NY
Studio: MGM   Awards: Oscar
Related to Vincente Minelli (spouse), Liza Minelli (daughter)

Garland, Judy....{36/50}
6764 Hollywood Boulevard (South)
Near: Guiness World of Records
Category/As: Recording as Singer
For: Somewhere Over the Rainbow

Garner, Erroll....{14/26}
6371 Hollywood Boulevard (North)
Near: Antenna of Hollywood
Category/As: Recording as Pianist
Real name: same or unknown
Born: June 15, 1923 in Norman, OK   Died: 1977

Garner, James...{05/34}
6925 Hollywood Boulevard (North)
Near: Mann's Chinese Theater
Category/As: Television as Actor
For: The Rockford Files (1974) NBC
Real name: James Scott Baumgarner

Born: April 7, 1928 in Norman, OK

Garner, Peggy Ann...{33/48}
6608 Hollywood Boulevard (South)
Near: Frederick's of Hollywood
Category/As: Motion Pictures as Actress
For: Jane Eyre (1944)
Born: February 3, 1932 in Canton, OH
Died: October 16, 1984, from cancer
Studio: 20th Century-Fox   Awards: Oscar

Garnett, Tay...{33/24}
6558 Hollywood Boulevard (South
Near: Body Image
Category/As: Motion Pictures as Director
For: The Postman Always Rings Twice (1946)
Real name: William Garnett
Born: June 13, 1898 in Los Angeles, CA   Died: 1977

Garroway, Dave...{14/44}
6357 Hollywood Boulevard (North)
Near: Star Fashion
Category/As: Radio as Host
For: Today (1952)
Real name: same or unknown
Born: July 13, 1913 in Schenectady, NY
Died: 1982, from suicide (gunshot)

Garroway, Dave...{23/27}
6274 Hollywood Boulevard (South)
Near: parking lot
Category/As: Television as Host
For: The Dave Garroway Show (1947)
Real name: same or unknown
Born: July 13, 1913 in Schenectady, NY
Died: 1982, from suicide (gunshot)

Garson, Greer...{27/93}
1645 Vine Street (West)
Near: Hollywood Vine Building
Caregory/As: Motion Pictures as Actress
For: Mrs. Miniver (1942) MGM
Born: September 29, 1908 in County Down, Ireland
Related to Richard May (spouse)

Gaye, Marvin...{25/41}
1560 Vine Street (East)
Near: parking lot
Caregory/As: Recording as Singer
For: Ain't No Mountain High Enough
Dedicated on September 27, 1990
Real name: Marvin Gaye,Jr.
Born: 1940   Died: 1984, murdered by his father, ashes scattered

Gaynor, Janet...{23/51}
6286 Hollywood Boulevard (South)
Near: Metro Rail Field Office
Category/As: Motion Pictures as Actress
For: Seventh Heaven (1927)
Real name: Laura Gainer
Born: October 6,1906 in Philadelphia, PA
Died: 1984, from pneumonia and buried in Hollywood, CA
Awards: Oscar

Gaynor, Mitzi...{23/31}
6274 Hollywood Boulevard (South)
Near: parking lot
Category/As: Motion Pictures as Actress
For: South Pacific (1958) Paramount
Real name: Francesca Mitzi Marlene de Charney von Gerber

Gibbons, Floyd...{27/58}
1635 Vine Street (West)
Near: Futurama Furniture
Category/As: Radio as Newscaster

For: Headline Hunters (1929) NBC
Real name: same or unknown
Born: 1887   Died: 1939

Gibbs, Georgia...{31/13}
6406 Hollywood Boulevard (South)
Near: Fox Cosmetics
Category/As: Recording as Vocalist
For: Tweedle Dee
Real name: Fredda Gibbins
Born: August 17, 1926

Gibson, Hoot...{16/108}
1777 Vine Street (West)
Near: Vine Street Building
Category/As: Motion Pictures as Actor
For: Ocean's Eleven (1961)
Real name: Edmond Richard Gibson
Born: August 6, 1892 in NE
Died: 1962, from cancer and buried in Inglewood, CA

Gigli, Beniamino...{05/62}
6925 Hollywood Boulevard (North)
Near: Mann's Chinese Theater
Category/As: Recording as Singer
For: Pagliacci
Real name: same or unknown
Born: March 20 1890 in Italy   Died: 1957

Gilbert, Billy...{18/04}
6263 Hollywood Boulevard (North)
Near: Equitible Building
Category/As: Motion Pictures as Actor
For: The Music Box (1932)
Real name: same or unknown
Born: September 12, 1894 in Louisville, KY
Died: 1971 from a stroke

Gilbert, John...{16/96}
1749 Vine Street (West)
Near: parking lot
Category/As: Motion Pictures as Actor
For:The Merry Widow (1925)
Real name: John Pringle
Born: July 10, 1895 in Logan, UT
Died: 1936, from a heart attack and buried in Glendale, CA
Studio: Triangle
Related to Ina Claire, Leatrice Joy (spouses)

Gilbert, Melissa...{13/22}
6433 Hollywood Boulevard (North)
Near: Pacific Theater
Category/As: Television as Actress
For: Little House on the Prairie (1974) as Laura Ingalls
Dedicated on March 13, 1985
Real name: same or unknown
Born: May 8, 1964 in Los Angeles, CA

Gilbert, Paul...{28/59}
6340 Hollywood Boulevard (South)
Near: Mr. Submarine
Category/As: Television as Actor
For: The Duke (1954)
Real name: Paul MacMahon
Born: 1917   Died: 1976

Gilley, Mickey...{37/117}
6922 Hollywood Boulevard (South)
Near: Hollywood Center
Catrgory/As: Recording as Singer
For: Room Full of Roses
Dedicated on October 18, 1984
Born: March 9, 1937

Gish, Dorothy...{14/02}
6385 Hollywood Boulevard (North)
Near: Security Pacific Bank
Category/As: Motion Pictures as Actress
For: Orphans of the Storm (1921)
Real name: Dorthy de Guiche
Born: March 11, 1898 in Massillon, OH   Died: 1968 from Pneumonia
Related to Lillian Gish (sister)

Gish, Lillian...{17/72}
1722 Vine Street (East)
Near: Nick's Diner
Category/As: Motion Pictures as Actress
For: Intolerance (1916)
Real name: Lillian de Guiche
Born: October 14, 1896 in Springfield, OH
Related to Dorothy Gish (sister)

Glaum, Louise...{37/38}
6834 Hollywood Boulevard (South)
Near: El Capitan Building
Category/As: Motion Pictures as Actress
For: I Am Guilty (1921)
Real name: same or unknown
Died: 1970, from pneumonia

Gleason, Jackie...{18/56}
6225 Hollywood Boulevard (North)
Near: vacent store
Category: Recording
Real name: Herbert John Gleason
Born: Februrary 26, 1916 in Brooklyn, NY   Died: 1987, fron cancer
Awards: Tony

Gleason, Jackie...{28/15}
6306 Hollywood Boulevard (South)
Near: Exotic Hair and Nail
Category/As: Television as Actor
For: The Honeymooners (1955-1966)
Note: The Honeymooners originally aired for only one year

Gleason, James...{38/66}
7038 Hollywood Boulevared (South)
Near: Andrea's Pizza
Category/As: Motion Pictures as Actor
For: Suddenly (1944)
Born: May 23, 1886   Died: 1959, from asthma

Globtrotters, The Harlem...{37/107}
6922 Hollywood Boulevard (South)
Near: Hollywood Center
Category/As: Television as Basketball Players
Dedicated on January 19, 1982

Gobel, George...{37/58}
6840 Hollywood Boulevard (South)
Near: Masonic Temple
Category/As: Television as Comedian
For: The George Gobel Show (1957-1959) NBC
Real name: same or unknown
Born: May 20, 1919   Died: 1919, from arterial leg surgery

91

Goddard, Paulette...{24/18}
1650 Vine Street (East)
Near: (closed)
Category/As: Motion Pictures as Actress
For: Modern Times (1930)
Real name: Marion Levy
Born: June 3, 1911 in Whitestone, NY   Died: 1990, from heart failure
Related to Charlie Chaplin, Burgess Meredith (spouses)

Godfrey, Arthur...{18/50}
6233 Hollywood Boulevard (North)
Near: Pantages Theater
Category/As: Radio as Host
For: Arthur Godfrey Time (1945) CBS

Born: August 31, 1903 in New York, NY   Died: 1983, from emphysema

Godfrey, Arthur...{33/62}
6612 Hollywood Boulevard (South)
Near: burned out store
Category/As: Recording as Singer

Godfrey, Arthur...{26/90}
1555 Vine Street (West)
Near: TAV Celebrity Center
Category/As: Television as Host
For: Arthur Godfrey's Talent Scouts (1948-1958)

Godwin, Earl...{19/15}
6211 Hollywood Boulevard (North)
Near: Capitol Records annex office
Category/As: Radio as Newsacster
For: White House Correspondent
Real name: same or unknown
Born: 1881   Died: 1956

Gold, Ernest...{31/54}
6434 Hollywood Boulevard (South)
Near: Picway Shoes
Category/As: Motion Pictures as Composer
For: Exodus (1960)
Born: July 13, 1921 in Vienna

Goldberg, Leonard...{05/73}
6925 Hollywood Boulevard (North)
Near: Mann's Chinese Theater
Category/As: Television as Producer
For: Fantasy Island (1973)
Dedicated on December 9, 1986
Real name: same or unknown
Born: January 24,1934 in New York, NY

Goldman, Edwin F. ...{31/21}
6410 Hollywood Boulevard (South)
Near: F.W. Woolworth
Category/As: Radio as Composer
Real name: same or unknown
Born: January 1, 1878   Died: 1956

Goldwyn, Samuel...{27/59}
1635 Vine Street (West)
Near: Futurama Furniture
Category/As: Motion Pictures as Pioneer
For: Co-founder MGM
Real name: Samuel Goldfish
Born: August 27, 1882 in Warsaw, Poland
Died: 1973, from cancer and buried in Glendale, CA

Goodman, Al...{28/18}
6310 Hollywood Boulevard (South)
Near: Olympic Electronics
Category/As: Recording as Composer
Born: March 1, 1920

Goodman, Benny...{20/98}
6125 Hollywood Boulevard (North)
Near: Pep Boys
Category/As: Recording as Musician
For: music for The Benny Goodman Story (1955)
Born: May 30, 1901   Died: 1986, from a heart attack

Goodson, Mark...{30/13}
6378 Hollywood Boulevard (South)
Near: burned out building
Category/As: Television as Producer
For: The Price is Right (1957)
Dedicated on June 23, 1982
Born: January 24, 1915   Died: December 18, 1992

Goodwin, Bill...{37/16}
6808 Hollywood Boulevard (South)
Near: vacant
Category/As: Radio as announcer
For: Blondie (1939)
Real name: same or unknown
Born: 1910   Died: 1958, from a heart attack

Gordon, Gale...{28/62}
6340 Hollywood Boulevard (North)
Near: Mr. Submarine
Category/As: Radio as Actor
For: Fibber McGee and Molly (1934) as The Old Timer
Real name: Charles Gaylord Aldrich
Born: February 2, 1906

Gore, Mike...{15/35}
6315 1/2 Hollywood Boulevard (North)
Near: Le Sex Shoppe
Category/As: Motion Pictures as Exhibitor
For: Theater Chain Owner
Real name: same or unknown
Born: in Russia

Gosden, "Amos" Freeman...{16/93}
1749 Vine Street (West)
Near: parking lot
Category/As: Radio as Actor
For: Amos 'n' Andy Show (1929)
Real name: Freeman F. Gosden
Born: May 5, 1899 in Richmond , VA
Died: 1982, from heart failure

Gossett, Jr., Louis...{38/49}
7024 Hollywood Boulevard (South)
Near: Roosevelt Hotel parking structure
Category/As: Motion Pictures as Actor
For: Iron Eagle (1986)
Dedicated on May 20, 1992
Born: 1936

Goudal, Jetta...{15/08}
6331 Hollywood Boulevard (North)
Near: Guaranty Building
Category/As: Motion Pictures as Actress
For: White Gold (1927)
Real name: same or unknown
Born: July 12, 1901 in France   Died: 1985

Gould, Morton...{11/53}
6533 Hollywood Boulevard (North)
Near: vacant
Category/As: Recording as Composer
For: America Sing
Real name: same or unknown
Born: December 10, 1913 in NY
Awards: Grammy

Goulet, Robert...{30/05}
6370 Hollywood Boulevard (South)
Near: vacant lot
Category/As: Motion Pictures as Actor
For: Carousel (1956)
Real name: Stanley Applebaum
Born: 1933 in Canada

Grable, Betty...{12/07}
6525 Hollywood Boulevard (North)
Near: Steve's Gifts
Category/As: Motion Pictures as Actress
For: Four Jills in a Jeep (1944)
Real name: Ruth Elizabeth Grable
Born: December 18, 1916 in St. Louis, MO
Died: July2, 1973 from cancer and buried in Inglewood, CA
Studio: 20th Century Fox

Related to Jackie Coogan, Harry James (spouses)

Graham, Billy...{05/63}
6925 Hollywood Boulevard (North)
Near: Mann's Chinese Theater
Category/As: Radio as Evangelist
For: Billy Graham Crusades
Dedicated on October 15, 1989
Real name: ~~Wolfgang Grajonca~~ ← this is the rock promoter

Grahame, Gloria...{32/37}
6522 Hollywood Boulevard (South)
Near: Newberry School of Beauty
Category/As: Motion pictures as Actress
For: The Bad and the Beautiful (1952)
Real name: Gloria Grahame Hallward
Born: November 28, 1925 in Pasadena, CA
Died: October 5, 1981 from cancer
Studio: MGM   Awards: Oscar
Related to Nicholas Ray, Tony Ray, Cy Howard
       and Stanley Clem (spouses)
       CLEMETS

Granger, Farley...{26/86}
1549 Vine Street (West)
Near: TAV Celebrity Center
Category/As: Television as Actor
For: Arrowsmith (19__)
Real name: Farley Earle Granger III
Born: July 1, 1925 in San Jose, CA

Grant, Cary...{24/80}
1610 Vine Street (East)
Near: Vine Street Bar and Grill
Category/As: Motion Pictures as Actor
For: Bringing Up Baby (1938)
Real name: Archibald Alexander Leach
Born: January 18, 1904 in Bristol, England
Died: 1986 from a stroke
Related to Virginia Cherrill, Dyan Cannon (spouses)

Grant, Johnny...{05/47}
6925 Hollywood Boulevard (North)
Near: Mann's Chinese Theater
Category/As: Television as Host
For: Johnny Grant at Universal Studios (1969-1971)
Dedicated on May 9, 1980
Born: May 9, 1923 in LaGrange, North Carolina
Awards: Emmy, LA Area's Governor Award
Notes: VP of Public Affairs and Special Projects (KTLA-TV)
       Honorary Mayor of Hollywood, CA
       Producer of Holywood Christmas Parade
       Chairman of the Walk of Fame Selection Committee

Granville, Bonita...{10/53}
6607 Hollywood Boulevard (North)
Near: vacant store
Category/As; Motion Pictures as Actress
For: Nancy Drew (1938)
Born: February 2, 1923 in Chicago, IL
Died: 1988 and buried in Culver City, CA

Grauman, Sid...{14/18}
6379 Hollywood Boulevard (North)
Near: vacant store
Category/As: Motion Pictures as Theater Owner
For: Chinese Theater Forecourt footprint collection
Born: March 17, 1879 in Indianapolis, IN   Died: 1950

Gray, Gilda...{33/72}
6620 Hollywood Boulevard (South)
Near: burned out store
Category/As: Motion Pictures as Actress
For: Rose Marie (1936)
Real name: Marianne Michaelska
Born: October 24, 1901 in Poland   Died: 1959 from food poisioning

Gray, Glen...{16/19}
1713 Vine Street (West)
Near: Dan Dee Shoe Repair
Category/As: Recording as Bandleader
Real name: Glen G. Knoblaough
Born: June 7, 1906 in Roanoke, VA   Died: 1963

Grayson, Kathryn..{24/94}
1600 Vine Street (East)
Near: D M V
Category/As: Motion Pictures as Actress
For: Kiss Me Kate (1953)   MGM
Real name: Zelma Kathryn Hedrick
Born: February 9, 1922 in Winston-Salem, NC

Green, Alfred...{12/01}
6529 Hollywood Boulevard (North)
Near: Hollywood Bargain
Category/As: Motion Pictures as Director
For: The Jolson Story (1940)
Real name: Alfred E. Green
Born: 1889   Died: 1960 from a long illness

Green, John...{05/38}
6925 Hollywood Boulevard (North)
Near: Mann's Chinese Theater
Category/As: Motion Pictures as Composer
For: Easter Parade (1948)
Real name: same or unknown
Born: October 10, 1908
Awards: Oscar

Green, Mitzi...{31/49}
6430 Hollywood Boulevard (South)
Near: Power Sports
Category/As: Motion Pictures as Actress
For: Little orphan Annie (1932)
Real name: Elizabeth Keno
Born: October 22, 1920   Died: May 24, 1969 from cancer

Greene, Lorne...{26/91}
1555 Vine Street (West)
Near: TAV Celebrity Center
Category/As: Television as Actor
For: Bonanza (1959) as Ben Cartwright
Dedicated on February 12, 1985
Real name: Lorne Green
Born: February 12, 1915 in Ottawa, Canada
Died: 1987 from ulcer surgery
Note: Star dedicated on birthday

Greenwood, Charlotte...{27/14}
1605 Vine Street (West)
Near: Molly Coney Island
Category/As: Radio as Actress
For: Oklahoma (1956)
Real name: Frances Charlotte Greenwood
Born: June 25, 1890 in Philadelphia, PA
Died: January 18, 1978
Studio: 20th Century Fox

Greer, Jane...{24/43}
1630 Vine Street (East)
Near: parking lot
Category/As: Motion Pictures as Actress
For: Man of a Thousand Faces (1957) RKO
Real name: Bettyjane Greer
Born: September 9, 1924 in Washington, D.C.   Died: 1972
Related to Rudy Vallee (spouse)

Grey, Joel...{07/47}
6755 Hollywood Boulevard (North)
Near: vacant
Category/As: Live Theater as Actor
For: Cabaret (1972)

Dedicated on October 9, 1985
Real name: Joel Katz
Born: April 11, 1932 in Cleveland, OH
Awards: Tony, Oscar
Related to Jennifer Grey (daughter)

Griffin, Merv...{26/65}
1541 Vine Street (West)
Near: TAV Celebrity Center
Category/As: Television as Executive
For: Creator of Wheel of Fortune and Jeopardy
Born: June 6, 1925 in San Mateo, CA
Awards: Emmy

Griffith, Andy...{31/32}
6418 Hollywood Boulevard (South)
Near: Hollywood Discount Center
Category/As: Television as Actor
For: The Andy Griffith Show (1960-1968)   CBS
Real name: same or unknown
Born: 1926

Griffith, Corinne...{25/34}
1560 Vine Street (East)
Near: parking lot
Category/As: Motion Pictures as Actress
For: Lillies of the Field (1924)
Born: November 24, 1896 in Texarkana, TX
Died: 1979 from cardiac arrest

*Griffith, David W. *...{11/47}
6535 Hollywood Boulevard (North)
Near: Jean Machine
Category/As: Motion Pictures as Director
For: Intolerence (1916)
Real name: David Lleweyn Wark Griffith
Born: January 22, 1874 in Crestwood, KY
Died: 1948 from a cerebral hemorrhage and buried in Crestwood, KY

Griffith, Raymond...{21/35}
6124 Hollywood Boulevard (south)
Near: Doug's Sports Corner
Category/As: Motion Pictures Actor
For: All Quiet on the Western Front (1930)
Real name: same or unknown
Born: January 23, 1890 in Boston, MA
Died: 1957 from a heart attack

Guillaume, Robert...{09/19}
6675 Hollywood Boulevard (North)
Near: Vogue Theater
Category/As: Television as Actor
For: Benson (1979) as Benson
Dedicated on November 22, 1984
Real name: Robert Williams
Born: November 30, 1937 in St. Louis, Mo
Awards: Emmy

Guinan, Texas...{16/116}
1779 Vine Street (West)
Near: Capezio Dance Studio
Category/As: Motion Pictures as Actress
For: Little Miss Deputy (1919)
Real name: Mary Louise Cecelia Guinan
Born: 1888 in TX   Died: 1933 from colitis operation

Guiness, Alec...{26/94}
1555 Vine Street (West)
Near: TAV Celebrity Center
Category/As: Motion Pictures as Actor
For: The Bridge on the River Kwai (1957)
Real name: same or unknown
Born: April 2, 1914 in London, England
Awards: Oscar

Gwenn, Edmund...{16/100}
1749 Vine Street (West)
Near: parking lot
Category/As: Motion Pictures as Actor
For: Miracle on 34th Street (1947) as Kris Kringle
Born: September 26, 1875 in Glamorgan, Wales
Died: September 6, 1959
Awards: Oscar

Hadley, Reed...{11/19}
6553 Hollywood Boulevard (North)
Near: London Connection
Category/As: Television as Actor
For: The Public Defender (1954) as Bart Matthews
Real name: Reed Herring
Born: January 8, 1911 in Texas   Died: 1974, from heart attack

Hagen, Jean...{25/40}
1560 Vine Street (East)
Near: parking lot
Category/As: Television as Actress
For: Make Room for Daddy (1953) as Margaret Williams
Real name: Jean Shirley Verhagen
Born: August 3, 1923 in Chicago, IL   Died: 1977, from cancer

Haggerty, Don...{21/63}
6140 Hollywood Boulevard (South)
Near: Henry Fonda Theater
Category/As: Television as Actor
For: Grizzly Adams (1977)
Real name: same or unknown
Born: November 19, 1941

Hagman, Larry...{25/43}
1560 Vine Street (East)
Near: parking lot
Category/As: Television as Actor
For: Dallas (1978) CBS as J.R Ewing
Dedicated on September 9, 1981
Real name: same or unknown
Born: September 21, 1931 in Texas
Related to Mary Martin (mother)

Haines, William...{38/24}
7000 Hollywood Boulevard (South)
Near: Roosevelt Hotel
Category/As: Motion Pictures as Actor
For: Tower of Lies (1924)
Real name: Federico Nobile
Born: January 1, 1900   Died: 1973, from cancer

Hairston, Jester...{20/25}
6161 Hollywood Boulevard (North)
Near: Network Body Shop
Category: Television as Actor
For: Amen (19__) as Deacon Rolly Forbes
Dedicated on February 12, 1992
Born: July 9, 1901 in Blews Creek, NC

Hale, Alan...{32/51}
6530 Hollywood Boulevard (South)
Near: Georgio's Pizza
Category/As: Motion Pictures as Actor
For: The Adventures of Robin Hood (1938)
Real name: Rufus Alan McKahan
Born: February 10, 1892
Died: 1950, from liver ailment and buried in Glendale, CA
Related to Alan Hale, Jr. (son)

Hale, Jr., Alan...{09/56}
6655-4 Hollywood Boulevard (South)
Near: Star Search
Category/As: Television as Actor
For: Gilligan's Island (1964-1966) CBS as the Skipper
Real name: Alan MacKahan
Born: March 8, 1918 in Los Angeles, CA   Died: 1990, from cancer
Related to Alan Hale (father)

Hale, Barbara...{24/56}
1630 Vine Street (East)
Near: parking lot
Category/As: Television as Actress
For: Perry Mason (1957-1966) as Della Street
Born: April 18, 1921 in DeKalb, IL
Related to Bill Williams (spouse), William Katt (son)
Awards: Emmy

Hale, Creighton...{05/50}
6925 Hollywood Boulevard (North)
Near: Mann's Chinese Theater
Category/As: Motion Pictures as Actor
For: The Perils of Pauline (1947)
Real name: Patrick Fitzgerald
Born: May 13, 1883 in Ireland   Died: 1965

Haley, Bill...{29/02}
6350 Hollywood Boulevard (South)
Near: Combo's Pizza
Category/As: Recording as Singer
For: Rock Around the Clock
Born: July 6, 1925   Died: 1981

Hale, Creighton...{05/50}
6925 Hollywood Boulevard (North)
Near: Mann's Chinese Theater
Category/As: Motion Pictures as Actor
For: The Perils of Pauline (1947)
Real name: Patrick Fitzgerald
Born: May 13, 1883 in Ireland   Died: 1965

Haley, Bill...{29/02}
6350 Hollywood Boulevard (South)
Near: Combo's Pizza
Category/As: Recording as Singer
For: Rock Around the Clock
Born: July 6, 1925   Died: 1981

Haley, Jack...{13/13}
6435 Hollywood Boulevard (North)
Near: By George, For Men
Category/As: Radio as Actor
For: The Sealtest Village Store (1942) NBC
Real name: John Joseph Haley
Born: August 10, 1989 in Boston MA   ｟89? ?｠
Died: June, 1979 and buried in Culver City, CA

Hall, Arsenio...{36/65}
6776 Hollywood Boulevard (South)
Near: McDonald's
Category/As: Televison as Host
For: The Arsenio Hall Show (19__) Fox
Dedicated on November 7, 1990
Real name: same or unknown

Hall, Jon...{17/56}
1724 Vine Street (East)
Near: parking lot
Category/As: Motion Pictures as Actor
For: Hurricane (1937)
Real name: Charles Hall Locher
Born: February 26, 1913 in Fresno, CA
Died: December 13, 1980, from suicide (gunshot) buried in Glendale, CA
Studio: Goldwyn
Related to Frances Langford, Raquel Torres (spouses)

Hall, Jon...{05/56}
6935 Hollywood Boulevard (North)
Near: Mann's Chinese parking
Category/As: Televsion as Actor
For: Ramar of the Jungle (1952)

Hall, Monty...{06/70}
6801 Hollywood Boulevard (North)
Near: vacant
Category/As: Television as Host
For: Let's Make A Deal (1963-1976)
Real name: Monte Halparin
Born: August 25, 1923 in Winnipeg, Canada
Studio: ABC

Hamblen, Stuart...{06/14}
6841 Hollywood Boulevard (North)
Near: Budget Rent-A-Car
Category/As: Recording as Singer
For: This Ole House
Real name: Carl S. Hamblen
Born: October 20, 1908 in TX   Died: 1989, from cancer

Hamer, Rusty...{15/26}
6323 Hollywood Boulevard (North)
Near: A AALL Hollywood Key
Category/As: Television as Actor
For: The Danny Thomas Show (1953) as Rusty Williams
Real name: Russell Craig Hamer
Born: February 15, 1947 in Tenafly, NJ   Died: 1990, from suicide
Studio: CBS

Hamilton, Lloyd...{20/40}
6141 Hollywood Boulevard (North)
Near: Mid-Town Towing
Category/As: Motion Pictures as Actor
For: Various Silent Movies
Real name: same or unknown
Born: August 19, 1891 in CA   Died: 1935, from stomach disorder

Hamilton, Neil...{33/100}
6630 D Hollywood Boulevard (South)
Near: European Menswear
Category/As: Motion Pictures as Actor
For: Beau Geste (1926)
Real name: James Neil Hamilton
Born: September 9, 1899   Died: 1984, from asthma

Hampton, Lionel...{38/29}
7000 Hollywood Boulevard (South)
Near: Roosevelt Hotel
Category/As: Recording as Musician
Dedicated on June 14, 1982
Real name: same or unknown
Born: April 12, 1913

Hanks, Tom...{38/58} *
7024 Hollywood Boulevard (South)
Near: Roosevelt Hotel parking
Category/As: Motion Pictures as Actor
For: Big (1988)
Dedicated on June 30, 1992
Real name: same or unknown

Hanna-Barbera...{07/51}
6751 Hollywood Boulevard (North)
Near: vacant
Category/As: Motion Pictures as Animators
For: The Flintstones
Real name: William Hanna, Joseph Barbera
Born: July 14, 1920, March 24, 1911 in Melrose, NM; New York
Awards: Oscar, Emmy

Harding, Ann...{19/17}
6207 Hollywood Boulevard (North)

Near: parking lot
Category/As: Motion Pictures as Actress
For: Love From a Stranger (1937)
Real name: Dorothy Walton Gatley
Born: August 7, 1901 in Houston, TX   Died: 1981, from short illness

Harding, Ann...{37/60}
6840 Hollywood Boulevard (South)
Near: Masonic Temple
Category/As: Television as Actress
For: Dr. Kildare (1961)

Hardwicke, Sir Cedric...{19/01}
6211 Hollywood Boulevard (North)
Near: Capitol Records annex office
Category/As: Motion Pictures as Actor
For: Nicholas Nickleby (1947)
Born: February 19, 1883 in England   Died: 1964, from lung ailment

Hardwicke, Sir Cedric...{33/44}
Near: J.J. Newberry
Category/As: Television as Actor
For: Mrs. G Goes to College (1961)

Hardy, Oliver...{25/92}
1500 Vine Street (East)
Near: Home Savings
Category/As: Motion Pictures as Comedian
For: Music Box (1932)
Real name: Oliver Nowell Hardy
Born: January 18, 1892 in Harlem, GA
Died: 1957, from stroke and buried in Burbank, CA
Studio: Hal Roach

Harlow, Jean...{37/86}
6912 Hollywood Boulevard (South)
Near: Harley Davidson Shop
Category/As: Motion Pictures as Actress
For: Hell's Angels (1930)
Real Name: Harlean Carpenter
Born: March 3, 1911 in Kansas City, MO
Died: June 7, 1937, from acute sunburn poisoning and buried in Glendale,
Studio: MGM
Related to Paul Bern (spouse)

Harris, Arlene...{23/03}
6250 Hollywood Boulevard (South)
Near: Stella Adler Theater
Category/As: Radio as Actress
For: The Baby Snooks Show (1939) as Mrs. Higgins
Real name: same or unknown
Born: in Canada
Studio: NBC

Harris, Mildred...{15/49}
6307 Hollywood Boulevard (North)
Near: Last Moving Picture
Category/As: Motion Pictures as Actress
For: Intolerance (1916)
Real name: same or unknown
Born: November 29, 1901 in WY   Died: 1944, from abdominal surgery
Related to Charlie Chaplin (spouse)

Harris, Phil...{09/62}
6655-F5 Hollywood Boulevard (North)
Near: Souvenir Shop
Category/As: Radio as Orchestra Leader
For: The Phil Harris-Alice Faye Show (1946)
Real name: same or unknown
Born: June 24, 1906 in Linton, IN
Related to Alice Faye (spouse)

Harris, Phil...{32/19}
6508 Hollywood Boulevard (South)
Near: Fox Theater (closed)
Category/As: Recording as Singer

For: Some Little Bug (Is Gonna Get You Someday)

Harrison, Rex...{37/78}
6906 Hollywood Boulevard (South)
Near: Juice Master
Ceategory/As: Motion Pictures as Actor
For: My Fair Lady (1964)
Real name: Reginald Carey Harrison
Born: March 5, 1908 in Huyton, England   Died: 1990, from cancer
Awards: Oscar
Related to Lillie Palmer, Carole Landis (spouses)

Harrison, Rex...{30/20}
6380 Hollywood Boulevard (South)
Near: No Problem
Category/As: Television as Actor
For: Don Quixote (1972)

Hart, John...{31/53}
6434 Hollywood Boulevard (South)
Near: Picway Shoes
Category/As: Television as Actor
For: The Lone Ranger (1952)
Real name: same or unknown

Hart, Mary...{38/43}
7024 Hollywood Boulevard (South)
Near: Roosevelt Hotel parking
Category/As: Television as Host
For: Entertainment Tonight (19__)
Dedicated on May 12, 1989

Hart, William S....{14/34}
6371 Hollywood Boulevard (North)
Near: Antenna of Hollywood
Category/As: Motion Pictures as Actor
For: Tumbleweeds (1925)
Born: December 6, 1870 in Newburgh, NY
Died: 1946, from stroke and buried in Brooklyn, NY

Hartley, Mariette...{38/33}
7000 Hollywood Boulevard (South)
Near: Roosevelt Hotel
Category/As: Television as Actress
Dedicated on June 11, 1987
Real name: same or unknown
Born: 1940

Hathaway, Henry...{24/33}
1638 Vine Street (East)
Near: Hollywood Import House
Category/As: Motion Pictures as Director
For: Lives of a Bengal Lancer (1935)
Real name: same or unknown
Born: March 13, 1898 in Sacramento, CA   Died: 1985, from heart attack
Awards: Oscar

Hatton, Raymond...{17/100}
1704 Vine Street (East)
Near Krisseli's Center
Category/As: Motion Pictures as Actor
For: We're in the Navy Now (1926)
Real name: same or unknown
Born: July 7, 1887 in Red Oak, IA   Died: 1971, from heart attack

Haver, June...{16/107}
1777 Vine Street (West)
Near: Vine Street Bldg.
Category/As: Motion Pictures as Actress
For: Look for the Silver Lining (1949)
Real name: June Stovenour
Born: June 10, 1926 in Rock Island, IL
Studio: 20th Century Fox
Related to Fred MacMurray (spouse)

Havoc, June...{33/66}
6618 Hollywood Boulevard (South)
Near: burned out
Category/As: Motion Pictures as Actress
For: Four Jacks and a Jill (1942)
Real name: Ellen Evangeline Hovick
Born: November 8, 1916 in Seattle, WA
Related to Gypsy Rose Lee (sister)

Havoc, June...{13/45}
6411-A Hollywood Boulevard (North)
Near: Hollywood Boots
Category/As: Television as Actress
For: Willy (1954)

Hawk, Bob...{13/21}
6433 Hollywood Boulevard (North)
Near: Pacific Theater
Category/As: Radio as Host
For: Take It or Leave It (1940)
Real name: same or unknown
Born: in Iowa

Hawks, Howard...{17/104}
1702 Vine Street (East)
Near: H & V Dentistry
Category/As: Motion Pictures as Director
For: His Girl Friday (1940)
Real name: Howard Winchester Hawks
Born: May 30, 1896 in Goshen, IN   Died: 1977, from fall & concussion
Studio: Fox   Awards: Oscar

Hay, Bill...{37/36}
6822 Hollywood Boulevard (South)
Near: Starline Tours & Gifts
Category/As: Radio as Announcer
For: The Amos 'n Andy Show (1926)

Hayakawa, Sessue...{27/80}
1645 Vine Street (West)
Near: Hollywood Vine Building
Category/As: Motion Pictures as Actor
For: The Bridge on the River Kwai (1957)
Real name: Kintaro Hayakawa
Born: June 10, 1889   Died: 1973, from cerebral thrombosis

Hayes, Gabby...{13/25}
6427 Hollywood Boulevard (North)
Near: 13th District
Category/As: Radio as Actor
For: The Roy Rogers Show (1944) as Gabby
Real name: George Francis Hayes
Born: May 7, 1885 in NY
Died: 1969, from heart ailment and buried in Los Angeles, CA

Hayes, George "Gabby"...{17/61}
1724 Vine Street (East Side)
Near: parking lot
Category/As: Television as Actor
For: The Roy Rogers Show (1951-1956)

Hayes, Helen...{23/15}
6256 Hollywood Boulevard (South)
Near: vacant lot
Category/As: Motion Pictures as Actress
For: Airport (1970) as Ada Quonsett
Real name: Helen B. Brown
Born: October 10, 1900 in WA   Died: March 17, 1993, from heart failure
Awards: Oscar
Related to James McArthur (son)

Hayes, Helen...{11/23}
6551 Hollywood Boulevard (North)
Near: Bruce Fashion
Category: Radio
For: The Helen Hayes Theater (1935)

Hayman, Richard...{16/112}
1779 Vine Street (West)
Near: Capezio Dance
Category/As: Recording as Musician
For: Ruby Gentry (1935)
Real name: same or unknown
Born: March 27, 1920
Studio: MGM

Haymes, Dick...{06/12}
6841 Hollywood Boulevard (North)
Near: Budget Rent-A-Car
Category/As: Radio as Host
For: I Fly Away (1950)
Real name: Richard Benjamin Haymes
Born: September 13, 1916 in Buenos Aires, Argentina
Died: March 28, 1980, from cancer
Studio: ABC
Related to Joanne Dru, Rita Hayworth (spouses)

Haymes, Dick...{21/27}
6100 Hollywood Boulevard (South)
Near: Chevron Gas Station
Category/As: Radio as Host
For: The Dick Haymes Show (1944)
Studio: NBC

Haymes, Dick...{17/55}
1724 Vine Street (East)
Near: parking lot
Category/As: Recording as Singer
For: Irish Eyes Are Smiling

Hays, Will H. ...{21/19}
6100 Hollywood Boulevard (South)
Near: Chevron Gas Station
Category/As: Motion Pictures as Censor
For: Motion Picture Production Code (1930)
Born: 1879 in Sullivan, IN   Died: 1954

Hayward, Louis...{25/58}
1550 Vine Street (East)
Near: parking lot
Category/As: Motion Pictures as Actor
For: My Son, My Son (1940)
Real name: Seafield Grant
Born: March 19, 1909 in Johnnesburg, South Africa
Died: 1985, from lung cancer
Related to Ida Lupino (spouse)

Hayward, Louis...{24/12}
1680 Vine Street (East)
Near: Taft Building
Category: Television
For: The Survivors (1969)

Hayward, Susan...(18/24}
6251 Hollywood Boulevard (North)
Near: parking lot
Category/As: Motion Pictures as Actress
For: I Want to Live (1958)
Real name: Edythe Marreanner   *MARRENER*
Born: June 30, 1918 in Brooklyn, NY
Died: March 14, 1975, from brain tumor and buried in Carrolton, GA
Awards: Oscar

Hayworth, Rita...{27/82}
1645 Vine Street (West)
Near: Hollywood Vine Building
Category/As: Motion Pictures as Actress
For: Gilda (1946)
Real name: Margarita Carmen Cansino
Born: October 17, 1918 in Brooklyn, NY
Died: 1987, from Alzheimer's disease and buried in Culver City, CA
Studio: Columbia
Related to: Dick Haymes, Orson Welles (spouses)

Head, Edith...{32/06}
6500 Hollywood Boulevard (South)
Near: Nikki's
Category/As: Motion Pictures as Costume Designer
For: The Sting (1973)
Born: October 28, 1907   Died: 1981

Healy, Jim...{36/23}
6740 Hollywood Boulevard (South)
Near: Sports Emporium
Category: Radio
For: Wizard of Oz (1939)
Dedicated on November 7, 1991

Hearn, Chick...{07/27}
6765 Hollywood Boulevard (North)
Near: Runkel's Jewelers
Category/As: Radio as Sportscaster
For: L.A. Lakers Announcer (since 1961)
Dedicated on September 24, 1986
Real name: Francis Hearn
Born: in IL

Heckart, Eileen...{21/59}
6140 Hollywood Boulevard (South)
Near: Henry Fonda Theater
Category/As: Motion Pictures as Actress
For: Butterflies Are Free (1972)
Real name: same or unknown
Born: March 29, 1919 in Columbus, OH
Awards: Oscar

Heflin, Van...{15/46}
6309 Hollywood Boulevard (North)
Near: Hollywood Recovery Center
Category/As: Motion Pictures as Actor
For: Johnny Eagar (1941)
Real name: Emmett Evan Heflin, Jr.
Born: December 13, 1910 in Walters, OK
Died: July 23, 1971, from stroke
Studio: MGM   Awards: Oscar

Heflin, Van...{20/62}
6125 Hollywood Boulevard (North)
Near: Pep Boys
Category/As: Television as Actor
For: Rank & File (1959)

Hefner, Hugh M. ...{38/11}
7000 Hollywood Boulevard (South)
Near: Roosevelt Hotel
Category/As: Television as Host
For: Playboy After Dark (1969)
Born: April 9, 1926

Heidt, Horace...{27/55}
1633 Vine Street (West)
Near: (closed) in Plaza Bldg
Category/As: Radio as Orchestra Leader
For: Pot 'O Gold (1939)
Born: May 21, 1901 in Alameda, CA
Died: 1986, from pneumonia and buried in Los Angeles, CA
Studio: NBC

Heidt, Horace...{33/90}
6630 A Hollywood Boulevard (South)
Near: Ventzia
Category/As: Television as Bandleader
For: The Horace Heidt Show (1950)

Heifetz, Jascha...{07/06}
6777 Hollywood Boulevard (North)
Near: Hollywood First National Bldg
Category/As: Recording as Violinist
Real name: same or unknown
Born: February 2, 1901 in Russia

Died: 1987, from brain surgery after fall
Awards: Grammy

Hendrix, Jimi...{10/14}
6631 Hollywood Boulevard (North)
Near: Hollywood Book City
Category/As: Recording as Musician
For: Purple Haze
Dedicated on November 21, 1991
Real name: James Marshall Hendrix
Born: 1943   Died: 1970, from inhalation of vomit and buried in Renton, WA

Henie, Sonja...{20/88}
6125 Hollywood Boulevard (North)
Near: Pep Boys
Category/As: Motion Pictures as Actress
For: Happy Landing (1938)
Born: April 8, 1912 in Oslo, Norway   Died: 1969, from leukemia

Henried, Paul...{29/26}
6366 Hollywood Boulevard (South)
Near: Kassfy Sportswear
Category/As: Motion Pictures as Actor
For: Casablanca (1942)
Real name: Paul George Julius Henreid Ritter von Wasel Waldingau
Born: January 10, 1908 in Trieste, Italy   Died: 1992, from stroke
Studio: Warner Brothers

Henried, Paul...{17/65}
1724 Vine Street (East)
Near: parking lot
Category/As: Television as Actor
For: The Failing of Raymond (1971)

Henson, Jim...{10/08}
6633 Hollywood Boulevard (North)
Near: Fame of Hollywood Cafe
Category/As: Television as Puppeteer
For: Muppet Show (1976)
Dedicated on September 24, 1991
Born: 1937   Died: 1990, from pneumonia
Studio: CBS

Hepburn, Audrey...{24/20}
1650 Vine Street (East)
Near: (closed)
Category/As: Motion Pictures as Actress
For: My Fair Lady (1964) as Eliza Doolittle
Real name: Edna Van Heemstra Hepburn-Ruston
Born: May 4, 1929 in Arnhem, Holland   Died: January 20, 1992, from cancer
Awards: Oscar
Related to Mel Ferrer (spouse)

Hepburn, Katharine...{23/54}
6288 Hollywood Boulevard (Soutj)
Near: Subway Sandwich Shop
Category/As: Motion Pictures as Actress
For: The African Queen (1951)
Real name: Katharine Houghton Hepburn
Born: May 12, 1907 in Hartford, CT

Herbert, Hugh...{18/22}
6251 Hollywood Boulevard (North)
Near: parking lot
Category/As: Motion Pictures as Actor
For: Sitting Pretty (1948)
Real name: F. Huge Herbert
Born: August 10, 1887 in NY   Died: 1952, from a heart attack

Herman, Pee Wee...{33/29}
6562 Hollywood Boulevard (South)
Near: Hollywood Toys Inc.
Category/As: Television as Actor
For: Pee Wee's Plathouse (1986) CBS
Dedicated on July 20, 1988
Real name: Paul Rubenfeld

Born: August 27, 1952

Herman, Woody...{37/14}
6806 Hollywood Boulevard (South)
Near: Misfits T-Shirts
Category/As: Recording as Musician
Real name: Woodrow Herman
Born: May 16,1913
Died: 1987, From emphysema and buried in Hollywood CA

Hersholt, Jean...{12/45}
6501 Hollywood Boulevard (North)
Near: burned out building
Category/As: Motion Pictures as Actor
For: Heidi (1937)
Born: July 12, 1886 in Copenhagen, Denmark
Died: 1956, from cancer and buried in Glendale, CA

Hersholt, Jean...{08/57}
6701 Hollywood Boulevard (North)
Near: Best Mini-Mart
Category/As: Radio as Production Executive

Hervey, Irene...{28/55}
6338 Hollywood Boulevard (South)
Near: El Golfo de Fonseca
Category/As: Motion Pictures as Actress
For: The Count os Monte Cristo (1934) MGM
Real name: Irene Herwick
Born: July 11, 1910 in Los Angeles, CA

Heston, Charlton...{24/59}
1628 Vine Street (East)
Near: Brown Derby ruins
Category/As: Motion Pictures as Actor
For: Ben Hur (1959)
Real name: John Charlton Carter
Born: October 4, 1923 in Evanston, IL
Studio: Paramount   Awards: Oscar

Heywood, Eddie...{16/14}
1711 Vine Street (West)
Near: vacant restaurant
Category/As: Recording as Pianist
Real name: same or unknown
Born: December 4, 1915 in Atlanta, GA
Died: 1989, from alzheimer's disease

Hibbler, Al...{24/22}
1650 Vine Street (East)
Near: vacant store
Category/As: Recording as Singer
For: Duke Ellington recordings
Real name: same or unknown
Born: August 16, 1915 in AR

Hicks, George...{28/25}
6314 Hollywood Boulevard (South)
Near: DAV Tech Computers
Category/As: Radio as Announcer
For: Death Valley Days (1930)

Hildegarde...{20/34}
6161 Hollywood Boulevard (North)
Near: Network Body Shop
Category/As: Radio as Singer
For: Beat the Band (1943) as the Incomparable Hildegarde
Real name: Hildegarde Loretta Sell
Born: February 1, 1906 in Milwaukee, WI

Hitchcock, Alfred...{32/13}
6506 Hollywood Boulevard (South)
Near: Misha Impex
Category/As: Motion Pictures as Director
For: Psycho (1960)
Real name: Sir Alfred Hitchcock

Born: August 13, 1899 in London, England   Died: 1980, from heart attack

Hitchcock, Alfred...{04/49}
7013 Hollywood Boulevard (North)
Near: Shelly's Cafe
Category/As: Television as Producer
For: Alfred Hitchcock Presents (1955-1962)
Studio: CBS & NBC

Hodiak, John...{20/82}
6125 Hollywood Boulevard (North)
Near: Pep Boys
Category/As: Radio as Actor
For: Li'l Abner (1939)
Born: April 16, 1914 in Pittsburg, PA
Died: October 19, 1955, from heart attack and buried in Los Angeles, CA
Related to Anne Baxter (spouse)

Hoffa, Portland...{24/31}
1642 Vine Street (East)
Near: Bernard Luggage
Category/As: Radio as Actress
For: The Fred Allen Show (1932)
Real name: same or unknown
Related to Fred Allen (spouse)

Holden, William...{27/90}
1645 Vine Street (West)
Near: Hollywood Vine Building
Category/As: Motion Pictures as Actor
For: Sunset Boulevard (1950)
Real name: William Franklin Beedle, Jr.
Born: April 17, 1918 in O'Fallon, MO
Died: November 16, 1981, from head injury from fall
Awards: Oscar

Holiday, Billie...{25/07}
1560 Vine Street (East)
Category/As: Recording as Singer
For: Gloomy Sunday
Dedicated on April 7, 1986
Real name: Eleanor McKay
Born: April 15, 1915 in Baltimore, MD
Died: 1959, from liver ailment and buried in the Bronx, NY
Awards: Grammy

Holliday, Judy...{05/64}
6925 Hollywood Boulevard (North)
Near: Mann's Chinese Theater
Category/As: Motion Pictures as Actress
For: Born Yesterday (1950)
Real name: Judith Tuvim
Born: June 21, 1922 in New York
Died: 1965, from cancer and buried in Hastings, NY
Studio: Columbia   Awards: Oscar

Holliman, Earl...{05/69}
6925 Hollywood Boulevard (North)
Near: Mann's Chinese Theater
Category/As: Television as Actor
For: Police Woman (1974) as Lt. Bill Crowley
Real name: Anthony Numkena
Born: September 11, 1928 in LA

Hollingshead, Gordon...{22/39}
6200 Hollywood Boulevard (South)
Near: parking lot
Category/As: Motion Pictures as Director
For: Various Silent Films
Real name: same or unknown
Born: January 8, 1892 in NJ   Died: 1952

Holm, Celeste...{25/54}
1550 Vine Street (East)
Near: parking lot
Category/As: Motion Pictures as Actress
For: All About Eve (1950)

Real name: same or unknown
Born: April 29, 1919 in New York
Awards: Oscar
Related to Wesley Addy (spouse)

Holm, Celeste...{06/11}
6841 Hollywood Boulevard (North)
Near: Budget Rent-A-Car
Category/As: Television as Actress
For: Nancy (1970)

Holmes, Burton...{33/46}
6602 Hollywood Boulevard (South)
Near: J.J. Newberry
Category/As: Motion Pictures as Producer
For: Various Travelogues
Real name: same or unknown
Born: January 8, 1870   Died: 1958

Holmes, Phillips...{37/84}
6908 Hollywood Boulevard (South)
Near: Hollywood Emporium
Category/As: Motion Pictures as Actor
For: An American Tragedy (1931)
Real name: same or unknown
Born: July 22, 1907   Died: August 12, 1942 from air collision

Holmes, Taylor...{06/17}
6821 Hollywood Boulevard (North)
Near: Hollywood Hamburger
Category/As: Motion Pictures as Actor
For: Ruggles of Red Gap (1918)
Real name: same or unknown
Born: May 18, 1872 in NJ   Died: 1959

Holt, Jack...{15/38}
6315 Hollywood Boulevard (North)
Near: Cave Theater
Category/As: Motion Pictures as Actor
For: Across the Wide Missouri (1951)
Real name: Charles John Holt II
Born: May 31, 1888 in Winchester, VA   Died: 1951, from coronary thrombosis

Hope, Bob...{04/28}
7021 Hollywood Boulevard (North)
Near: Hollywood Galaxy
Category/As: Live Theater as Entertainer
Dedicated on May 13, 1993
Real name: Leslie Townes Hope
Born: May 29, 1903 in Eltham, England

Hope, Bob...{11/35}
6541 Hollywood Boulevard (North)
Near: Janes House
Category/As: Motion Pictures as Comedian
For: "Road" series of films
Studio: Paramount   Awards: Oscar, Emmy

Hope, Bob...{20/36}
6141 Hollywood Boulevard (North)
Near: Mid-Town Towing
Category/As: Radio as Host
For: Pepsodent Show (1938)
Studio: NBC

Hope, Bob...{36/40}
6756 Hollywood Boulevard (South)
Near: The Dome
Category/As: Television as Comedian
For: The Bob Hope Show (1952-1955)
Studio: NBC

Hopkins, Miriam...{16/05}
1711 Vine Street (West)
Near: vacant

Category/As: Motion Pictures as Actress
For: The Richest Girl in the World (1934)
Real name: Ellen Miriam Hopkins
Born: October 18, 1902 in Bainbridge, GA
Died: October, 1972, from heart attack
Related to Anatole Litvak (spouse)

Hopkins, Miriam...{17/88}
1708 Vine Street (East)
Near: Collectors Book Store
Category/As: Television as Actress
For: Lux Video Theater (1954)

Hopper, Hedda...{15/40}
6315 Hollywood Boulevard (North)
Near: Cave Theater
Category/As: Motion Pictures as Columnist
For: Celebrity "gossip" columnist
REal name: Elda Furry
Born: June 2, 1890 in Hollidaysburg, PA
Died: 1966, from double pneumonia and buried in Altoona, PA

Horne, Lena...{23/49}
6284 Hollywood Boulevard (South)
Near: India Tandor
Category/As: Motion Pictures as Singer
For: Swing Fever (1943)
Real name: same or unknown
Born: June 30, 1917 in Brooklyn, NY
Awards: Tony, Grammy

Horne, Lena...{23/01}
6250 Hollywood Boulevard (South)
Near: Stella Adler Theater
Category/As: Recording as Singer
For: Various pop recordings

Horowitz, Vladimir...{24/04}
1680 Vine Street (East)
Near: Taft Building
Category/As: Recording as Pianist
Real name: Vladimir Gorwicz
Born: October 1, 1904 in Russia   Died: 1989, from heart attack

Horton, Edward Everett...{13/27}
6427 Hollywood Boulevard (North)
Near: 13th District
Category/As: Motion Pictures as Actor
For: Trouble in Paradise (1932)
Real name: same or unknown
Born: March 18, 1886 in New York
Died: 1970, from cancer and buried in Glendale, CA
Studio: RKO

Houdini...{04/69}
7001 Hollywood Boulevard (North)
Near: Hollywood Souvenirs
Category/As: Motion Pictures as Magician
For: The Man from Beyond (1922)
Real name: Ehrich Weiss
Born: March 24, 1874
Died: 1926, from ruptured appendix and buried in Ridgewood, NY

Howard, Eddy...{36/04}
6724 Hollywood Boulevard (South)
Near: Scientology
Category/As: Recording as Conductor
Real name: same or unknown
Born: September 12, 1914   Died: 1963

Howard, John...{12/23}
6515 Hollywood Boulevard (North)
Near: Tony's Sports
Category/As: Television as Host
For: Dr. Hudson's Secret Journal (1955-1957) as Dr. Wayne Hudson

Real name: Jack Cox
Born: April 14, 1913 in Cleveland, OH

Howard, Leslie...{33/14}
6550 Hollywood Boulevard (South)
Near: Chalame
Category/As: Motion Pictures as Actor
For: Gone With The Wind (1939) as Ashley Wilkes
Real name: Leslie Howard Stainer
Born: April 24, 1893 in London, England
Died: 1943, in an airplane crash
Studio: MGM

Howard, Ron...{37/55}
6838 Hollywood Boulevard (South)
Near: El Capitan
Category/As: Television as Actor
For: Happy Days (1977) as Richie Cunningham
Real name: same or unknown
Born: March 1, 1954

Howard, William K.....{25/60}
1550 Vine Street (East)
Near: parking lot
Category/As: Motion Pictures as Director
For: Sherlock Holmes (1932)
Born: June 16, 1899 in OH   Died: 1954, from throat cancer
Studio: Fox

Hudson, Rochelle...{22/43}
6200 Hollywood Boulevard (South)
Near: parking lot
Category/As: Motion Pictures as Actress
For: Rebel Without A Cause (1955)
Real name: same or unknown
Born: March 6, 1914 in Oklahoma City, OK   Died: 1972

Hudson, Rock...{21/31}
6100 Hollywood Boulevard (South)
Near: Chevron Gas Station
Category/As: Motion Pictures as Actor
For: Pillow Talk (1959)
Real name: Roy Scherer, Jr.
Born: November 17, 1925 in Winnetka, IL
Died: 1985, from AIDS and ashes scattered

Hull, Josephine...{32/05}
6500 Hollywood Boulevard (South)
Near: Nikki's
Category/As: Motion Pictures as Actress
For: Arsenic and Old Lace (1950)
Real name: Josephine Sherwood
Born: May 30, 1884   Died: 1957, from cerebral hemorrhage
Awards: Oscar

Hull, Warren...{23/35}
6274 Hollywood Boulevard (South)
Near: parking lot
Category/As: Radio as Host
For: Strike It Rich (1947)
Born: January 17, 1903 in NY   Died: 1974, from heart failure

Hull, Warren...{20/48}
6141 Hollywood Boulevard (North)
Near: Mid-Town Towing
Category/As: Television as Host
For: Strike It Rich (1951)

Humberstone, Bruce...{17/24}
1750 Vine Street (East)
Near: Capitol Record Bldg
Category/As: Motion Pictures as Director
For: Charlie Chan Series of movies
Born: November 18, 1903 in Buffalo, NY

Humperdinck, Englebert...{38/44}
7024 Hollywood Boulevard (South)
Near: Roosevelt Hotel parking
Category/As: Recording as Singer
Dedicated on October 21, 1989
Real name: Arnold Gerry Dorsey

Hunt, Frazier...{17/95}
1708 Vine Street (East)
Near: Collectors Book Store
Category/As: Radio as Newscaster
Real name: same or unknown

Hunt, Marsha...{34/17}
6658 Hollywood Boulevard (South)
Near: In-Step Shoes
Category/As: Television as Actress
For: Peck's Bad Girl (1959)
Real name: same or unknown
Born: October 17, 1917

Hunt, Pee Wee...{37/52}
6838 Hollywood Boulevard (South)
Near: El Capitan
Category/As: Recording as Musician
For: 12th Street Rag
Real name: Walter Hunt
Born: May 10, 1907   Died: 1979

Hunter, Jeffery...{37/98}
6916 Hollywood Boulevard (South)
Near: Gulliver's Travel
Category/As: Television as Actor
For: King of Kings (1961)
Real name: Henry Herman McKinnies
Born: November 25, 1925 in New Orleans, LA
Died: 1969, from head injury from fall
Related to Barbara Rush (spouse)

Hunter, Kim...{27/34}
1615 Vine Street (West)
Near: Doolittle Theater
Category/As: Motion Pictures as Actress
For: A Streetcar Named Desire (1951)
Real name: Janet Cole
Born: November 12, 1922 in Detroit, MI

Hunter, Kim...{16/24}
1715 Vine Street (West)
Near: Hair Vine
Category/As: Television as Actress
For: Ellery Queen (1975)

Hunter, Tab...{28/32}
6320 Hollywood Boulevard (South)
Near: Hollywood Bazaar
Categroy/As: Recording as Singer
For: Various Pop Recordings
Real name: Arthur Andrew Gelien
Born: July 11, 1931

Hurt, Marlin...{32/27}
6512 Hollywood Boulevard (South)
Near: Roma Fashions
Category/As: Radio as Actor
For: Beulah
Real name: same or unknown
Born: 1906   Died: 1946, from heart attack and buried in Glendale, CA

Husing, Ted...{06/47}
6819 Hollywood Boulevard (North)
Near: Hollywood Tours & Gifts
Category/As: Radio as Sportscaster
For: The March of Time (1931)
Real name: same or unknown

Born: November 27, 1901 in New York   Died: 1962
Studio: CBS

Husky, Ferlin...{09/22}
6675 Hollywood Boulevard (North)
Near: Vogue Theater (closed)
Category/As: Recording as Singer
For: On The Wings of a Dove
Real name: same or unknown
Born: December 3, 1927 in Flat River, MO

Hussey, Ruth...{26/84}
1549 Vine Street (West)
Near: TAV Celebrity Center
Category/As: Motion Pictures as Actress
For: The Philadelphia Story (1940)
Real name: Ruth Carol O'Rourke
Born: October 30, 1914 in Providence, RI

Huston, John...{16/114}
1779 Vine Street (West)
Near: Capezio Dance
Category/As: Motion Pictures as Director
For: The Treasure of Sierra Madre (1948)
Real name: same or unknown
Born: August 5, 1906 in Nevada, MO
Died: 1987, from emphysema and buried in Hollywood, CA
Awards: Oscar
Related to Walter Huston (father), Anjelica Huston (daughter)

Huston, Walter...{33/82}
6626 Hollywood Boulevard (South)
Near: Wig Outfitters
Category/As: Motion Pictures as Actor
For: The Treasure of Sierra Madre (1948)
Real name: Walter Houghston
Born: April 6, 1884 in Toronto, Canada   Died: 1950, and ashes to family
Awards: Oscar
Related to John Huston (son)

Hutton, Betty...{18/12}
6253 Hollywood Boulevard (North)
Near: Equitible Building Entrance
Category/As: Motion Pictures as Actress
For: Annie Get Your Gun (1950)
Real name: Elizabeth Jane Thornburg
Born: February 26, 1921 in Battle Creek, MI
Studio: Paramount

I

Iglesias, Julio...{38/13}
7000 Hollywood Boulevard (South)
Near: Roosevelt Hotel
Category: Recording as Singer
Dedicated on November 7, 1985
Real name: same or unknown
Born: September 23, 1943

Ince, Thomas H. ...{08/23}
6727 Hollywood Boulevard (North)
Near: Artesian Patio
Category/As: Motion Pictures as Producer
For: A Call to Arms (1913)
Born: November 6, 1882 in Newport, RI
Died: 1924, accidental gunshot (murdered ?)

Ingram, Rex...{27/97}
1645 Vine Street (West)
Near: Hollywood Vine Building
Category/As: Motion Pictures as Actor

For: The Prisioner of Zenda (1922)
Real name: Reginald Ingram Montogomery Hitchcock
Born: October 20, 1895 in Dublin, Ireland
Died: 1969, and buried in Los Angeles, CA
Related to Alice Terry (spouse)

Ireland, Jill...{07/49}
6755 Hollywood Boulevard (North)
Near: vacant
Category/As: Motion Pictures as Actress
Dedicated on April 25, 1990
Real name: same or unknown
Born: 1936   Died: 1990, from cancer
Related to Charles Bronson (Spouse)

Ireland, John...{24/84}
1610 Vine Street (East)
Near: Vine Street Bar and Grill
Category/As: Television as Actor
For: Rawhide (1965) as Jed Colby
Real name: same or unknown
Born: January 30, 1914 in Victoria, Canada Died: 1992, from leukemia

Iturbi, Jose...{37/44}
6834 Hollywood Boulevard (South)
Near: Rockrt Hollywood
Category/As: Recording as Pianist
For: Song to Remember (1944)
Born: November 28, 1895
Died: 1980, from heart attack and buried in Culver City, CA

Jackson, Janet...{25/49}
1550 Vine Street (East)
Near: parking lot
Category/As: Recording as Singer
Dedicated on April 2, 1990

Jackson, Mahalia...{37/69}
6840 Hollywood Boulevard (South)
Near: Masonic Temple
Category/As: Recording as Singer
Dedicated on September 1, 1988
Real name: same or unknown
Born: 1912   Died: 1972, from heart disease and buried in Metairie, LA

Jackson, Michael...{26/71}
1549 Vine Street (West)
Near: Tav Celeberity Center
Category/As: Radio as Host
For: Radio Talk Show
Dedicated on August 22, 1984
Born: April 16, 1934 in England
Awards: Emmy, Golden Mike

Jackson, Michael...{05/30}
6925 Hollywood Boulevard (North)
Near: Mann's Chinese Theater
Category/As: Recording as Singer
For: Billie Jean
Dedicated on November 10, 1984
Born: August 29,1958

Jackson, Sherry...{28/38}
6324 Hollywood Boulevard (South)
Near: vacant
Category/As: Television as Actress
For: The Danny Thomas Show (1953)

Born: February 15, 1942

Jacksons, The...{25/81}
1500 Vine Street (East)
Near: Home Savings
Category/As: Recording as Singers

Jagger, Dean...{27/44}
1627 Vine Street (West)
Near: parking lot
Category/As: Motion Pictures as Actor
For: 12 O'Clock High (1949)
Real name: Dean Jeffries
Born: November 7, 1903 in Columbus Grove, OH
Awards: Oscar, Emmy

Jam, Jimmy and Terry Lewis...{14/49}
6371 Hollywood Boulevard (North)
Near: Antenna of Hollywood
Category/As: Recording as Songwriters
Dedicated on March 10, 1993
Real name: same or unknown

James, Dennis...{07/45}
6753 Hollywood Boulevard (North)
Near: vacant
Category/As: Television as Host
Dedicated on September 10, 1993

James, Harry...{09/10}
6683 Hollywood Boulevard (North)
Near: Lazer Shoes
Category/As: Recording as Musician
For: I'll Get By
Real name; same or unknown
Born: May 15, 1916   Died: 1983, from lymphatic cancer

James, Joni...{37/20}
6814 Hollywood Boulevard (North)
Near: Greco's Pizza
Caregory/As: Recording as Singer
For: Your Cheatin' Heart
Real name: Joan Carmella Babbo
Born: September 22, 1930

James, Sonny...{33/94}
6630-B Hollywood Boulevard (South)
Near: Z Rock
Category/As: Recording as Singer
For: Young Love
Real name: James Loden
Born: May 1,1929

Janis, Elsie...{36/56}
6776 Hollywood Boulevard (South)
Near: Camera and Photo
Category/As: Motion Pictures as Actress
For: Betty in Search of a Thrill (1919)
Real name: Elsie Bierbaur
Born: March 16, 1889   Died: 1956

Jannings, Emil...{24/50}
1630 Vine Street (East)
Near: parking lot
Category/As: Motion Pictures as Actor
For: The Last Command (1928)
Real name: Theodor Friedrich Emil Janez
Born: July 22, 1884 in Rorschach, Switzerland   Died: 1950, from cancer

Janssen, David...{04/52}
7009 Hollywood Boulevard (North)
Near: Fame and Fortune
Category/As: Television as Actor
For: The Fugitive (1963-1967) ABC

Dedicated on May 11, 1989
Real name: David Harold Meyer
Born: 1931   Died 1980, from heart attack and buried in Los Angeles, CA

Jeffreys, Anne...{26/02}
1501 Vine Street (West)
Near: shopping center
Category/As: Television as Actress
For: Topper (1953-1955) as Marion Kirby
Real name: Anne Carmichael
Born: January 26, 1923 in NC

Jenkins, Gordon...{33/84}
6626 Hollywood Boulevard (South)
Near: Wig Outfitters
Category/As: Recording as Pianist
For: Bewitched
Born: May 12, 1910   Died: 1984, from lateral sclerosis

Jergens, Adele...{38/82}
7046 Hollywood Boulevard (South)
Near: X Building
Category/As: Television as Actress
For: Pantomine Quiz (1950)
Real name: same or unknown
Born: November 28, 1922

Jessel, George...{16/101}
1749 Vine Street (West)
Near: parking lot
Category/As: Motion Pictures as Actor
For: For Jills in a Jeep (1944)
Real name: same or unknown
Born: April 3, 1898 in New York, NY
Died: 1981, from heart attack and buried in Los Angeles, CA
Awards: Oscar

Jewell, Isabel...{25/20}
1560 Vine Street (East)
Near: parking lot
Category/As: Motion Pictures as Actress
For: Lost Horizon (1937)
Born: July 10, 1910 in NY   Died: 1972, from natural causes

Jewison, Norman...{38/35}
7000 Hollywood Boulevard (South)
Near: Roosevelt Hotel
Category/As: Motion Pictures as Director
For: In the Heat of the Night (1967)
Dedicated on November 14, 1988
Real name: same or unknown
Born: 1926 in Toronto, Canada

John, Elton...{05/43}
6925 Hollywood Boulevard (North)
Near: Mann's Chinese Theater
Category/As: Recording as Singer
For: Someone Saved My Life Tonight
Real name: Reginald Kenneth Dwight
Born: March 25, 1947

Johnson, Nunnally...{22/65}
6240 Hollywood Boulevard (South)
Near: West Coast Ensemble
Category/As: Motion Pictures as Screenwriter
For: The Grapes of Wrath (1940)
Real name: same or unknown
Born: December 5, 1897 in Columbus, GA
Died: 1977, and buried in Los Angeles, CA

Johnson, Van...{33/38}
6602 Hollywood Boulevard (South)
Near: J.J. Newberry
Category/As: Motion Pictures as Actor
For: The Caine Mutiny (1954)

Real name: Charles Van Dell Johnson
Born: August 25, 1916 in Newport, RI

Jolson, Al...{33/74}
6622 Holywood Boulevard (South)
Near: Galaxy DeLuxe Burger
Category/As: Motion Pictures as Actor
For: The Jazz Singer (1927)
Real name: Asa Yoelson
Born: May 26, 1886 in St. Petersburg, Russia
Died: 1950, from a heart attack and buried in Los Angeles, CA
Related to Ruby Keeler (spouse)

Jolson, Al...{36/28}
6740 Hollywood Boulevard (South)
Near: Sports Emporium
Category/As: Radio as Host
For: Kraft Music Hall (1933)

Jolson, Al... {17/81}
1718 Vine Street (East)
Near: Sun Palace Restaurant
Category/As: Recording as Singer
For: Sonny Boy

Jones, Allen...{21/07}
6100 Hollywood Boulevard (South)
Near: Chevron Gas Station
Category/As: Recording as Singer
For: Show Boat
Born: October 14, 1907 in Scranton, PA   Died: 1992

Jones, Buck...{37/40}
6834 Hollywood Boulevard (South)
Near: El Capitan Building
Category/As: Motion Pictures as Actor
For: Hearts and Spurs (1925)
Real name: Charles Gebhart
Born: December 4, 1889   Died: from burnes due to fire

Jones, Dick...{38/72}
7040 Hollywood Boulevard (South)
Near: Hollywood Liquor Store
Category/As: Television as Actor
For: The Range Rider (1951)
Real name: same or unknown
Born: Feburary 25, 1927

Jones, Gordon...{27/43}
1627 Vine Street (West)
Near: parking lot
Category/As: Television as Actor
For: Abbott and Costello Show (1951) as Mike (the cop)

Jones, Jack...(21/08)
6100 Hollywood Boulevard (South)
Near: Chevron Gas Station
Category/As: Recording as Singer
Dedicated on April 13, 1989
Real name: same or unknown
Related to Allan Jones (father)

Jones, Jennifer...{13/23}
6429 Hollywood Boulevard (North)
Near: Yaba'S Imports
Category/As: Motion Pictures as Actress
For: The Song of Beradette (1943)
Real name: Phyllis Lee Isley
Born: March 2, 1919 in Tulsa, OK
Related to David O. Selznick and Robert Walker (spouses)

Jones, Quincy...{25/87}
1500 Vine Street (25/87)
Near: Home Savings
Category/As: Recording as Arranger

Born: March 14, 1933 in Chicago, IL
Awards: Grammy, Emmy

Jones, Shirley...{26/67}
1549 Vine Street (West)
Near: TAV Celeberity Center
Category/As: Motion Pictures as Actress
For: Elmer Gantry (1960)
Dedicated on February 14, 1986
Born: March 31, 1935 in Smithton, PA

Jones, Spike...{23/61}
6290 Hollywood Boulevard (South)
Near: Holly Vine Shoppe
Category/As: Radio as Musical Satirist
For: The Spike Jones Show (1940)
Real name: Lindley Armstrong Jones
Born: December 14,1911 in Long Beach, CA
Died: 1956, from emphysems and buried in Culver City, CA

Jones, Spike...{25/86}
1500 Vine Street (Easr)
Near: Home Savings
Category/As : Recording as Bandleader
For: All I Want For Christmas is My Two Frount Teeth

Jones, Spike...{37/30}
6822 Hollywood Boulevard (South)
Near: Starline Tours and Gifts
Category/As: Television as Bandleader
For: The Spike Jones Show (1954)

Jones, Tom...{33/49}
6608 Hollywood Boulevard (South)
Near: Frederick's of Hollywood
Category/As: Recording as Singer
For: Whar's New Pussycat?
Dedicated on June 29,1989
Real name: Thomas Jones Woodward

Jordan, Louis...{13/05}
6445 Hollywood Boulevard (North)
Near: Best Tomy # 21
Category/As: Television as Musician
Real name: same or unknown

Jory, Victor...{10/55}
6605 Hollywood Boulevard (North)
Near: U.T.B. Building
Category/As: Motion Pictures as Actor
For: The Miracle Worker
Born: November 23, 1902 in Canada
Died: 1982, from heart attack and buried in Los Angeles, CA

Jourdan, Louis...{20/18}
6161 Hollywood Boulevard (North)
Near: Network Body Shop
Category/As: Recording as Singer
For: Three Coins in the Fountain (1954)
Real name: Louis Gendre
Born: June 19, 1919 in Marseilles, France

Joy, Leatrice...{12/19}
6519 Hollywood Boulevard (North)
Near: Kalypso Gigts
Category/As: Motion Pictures as Actress
For: The Ten Commandments (1923)
Real name: Leatrice Joy Zeidler
Born: November 7, 1896 in New Orleans, LA   Died: 1985
Related to John Gilbert (spouse)

Kallen, Kitty...{04/15}
7021 Hollywood Boulevard (North)
Near: Hollywood Galaxy
Category/As: Recording as Singer
For: Little Things Mean a Lot
Born: May 25, 1926

Kalmus, Herbert...{20/08}
6161 Hollywood Boulevard (North)
Near: Network Body Shop
Category/As: Motion Pictures as Inventor
For: Patented Technicolor
Born: November 9,1881 in Chelsea, MA   Died: 1963
Related to Natalie Kalmus (spouse)

Karloff, Boris...{16/63}
1735 Vine Street (West)
Near: Palace
Category/As: Motion Pictures as Actor
For: Frankenstein (1931)
Real name: William Henry Pratt NBC
Born: November 23, 1887 in London, England
Died: February 2, 1969 from respiratory ailment

Karloff, Boris...{34/25}
6664 Hollywood Boulevard (South)
Near: Supply Sergeant
Category/As: Television as Host
For: Thriller (1960-1961)

Kasem, Casey...{05/22}
6935 Hollywood Boulevard (North)
Near: Mann's Chinese parking
Category/As: Radio as Disc Jockey
For: American Top 40
Dedicated on April 27, 1981
Real name: Karmal Amin Kasem
Born: Detroit, MI

Kaye, Danny...{11/05}
6566 Hollywood Boulevard (North)
Near: Cash It Here
Category/As: Motion Pictures as Actor
For: The Secret Life of Walter Mitty (1947) as Walter Mitty
Real name: David Daniel Kaminsky
Born: January 18, 1913 in Brooklyn, NY   Died: 1987, from hepatitis
Related to Sylvia Fine (spouse)

Kaye, Danny...{20/86}
6125 Hollywood Boulevard (North)
Near: Pep Boys
Category/As : Radio as Host
For: The Danny Kaye Show (1945)

Kaye, Danny...{37/46}
6834 Hollywood Boulevard (South)
Near: Rocket Hollywood
Category/As: Recording as Singer

Kaye, Sammy...{06/03}
6845 Hollywood Boulevard (North)
Near: Starline Tours & Gifts
Category/As: Radio as Orchestra Leader
For: The Sammy Kaye Show (1944)
Real name: same or unknown
Born: March 13, 1910 in OH   Died: 1987

Kaye, Sammy...{07/26}
6765 Hollywood Boulevard (North)
Near: Runkel's Jewelers
Category/As: Recording as Composer
For: Moondust

Kaye, Sammy...{13/37}
6419 Hollywood Boulevard (North)
Near: Haunted Studio
Category/As: Television as Orchestra Leader
For: The Sammy Kaye Show (1950)

Kazan, Elia.{37/08}
6800 Hollywood Boulevard (South)
Near: Souvenirs of Hollywood
Category/As: Motion Pictures as Producer
For: East of Eden (1955)
Real name: Elia Kazanjoglous
Born: September 7, 1909

Keaton, Buster...{10/27}
6621 Hollywood Boulevard (North)
Near: Stairway Fashion
Category/As: Motion Pictures as Comedian
For: The Navigator (1924)
Real name: Joseph Frank Keaton
Born: October 4, 1895 in Piqua, KS
Died: 1966, from cancer and buried in Los Angeles, CA

Keaton, Buster...{18/57}
6225 Hollywood Boulevard (North)
Near: vacant store
Category/As: Television as Actor

Keel, Howard...{18/14}
6253 Hollywood Boulevard (North)
Near: Equitible Building
Category/As: Motion Pictures as Actor
For: Annie Get Your Gun (1950)
Real name: Harold Clifford Leek
Born: April 13, 1917 in Gillespie, IL
Studio: MGM

Keeler, Ruby...{36/16}
6730 Hollywood Boulevard (South)
Near: parking lot
Category/As: Motion Pictures as Dancer
For: 42nd Street (1933)
Real name: Ethel Hilda Keeler
Born: August 25, 1909 in Halifax, Nova Scotia
Related to Al Jolson (spouse)

Keene, Bill...{26/79}
1549 Vine Street (West)
Near: TAV Celebrity Center
Category: Radio
Dedicated on May 21, 1992
Real name: same or unknown

Keeshan, Bob Captain Kangaroo...{25/75}
1500 Vine Street (East)
Near: Home Savings
Category/As: Telrvision as Host
For: Captain Kangaroo (1955) CBS
Born: June 27,1927 in NY

Kellerman, Annette...{33/50}
6608 Hollywood Boulevard (South)
Near: Frederick's of Hollywood
Category/As: Motion Pictures as Actress
For: Queen of the Sea (1918)
Real name: same or unknownFor: Star Trek
Born: December 1, 1887 in Australia   Died: 1975

Kelley, DeForest...{04/18}
7021 Hollywood Boulevard (North)
Near: Hollywood Galaxy
Category/As: Motion Pictuers as Actor
For: Star Trek (1979) as Dr. McCoy
Dedicated on December 18, 1991
Born: 1920

Kelly, Gene...{20/20}
6161 Hollywood Boulevard (North)
Near: Network Body Shop
Category/As: Motion Pictures as Actor
For: Singing in th Rain (1952)
Real name: Eugene Curran Kelly
Born: August 23, 1912 in Pittsburg, PA
Stuido: MGM   Awards: Oscar

Kelly, Grace...{15/17}
6329 Hollywood Boulevard (North)
Near: Fantasy T-Shitrs
Category/As: Motion Pictures as Actress
For: Rear Window (1954)
Born: November 12, 1928 in Philadelphia, PA
Died: 1982 in an automobile accident

Kelly Nancy...{04/27}
7021 Hollywood Boulevard (North)
Near: Hollywood Galaxy
Category/As: Motion Pictures as Actress
For: The Bad Seed (1956)
Born: March 25, 1921 in Lowell, MA

Kelly, Patsy...{09/30}
6669 Hollywood Boulevard (North)
Near: Asia Imports
Category/As: Motion Pictures as Actress
For: Topper Returns (1941)
Real name: same or unknown
Born: January 10, 1910 in Brooklyn, NY   Died: 1981

Kennedy, Arthur...{09/14}
6681 Hollywood Boulevard (North)
Near: Dynamite Boutique
Category/As: Motion Pictures as Actor
For: High Sierra (1941)
Real name: John Arthur Kennedy
Born: February 17, 1914 in Worchester, MA
Died: 1990, From a brain tumor
Studio: Warner Brothers

Kennedy, Arthur...{24/64}
1628 Vine Street (East)
Near: Brown Derby ruins
Category/As: Television as actor
For: The President's Plane is Missing (1973)

Kennedy, Edgar...{05/66}
6925 Hollywood Boulevard (North)
Near: Mann's Chinese Theater
Category/As: Motion Pictures as Actor
For: Duck Soup (1933)
Real name: same or unknown
Born: April 26, 1890 in Monterey, CA
Died: 1948, from cancer and buried in Culver City, CA

Kennedy, George...{29/13} *
6358 Hollywood Boulevard (South)
Near: Glad's discount Mini-Mart
Category/As: Motion Pictors as Actor
For: Airport (1970) as Patroni, Universal
Dedicated on October 17, 1991
Real name: same or unknown
Born: 1925 in New York, NY
Awards: Oscar

Kennedy, John B. ...{27/19}
1605 Vine Street (West)
Near: Molly Coney Island
Category/As: Radio as Newscaster
For: The Collier Hour (1927)
Real name: same or unknown

Kennedy, Madge...{24/97}
1600 Vine Street (East)
Near: D M V
Category/As: Motion Pictures as Actress
Real name: same or unknown
Born: August 1, 1892 in Chicago, IL   Died: 1987, from resptratory failure

Kenton, Stan...{28/50}
6338 Hollywood Boulevard (South)
Near: El Golfo De Fonseca
Category/As: Recording as Composer
For:007
Real name: Stanley Newcombe Kenton
Born: February 19,1912
Died: 1979, from a stroke and buried in Los Angeles, CA

Kerr, Deborah...{16/07}
1711 Vine Street (West)
Near: vacant
Category/As: Motion Pictures as Actress
For: From Here to Eternity (1953) MGM
Real name: Deborah Kerr-Trimmer
Born: September 30 1921 in Helensburg, Scotland

Kerrigan, J.M. ...{10/25}
6621 Hollywood Boulevard (North)
Near: Stairway Fashion
Category/As: Motion Pictures as Actor
For: Captain Blood (1935
Real name: same or unknown
Born: July 25, 1889 in Louisville, KY   Died: 1947

Kerry, Norman...{36/02}
6724 Hollywood Boulevard (South)
Near: Scientology
Category/As: Motion Pictures as Actor
For: Phantom of the Opera (1925)
Real name: Arnold Kaiser
Born: June 16, 1889   Died: 1956

Kilgallen, Dorothy...{36/70}
6780 Hollywood Boulevard (South)
Near: Ripley's Museum
Category/As: Television as Panelist
For: What's My Line (1950)
Real name: same or unknown
Born: July 3, 1913 in Chicago, IL
Died: 1965, from seconal and alcohol and buried in Hawthorne, NY

King, Andrea...{26/78}
1549 Vine Street (West)
Near: TAV Celebrity Center
Category/As: Television as Actress
For: The Days of Our Lives
Real name: Georgette Barry
Born: Feburary 7, 1915

King, B.B. ...{07/17}
6771 Hollywood Boulevard (North)
Near: Hollywood Leather and Gift
Category/As: Recording as Musician
Dedicated on September 5, 1990
Real name: Riley B. King

King, Henry...{15/19}
6327 Hollywood Boulevard (North)
Near: Chicken Delight
Category/As: Motion Pictures as Director

For: In Old Chicago (1938)
Born: June 24, 1888 in Christianburg, VA
 Died: 1982, from natural causes

King, John Reed...{31/09}
6402 1/2 Hollywood Boulevard (South)
Near: Black & White
Category/As: Radio as Host
For: Break the Bank (1945)
Born: October 25, 1914   Died: 1979

King, Pee Wee...{16/26}
1715 Vine Street (West)
Near: Hair Vine
Category/As: Recording as Bandleader
For: Slow Poke
Real name: Frank King
Born: Feburary 18, 1974 in Abrams, WI

King, Peggy...{11/01}
6565 Hollywood Boulevard (North)
Near: Cash it Here
Category/As: Television as Singer
For: George Gobel Show (1954)
Real name: same or unknown
Born: 1931 in PA

King, Wayne...{18/23}
6251 Hollywood Boulevard (North)
Near: parking lot
Category/As: Radio as Conductor
For: Baby Shoes
Real name: same or unknown
Born: Feburary 16, 1901 in Savannah, IL   Died: 1985, from a heart attack

Kirkwood, Jr, Joe...{24/49}
1630 Vine Street (East)
Near: parking lot
Category/As: Television as Actor
For: Joe Palooka (1946)
Real name: same or unknown
Born: March 22, 1897

Kirsten, Dorothy...{15/14}
6331 Hollywood Boulevard (North)
Near: Guaranty Building
Category/As: Recording as Singer
Real name: same or unknown
Born: July 6, 1919 in Trenton, NJ

Kitt, Eartha...{34/15}
6656 Hollywood Boulevard (South)
Near: Ritz Theater
Category/As: Recording as Singer
Real name: same or unknown
Born: January 26, 1928

Klugman, Jack...{11/16}
6555 Hollywood Boulevard (North)
Near: Legends of Hollywood
Category/As: Motion Pictures as Actor
For: Twelve Angry Men (1957)
Dedicated on January 7, 1988
Real name: same or unknown
Born: 1922

Knight, Evelyn...{21/49}
6140 Hollywood Boulevard (South)
Near: Henry Fonda Theater
Category/As: Recording as Singer
Real name: same or unknown

Knight, June...{18/29}
6247 Hollywood Boulevard (North)
Near: Ronnie's Donuts

Category/As: Motion Pictures as Actress
For: Broadway Melody of 1936 (1935)
Real name: Margaret Rose Vallikett
Born: January 22, 1913 in Los Angeles, CA
Died: June 16, 1987 from a stroke

Knight, Raymond...{21/47}
6128 Hollywood Boulevard (South)
Near: Hollywood Psychic
Category/As: Radio as Actor
For: The Cuckoo Hour (1930)
Real name: same or unknown
Studio: NBC

Knight, Ted...{09/27}
6673 Hollywood Boulevard (North)
Near: Star Deli
Category/As: Television as Actor
For: The Mary Tyler Moore Show (1970)
Dedicated on January 30, 1985
Real name: Tadeus Wladyslaw Konopka
Born: December 7, 1925 in Terryville, CT
Died: 1986, from Urinary tract growth and buried in Glendale, CA
Studio: CBS   Awards: Emmy

Knowles, Patric...{33/08}
6542 Hollywood Boulevard (South)
Near: Consumer's Discount
Category/As: Television as Actor
For: The Adventures of Robin Hood (1938)
Real name: Reginald Knowles
Born: November 11, 1911

Knudsen, Peggy...{23/24}
6274 Hollywood Boulevard (South)
Near: parking lot
Category/As: Television as Actress
For: Humoresque (1947)
Born: April 27, 1923 in Duluth, MN   Died: 1980

Kosloff, Theodore...{27/28}
1615 Vine Street (West)
Near: Doolittle Theater
Category/As: Motion Pictures as Dancer
For: Feet of Clay (1924)
Born: April 5, 1882 in Russia   Died: 1956

Kostelanetz, Andre...{33/06}
6542 Hollywood Boulevard (South)
Near: Consumer's Discount
Category/As: Recording as Conductor
Real name: same or unknown
Born; December 22, 1901 in St. Petersburg, Russia   Died: 1980

Koster, Henry...{36/46}
6305 Hollywood Boulevard (South)
Near: The Dome
Category/As: Motion Pictures as Director
For: It Started With Eve (1941)
Real name: Herman Kosterlitz
Born: May 1, 1905 in Berlin, Germany   Died: 1988

Kovacs, Ernie...{15/50}
6305 Hollywood Boulevard (North)
Near: Vetas
Category/As: Television as Actor
For: The Ernie Kovacs Show (1955) NBC
Real name: same or unknown
Born: January 23, 1919 in Trenton, NJ
Died: 1962 in an automobile accident and buried in Los Angeles, CA

Kramer, Stanley...{21/01}
6100 Hollywood Boulevard (South)
Near: Chevron Gas Station
Category/As: Motion Pictures as Producer
For: Guess Who's Coming to Dinner (1967)
Real name: same or unknown

Born: September 29, 1913 in New York, NY

Kreisler, Fritz..(09/52)
6655-3 Hollywood Boulevard (North)
Near: USA Jeans Factory
Category/As: Recording as Musician
Real name: same or unknown
Born: February 2, 1875 Austria
Died: 1962, from a heart attack and buried in The Bronx, NY

Kreuger, Kurt...{25/38}
1560 Vine Street (East)
Near: parking lot
Category/As: Motion Pictures as Actor
For: The Enemy Below (1957)
Born: July 23, 1916 in Michenberg, Germany

Kruger, Otto...{16/66}
1735 Vine Street (West)
Near: Palace
Category/As: Motion Pictures as Actor
For: High Noon (1952)
Real name: same unknown
Born: September 6, 1885 in Toledo, OH
Died: September 6, 1974 from a stroke and buried in Los Angeles, CA

Kruger, Otto...{15/13}
6331 Hollywood Boulevard (North)
Near: Guaranty Building
Category/As: Television as Actor

Kyser, Kay...{27/12}
1601 Vine Street (West)
Near: parking lot
Category/As: Radio as Bandleader
For: Kollege of Musical Knowledge

Kyser, Kay...{17/106}
1700 Vine Street (East)
Near: Equitible Building
Category/As: Recording as Bandleader
For: Don't Sit Under the Apple Tree
Real name: James Kern Kyser
Born: June 18, 1906 in Rocky Mount, NC
Died: 1985, from a heart attack

La Cava, Gregory...{37/82}
6908 Hollywood Boulevard (South)
Near: Hollywood Emporium
Category/As: Motion Pictures as Director
For: My Man Godfrey (1936)
Born: March 10, 1892 inTowanda, PA   Died: 1952
Studio: RKO

LaPlante, Laura...{30/16}
6376 Hollywood Boulevard (South)
Near: Demain
Category/As: Motion Pictures as Actress
For: The Cat & The Canary (1927) Universal
Real name: same or unknown
Born: November 1, 1904 in St. Louis, MO
Related to William Seiter, Irving Asher (spouses)

La Rocque, Rod...{25/24}
1560 Vine Street (East)
Near: parking lot
Category/As: Motion Pictures as Actor
For: The Hunchback of Notre Dame (1939)

Real name: Rodrique la Rocque de la Rour
Born: in Chicago, IL   Died: 1969
Related to Vilma Banky (spouse)

La Rosa, Julius...{23/64}
5290 Hollywood Boulevard (South)
Near: Holly Vine Shoppe
Category/As: Television as Singer
For: Arthur Godfrey and Friends (1953)
Real name: same or unknown
Born: January 2, 1930 in New York, NY

LaBelle, Patti...{38/61}
7024 Hollywood Boulevard (South)
Near: Roosevelt Hotel parking
Category/As: Recording as Singer
Dedicated on March 4, 1993
Real name: Patricia Louise Holt

Laboe, Art...{37/01}
6800 Hollywood Boulevard (South)
Near: Souvenirs of Hollywood
Category/As: Radio as Disc Jockey
Dedicated on July 17, 1981
Born: August 7, 1925

Ladd, Alan...{27/03}
1601 Vine Street (West)
Near: parking lot
Category/As: Motion Pictures as Actor
For: This Gun for Hire (1942)
Real name: Alan Waldridge Ladd
Born: September 3, 1913 in Hot Springs, AR
Died: 1964, from alcohol & drug mix and buried in Glendale, CA
Studio: Paramount
Related to Sue Carol Ladd (spouse)

Ladd, Sue Carol...{27/68}
1637 Vine Street (West)
Near: Early World Restaurant
Category/As: Motion Pictures as Actress
For: Secret Sinners (1933)
Dedicated on September 8, 1982
Real name: Evelyn Lederer
Born: October 30, 1907 in Chicago, IL
Died: February 4, 1982, from heart attack and buried in Glendale, CA
Related to Alan Ladd (spouse)

Laemmle, Carl...{15/63}
6301 Hollywood Boulevard (North)
Near: vacant
Category/As: Motion Pictures as Pioneer
For: Founder of Universal Pictures
Real name: same or unknown
Born: January 17, 1867 in Laupheim, Germany
Died: 1939, from heart attack and buried in Los Angeles, CA

Laine, Frankie...{14/04}
6385 Hollywood Boulevard (North)
Near: Security Pacific Bank
Category/As: Recording as Singer
For: Rawhide theme song
Real name: Frank Paul Lo Vecchio
Born: March 30, 1913

Laine, Frankie...{27/73}
1645 Vine Street (West)
Near: Hollywood Vine Building
Category/As: Television as Singer
For: Rawhide Theme Song

Lake, Alice...{24/62}
1628 Vine Street (East)
Near: Brown Derby (Ruins)
Category/As: Motion Pictures as Actress

For: The Price of Success (1925)
Real name: same or unknown
Born: March 23, 1897 inBrooklyn, NY   Died: 1967

Lake, Arthur...{33/114}
6644 Hollywood Boulevard (South)
Near: Larry Edmunds Book Store
Category/As: Radio as Actor
For: Blondie (1939) as Dagwood Bumsted
Real name: Arthur Silverlake
Born: April 17, 1905 in Corbin, KY
Died: 1987, from heart attack and buried in Hollywood, CA
Studio: NBC
Related to Marion Davies (aunt)

Lake, Veronica...{37/96}
6914 Hollywood Boulevard (South)
Near: Hamburger Hamlet
Category/As: Motion Pictures as Actress
For: This Gun for Hire (1942)
Real name: Constance Frances Marie Ockleman
Born: November 14, 1920 in Brooklyn, NY
Died: July 7, 1973, from acute hepatitis

Lamarr, Barbara...{27/39}
1627 Vine Street (West)
Near: parking lot
Category/As: Motion Pictures as Actress
For: Heart of a Siren (1925)
Real name: Rheatha Watson
Born: July 28, 1896 in Richmond, VA
Died: 1926, from over-dieting and buried in Hollywood, CA

Lamarr, Hedy...{18/28}
6249 Hollywood Boulevard (North)
Near: RTD Customer Service
Category/As: Motion Pictures as Actress
For: Samson & Delilah (1949)
Real name: Hedwig Eva Maria Kiesler
Born: November 9, 1913 in Vienna, Austria
Studio: Paramount

Lamour, Dorothy...{28/48}
6332 Hollywood Boulevard (South)
Near: Photo City
Category/As: Motion Pictures as Actress
For: "Road" series of films
Real name: Mary Dorothy Kaumeyer
Born: December 10, 1914 in New Orleans, LA

Lamour, Dorothy...{22/55}
6200 Hollywood Boulevard (South)
Near: parking lot
Category/As: Radio as Actress

Lancaster, Burt...{06/59}
6801 Hollywood Boulevard (North)
Near: vacant
Category/As: Motion Pictures as Actor
For: From Here to Eternity (1953)
Real name: Burton Stephen Lancaster
Born: November 2, 1913 in New York, NY
Awards: Oscar

Landi, Elissa...{27/25}
1615 Vine Street (West)
Near: Doolittle Theater
Category/As: Motion Pictures as Actress
For: The Sign of the Cross (1932)
Real name: Elisabeth Marie Kuhnelt
Born: December 6, 1904 in Italy   Died: October 21, 1948, from cancer

Landis, Carole...{16/102}
1777 Vine Street (West)
Near: Vine Street Bldg

Category/As: Motion Pictures as Actress
For: Topper Returns (1941)
Real name: Frances Lillian Mary Ridste
Born: January 1, 1919 in Fairchild, WI
Died: July 4, 1948, from suicide and buried in Glendale, CA
Studio: 20th Century
Related to Rex Harrison (spouse)

Landon, Michael...{25/61}
1550 Vine Street (East)
Near: parking lot
Category/As: Television as Actor
For: Little House on the Prairie (1974)
Dedicated on August 15, 1984
Real name: Eugene Maurice Orowitz
Born: October 31, 1937 in Forest Hills, NY
Died: 1991 from liver cancer and buried in Los Angeles, CA

Landsberg, Klaus...{25/57}
1550 Vine Street (East)
Near: parking lot
Category/As: Television as Executive
For: KTLA-TV Executive
Dedicated on May 13, 1985
Real name: same or unknown
Born: July 7, 1916

Lane, Abbe...{14/14}
6385 Hollywood Boulevard (North)
Near: Security Pacific Bank
Category/As: Television as Singer
For: The Xavier Cugat Show (1957)
Real name: same or unknown
Born: December 14, 1932 in New York, NY
Related to Xavier Cugat (spouse)

Lane, Dick...{15/34}
6317 Hollywood Boulevard (North)
Near: Hollywood Tattoo
Category/As: Television as Sportscaster
For: L.A. Newscaster
Real name: same or unknown
Born: May 28, 1899 in Rice Lake, WI   Died: 1982
Studio: KTLA-TV5

Lanfield, Sidney...{20/74}
6125 Hollywood Boulevard (North)
Near: Pep Boys
Category/As: Motion Pictures as Director
For: The Hound of the Baskervilles (1939)
Real name: same or unknown
Born: April 20, 1898 in Chicago, IL   Died: 1972

Lang, Fritz...{24/93}
1600 Vine Street (East)
Near: DMV
Category/As: Motion Pictures as Director
For: Metropolis (1926)
Real name: same or unknown
Born: December 5, 1890 in Germany   Died: 1976 and buried in Glendale, CA

Lang, Walter...{32/35}
6520 Hollywood Boulevard (South)
Near: Star Electronics
Category/As: Motion Pictures as Director
For: The King and I (1956)
Real name: same or unknown
Born: August 10, 1898 in Memphis, TN   Died: 1972, from kidney failure
Studio: Columbia

Langdon, Harry...{05/37}
6925 Hollywood Boulevard (North)
Near: Mann's Chinese Theater
Category/As: Motion Pictures as Comedian
For: Three's A Crowd (1927)

Real name: same or unknown
Born: June 15, 1884 in Council Bluffs, IA   Died: 1944, from heart attack
Studio: Mack Sennett

Langford, Frances...{25/72}
1500 Vine Street (East)
Near: Home Savings
Category/As: Motion Pictures as Actress
For: The Glenn Miller Story (1954)
Real name: Frances Newbern
Born: April 6, 1914 in Lakeland, FL

Langford, Frances...{26/44}
1501 Vine Street (West)
Near: West Sunset Offices
Category/As: Radio as Actress
For: The Bickersons (1946)
Studio: NBC

Lansbury, Angela...{10/19}
6623 Hollywood Boulevard (North)
Near: Mona Lisa Tops
Category/As: Motion Pictures as Actress
For: The Manchurian Candidate (1961)
Real name: Angela Brigid Lansbury
Born: October 16, 1925 in London, England
Related to Richard Cromwell (spouse)

Lansbury, Angela...{26/36}
1501 Vine Street (West)
Near: Shopping Center
Category/As: Television as Actress
For: Murder, She Wrote (1984)

Lansing, Joi...{18/13}
6253 Hollywood Boulevard (North)
Near: Equitable Building Entrance
Category/As: Television as Actress
For: The Beverly Hillbillies (1962) as Gladys Flatt
Real name: Joyce Wassmandoff
Born: April 6, 1928   Died: 1972, from cancer

Lantz, Walter...{38/17}
7000 Hollywood Boulevard (South)
Near: Roosevelt Hotel
Category/As: Motion Pictures as Animator
For: Woody Woopecker creator
Dedicated on March 5, 1986
Born: April 27, 1900 in New York
Studio: Universal   Awards: Oscar

Lanza, Mario...{06/25}
6821 Hollywood Boulevard (North)
Near: Hollywood Hamburger
Category/As: Motion Pictures as Actor
For: The Great Caruso (1951)
Real name: Alfred Arnold Cocozza
Born: January 31, 1921 in New York
Died: 1959, from over-dieting and buried in Culver City, CA
Studio: MGM

Lanza, Mario...{16/89}
1749 Vine Street (West)
Near: parking lot
Category/As: Recording as Singer
For: Soloist w/Boston Symphony Orchestra
Studio: Victor Records

Larson, Glen A. ...{09/25}
6671 Hollywood Boulevard (North)
Near: Studio 2
Category/As: Televsion as Producer
For: It Takes A Thief (1968)
Dedicated on October 23, 1985
Real name: same or unknown

Lasky, Jesse...{13/17}
6433 Hollywood Boulevard (North)
Near: Pacific Theater
Category/As: Motion Pictures as Producer
For: The Gay Deception
Real name: Jesse L. Lasky
Born: September 13, 1880 in San Francisco, CA
Died: 1958, and buried in Hollywood, CA

Lassie...{30/04}
6370 Hollywood Boulevard (South)
Near: vacant lot
Category/As: Motion Pictures as Dog
For: Lassie Come Home (1943)
Real name: Pal
Born: 1941   Died: 1959

Laughton, Charles...{17/36}
1750 Vine Street (East)
Near: Capitol Record Bldg
Category/As: Motion Pictures as Actor
For: Mutiny on the Bounty (1935) as Captain Bligh
Real name: same or unknown
Born: July 1, 1899 in Scarborough, Yorkshire
Died: 1962, from cancer and buried in Los Angeles, CA
Studio: MGM   Awards: Oscar

Laurel, Stan...{04/43}
7021 Hollywood Boulevard (North)
Near: Hollywood Galaxy
Category/As: Motion Pictures as Actor
For: Music Box (1930)
Real name: Arthur Stanley Jefferson
Born: June 16, 1890 in Ulverson, Lancashire
Died: 1965, from heart attack and buried in Los Angeles, CA
Studio: MGM   Awards: Oscar

Lawford, Peter...{37/102}
6920 Hollywood Boulevard (South)
Near: Pro Electronics
Category/As: Television as Actor
For: The Thin Man (1957-1958)
Real name: Peter Sydney Ernest Lawford
Born: September 7, 1923 in London, England
Died: December 24, 1984, from cardiac arrest and ashes scattered
Studio: NBC
Related to Betty Lawford (cousin)

Lawrence, Barbara...{16/61}
1735 Vine Street (West)
Near: Palace
Category/As: Television as Actress
For: Oklahoma (1955)
Real name: same or unknown
Born: February 24, 1930 in Oklahoma

Lawerence, Carol...{19/06}
6211 Hollywood Boulevard (North)
Near: Capitol Records annex office
Category/As: Live Theater as Actress
For: South Pacific
Dedicated on February 27, 1985
Real name: same or unknown
Born: September 5, 1934 in Chicago, IL

Lawrence, Steve & Eydie Gorme...{26/63}
1541 Vine Street (West)
Near: TAV Celebrity Center
Category/As: Recording as Singers
For: Various
Real name: Sidney Liebowitz (Steve)
Born: Steve, July 8, 1935; Eydie, August 16, 1931 in New York, NY

LeRoy, Mervyn...{25/06}
1560 Vine Street (East)
Near: parking lot
Category/As: Motion Pictures as Producer
For: The Wizard of Oz (1939)
Born: October 15, 1900 in San Francisco, CA   Died: 1987, from heart fail
Studio: MGM

Leachman, Cloris...{13/14}
6435 Hollywood Boulevard (North)
Near: By George, For Men
Category/As: Television as Actress
For: The Mary Tyler Moore Show (1970) as Phyliss Lindstrom
Real name: same or unknown
Born: April 30, 1930 in DesMoines, IA

Lear, Norman...{10/34}
6615 Hollywood Boulevard (North)
Near: China King
Category/As: Television as Producer
For: All in the Family (1971)
Real name: same or unknown
Born: July 27, 1922 in CT
Studio: CBS   Awards: Emmy

Lederer, Francis...{37/72}
6904 Hollywood Boulevard (South)
Near: Hollywood Tourist & Gifts
Category/As: Motion Pictures as Actor
For: My American Wife (1936)
Real name: Frantisek Lederer
Born: November 6, 1906 in Prague
Studio: RKO

Lee, Anna...{07/11}
6777 Hollywood Boulevard (North)
Near: Hollywood First National Bldg
Category/As: Motion Pictures as Actress
Dedicated on January 11, 1993
Real name: same or unknown

Lee, Bruce...{05/24}
6935 Hollywood Boulevard (North)
Near: Mann's Chinese parking
Category/As: Motion Pictures as Actor
For: Enter The Dragon
Dedicated on April 28, 1993
Real name: Lee Siu Loong
Born: November 27, 1940 in San Francisco, CA
Died: From brain aneurysm
Related to Brandon Lee (son)

Lee, Gypsy Rose...{14/52}
6351 Hollywood Boulevard (North)
Near: Hardy Shoes
Category/As: Motion Pictures as Actress
For: The Stripper (1963)
Real name: Rose Louise Hovick
Born: February 19, 1914 in Seattle, WA
Died: 1970, from cancer and buried in Inglewood, CA
Related to June Havoc (sister)

Lee, Lila...{17/82}
1718 Vine Street (East)
Near: Sun Palace Restaurant
Category/As: Motion Pictures as Actress
For: The Ex-Mrs. Bradford (1936)
Real name: Augusta Appel
Born: July 25, 1901 in NY   Died: 1973, from stroke

Lee, Peggy...{15/31}
6319 Hollywood Boulevard (North)
Near: Sandy Burger
Category/As: Recording as Singer
For: Fever
Real name: Norma Egstrom   *Engstrom*
Born: May 26, 1920 in Jamestown, MD   *ND*

Lee, Pinky...{19/19}
6207 Hollywood Boulevard (North)
Near: parking lot
Category/As: Television as Actor
For: The Pinky Lee Show (1950)
Real name: Pincus Leff
Born: 1916 in MN
Studio: NBC

Lee, Rowland...{28/26}
6314 Hollywood Boulevard (South)
Near: DAV Tech Computers
Category/As: Motion Pictures as Director
For: Son of Frankenstein (1939)
Real name: same or unknown
Born: September 6, 1891   Died: 1975

Lehmann, Lottie...{16/60}
1735 Vine Street (West)
Near: Palace
Category/As: Recording as Singer
For: Various Opera Recordings
Real name: same or unknown
Born: February 27, 1888 in Germany   Died: 1976

Leigh, Janet...{16/109}
1777 Vine Street (West)
Near: Vine Street Bldg
Category/As: Motion Pictures as Actress
For: Psycho (1960)
Real name: Jeanette Helen Morrison
Born: July 6, 1927 in Merced, CA
Studio: MGM
Related to Tony Curtis (spouse), Jamie Lee Curtis (daughter)

Leigh, Vivien...{07/16}
6773 Hollywood Boulevard (North)
Near: Hollywood Fantasy Tours
Category/As: Motion Pictures as Actress
For: Gone With The Wind (1939) as Scarlett O'Hara
Real name: Vivian Mary Hartley
Born: November 5, 1913 in Darjeeling, India   Died: 1967, from tuberculosis
Awards: Oscar
Related to Laurence Olivier (spouse)

Leisen, Mitchell...{18/43}
6233 Hollywood Boulevard (North)
Near: Pantages Theater
Category/As: Motion Pictures as Director
For: Death Takes a Holida (1934)
Born: October 6, 1897 in Menominee, MI
Died: 1972, from coronary complications

Lemmon, Jack...{14/42}
6357 Hollywood Boulevard (North)
Near: Star Fashion
Category/As: Motion Pictures as Actor
For: Mr. Roberts (1955) as Ensign Pulver
Real name: John Uhler Lemmon III
Born: February 8, 1925 in Boston, MA
Awards: Oscar, Emmy
Related to Felicia Farr (spouse), Chris Lemmon (son), Courtney (daughter)

Lennon, John...{17/06}
1770 Vine Street (East)
Near: parking lot
Category/As: Recording as Singer
For: 1/4 of The Beatles
Dedicated on September 30, 1988
Died: 1980, from murder (gunshot) and ashes to wife

Lennon Sisters, The...{25/55}
1550 Vine Street (East)
Near: parking lot
Category/As: Television as Singers

For: The Lawrence Welk Show
Dedicated on December 15, 1987

Leonard, Robert Z. ..{30/06}
6370 Hollywood Boulevard (South)
Near: vacant lot
Category/As: Motion Pictures as Director
For: The Great Ziegfeld (1936)
Real name: same or unknown
Born: October 7, 1889 in Chicago, IL   Died: 1968, from aneurysm
Studio: Universal

Lescoulie, Jack...{32/03}
6500 Hollywood Boulevard (South)
Near: Nikki's
Category/As: Television as Host
For: Today Show (1958)
Real name: same or unknown
Born: November 17, 1912   Died: 1987, from cancer
Studio: NBC

Leslie, Joan...{25/18}
1560 Vine Street (East)
Near: parking lot
Category/As: Television as Actress
For: Sergeant York (1941)
Real name: Joan Agnes Theresa Sadie Brodell
Born: January 26, 1925 in Pittsburg, PA
Studio: Warner Brothers

Lesser, Sol...{11/51}
6535 Hollywood Boulevard (North)
Near: Jean Machine
Category/As: Motion Pictures as Producer
For: Tarzan movies
Real name: same or unknown
Born: February 17, 1890 in Spokane, WA   Died: 1980

Levant, Oscar...{36/10}
6730 Hollywood Boulevard (South)
Near: parking lot
Category/As: Recording as Pianist
For: An American in Paris
Real name: same or unknown
Born: December 27, 1906
Died: 1972, from heart attack and buried in Los Angeles, CA

Lewis, Fulton...{23/13}
6256 Hollywood Boulevard (South)
Near: vacant lot
Category/As: Radio as Commentator
Real name: Fulton Lewis, Jr.
Born: in DC

Lewis, Jerry...{06/33}
6819 Hollywood Boulevard (North)
Near: Hollywood Tours & Gifts
Category/As: Motion Pictures as Actor
For: The Bellboy (1960)
Real name: Joseph Levitch
Born: March 16, 1926 in Newark, NJ
Studio: Paramount

Lewis, Jerry...{22/03}
6150 Hollywood Boulevard (South)
Near: Network Body Shop
Category/As: Television as Actor
For: The Colgate Comedy Hour (1950) NBC

Lewis, Jerry Lee...{10/10}
6631 Hollywood Boulevard (North)
Near: Hollywood Book City
Category/As: Recording as Singer
For: Great Balls of Fire
Dedicated on June 13, 1989

Real name: same or unknown
Born: September, 1936

Lewis, Robert Q. ...{16/06}
1711 Vine Street (West)
Near: vacant
Category/As: Television as Host
For: The Show Goes On (1950)
Real name: Robert Lewis
Born: April 5, 1924 in New York, NY   Died: 1991, from emphysema

Lewis, Shari...{08/08}
6743 Hollywood Boulevard (South)
Near: Henry Fonda Theater
Category/As: Television as Host
For: It Could Be You (1956)
Real name: same or unknown

Leyden, Bill...{21/51}
6140 Hollywood Boulevard (South)
Near: Henry Fonda Theater
Category/As: Television as Host
For: It Could Be You (1956)
Real name: same or unknown

Liberace...{12/05}
6529 Hollywood Boulevard (North)
Near: Hollywood Bargain
Category/As: Recording as Musician
Real name: Wladziu Valentino Liberace
Born: May 16, 1919 in West Allis, WI
Died: 1987 from AIDS and buried in Los Angeles, CA
Awards: Emmy

Liberace...{08/13}
6739 Hollywood Boulevard (North)
Near: Capitol Rock
Category/As: Television as Pianist
For: The Liberace (1953-1955)

Lichtman, Al...{06/09}
6841 Hollywood Boulevard (North)
Near: Budget Rent-A-Car
Category/As: Motion Pictures as Executive
For: President of United Artists
Real name: same or unknown
Born: April 9, 1888 in Hungary

Lillie, Beatrice...{31/11}
6404 Hollywood Boulevard (South)
Near: Hollywood Building
Category/As: Motion Pictures as Comedienne
For: Thoroughly Modern Millie (1967)
Real name: Constance Sylvia Munston
Born: May 29, 1896 in Toronto, Canada   Died: 1989

Lincoln, Elmo...{38/76}
7042 1/2 Hollywood Boulevard (South)
Near: Souvenir Stop
Category/As: Motion Pictures as Actor
For: Tarzan of the Apes (1918)]
Real name: Otto Elmo Linkenhelter
Born: June 14, 1899   Died: 1952, from heart attack

Linden, Eric...{24/27}
1648 Vine Street (East)
Near: Jerimiha Comey Studios
Category/As: Motion Pictures as Actor
For: Are These Our Children? (1931)
Born: September 15, 1909 in New York, NY

Lindsay, Margaret...{28/29}
6320 Hollywood Boulevard (South)
Near: Hollywood Bazaar
Category/As: Motion Pictures as Actress
For: The House of Seven Gables (1940)

Real name: Margaret Kies
Born: September 19, 1910
Died: 1891, from emphysema and buried in Culver City, CA

Linkletter, Art...{25/01}
1560 Vine Street (East)
Near: parking lot
Category/As: Radio as Host
For: People Are Funny (1943)
Born: July 17, 1912 in Saskatchewan, Canada
Studio: NBC   Awards: Grammy

Linkletter, Art...{14/22}
6371 Hollywood Boulevard (North)
Near: Antenna of Hollywood
Category/As: Radio as Host
For: House Party (1945)
Studio: CBS

Little, Little Jack...{33/68}
6618 Hollywood Boulevard (South)
Near: Burned Out
Category/As: Radio as Composer
Real name: same or unknown
Born: May 28, 1900   Died: 1956

Little, Rich...{30/09}
6370 Hollywood Boulevard (South)
Near: vacant lot
Category/As: Television as Impressionist
Dedicated on July 27, 1983
Born: November 26, 1938 in Ottawa, Canada

Little Richard...{37/71}
6904 Hollywood Boulevard (South)
Near: Hollywood Tourist & Gifts
Category/As: Recording as Singer
Dedicated on June 21, 1990
Real name: unknown

Litvak, Anatole...{10/04}
6633 Hollywood Boulevard (North)
Near: Fame of Hollywood Cafe
Category/As: Motion Pictures as Director
For: The Snake Pit (1948)
Real name: Michael Anatole Litwak
Born: May 10, 1902 in Kiev, Russia   Died: 1974
Studio: Fox
Related to Miriam Hokins (spouse)

Livingston, Mary...{08/51}
6701 Hollywood Boulevard (North)
Near: Best Mini-Mart
Category/As: Radio as Actress
For: The Jack Benny Show (1932)
Real name: Sadye Marks
Born: June 22, 1909 in Vancouver, BC   Buried in Los Angeles, CA

Lloyd, Frank...{09/32}
6667 Hollywood Boulevard (North)
Near: Musso & Frank Grill
Category/As: Motion Pictures as Director
For: Mutiny on the Bounty (1935)
Real name: same or unknown
Born: February 2, 1888 inGlasgow, Scotland
Died: 1960 and buried in Glendale, CA
Studio: First National   Awards: Oscar

Lloyd, Harold...{37/65}
6840 Hollywood Boulevard (South)
Near: Masonic Temple
Category/As: Motion Pictures as Producer
For: My Favorite Spy (1942)
Real name: Harold Clayton Lloyd
Born: April 20, 1893 in Burchard, NE   Died: 1971, from cancer
Related to Mildred Davis (spouse)

Lloyd, Harold...{26/08}
1501 Vine Street (West)
Near: Shopping Center
Category/As: Motion Pictures as Producer
For: The Kid Brother (1927)
Awards: Oscar

Lockhart, Gene...{15/52}
6305 Hollywood Boulevard (North)
Near: Ventas
Category/As: Motion Pictures as Actor
For: Algiers (1938) as Regis
Real name: same or unknown
Born: July 18, 1891 in London, Ontario
Died: 1957, from coronary thrombosis and buried in Culver City, CA
Related to Kathleen Lockhart (spouse), June Lockhart (daughter)

Lockhart, Gene...{09/12}
6681 Hollywood Boulevard (North)
Near: Dynamite Boutique
Category/As: Television as Actor
For: Fireside Theater (1953)

Lockhart, June...{15/27}
6321 Hollywood Boulevard (North)
Near: Vine Theater
Category/As: Motion Pictures as Actress
For: Meet Me in St. Louis (1944)
Born: June 25, 1925
Related to Kathleen and Gene Lockhart (parents)

Lockhart, June...{29/18}
6362 Hollywood Boulevard (South)
Near: Palmer Building
Category/As: Television as Actress
For: Lost in Space (1965-1968)
Studio: CBS

Lockhart, Kathleen...{18/47}
6233 Hollywood Boulevard (North)
Near: Pantages Theater
Category/As: Motion Pictures as Actress
For: the Glenn Miller Story (1954)
Real name: Kathleen Arthur
Born: in England   Died: 1978
Related to Gene Lockhart (spouse), June Lockhart (daughter)

Loew, Marcus...{27/35}
1615 Vine Street (West)
Near: Doolittle Theater
Category/As: Motion Pictures as Executive
For: CEO of MGM
Born: May 7, 1870 in New York, NY   Died: 1927, from heart failure
Studio: MGM

Logan, Joshua...{18/49}
6233 Hollywood Boulevard (North)
Near: Pantages Theater
Category/As: Motion Pictures as Director
For: Bus Stop (1956)
Real name: same or unknown
Born: October 5, 1908 in Texarkana, TX   Died: 1988, from supranuclear palsy
Studio: United Artists

Lohman, Al & Roger Barkley...{25/11}
1560 Vine Street (East)
Near: parking lot
Category/As: Radio as Comedians
Dedicated on December 4, 1985
Born: 1935 in IA (Al), 1936 in IA (Roger)
Awards: Emmy

Lombard, Carole...{37/114}
6922 Hollywood Boulevard (South)
Near: Hollywood Center
Category/As: Motion Pictures as Actress
For: My Man Godfrey (1936)
Real name: Jane Alice Peters
Born: October 6, 1908 in Ft. Wayne, IN
Died: January 16, 1942, from airplane crash and buried in Glendale, CA
Studio: Universal
Related to William Powell, Clark Gable (spouses)

Lombardo, Guy...{09/18}
6679 Hollywood Boulevard (North)
Near: Los Burritos
Category/As: Radio as Bandleader
For: New Year's Eve (1929)
Real name: Gaetano Albert Lombardo
Born: June 19, 1902 in London, Ontario
Died: 1977, from heart failure and buried in Farmingdale, NY

Lombardo, Guy...{34/33}
6666 Hollywood Boulevard (South)
Near: vacant
Category/As: Recording as Orchestra Leader

Lombardo, Guy...{14/32}
6371 Hollywood Boulevard (North)
Near: Antenna of Hollywood
Category/As: Television as Bandleader
For: New Year's Eve Broadcasts since 1936

London, Julie...{38/06}
7000 Hollywood Boulevard (South)
Near: Roosevelt Hotel
Category/As: Recording as Singer
For: Cry Me a River
Real name: Julie Peck
Born: September 26, 1926
Related to Jack Webb (spouse)

Lopez, Vincent...{10/49}
6609 Hollywood Boulevard (North)
Near: Gift Island
Category/As: Radio as Bandleader
For: Nola
Real name: same or unknown
Born: December 30, 1895 in Brooklyn, NY   Died: 1975, from liver failure

Lord, Marjorie...{15/33}
6317 Hollywood Boulevard (North)
Near: Hollywood Tattoo
Category/As: Television as Actress
For: Make Room For Daddy (1957) as Kathy Williams
Real name: Marjorie Wollenberg
Born: July 26, 1918 in San Francisco, CA
Related to Anne Archer (daughter)

Lord, Phillips...{37/88}
6914 Hollywood Boulevard (South)
Near: Hamburger Hamlet
Category/As: Radio as Narrator
For: Gangbusters (1935)
Born: October 1, 1897   Died: 1968

Lorre, Peter...{10/29}
6619 Hollywood Boulevard (North)
Near: Hollywood Styles
Category/As: Motion Pictures as Actor
For: The Maltese Falcon (1941)
Real name: Laszlo Lowenstein
Born: June 26, 1904 in Rosenburg, Hungary
Died: 1964, from stroke and buried in Hollywood, CA

Louise, Anita...{06/31}
6819 Hollywood Boulevard (North)
Near: Hollywood Tours & Gifts
Category/As: Motion Pictures as Actress
For: Madame DuBarry (1934)
Real name: Anita Louise Fremault

Born: January 9, 1915 in New York
Died: April 25, 1970, from stroke and buried in Glendale, CA
Related to Buddy Adler (spouse)

Love, Bessie...{07/08}
6777 Hollywood Boulevard (North)
Near: Hollywood First National Bldg
Category/As: Motion Pictures as Actress
For: Intolerance (1916)
Real name: Juanita Horton
Born: September 10, 1898 in Texas   Died: 1986

Lovejoy, Frank...{15/23}
6325 Hollywood Boulevard (North)
Near: Dr. Pachman Optometrist
Category/As: Television as Actor
For: Meet McGraw (1957)
Real name: same or unknown
Born: March 28, 1914 in NY
Died: 1962, from heart attack and buried in Culver City, CA

Lowe, Edmund...{14/30}
6371 Hollywood Boulevard (North)
Near: Antenna of Hollywood
Category/As: Motion Pictures as Actor
For: What Price Glory? (1926)
Real name: same or unknown
Born: March 3, 1890 in San Jose, CA   Died: 1971, from lung ailment

Lowe, Edmund...{10/59}
6601 Hollywood Boulevard (North)
Near: Station Market
Category/As: Television as Actor
For: Front Page Detective (1951) as David Chase
Born: March 3, 1890   Died: 1971, from a lung ailment

Lowe, Jim...{15/04}
6331 Hollywood Boulevard (North)
Near: Guarantee Building
Category/As: Recording as Songwriter
For: The Green Door
Real name: same or unknown
Born: May 7, 1927 in Springfield, MO

Loy, Myrna...{09/08}
6683 Hollywood Boulevard (North)
Near: Lazer Shoes
Category/As: Motion Pictures as Actress
For : The Thin Man (1934)
Real name: Myrna Williams
Born: August: 2, 1905 in Helena, MT

Lubin, Sigmund...{21/21}
6100 Hollywood Boulevard (South)
Near: Chevron Gas Station
Category/As: Motion Pictures as Producer
For: The Battle of Gettysburg (1912)
Real name: same or unknown   Died: 1923

Lubitsch, Ernst...{38/74}
7040 Hollywood Boulevard (South)
Near: Hollywood Liquor Store
Category/As: Motion Pictures as Director
For: Heaven Can Wait (1943) Paramount
Born: January 28, 1892 in Berlin, Germany
Died: 1947, from cancer and buried in Glendale, CA

Luboff, Norman...{24/74}
1614 Vine Street (East)
Near: parking lot
Category/As: Recording as Musician
Real name: same or unknown
Born: May 14, 1917 in Chicago, IL   Died: 1987, from cancer

Ludden, Allen...{08/02}
6743 Hollywood Boulevard (North)
Near: B. Dalton Book Store
Category/As: Television as Host
For: Password (19__)
Dedicated on March 31, 1988
Born: 1981 Died: 1981, from cancer
Related to Betty White (spouse)

Lugosi, Bella...{28/64}
6340 Hollywood Boulevard (South)
Near: Mr. Submarine
Category/As: Motion Pictures as Actor
For: Dracula (1931)
Real name: Bela Lugosi Blasko
Born: October 20, 1882 in Hungary
Died: 1956, from a heart attack and buried in Culver City, CA

Lukas, Paul...{06/13}
6841 Hollywood Boulevard (North)
Near: Budget Rent-A-Car
Category/As: Motion Pictures as Actor
For: Watch on the Rhine (1943)
Real name: Pal Lucacs
Born: May 26, 1894 in Bugapest, Hungary
Died: August 16, 1971, from a heart attack
Studio: Paramount   Awards: Oscar

Luke, Keye...{38/51}
7024 Hollywood Boulevard (South)
Near: Roosevelt Hotel parking structure
Cayegory/As: Motion Pictures as Actor
For: Gremlins (1984) as Grandfather Warner Brothers
Dedicated on December 5, 1990
Real name: same or unknown
Born: 1905   Died: 1991, from a stroke

Lumiere, August...{28/31}
6320 Hollywood Boulevard (South)
Near: Hollywood Bazaar
Category/As: Motion pictures as Inventor
For: Invented motion picture projector
Real name: Auguste Lumiere
Born: October 19, 1862 in Besancon, France   Died: 1954
Related to Louis Lumiere (brother)

Lumiere, Louis...{26/46}
1541 Vine Street (West)
Near: TAV Celebrity Center
Category/As: Motion Picture as Inventor
For: Invented motion picture projector
Born: October 5, 1864 in Besancon, France   Died: 1948
Related to Auguste Lumiere (brother)

Luna, Humberto...{25/17}
1560 Vine Street (East)
Near: parking lot
Category: Radio
Dedicated on October 12, 1990
Real name: same or unknown

Lund, Art...{21/41}
6126 Hollywood Boulevard (South)
Near: Henry Fonda Theater
Category/As: Recording as Singer
Real name: same or unknown
Born: April 1, 1920 in Salt Lake City, UT   Died: 1990, from liver cancer

Lundigan, William...{34/37}
6670 Hollywood Boulevard (South)
Near: vacant store
Category/As: Television as Actor
For: Men Into Space (1959)
Born: June 12, 1914 in Syracuse,
Died: December 20, 1975 from lung congestion and buried in Culver City,

Lupino, Ida...{06/07}
6845 Hollywood Boulevard (North)
Near: Starline Tours & Gifts
Category/As: Motion Pictures as Actress
For: High Sierra (1941)
Born: January 1, 1914 in London, England
Studio: Paramount
Related to Howard Duff, Louis Hayward (spouses), Lupino Lane (cousin)

Feb 4 18

Lupino, Ida...{17/53}
1724 Vine Street (East)
Near: parking lot
Category/As: Television as Actress
For: Mr. Adams and Mrs. Eve (1957-1958) CBS

Lupton, John...{16/23}
1713 Vine Street (West)
Near: Dan Dee Shoe Repair
Category/As: Television as Actor
For: Broken Arrow (1956-1960) as Tom Jeffords
Real name: same or unknown
Born: August 22, 1926 in Highland Park, IL

Luther, Frank...{17/110}
1700 Vine Street (East)
Near: Equitible Building
Category/As: Recording as Singer
For: Barnacle Bill and the Sailors
Real name: Frank L. Crow
Born: August 5, 1905 in KS   Died: 1980

Lyles, A.C. ...{37/61}
6840 Hollywood Boulevard (South)
Near: Masonic Temple
Category/As: Motion Pictures as Producer
For: Johnny Reno (1966)
Dedicated on March 3, 1988
Born: 1918

Lynn, Diana...{27/52}
1627 Vine Street (West)
Near: parking lot
Category/As: Motion Pictures as Actress
For: The Major and the Minor (1943)
Real name: Dolores Loehr
Born: October 7, 1926 in Los Angeles, CA
Died: December 19, 1971 from a brain hemorrhage

Lynn, Diana...{29/06}
6350 Hollywood Boulevard (South)
Near: Combo's Pizza
Category/As: Television as Actress
For: The Company of Killers (1971)

Lynn, Loretta...{26/23}
1501 Vine Street (West)
Near: Shopping Center
Category/As: Recording as Singer
For: Coal Miner's Daughter
Real name: Loretta Webb
Born: April 14,1935 in Butcher's Hollow, KY
Awards: Grammy

Lyon, Ben...{17/50}
1724 Vine Street (East)
Near: parking lot
Category/As: Motion Pictures as Actor
For: Hell's Angels (1930)
Real name: same or unknown
Born: February 6, 1901 in Atlanta, GA
Died: March, 1979 from a heart attack and buried in Hollywood, CA
Related to Bebe Daniels, Marion Nixon (spouses)

Lytell, Bert...{13/39}
6417 Hollywood Boulevard (North)

Near: Donner's Donuts
Category/As: Motion Pictures as Actor
For: Stage Door Canteen (1943)
Real name: same or unknown
Born: February 24, 1885 in NY
Died: 1954, following surgery

M

MacDonald, Jeanette...{20/02}
6161 Hollywood Boulevard (North)
Near: Network Body Shop
Category/As: Motion Pictures as Actress
For: Rose Marie (1936)
Real name: Jeanette Anna MacDonald
Born: June 18, 1901 in Philadelphia, PA.
Died: 1965, from heart attack and buried in Glendale, CA
Related to Gene Raymond (spouse)

MacDonald, Jenette...{24/52}
1630 Vine Street (East)
Near: Parking Lot
Category/As: Recording as Singer
For: Rose Marie (1930)

MacDonald, Katherine...{07/36}
6759 Hollywood Boulevard (North)
Near: This is Hollywood
Category/As: Motion Pictures as Actress
For: Untamed Women (1925)
Real name: same or unknown
Born: December 14, 1891 in Philadelphia, PA.
Died: 1956

Mack, Helen...{28/21}
6312 Hollywood Boulevard (South)
Near: Vacant
Category/As: Motion Pictures as Actress
For: Strange Holiday (1945)
Real name: Helen McDougall
Born: November 13, 1913
Died: 1986, from cancer.

Mack, Ted...{28/12}
6306 Hollywood Boulevard (South)
Near: Exotic Hair and Nail
Category/As: Television as Host
For: The Original Amateur Hour (1946) CBS
Real name: William Edward Maguinness
Born: February 12, 1904
Died: 1976

MacKenzie, Gisele...{27/08}
1601 Vine Street (West)
Near: Parking Lot
Category/As: Television as Singer
For: Your Hit Parade (1953)
Real name: Marie Marguerite Gisele LaFlenche
Born: January 10, 1927 in Winnipeg, Canada

MacLaine, Shirley...{27/26}
1615 Vine Street (West)
Near: Doolittle Theater
Category/As: Motion Pictures as Actress
For: Sweet Charity (1968)
Real name: Shirley MacLean Beaty
Born: April 24, 1934 in Richmond, VA.
Studio: Paramount   Awards: Oscar, Emmy
Related to Warren Beatty (brother)

MacLane, Barton...{08/35}
6719 Hollywood Boulevard (North)
Near: Hollywood Natural Food
Category/As: Television as Actor
For: I Dream of Jeannie (1965-1969) as General Peterson
Real name: same or unknown
Born: December 25, 1902 in SC
Died: 1969, from double pneumonia

MacMurray, Fred...{13/33}
6421 Hollywood Boulevard (North)
Near: Four M Shoes
Category/As: Motion Pictures as Actor
For: Double Indemnity (1944)
Real name: Fredrick Martin Mac Murray
Born: August 30, 1908 in Kankakee, IL
Died: 1991, from pneumonia
Studio: Paramount
Related to June Haver (spouse)

MacPherson, Jeanie...{22/15}
6150 Hollywood Boulevard (South)
Near: Network Body Shop
Category/As: Motion Pictures as Screenwriter
For: The King of Kings (1927)
Real name: same or unknown
Born: Boston, MA

Macrae, Gordon...{15/24}
6325 Hollywood Boulevard (North)
Near: Dr. Pachman Optometrist
Category/As: Radio as Singer
For: The Railroad Hour (1949) NBC
Real name: same or unknown
Born: March 12, 1921 in Orange, NJ
Died: 1986, from cancer.

Maddox, Johnny...{13/61}
6401 Hollywood Boulevard (North)
Near: Community Check Cashing
Category/As: Recording as Pianist
For: Heart and Soul

Madison, Guy...{05/15}
6935 Hollywood Boulevard (North)
Near: Mann's Chinese Parking
Category/As: Radio as Actor
For: Wild Bill Hickok (19__)
Real name: Robert Moseley
Born: January 19, 1922
Related to Gail Russell (spouse)

Madison, Guy...{15/02}
6331 Hollywood Boulevaed (North)
Near: Guaranty Building
Category/As: Television as Actor
For: Wild Bill Hickok (1951)

Magnani, Anna...{14/16}
6385 Hollywood Boulevard (North)
Near: Security Pacific Bank
Category/As: Motion Pictures as Actress
For: The Rose Tattoo (1955)
Real name: same or unknown
Born: March 7, 1908 in Egypt   Died: 1973, from cancer
Awards: Oscar

Majors, Lee...{05/02}
6935 Hollywood Boulevard (North)
Near: Casablanca Tours
Category/As: Television as Actor
For: The Six Million Dollar Man (1974)
Dedicated on September 5, 1984
Real name: same or unknown
Born: April 23, 1942

Malden, Karl...{18/55}
6231 Hollywood Boulevard (North)
Near: vacant
Category/As: Motion Pictures as Actor
For: On the Waterfront (1954)
Real name: Malden Sekulovich
Born: March 22, 1914 in Gary, IN
Awards: Oscar

Malone, Dorothy...{17/85}
1718 Vine Street (East)
Near: Sun Palace Restaurant
Category/As: Motion Pictures as Actress
For: Written On The Wind (1956)
Real name: Dorothy E. Maloney
Born: January 30, 1925 in Chicago, IL
Studio: RKO   Awards: Oscar
Related to Jaques Bergerac (spouse)

Malone, Ted...{24/57}
1630 Vine Street (East)
Near: parking lot
Category/As: Radio as Host
For: Between The Bookends (1935) CBS
Real name: same or unknown

Mamoulian, Rouben...{16/13}
1711 Vine Street (West)
Near: vacant
Category/As: Motion Pictures as Director
For: Becky Sharp (1935)
Real name: same or unknown
Born: October 8, 1898 in Tiflis, Russia
Died: 1987, from natural causes

Mancini, Henry...{06/26}
6821 Hollywood Boulevard (North)
Near: Hollywood Hamburger
Category/As: Recording as Composer
For: Moon River
Dedicated on September 22, 1982
Real name: same or unknown
Born: April 16, 1924 in Cleveland, OH
Awards: Oscar, Grammy

Manilow, Barry...{18/42}
6233 Hollywood Boulevard (North)
Near: Pantages Theater
Category/As: Recording as Songwriter
For: I Write the Music
Real name: same or unknown
Born: June 17, 1946 in Brooklyn, NY

Mankiewicz, Joseph L.....{19/09}
6211 Hollywood Boulevard (North)
Near: Capitol Records annex office
Category/As: Motion Pictures as Director
Foir: All About Eve (1950)
Real name: Joseph Leo Mankiewicz
Born: February 11, 1909 in Wilkes Barrie, PA
Died: February 5, 1993
Awards: Oscar

Mann, Anthony...{18/58}
6225 Hollywood Boulevard (North)
Near: vacant
Category/As: Motion Pictures as Director
For: God's Little Acre (1958)
Real name: Emil Anton Bundsmann
Born: June 30, 1906 in San Diego, CA
Died: 1967, from heart attack
Studio: MGM

Mann, Delbert...{17/84}
1718 Vine Street (East)

Near: Sun Palace Restaurant
Category/As: Motion Pictures as Director
For: Marty (1955)
Born: January 30, 1920 in Lawrence, KS
Studio: United Artists   Awards: Oscar

Mann, Hank...{28/02}
6302 Hollywood B oulevard (South)
Near: New York Pizza Express
Category/As: Motion Pictures as Comedian
For: City Lights (1931)
Real name: David W. Liebermann
Born: 1913   Died: 1971

Mansfield, Jayne...{28/43}
6328 Hollywood Boulevard (South)
Near: Hollywood Cards
Category/As: Motion Pictures as Actress
For: Bus Stop (1956)
Real name: Vera Jane Palmer
Born: 1933 in Bryn Mawr, PA
Died: 1967: from auto accident and buried in Hollywood, CA
Related to Mickey Hargaity, Matt Cimber (spouses)

Mantovani...{17/94}
1708 Vine Street (East)
Near: Collectors Book Store
Category/As: Recording as Conductor
For: Mexicali Rose
Real name: Annunzio Mantovani
Born: November 5, 1905 in Italy

March, Fredrick...{24/68}
1616 Vine Street (East)
Near: Juice Fountain
Category/As: Motion Pictures as Actor
For: Dr. Jekyll & Mr. Hyde (1932)
Real name: Ernest Frederick McIntyre Bickel
Born: August 31, 1897 in Racine, WI
Died: 1975, from cancer
Studio: Paramont   Awards: Oscar
Related to Florence Eldridge (spouse)

March, Hal...{25/22}
1560 Vine Street (East)
Near: parking lot
Category/As: Radio as Actor
For: Hear Me Good (1957)
Real name: Harold Mendelson
Born: April 22, 1920 in CA.
Died: 1970, from lung cancer

March, Hal...32/55}
6538 Hollywood Boulevard (south)
Near: Ziganne
Category/As: Television as Actor
For: Burns & Allen Show 1950-1958)

Margret, Ann...{12/40}
6501 Hollywood Boulevard (Norh)
Near: burned out
Category/As: Motion Pictures as Actress
For: Viva Los Vegas (1964)
Real name: Ann Margret Olsson
Born: April 28, 1941 in Valsjobyn, Sweden

Marley, J. Peverell...{06/52}
6801 Hollywood Boulevard (North)
Near: vacant
Category/As: Motion Pictures as Cinematographer
For: The Ten Commandments (1923)
Real name: same or unknown
Born: August 14, 1901 in San Jose, CA   Died: 1964
Related to Linda Darnell (spouse)

Marsh, Mae...{24/85}
1610 Vine Street (East)
Near: Vine Street Bar & Grill
Category/As: Motion Pictures as Actress
For: Intolerance (1916) the Little Dear One
Real name: Mary Warne Marsh
Born: November 9, 1895 in Madrid, NM
Died: 1968, from heart attack

Marshall, Garry...{37/51}
6838 Hollywood Boulevard (South)
Near: El Capitan
Category/As: Television as Writer
For: Happy Days (1974)
Dedicated on November 23, 1983
Born: November 13, 1934

Marshall, George...{38/84}
7046 Hollywood Boulevard (South)
Near: Souvenir Stop
Category/As: Motion Pictures as Director
For: Destry Rides Again (1939)
Born: December 29, 1891   Died: 1975

Mashall, Herbert...{22/45}
6200 Hollywood Boulevard (South)
Near: parking Lot
Category/As: Motion Pictures as Actor
For: The Enchanted Cottage (1945)
Real name: same or unknown
Born: May 23, 1890 in London, England
Died: 1966, from heart attack
Studio: RKO
Related to Boots Malloy, Edna Best (spouses)

Martin, Dean...{12/17}
6519 Hollywood Boulevard (North)
Near: Kalypso Gifts
Category/As: Motion Pictures as Actor
For: Scared Stiff (1953)
Real name: Dino Crocetti
Born: June 17, 1917 in Steubenville, OH.

Martin, Dean...{27/33}
1615 Vine Street (West)
Near, Doolittle Theater
Category/As: Recording as Singer
For: That's Amore

Martin, Dean...{09/60}
6655-F5 Hollywood Boulevard (North)
Near: Souvenir Shop
Category/As: Television as Actor.
For: The Colgate Comedy Hour (1950)

Martin, Freddy...{32/53}
6536 Hollywood Boulevard (South)
Near: Jewelry Magic
Category/As: Recording as Bandleader
For: All or Nothing At All
Real name: same or unknown
Born: December 9, 190-6
Died: 1983, from stroke

Martin, Marion...{05/42}
6925 Hollywood Boulevard (North)
Near: Mann's Chinese Theater
Category/As: Motion Pictures as Actress
For: Angel on My Shoulder (1946) MGM
Real name: Marion Suplee
Born: June 7, 1916 in Philadelphia, PA
Died: August 13, 1985 from natural causes and buried in Culver City, CA

Martin, Mary...{10/47}
6609 Hollywood Boulevard (North)
Near: Gift Island

Category/As: Radio as Actress
Real name: Mary Virginia Martin
Born: December 1, 1913 in Weatherford, TX
Died: 1990, from cancer
Awards: Emmy, Tony
Related to Larry Hagman (son)

Martin, Mary...{25/42}
1560 Vine Street (East)
Near: parking lot
Category/As: Recording as Singer

Martin, Quinn...{09/37}
6667 Hollywood Boulevard (North)
Near: Musso & Frank Grill
Category/As: Television as Producer
For: The Fugitive (1963-1967)
Real name: same or unknown
Born: May 22, 1927 in Los Angeles, CA

Martin, Tony...{31/59}
6440 Hollywood Boulevard (South)
Near: Playmates
Category/As: Motion Pictures as Singer
For: Sing, Baby, Sing (1936)
Real name: Alvin Morris
Born: December 25, 1913 in San Francisco, CA
Related to Cyd Charisse, Alice Faye (spouses)

Martin, Tony...{17/09}
1770 Vine Street (East)
Near: parking lot
Category/As: Radio as Singer
For: The Burns & Allen Show (1931)

Martin, Tony...{15/12}
6331 Hollywood Boulevard (North)
Near: Guaranty Building
Category/As: Recording as Singer
For: I Get Ideas

Martin, Tony...{16/43}
1719 Vine Street (West)
Near: parking lot
Category/As: Television as Singer
For: The Tony Martin Show (1954)

Marx, Groucho...{06/45}
6819 Hollywood Boulevard (North)
Near: Hollywood Tours & Gifts
Category/As: Radio as Comedian
For: You Bet Your Life (1947)
Real name: Julius Henry Marx
Born: October 2, 1890 in New York NY
Died: August 19, 1977, from pneumonia and buried in San Fernando, CA
Studio: ABC, CBS, NBC

Marx, Groucho...{16/68}
1749 Vine Street (West)
Near: parking lot
Category/As: Television as Host
For: You Bet Your Life (1950)

Mason, James...{06/04}
6845 Hollywood Boulevard (North)
Near: Starline Tours 7 Gifts
Category/As: Television as Actor
For: 20,000 Leagues Under The Sea (1954)
Real name: James Neville Mason
Born: May 15, 1909 in Huddersfield, England
Died: July 27, 1984, from heart attack
Studio: Disney

Massey, Ilona...{27/45}
1627 vine Street (West)
Near: parking lot

Category/As: Motion Pictures as Actress
For: rosalie (1938)
Real name: Ilona Hajmassy
Born:June 16, 1910 in Budapest, Hungary
Died: August 10, 1974, from cancer and buried in Arlington, VA
Studio: MGM

Massey, Raymond...{16/39}
1719 Vine Street (West)
Near: parking lot
Category/As: Motion Pictures as Actor
For: Abe Lincoln in Illinois (1940)
Real name: same or unknown
Born: August 30, 1896 in Toronto, Canado.
Died: 1983, from pneumonia and buried in Hamden, CT

Massey, Raymond...{35/15}
6706 Hollywood Boulevard (South)
Near: burned out
Category/As: Television as Actor
For: Dr. Kildare (1961)

Mathis, Johnny...{26/03}
1501 Vine Street (West)
Near: Shopping Center
Category/As: Recording as Singer
For: Misty
Born: September 30, 1935 in San Francisco, CA

Matthau, Walter...{14/43}
6357 Hollywood Boulevard (North)
Near: Star Fashion
Category/As: Motion Pictures as Actor
For: The Odd Couple (1968)
Dedicated on March 9, 1982
Real name: Walter Matuschanskayasky
Born: October 1, 1920 in New York
Awards: Oscar

Mature, Victor...{36/68}
6780 Hollywood Boulevard (South)
Near: Ripley's Museum
Category/As: Motion Pictures as Actor
For: The Robe (1953)
Born: January 29, 1915 in Louisville, KY.   Died: 198?
Studio: 20th Century

Mayer, Louis B. ...{27/65}
1637 Vine Street (West)
Near: Plaza Hotel
Category/As: Motion Pictures as Pioneer
For: Co-founder MGM
Real name: Louis Burt Meyer
Born: July 4, 1885 in Minsk, Russia.
Died: 1957, from leukemia and buried in Los Angeles, CA
Studio: MGM   Awards: Oscar

Maynard, Ken...{07/52}
6751 Hollywood Boulevard (North)
Near: vacant
Category/As: Motion Pictures as Actor
For: Texas Gunfighter (1932)
Real name: same or unknown
Born: July 21, 1895 in IN
Died: 1973, from malnutrition

Mayo, Archie...{15/62}
6301 Hollywood Boulevard (North)
Near: vacant
Category/As: Motion Pictures as Director
For: Bordertown (1934)
Real name: Archie L. Mayo
Born: 1891 in Guadalajara, Mexico   Died: 1968, from cancer

Mayo, Virginia...{16/74}
1749 Vine Street (West)

Near: parking lot
Category/As: Television as Actress
For: The Secret Life of Walter Mitty (1947)
Real name: Virginia Clara Jones
Born: November 30, 1920 in St. Louis, MO
Related to Michael O'Shea (spouse)

McAvoy, May...{16/52}
1735 Vine Street (West)
Near: Palace
Category/As: Motion Pictures as Actress
For: The Jazz Singer (1927)
Real name: same or unknown
Born: September 8, 1901 in Manhattan, NY   Died: 1984
Studio: Warner Brothers

McBride, Mary Margaret...{38/32}
7000 Hollywood Boulevard (South)
Near: Roosevelt Hotel
Category/As: Radio as Interviewer
For: Celebrity Talk Show (1937) CBS
Born: November 16, 1899   Died: 1976

McCalla, Irish...{17/63}
1724 Vine Street (East)
Near: parking Lot
Category/As: Television as Actress
For: Sheena, Queen of the Jungle (1955)
Real name: same or unknown
Born: December 25, 1929 in Pawnee City, NE

McCambridge, Mercedes...{17/71}
1722 Vine Street (East
Near: Nick's Diner
Category/As: Motion Pictures as Actress
For: All the King's Men (1949)
Real name: Carlotta Mercedes McCambridge
Born: March 17, 1918 in Joliet, IL
Awards: Oscar

McCambridge, Mercedes...{18/35}
6243 Hollywood Boulevard (North)
Near: Ticketmaster
Category/As: Television as Actress
For: The Counterfiet Killer (1970)

McCarey, Leo...{25/82}
1500 Vine Street (East)
Near: Home Savings
Category/As: Motion Pictures as Director
For: Going My Way (1944)
Born: October 3, 1929 in Los Angeles, CA   Died: 1969
Awards: Oscar

McCarthy, Clem...{11/03}
6565 Hollywood B oulevard (North)
Near: Cash It Here
Category/As: Radio as Announcer
For: pioneer sportscaster
Real name: same or unknown

McConnell, Smilin' Ed...{34/05}
6650 Hollywood Boulevard (North)
Near: Hurricane
Category/As: Radio as Singer
For: The Buster Brown Show (1943)
Real name: James Ed McConnell
Died: 1954

McCormack, Patty...{28/22}
6312 Hollywood Boulevard (South)
Near: vacant
Category/As: Motion Pictures as Actress
For: The Bad Seed (1956)
Born: August 21, 1945

McCoy, Clyde...{31/43}
6426 Hollywood Boulevard (South)
Near: Hollywood Discount Center
Category/As: Recording as Musician
For: Sugar Blues
Real name: same or unknown
Born: December 29, 1903

McCoy, Tim...{24/91}
1600 Vine Street (East)
Near: D M V
Category/As: Motion Pictures as Actor
For: War Paint (1926)
Real name: same or unknown
Born: April 19, 1891 in Saginaw, MI   Died: 1978

McCrary, Tex...{24/54}
1630 Vine Street (East)
Near: parking lot
Category/As: Motion Pistures as Columnist
For: Tex & Jinx (1947)
Real name: John Reagan
Born: TX
Related to Jinx Falkenburg (spouse)

McCrea, Joel...{05/70}
6925 Hollywood Boulevard (North)
Near: Mann's Chinese Theater
Category/As: Motion Pictures as Actor
For: Sullivan's Travels (1941)
Born: November 5, 1905 in South Pasadena, CA
Died: 1990, from pulmonary complications
Studio: RKO
Related to Frances Dee (spouse)

McCrea, Joel...{18/39}
6233 Hollywood Boulevard (North)
Near: Pantages Theater
Category/As: Radio as Actor

McDaniel, Hattie...{16/35}
1719 Vine Street (West)
Near: parking lot
Category/As: Motion Pictures as Actress
For: Gone With The Wind (1939) as Mammy
Born: June 10, 1895 in Wichita, KA
Died: 1952, buried in Los Angeles, CA
Awards: Oscar

McDaniel, Hattie...{05/27}
6925 Hollywood Boulevard (North)
Near: Mann's Chinese Theater
Category/As: Radio as Actress
For: Amos 'n' Andy (1926}

McDowall, Roddy...{33/96}
6630-C Hollywood Boulevard (South)
Near: City Life Sports
Category/As: Television as Actor
For: Planet of the Apes (1967)
Real name: Roderick Andrew McDowall
Born: September 17, 1928 in London, England
Awards: Emmy

McGee, Fibber & Molly...{25/77}
1500 Vine Street (East)
Near: Home Savings
Category/As: Radio as Actors
For: Fibber McGee and Molly (1935) NBC
Dedicated on December 21, 1983
Real names: Jim Jordan and Marion Jordan
Born: 1887 (both) in Peoria, IL (both)
Died: 1968 (Jim), from blood clot after a fall

McGraw, Charles...{05/35}
6925 Hollywood Boulevard (North)
Near: Mann's Chinese Theater
Category/As: Television as Actor
For: The Narrow Margin (1950)
Real name: same or unknown
Born: May 10, 1914   Died: 1980

McGuire, Dorothy...{05/25}
6935 Hollywood Boulevard (North)
Near: Mann's Chinese Parking
Category/As: Motion Pictures as Actress
For: Three Coins in the Fountain (1954)
Real name: Dorothy Hackett McGuire
Born: June 14, 1918 in Omaha, NE
Studio: Fox

McKuen, Rod...{08/06}
6743 Hollywood Boulevard (North)
Near: B. Dalton Book
Category/As: Recording as Songwriter
For: Jean
Real name: same or unknown
Born: April 29, 1933 in Oakland, CA
Awards: Grammy

McLaglen, Victor...{16/59}
1735 Vine Street (West)
Near: Palace
Category/As: Motion Pictures as Actor
For: Beau Geste (1926)
Real name: same or unknown
Born: December 10, 1886 in Tunbridge Wells, Kent, England
Died: 1959, from heart failure and buried in Glendale, CA
Studio: Fox   Awards: Oscar

McLeod, Norman Z. ...{17/49}
1724 Vine Street (East)
Near: parking lot
Category/As: Motion Pictures as Director
For: Horse Feathers (1932)
Real name: same or unknown
Born: September 20, 1898 in Grayling, MI
Died: 1964, after a long illness
Studio: Paramount

McMahon, Ed...{38/09}
7000 Hollywood Boulevard (South)
Near: Roosevelt Hotel
Category/As: Television an Announcer
For: The Tonight Show (1962-1992) NBC
Dedicated on March 20, 1986
Born: March 6, 1923 in Detroit, MI

McNamee, Graham...{13/55}
6405 Hollywood Boulevard (North)
Near: Greco's Pizza
Category/As: Radio as Sportscaster
For: Originated sportscasting on NBC
Born: July 10, 1888 in Washington, DC   Died: 1942

McNeill, Don...{15/61}
6301 Hollywood Boulevard (North)
Near: vacant
Category/As: Radio as Host
For: The Breakfast Club (1933) NBC
Born: December 23, 1907 in Galena, IL

McQueen, Steve...{37/47}
6834 Hollywood Boulevard (South)
Near: Rocket Hollywood
Category/As: Motion Pictures as Actor
For: Bullitt (1968)
Dedicated on June 12, 1986
Real name: Terrence Stephen McQueen

Born: March 24, 1930 in Slater, MO
Died: 1980, from cancer

Meadows, Audrey...{21/09}
6100 Hollywood Boulevard (South)
Near: Chevron Gas Station
Category/As: Television as Actress
For: The Honeymooners (1955-1956) as Alice Kramden
Real name: Audrey Cotter
Born: February 8, 1924
Awards: Emmy
Note: Honeymooners originally aired only one year

Meek, Donald...{17/32}
1750 Vine Street (East)
Near: Catitol Record Building
Category/As: Motion Pictures as Actor
For: Stagecoach (1939)
Real name: same or unknown
Born: July 14, 1880 in Scotland
Died: 1946, from heart attack

Meeker, George...{20/78}
6125 Hollywood Boulevard (North)
Near: Pep Boys
Category/As: Motion Pictures as Actor
For: Back Street (1932)
Real name: same or unknown
Born: March 5, 1904 in Brooklyn, NY   Died: 1963

Meighan, Thomas...{16/38}
1719 Vine Street (West)
Near: parking lot
Category/As: Motion Pictures as Actor
For: Peck's Bad Boy (1934)
Real name: same or unknown
Born: April 9, 1878 in Pittsburgh, PA   Died: 1936, from cancer

Meiklejohn...{16/105
1777 Vine Street (West)
Near: Vine Street Building
Category/As: Motion Pictures as Actress
Real name: Charlotte Meiklejohn
Born: November 5, 1900

Melachrino...{27/46}
1627 Vine Street (West)
Near: parking lot
Category/As: Recording as Composer
Real name: George Melachrino
Born: May 1, 1909 in England Died: 1965

Melchior, Lauritz...{17/76}
1718 Vine Street (East)
Near: Sun Palace Restuarant
Category/As: Recording as Opera Singer
Real name: Lebrecht Hommel
Born: March 20, 1890 in Denmark.
Died: 1973, from gall bladder operation

Melton, James...{28/13}
6306 Hollywood Boulevard (South)
Near: Exotic Hair and Nail
Category/As: Radio as Singer
For: The James Melton Show (1943)
Born: January 2, 1904
Died: 1961, from pneumonia

Melton, James...{33/30}
6562 Hollywood Boulevard (South)
Near: Hollywood Toys Inc.
Category/As: Recording as Singer

Mendez, Rafael...{07/23}
6767 Hollywood Boulevard (North)
Near: Hollywood Wax Museum

Category/As: Recording as Musician
For: trumpet player with Rudy Vallee Orchestra
Dedicated on March 2, 1983
Real name: same or unknown
Born: March 26, 1906 in Mexico   Died: 1981

Menjou, Aldoph...{37/34}
6822 Hollywood Boulevard (South)
Near: Starline Tours & Gifts
Category/As: Motion Pictures as Actor
For: Little Miss Marker (1934)
Real name: same or unknown
Born: February 18, 1890 in Pittsburg, PA
Died: 1963, from hepatitis and buried in Hollywood, CA

Menuhin, Yehudi...{35/23}
6712 Hollywood Boulevard (South)
Near: Egyptian Theater
Category/As: Recording as Violinist
Born: April 22, 1916

Mercer, Johnny...{24/58}
1630 Vine Street (East)
Near: parking lot
Category/As: Television as Singer
For: Somethimg's Got To Give
Real name: same or unknown
Born: November 18, 1909 in GA.   Died: 1976
Awards: Oscar, Grammy

Meredith, Burgess...{37/77}
6906 Hollywood Boulevard (South)
Near: Juice Master
Category/As: Motion Pictures as Actor
For: Of Mice and Men (1939)
Dedicated on November 5, 1987
Real name: George Burgess
Born: 1907 in Cleveland, OH
Related to Paulette Goddard (spouse)

Merkel, Una...{23/22}
6262 Hollywood Boulevard (South)
Near: vacant lot
Category/As: Motion Pictures as Actress
Fro: Destry Rides Again (1939)
Real name: same or unknown
Born: December 10, 1903 in Covington, KY   Died: 1986

Merman, Ethel...{38/78}
7042 1/2 Hollywood Boulevard (South)
Near: Souvenir Stop
Category/As: Motion Pictures as Actress
For: Call Me Madam (1953)
Real name: Ethel Zimmerman
Born: January 16, 1909   Died: 1984, from brain tumor

Merman, Ethel...{16/70}
1749 Vine Street (West)
Near: parking lot
Category/As: Recording as Singer
For: There's No Business Like Show Business

Merrill, Robert...{07/32}
6763 Hollywood Boulevard (North)
Near: This Is Hollywood
Category/As: Recording as Singer
Real name: Robert Miller
Born: June 4, 1917 in NY

Micheaux, Oscar...{08/32}
6721 Hollywood Boulevard (North)
Near: vacant
Category/As: Motion Pictures as Writer
For: Body and Soul (1924)
Dedicated on February 13, 1987
Real name: same or unknown

Born: Approx. 1890 in IL   Died: 1951

Midler, Bette...{37/115}
6922 Hollywood Boulevard (South)
Near: Hollywood Center
Category/As: Recording as Singer
For: Wind Beneath My Wings
Dedicated on February 6, 1986
Real name: same or unknown
Born: December 1, 1945

Miles, Vera...{24/19}
1650 Vine Street (East)
Near: vacant store
Category/As: Television as Actress
For: Pepsi-Cola Playhouse (1951)
Real name: Vera Ralston
Born: August 23, 1930 in Boise City, OK

Milestone, Lewis...{04/37}
7021 Hollywood Boulevard (North)
Near: Hollywood Galaxy
Category/As: Motion Pictures as Director
For: All Quiet on the Western Front (1930)
Born: September 30, 1895 in Chisinau, Russia
Died: 1980, after abdominal surgery
Awards: Oscar

Milland, Ray...{27/36}
1627 Vine Street (West)
Near: parking lot
Category/As: Motion Pictures as Actor
For: The Lost Weekend (1945)
Real name: Reginald Truscott-Jones
Born: January 3, 1905 in Neath, Wales
Died: 1986, from cancer
Studio: Paramount   Awards: Oscar

Milland, Ray...{24/44}
1630 Vine Street (East)
Near: parking lot
Category/As: Television as Actor
For: Rich Man, Poor Man (1976)

Miller, Ann...{37/92}
6914 Hollywood Boulevard (South)
Near: Hamburger Hamlet
Category/As: Motion Pictures as Actress
For: Kiss Me Kate (1953)
Real name: Lucille Ann Collier
Born: April 12, 1919 in Houston, TX
Studio: MGM

Miller, Glenn...{05/48}
6925 Hollywood Boulevard (North)
Near: Mann's Chinese Theater
Category/As: Recording as Bandleader
For: In The Mood
Real name: Alton Glenn Miller
Born: March 1, 1904 in Clarinda, IA
Died: 1944, in an airplane crash

Miller, Marilyn...{15/64}
6301 Hollywood Boulevard (North)
Near: vacant
Category/As: Motion Pictures as Actress
For: Her Majesty's Love (1932)
Real name: Mary Lynn Reynolds
Born: September 1, 1898 in Evanston, IL
Died: 1936, from sinus infection and burried in Bronx, NY

Miller, Marvin...{20/92}
6125 Hollywood Boulevard (North)
Near: Pep Boys
Category/As: Television as Actor
For: The Millionaire (1955) CBS as Michael Anthony

Real name: Marvin Mueller
Born: July 19, 1913 in St. Louis, MO.
Died: 1985, and buried in Los Angeles, CA

Miller, Mitch...{04/47}
7013 Hollywood Boulevard (North)
Near: Shelly's Cafe
Category/As: Recording as Conductor
For: Sing Along With Mitch
Born: July 4, 1911

Miller Band, The Steve...{17/12}
1770 Vine Street (East)
Near: parking lot
Category/As: Recording as Musicians
Dedicated on July 14, 1987

Mills Brothers, The...{38/01}
7000 Hollywood Boulevard (South)
Near: Roosevelt Hotel
Category/As: Recording as Singers
For: Glow Worm
Real names: Harry, Donald, Herbert and John Mills

Milstein, Nathan...{14/20}
6377 Hollywood Boulevard (North)
Near: Beeper Store
Category/As: Recording as Violinist
Real name: same or unknown
Born: December 31, 1904 in Russia

Minnelli, Liza...{38/55}
7024 Hollywood Boulevard (South)
Near: Roosevelt Hotel Parking
Category/As: Live Theater as Entertainer
For Cabaret (1972)
Dedicated on September 30, 1991
Related to Judy Garland (mother), Vincentte Minelli (father)

Minnelli, Vincente...{34/49}
6674 Hollywood Boulevard (South)
Near: Explosion
Category/As: Motion Pictures as Director
For: Father of the Bride (1950)
Born: February 28, 1910   Died: 1986
Studio: MGM   Awards: Oscar
Related to Judy Garland (spouse), Liza Minelli (daughter)

Minter, Mary Miles...{17/48}
1724 Vine Street (East)
Near: parking lot
Category/As: Motion Pictures as Actress
For: The Trail of The Lonesome Pine (1923)
Real name: Juliet Riley
Born: April 1, 1902 in LA.
Died: 1984, from heart failure and ashes scattered

Minyard, Bob and Ken Arthur...{33/57}
6608 Hollywood Boulevard (South)
Near: Frederick's of Hollywood
Category/As: Radio as Host
For: Ken & Bob Company Program
Dedicated on August 6. 1986
Real name: same or unknown

Miranda, Carmen...{23/23}
6262 Hollywood Boulevard (South)
Near: vacant lot
Gategory/As: Motion Pictures as Singer
For: Down Argentine Way (1940)
Real name: Maria de Carmo Miranda de Cunha
Born: February 9, 1909 in Portugal
Died: August 5, 1955, from heart attack
Studio: 20th Century

Mitchell, Everett...{23/08}
6254 Hollywood Boulevard (South)
Near: burned out
Category/As: Radio as Host
For: National Farm & Home Hour (1928)
Real name: same or unknown

Mitchell, Guy...{38/02}
7000 Hollywood Boulevard (South)
Near: Roosevelt Hotel
Category/As: Recording as Singer
For: Red Garters (1954)
Real name: Al Cernick
Born: February 27, 1925 in Detroit, MI

Mitchell, Thomas...{27/84}
1645 Vine Street (West)
Near: Hollywood Vine Building
Category/As: Motion Pictures as Actor
For: Stagecoach (1939)
Real name: same or unknown
Born: July 11, 1892 in Elizabeth, NJ
Died: 1962, from cancer
Awards: Oscar

Mitchell, Thomas...{21/05}
6100 Hollywood Boulevard (South)
Near: Chevron Gas Station
Category/As: Television as Actor
For: O'Henry Playhouse (1956)

Mitchum, Robert...{22/60}
6240 Hollywood Boulevard (South)
Near: West Coast Ensemble
Category/As: Motion Pictures as Actor
For: The Big Sleep (1978) Philip Marlow
Dedicated on January 25, 1984
Born: August 6, 1917 in Bridgeport, CT
Studio: RKO

Mix, Tom...{17/108}
1700 Vine Street(East)
Near: Equitible Building
Category/As: Motion Pictures as Actor
For: Destry Rides Again (1927)
Real name: Thomas Hezikah Mix
Born: January 6, 1880 in Mix Run, PA
Died: 1940, in an automobile accident and buried in Glendale, CA
Studio: Universal
Note: buried in his automobile

Mohr, Hal...{13/20}
6433 Hollywood Boulevard (North)
Near: Pacific Theater
Category/As: Motion Pictures as Cinematographer
For: Phantom of The Opera (1943)
Real name: same or unknown
Born: August 2, 1894 in San Francisco, CA   Died: 1974
Studio: Universal   Awards: Oscar

Monkees, The...{09/17}
6679 Hollywood Boulevard (North)
Near: Los Burritos
Category/As: Television as Musicical Group
For: The Monkees (1966-1968) NBC
Dedicated on July 10, 1989
Real names: Peter Tork, Mike Nesmith, Mickey Dolenz, Davey Jones
Born: 1942, 1943, 1945, 1944

Monroe, Marilyn...{36/64}
6776 Hollywood Boulevard (South)
Near: McDonald's
Category/As: Motion Pictures as Actress
For: How to Marry a Millionaire (1953)
Real name: Norma Jean Mortenson (Baker)
Born: June 1, 1926 in Los Angeles, CA

Died: August 15, 1962, from drug overdose and buried in Los Angeles, CA
Studio: 20th Century
Related to Joe DiMagio, Arthur Miller (spouses)

Monroe, Vaughn...{16/98}
1749 Vine Street (West)
Near: parking Lot
Category/As: Radio as Singer
For: Singing Guns (1950) CBS
Real name: same or unknown
Born: October 7, 1911   Died: 1973

Monore, Vaughn...{24/96}
1600 Vine Street (East)
Near: D M V
Category/As: Recording as Singer
For: Ghost Riders in the Sky

Montalban, Ricardo...{04/29}
7021 Hollywood Boulevard (North)
Near: Hollywood Galaxy
Category/As: Television as Actor
For: Fantasy Island (1973)
Real name: same or unknown
Born: November 25, 1920 in Mexico City
Studio: MGM

Monteux, Pierre...{16/46}
1719 Vine Street (West)
Near: parking lot
Category/As: Recording as Conductor
Real name: same or unknown
Born: April 4, 1875 in Paris, France   Died: 1964

Montgomery, George...{15/55}
6440 Hollywood Boulevard (South)
Near: vacant
Category/As: Television as Actor
For: Cimarron City (1958)
Real name: George Mongomery Litz
Born: August 29, 1916 in Brady, MT
Studio: 20th Century
Related to Dinah Shore (spouse)

Montgomery, Robert...{31/65}
6440 Hollywood Boulevard (South)
Near: Playmates
Category/As: Motion Pictures as Actor
For: The Texas Rangers (1951)
Real name: Henry Montgomery, Jr.
Born: May 21, 1904 in Beacon, NY   Died: 1981, from cancer
Studio: MGM
Related to Elizabeth Montgomery (daughter)

Montgomery, Robert...{27/57}
1633 Vine Street (West)
Near: Plaza Building
Category/As: Television as Actor
For: Robert Montgomery Presents (1950)

Mooney, Art...{22/09}
6150 Hollywood Boulevard (South)
Near: Network Body Shop
Category/As: Recording as Bandleader
Real name: same or unknown

Moore, Clayton (The Lone Ranger)...{37/91}
6914 Hollywood Boulevard (South)
Near: Hamburger Hamlet
Category/As: Television as Actor
For: The Lone Ranger (1952) ABC
Dedicated on June 5, 1987
Real name: same or unknown
Born: 1908

Moore, Colleen...{26/80}
1549 Vine Street (West)
Near: TAV Celebrity Center
Category/As: Motion Pictures as Actress
For: The Perfect Flapper (1924)
Real name: Kathleen Morrison
Born: August 19, 1900 in Port Huron, MI
Died: 1988, from a long illness

Moore, Constance...{23/34}
6274 Hollywood Boulevard (South)
Near: parking lot
Category/As: Motion Pictures as Actress
For: I Wanted wings (1941)
Born; January 18, 1922 in Sious City, IA
Studio: Republic

Moore, Del...{13/59}
6403 Hollywood Boulevard (North)
Near: Hollywood Pants
Category/As: Television as Actor
For: Bachelor Father (1960) Cal Mitchell
Real name: same or unknown

Moore, Dudley...{38/31}
7000 Hollywood Boulevard (South)
Near: Roosevelt Hotel
Category/As: Motion Pictures as Actor
For: Arthur (1981)
Dedicated on September 23, 1987
Real name: same or unknown

Moore, Garry...{17/73}
1722 Vine Street (East)
Near: Nick's Diner
Category/As: Radio as Announcer
For: The Camel Caravan (1943) CBS
Real name: Thomas Garrison Morfit
Born: January 31, 1915 in Baltimore, MD

Moore, Garry...{24/08}
1680 Vine Street (East)
Near: Taft Building
Category/As: Television as Host
For: The Garry More Show (1958)

Moore, Grace...{23/37}
6274 Hollywood Boulevard (South)
Near: parking lot
Category/As: Motion Pictures as Singer
For: I'll Take Romance
Real name: same or unknown
Born: December 5,1901 in TN
Died: 1947 in an airplane crash

Moore, Mary Tyler...{04/14}
7021 Hollywood Boulevard (North)
Near: Hollywood Galaxy
Category/As: Television as Actress
For: The Mary Tyler Moore Show (1970-1977)
Real name: same or unknown
Studion: CBS-MTM
Related to. Grant Tinker (spouse)

Moore, Matt...{15/57}
6301 Hollywood Boulevard (North)
Near: vacant
Category/As: Motion Pictures as Actor
For: An Affair to Remember (1957)
Real name: same or unknown
Born: January 8, 1988 in Ireland   Died: 1960
Related to Tom Moore, Owen Moore (brothers)
Note: all three brothers have WOF Stars

Moore, Owen...{08/25}
6727 Hollywood Boulevard (North)
Near: Artesian Patio
Category/As: Motion Pictures as Actor
For: She Done Him Wrong (1933)
Real name: same or unknown
Born: December 12, 1886 in Ireland.   Died: 1939
Related to Mary Pickford (spouse), Tom Moore, Matt Moore (brothers)
Note: all three brothers have WOF Stars

Moore, Tom...{24/30}
1642 Vine Street (East)
Near: Bernard Luggage
Category/As: Motion Pictures as Actor
For: A Man and His Money (1919)
Real name: same or unknown
Born: November 14, 1884   Died: 1955, from cancer
Related to Matt Moore, Owen Moore (brothers)
Note: all three brothers have WOF Stars

Moore, Victor...{37/50}
6838 Hollywood Boulevard (South)
Near: El Capitan
Category/As: Motion Pictures as Actor
For: The Seven Year Itch (1955)
Real name: same or unknown
Born: February 24, 1876   Died: 1962, from heart attack

Moorehead, Agnes...{16/41}
1719 Vine Street (West)
Near: parking lot
Category/As: Motion Pictures as Actress
For: Citizen Kane (1941)
Real name: Agnes Robertson Morrison
Born: December 6, 1906 in Clinton, MA
Died: April 30, 1974, from cancer

Moran, Polly...{28/04}
6302 Hollywood Boulevard (South)
Near: New York Pizza Express
Category/As: Motion Pictures as Actress
For: Adam's Rib (1949)
Born: June 28, 1884   Died: 1952, from heart ailment

Moreno, Antonio...{09/58}
6655-5 Hollywood Boulevard (North)
Near: Camp Hollywood
Category/As: Motion Pictures as Actor
For: The Trail of the Lonesome Pine (1923)
Real name: same or unknown
Born: September 26, 1886   Died: 1867, from a long illness

Morgan, Frank...{17/96}
1708 Vine Street (East)
Near: Collectors Book Store
Category/As: Motion Pictures as Actor
For: The Wizard of Oz (1939) as The Wizard
Real name: Francis Wupperman
Born: June 1, 1890 in New York, NY
Died: 1949, and buried in Brooklyn, NY
Studio: MGM
Related to Ralph Morgan (brother)

Morgan, Frank...{35/03}
6700 Hollywood Boulevard (South)
Near: LA Tattoo
Category/As: Radio as Host
For: 21 Beacon Street (1959)

Morgan, Henry...{28/40}
6328 Hollywood Boulevard (South)
Near: Hollywood Cards
Category/As: Radio as Actor
For: The Henry Morgan Show (1946) ABC
Real name: Henry von Ost

Born: March 31, 1915 in Detroit, MI

Morgan, Michele...{27/79}
1645 Vine Street (West)
Near: Hollywood Vine Building
Category/As: Motion Pictures as Actress
For: L'Etrange madame X (1950)
Real name: Simone Roussel
Born: February 29, 1920 in France

Morgan, Ralph...{27/29}
1615 Vine Street (West)
Near: Doolittle Theater
Category/As: Motion Pictures as Actor
For: The Power and the Glory (1933)
Real name: Raphael Kuhner Wupperman
Born: July 6, 1882 in New York, NY   Died: 1956
Related to Frank Morgan (brother)

Morgan, Robert W. ...{06/10}
6841 Hollywood Boulevard (North)
Near: Budget Rent-A-Car
Category/As: Radio
Dedicated on April 8, 1993
Real name: same or unknown

Morgan, Russ...{16/87}
1749 Vine Street (West)
Near: parking lot
Category/As: Recording as Composer
For: You're Nobody 'Till Somebody Loves You
Real name: same or unknown
Born: April 29, 1904 in Scranton, PA
Died: 1969, from Cerebral Hemorrhag

Morse, Carlton E. ...{13/03}
6445 Hollywood Boulevard (North)
Near: Best Tomy #21
Category/As: Radio as Writer
For: One Man's Family (1932) NBC
Real name: same or unknown
Born: 1901 in LA

Morse, Ella Mae...{17/64}
1724 Vine Street (East)
Near: parking lot
Category/As: Recording as Singer
For: Cow-Cow Boogie
Real name: same or unknown
Born: September 12, 1926 in TX

Mouse, Mickey...{05/32}
6925 Hollywood Boulevard (North)
Near: Mann's Chinese Theater
Category/As: Motion Pictures as Animated Character
Real name: Steamboat Willie
Born: 1928, in Hollywood, CA

Muir, Jean...{23/45}
6282 Hollywood Boulevard (South)
Near: Original Coney Island
Category/As: Motion Pictures as Actress
For: A Midsummer Night's Dream (1935)
Real name: Jean M. Fullerton
Born: February 13, 1911 in Canada

Mulhall, Jack...{17/39}
1750 Vine Street (East)
Near: Capitol Record Building
Category/As: Motion Pictures as Actor
For: Hollywood Boulevard (1936)
Real name: same or unknown
Born: October 7, 1887 in NY
Died: 1979, from heart failure

Muni, Paul...{13/15}
6433 Hollywood Boulevard (North)
Near: Pacific Theater
Category/As: Motion Pictures as Actor
For: The Story of Louis Pasteur (1936)
Real name: Muni Weisenfruend
Born: September 22, 1897 in Lwow, Poland
Died: 1967, from heart trouble and buried in Hollywood CA
Studio: Warner Brothers   Awards: Oscar

Munson, Ona...{23/02}
6250 Hollywood Boulevard (South)
Near: Stella Adler Theater
Category/As: Motion Pictures as Actress
For: Gone With The Wind (1939)
Real name: Ona Wolcott
Born: June 16, 1906 in Portland, OR
Died: 1955, from suicide (pills) and buried in Hartsdale, NY

Murphy, Audie...{27/04}
1601 Vine Street (West)
Near: parking lot
Category/As: Motion Pictures as Actor
For: The Red Badge of Courage (1951)
Born: June 20, 1924 in Kingston, TX
Died: 1971, in an airplane crash
Studio: Universal

Murphy, George...{27/18}
1605 Vine Street (West)
Near: Molly Coney Island
Category/As: Motion Pictures as Actor
For: Bataan (1943)
Real name: same or unknown
Born: July 4, 1902 in New Haven, CT
Died: 1992, from leukemia
Awards: Oscar

Murray, Anne...{17/16}
1750 Vine Street (East)
Near: Capitol Record Building
Category/As: Recording as Singer
For: Snow Bird
Born: June 20, 1946 in Nova Scotia
Awards: Grammy

Murray, Charlie...{16/33}
1719 Vine Street (West)
Near: parking lot
Category/As: Motion Pictures as Actor
For: Soldiers of Misfortune (1914)
Real name: same or unknown
Born: June 22, 1872 in Laurel, IN
Died: 1941, from pneumonia
Studio: Biograph

Murray, Don...{14/08}
6385 Hollywood Boulevard (North)
Near: Security Pacific Bank
Category/As: Motion Pictures as Actor
For: Bus Stop (1956)
Real name: same or unknown
Born: July 31, 1929 in Hollywood, CA
Related to Hope Lang (spouse)

Murray, Jan...{20/12}
6161 Hollywood Boulevard (North)
Near: Network Body Shop
Category/As: Television as Host
For: Treasure Hunt (1956)
Real name: Murray Janofsky
Born: New York, NY

Murray, Ken...{17/37}
1750 Vine Street (East)
Near: Capitol Record Building
Category/As: Radio as Actor
For: The Ken Murray Show (1933)
Real name: Ken Doncourt
Born: July 14, 1903 in New York, NY   Died: October 12, 1988
Studio: CBS   Awards: Oscar

Murray, Mae...{28/30}
6320 Hollywood Boulevard (South)
Near: Hollywood Bazaar
Category/As: Motion Pictures as Actress
For: The Merry Widow (1925)
Real name: Marie Adrienne Koenig
Born: May 10, 1889   Died: 1965, from heart condition

Murrow, Edward R....{18/01}
6263 Hollywood Boulevard (North)
Near: Equitible Building
Category/As: Radio as Newscaster
For: Chief of Foreign Staff
Real name: Egbert Roscoe Murrow
Born: April 25, 1908
Died: 1965, from lung cancer and buried in Brooklyn, NY
Studio: CBS

Murrow, Edward R....{31/29}
6414 Hollywood Boulevard (South)
Near: Alley
Category/As: Television as Host

Myers, Carmel...{16/80}
1749 Vine Street (West)
Near: parking lot
Category/As: Motion Pictures as Actress
For: Ben Hur (1925) as Iras   Studio: Universal
Born: April 9, 1899 in San Francisco, CA
Died: November 9, 1980 from heart attack, ashes scattered at Pickfair
Related to A.W. Schwalberg (spouse)

N

Nabors, Jim...{13/12}
6439 Hollywood Boulevard (North)
Near: Schtromberg Jewelers
Category/As: Live Theater as Actor
Dedicated on January 31, 1991
Real name: same or unknown

Nagel, Conrad...{16/42}
1719 Vine Street (West)
Near: parking lot
Category/As: Motion Pictures as Actor
For: Little Women (1918)
Born: March 16, 1897 in Keokuk, IA   Died: 1970
Awards: Oscar

Nagel, Conrad...{17/38}
1750 Vine Street (East)
Near: Capitol Record Bldg
Category/As: Radio as Host
For: The Radio Reader's Digest (1942-1945)

Nagel, Conrad...{17/19}
1750 Vine Street (East)
Near: Capitol Record Bldg
Category/As: Television as Actor

Naish, J. Carrol...{20/32}
6161 Hollywood Boulevard (North)
Near: Network Body Shop
Category/As: Television as Actor

For: Life With Luigi (1948) CBS
Real name: Joseph Carrol Naish
Born: January 21, 1897   Died: 1973

Naldi, Nita...{28/27}
6314 Hollywood Boulevard (South)
Near: DAV Tech Computers
Category/As: Motion Pictures as Actress
For: Blood & Sand (1922)
Real name: Anita Donna Dooley
Born: April 1, 1899   Died: 1961, and buried in Woodside, NY

Nash, Ogden...{23/25}
6274 Hollywood Boulevard (South)
Near: parking lot
Category/As: Television as Panelist
For: Masquerade Party (1953)
Ral name: Frederich O. Nash
Born: August 19, 1902   Died: 1971

Nazimova...{21/61}
6140 Hollywood Boulevard (South)
Near: Henry Fonda Theater
Category/As: Motion Pictures as Actress
For: Camille (1921)
Real name: Alla Nazimoffa
Born: June 4, 1879 in Yalta, Russia
Died: 1945, from coronary thrombosis and buried in Glendale, CA

Nederlander, James...{18/44}
6233 Hollywood Boulevard (North)
Near: Pantages Theater
Category/As: Live Theater as Producer
For: Annie
Dedicated on November 7, 1986
Real name: same or unknown
Born: 1922 in Detroit, MI

Negri, Pola...{05/01}
6935 Hollywood Boulevard (North)
Near: Casablanca Tours
Category/As: Motion Pictures as Actress
For: Forbidden Paradise (1929)
Real name: Apolonia Mathias-Chalupec
Born: December 31, 1894 in Janowa, Poland
Died: 1987, from brain tumor and buried in Los Angeles, CA

Negulesco, Jean...{22/49}
6200 Hollywood Boulevard (South)
Near: parking lot
Category/As: Motion Pictures as Director
For: Johnny Belinda (1948)
Real name: same or unknown
Born: February 29, 1900 in Craiova, Rumania
Studio: Fox

Neilan, Marshall...{18/45}
6233 Hollywood Boulevard (North)
Near: Pantages Theater
Category/As: Motion Pictures as Director
For: Rebecca of Sunnybrook Farm (1917)
Real name: Marshall A. Neilan
Born: April 11, 1891 in San Bernadino, CA   Died: 1958, from cancer
Studio: MGM

Nelson, Barry...{18/11}
6263 Hollywood Boulevard (North)
Near: Equitible Building
Category/As: Television as Actor
For: My Favorite Husband (1953) George Cooper
Real name: Robert Haakon Nielson
Born: April 16, 1920 in San Francisco, CA

Nelson, Gene...{04/61}
7005 Hollywood Boulevard (North)

Near: Hollywood Momentos
Category/As: Motion Pictures as Director
For: Harum Scarum (1965)
Dedicated on September 24, 1990
Real name: Leander Berg
Born: 1920

Nelson, Harriet...{06/41}
6819 Hollywood Boulevard (North)
Near: Hollywood Tours & Gifts
Category/As: Television as Actress
For: Ozzie & Harriett (1952-1960) ABC
Real name: Harriet Hilliard
Born: July 18, 1914 in Des Moines, IA
Related to Ozzie Nelson (spouse), Rick Nelson, David Nelson (sons)

Nelson, Ozzie...{11/13}
6555 Hollywood Boulevard (North)
Near: Legends of Hollywood
Category/As: Television as Actor
For: Ozzie and Harriet (1952-1960)
Real name: Oswald Nelson
Born: March 20, 1907 in Jersey City, NJ
Died: 1975, from cancer and buried in Los Angeles, CA
Related to Harriet Nelson (spouse), Rick Nelson, David Nelson (sons)

Nelson, Ozzie & Harriet...{23/16}
6256 Hollywood Boulevard (South)
Near: vacant lot
Category/As: Radio as Actors
For: Adventures of Ozzie & Harriet Show (1944)
Real name: (see individual stars)
Studio: CBS
Related to David and Rick Nelson (sons)

Nelson, Rick...{26/09}
1501 Vine Street (West)
Near: shopping center
Category/As: Recording as Singer
For: Hello, Mary Lou
Real name: Eric Nelson
Born: May 8, 1940 in New Jersey
Died: 1985, from airplane crash and buried in Los Angeles, CA
Related to Ozzie & Harriet Nelson (parents), David Nelson (brother)

Nesbitt, John...{16/28}
1719 Vine Street (West)
Near: parking lot
Category/As: Motion Pictures as Narrator
For: Main Street on the March (1941)
Real name: same or unknown
Born: August 23, 1910 in B.C. Canada   Died: 1960, from heart attack
Studio: MGM

Nesbitt, John...{22/41}
6200 Hollywood Boulevard (South)
Near: parking lot
Category/As: Radio as Narrator
For: Passing Parade (1936-1948)

Newman, Alfred...{17/93}
1708 Vine Street (East)
Near: Collectors Book Store
Category/As: Recording as Composer
For: Love is a Many Splendored Thing
Real name: same or unknown
Born: March 17, 1901 in New Haven, CT
Died: 1970, from emphysema and buried in Glendale, CA
Awards: Oscar

Newton, Wayne...{05/61}
6925 Hollywood Boulevard (North)
Near: Mann's Chinese Theater
Category/As: Recording as Singer
For: Danke Schoen

Real name: same or unknown
Born: April 3, 1942 in VA

Newton-John, Olivia...{05/67}
6925 Hollywood Boulevard (North)
Near: Mann's Chinese Theater
Category/As: Recording as Singer
For: I Honestly Love You
Dedicated on August 5, 1981
Real name: same or unknown
Born: September 26, 1948 in England

Niblo, Fred...{38/26}
7000 Hollywood Boulevard (South)
Near: Roosevelt Hotel
Category/As: Motion Pictures as Director
For: Ben Hur (1926)
Real name: Frederico Nobile
Born: January 6, 1874 in New York, NY
Died: 1948, from pneumonia and buried in Glendale, CA

Nichols, Nichelle...{10/03}
6633 Hollywood Boulevard (North)
Near: Fame of Hollywood Cafe
Category/As: Television as Actress
For: Star Trek (1966) as Commander Ohura
Dedicated on January 9, 1992
Real name: same or unknown

Nielsen, Leslie...{11/38}
6541 Hollywood Boulevard (North)
Near: Janes House
Category/As: Motion Pictures as Actor
For: Airplane (1980) as Dr. Rumack
Dedicated on December 9, 1988
Real name: same or unknown
Born: 1925   Studio: Paramount

Niles, Ken...{08/41}
6715 Hollywood Boulevard (North)
Near: Outpost Building
Category/As: Radio as Announcer
For: Big Town (1937) CBS
Real name: same or unknown
Born: December 9, 1906 in Livingston, MT   Died: 1988

Niles, Wendell...{16/44}
1719 Vine Street (West)
Near: parking lot
Category/As: Radio as Actor
For: The Adventures of Philip Marlow (1947)
Real name: same or unknown
Born: December 29, 1904 in Livingston, MT
Studio: NBC

Nilsson, Anna Q. ...{22/11}
6150 Hollywood Boulevard (South)
Near: Network Body Shop
Category/As: Motion Pictures as Actress
For: Sunset Boulevard (1950)
Real name: Anna Querentia Nilsson
Born: March 30, 1890 in Sweden   Died: 1974, from natural causes

Nimoy, Leonard...{09/63}
6655-F5 Hollywood Boulevard (North)
Near: Souvenir Shop
Category/As: Motion Pictures as Actor
For: Star Trek (1979) as Mr. Spock
Dedicated on January 16, 1985
Real name: same or unknown
Born: March 26, 1931 in Boston, MA

Niven, David...{30/24}
6384 Hollywood Boulevard (South)
Near: Popeye Chicken

Category/As: Motion Pictures as Actor
For: Separate Tables (1958)
Real name: James David Niven
Born: March 15, 1909 in Kirrkmuir, Scotland
Died: 1983, from lateral sclerosis
Awards: Oscar

Niven, David...{27/49}
1627 Vine Street (West)
Near: parking lot
Category/As: Television as Actor
For: The Rogues (1964)

Nixon, Marian...{17/41}
1750 Vine Street (East)
Near: Capitol Record Bldg
Category/As: Motion Pictures as Actress
For: Rebecca of Sunnybrook Farm (1932)
Born: October 20, 1904 in Superior, WI
Died: February 13, 1983 after heart surgery
Related to Ben Lyon, William Seiter (spouses)

Nolan, Lloyd...{17/35}
1750 Vine Street (East)
Near: Capitol Record Bldg
Category/As: Television as Actor
For: Bataan (1943)
Real name: same or unknown
Born: August 11, 1902 in San Francisco, CA
Died: 1985, from cancer and buried in Los Angeles, CA
Studio: Fox   Awards: Emmy

Normand, Mabel...{06/35}
6819 Hollywood Tours & Gifts
Category/As: Motion Pictures as Comedienne
For: Barney Oldfield's Race for Life (1912)
Real name: Mabel Fortescue
Born: November 16, 1894 in Boston, MA
Died: 1930, from tuberculosis and buried in Los Angeles, CA
Studio: Mack Sennett

Norris, Chuck...{38/48}
7024 Hollywood Boulevard (South)
Near: Roosevelt Hotel parking
Category/As: Motion Pictures as Actor
For: Various kung fu movies
Dedicated on December 15, 1989
Real name: Carlos Ray Norris

Novak, Kim...{28/49}
6336 Hollywood Boulevard (South)
Near: Alberts Hosery
Category/As: Motion Pictures as Actress
For: Picnic (1955)
Real name: Marilyn Novak
Born: February 13, 1933 in Chicago, IL
Studio: Columbia

Novarro, Ramon...{29/04}
6350 Hollywood Boulevard (South)
Near: Combo's Pizza
Category/As: Motion Pictures as Actor
For: Ben Hur (1926)
Real name: Jose Ramon Samaniegos
Born: February 6, 1889 in Durango, Mexico
Died: 1968, murdered and buried in Los Angeles, CA
Studio: MGM

O'Brian, Hugh...{10/39}
6613 1/2 Hollywood Boulevard (North)
Near: L.A. Roxx

Category/As: Television as Actor
For: Wyatt Earp (1955)
Real name: Hugh Krampe
Born: April 19, 1925 in NY

O'Brien, Dave...{18/19}
6251 Hollywood Boulevard (North)
Near: Dos Burritos
Category/As: Motion Pictures as Actor
For: Phantom of 42nd Street (1945)
Real name: David Barclay
Born: May 31, 1912 in TX   Died: 1969
Awards: Emmy

O'Brien, Edmond...{16/48}
1719 Vine Street (West)
Near: parking lot
Category/As: Motion Pictures as Actor
For: The Barefoot Contessa (1954)
Real name: same or unknown
Born: September 10, 1915 in New York, NY
Died: 1985, from Alzheimer's disease and buried in Culver City, CA
Awards: Oscar

O'Brien, Edmond...{12/11}
6523 Hollywood Boulevard (North)
Near: Maya Shoes
Category/As: Television as Actor
For: Sam Benedict (1962) NBC

O'Brien, Eugene...{24/73}
1614 Vine Street (East)
Near: parking lot
Category/As: Motion Pictures as Actor
For: The Perfect Lover (1919)
Real name: same or unknown
Born: November 14, 1882 in Boulder, CO   Died: 1966, from pneumonia

O'Brien, George...{19/21}
6207 Hollywood Boulevard (North)
Near: parking lot
Category/As: Motion Pictures as Actor
For: She Wore a Yellow Ribbon (1949)
Real name: same or unknown
Born: April 19, 1900 in San Francisco, CA   Died: 1985, from stroke
Studio: RKO

O'Brien, Margaret...{33/52}
6608 Hollywood Boulevard (South)
Near: Frederick's of Hollywood
Category/As: Motion Pictures as Actress
For: Meet Me in St. Louis (1944)
Real name: Angela Maxine O'Brien
Born: January 15, 1937 in Los Angeles, CA
Awards: Oscar

O'Brien, Margaret...{24/45}
1630 Vine Street (East)
Near: parking lot
Category/As: Television as Actress

O'Brien, Pat...{26/52}
1541 Vine Street (West)
Near: TAV Celebrity Center
Category/As: Motion Pictures as Actor
For: Some Like It Hot (1959)
Real name: William Joseph O'Brien, Jr.
Born: November 11, 1899 in Milwaukee, WI
Died: 1983, from heart attack and buried in Culver City, CA

O'Brien, Pat...{22/63}
Near: West Coast Ensemble
Category/As: Television as Actor
For: Harrigan and Son (1960)

O'Connor, Donald...{24/02}
1680 Vine Street (East)
Near: Taft Building
Category/As: Motion Pictures as Actor
For: Francis Talking Mule Series (1950)
Real name: Donald David Dixon Ronald O'Connor
Born: August 28, 1925 in Chicago, IL
Studio: Universal

O'Connor, Donald...{04/31}
7021 Hollywood Boulevard (North)
Near: Hollywood Galaxy
Category/As: Television as Dancer
For: The Donald O'Connor Show (1953)

O'Day, Molly...{17/109}
1700 Vine Street (East)
Near: Equitible Building
Category/As: Motion Pictures as Actress
For: Various B Movies
Real name: Molly Noonan
Born: February 11, 1911 in NJ   Died: 1987, from cancer

O'Hanlon, George...{31/47}
6426 Hollywood Boulevard (South)
Near: Hollywood Discount Center
Category/As: Motion Pictures as Actor
For: Battle Stations (1955)
Real name: George Rice
Born: November 23, 1917   Died: 1989, from stroke

O'Hara, Maureen...{38/08}
7000 Hollywood Boulevard (South)
Near: Roosevelt Hotel
Category/As: Motion Pictures as Actress
For: Miracle on 34th Street (1947)
Real name: Muareen Fitzsimmons
Born: August 17, 1920 in Milltown, Ireland
Studio: RKO

O'Keefe, Walter...{20/16}
6161 Hollywood Boulevard (North)
Near: Network Body Shop
Category/As: Radio as Host
For: Double or Nothing (1940)
Real name: same or unknown
Born: August 18, 1900 in Hartford, CT
Studio: CBS

O'Neill, Henry...{06/48}
6819 Hollywood Boulevard (North)
Near: Hollywood Tours & Gifts
Category/As: Motion Pictures as Actor
For: Billy the Kid (1941)
Real name: same or unknown
Born: August 10, 1891 in NJ   Died: 1961

O'Shea, Michael...{24/10}
1680 Vine Street (East)
Near: Taft Building
Category/As: Television as Actor
For: It's A Great Life (1954) as Denny
Real name: Edward Francis Michael Joseph O'Shea
Born: March 17, 1906 in Long Island, NY
Died: December, 1973, from heart condition
Related to: Virginia Mayo

O'Sullivan, Maureen...{11/44}
6541 Hollywood Boulevard (North)
Near: Janes House
Category/As: Motion Pictures as Actress
For: Pride and Prejudice (1940)
Dedicated on February 27, 1991
Real name: same or unknown
Born: May 17, 1911 in County Roscommon, Ireland

Related to John Farrow (spouse), Mia Farrow (daughter)

Oakie, Jack...{36/34}
6752 8A Hollywood Boulevard (South
Near: International Kitchen
Category/As: Motion Pictures as Actor
For: Million Dollar Legs (1932)
Real name: Lewis Delany Offield
Born: November 12, 1903   Died: 1978, from aneurysm

Oberon, Merle...{23/39}
6274 Hollywood Boulevard (South)
Near: parking lot
Category/As: Motion Pictures as Actress
For: Wuthering Heights (1939)
Real name: Estelle Merle O'Brien Thompson
Born: February 19, 1911 in Tasmania
Died: 1979, from stroke and buried in Glendale, CA
Related to Lucien Ballard (spouse)

Oliver, Edna May...{27/47}
1627 Vine Street (West)
Near: parking lot
Category/As: Motion Pictures as Actress
For: Alice in Wonderland (1933)
Real name: Edna May Cox-Oliver
Born: November 1883 in Malden, MA
Died: November 8, 1842, from intestinal disorder and buried in Glendale, CA
Studio: RKO

Olivier, Laurence...{15/30}
6321 Hollywood Boulevard (North)
Near: Vine Theater
Category/As: Motion Pictures as Actor
For: Hamlet (1948)
Real name: Laurence Kerr Olivier
Born: May 22, 1907 in England   Died: 1989, from natural causes
Awards: Oscar
Related to Vivien Leigh, Joan Plowright (spouses)

Olmos, Edward James...{04/24}
7021 Hollywood Boulevard (North)
Near: Hollywood Galaxy
Category/As: Motion Pictures as Actor
For: Stand and Deliver
Dedicated on February 24, 1992

Orlando, Tony...{14/11}
6385 Hollywood Boulevard (North)
Near: Security Pacific Bank
Category/As: Recording as Singer
For: Tie a Yellow Ribbon
Dedicated on March 21, 1990
Real name: Michael Anthony Orlando Cassavitis

Ormandy, Eugene...{37/108}
Near: Hollywood Center
Category/As: Recording as Conductor
Real name: Eugene Blau
Born: November 18, 1899   Died: 1985

Owens, Buck...{09/35}
6667 Hollywood Boulevard (North)
Near: Musso & Frank Grill
Category/As: Recording as Singer
For: Waitin' In Your Welfare Line
Real name: same or unknown
Born: August 12, 1929 in Sherman, TX

Owens, Gary...{08/04}
6743 Hollywood Boulevard (North)
Near: B. Dalton Book
Category/As: Radio as Announcer
For: L.A. radio show
Real name: Gary Altman
Born: May 10, 1936 in SD

P

Paar, Jack...{22/47}
6200 Hollywood Boulevard (South)
Near: parking lot
Category/As: Television as Host
For: Tonight Show (1957-1962) NBC
Real name: same or unknown
Born: May 1, 1918 in Canton, OH

Paderewski...{23/52}
6286 Hollywood Boulevard (South)
Near: Metro Rail Field Office
Category/As: Recording as Composer
For: Moonlight Sanata (1937)
Real name: Ignace Jan Paderewski
Born: November 6, 1860 in Kuilovka, Pland
Died: 1941, from pneumonia and buried in Arlington, VA

Page, Anita...{21/23}
6100 Hollywood Boulevard (South)
Near: Chevron Gas Station
Category/As: Motion Pictures as Actress
For: Jungle Bride (1933)
Real name: Anita Pomares
Born: August 4, 1910 in NY

Page, Patti...{36/44}
6760 Hollywood Boulevard (South)
Near: The Dome
Category/As: Recording as Singer
For: How Much Is That Doggie In The Window?
Real name: Clara Ann Fowler
Born: November 8, 1927

Paige, Janis...{33/80}
6624 Hollywood Boulevard (South)
Near: The Gallery
Category/As: Motion Pictures as Actress
For: Silk Stockings (1957)
Real name: Donna Mae Jaden
Born: September 16, 1923

Pal, George...{17/68}
1724 Vine Street (East)
Near: parking lot
Category/As: Motion Pictures as Puppeteer
For: Tom Thumb (1958)
Born: February 1, 1908 in Ceglad, Hungary   Died: 1980
Studio: MGM   Awards: Oscar

Palance, Jack...{33/56}
6608 Hollywood Boulevard (South)
Near: Frederick's of Hollywood
Category/As: Television as Actor
For: Ripley's Believe it or Not (1982)
Real name: Vladmir J. Palahnuik
Born: February 18, 1920 in Lattimer, PA
Awards: Oscar

Pallette, Eugene...{35/05}
6702 Hollywood Boulevard (South)
Near: Hollywood Beauty
Category/As: Motion Pictures as Actor
For: My Man Godfrey (1936)
Real name: same or unknown
Born: July 8, 1889   Died: 1954, from long illness

Palmer, Lilli...{04/51}
7013 Hollywood Boulevard (North)
Near: Shelly's Cafe
Category/As: Television as Actress

For: Body and Soul (1947)
Real name: Marcia Lilli Peiser
Born: May 24, 1914 in Posten, Germany
Died: 1986, from cancer and buried in Glendale, CA
Related to Rex Harrision, Carlos Thompson (spouses)

Pangborn, Franklin...{25/94}
1500 Vine Street (East)
Near: Home Savings
Category/As: Motion Pictures as Actor
For: The Bank Dick (1940)
Born: January 23, 1893 in Newark, NJ
Died: 1958, and buried in Glendale, CA

Parker, Eleanor...{28/63}
6340 Hollywood Boulevard (South)
Near: (closed) Mr. Submarine
Category/As: Motion Pictures as Actress
For: Of Human Bondage (1946)
Born: June 26, 1922 in Cedarville, OH
Studio: MGM   Awards: Oscar (3)

Parker, Frank...{06/21}
6821 Hollywood Boulevard (North)
Near: Hollywood Hamburger
Category/As: Recording as Singer
For: Arthur Godfrey Show (1945)
Real name: same or unknown
Born: November 8, 1900 in MO   Died: 1962

Parker, Jean...{34/35}
Near: vacant
Category/As: Motion Pictures as Actress
For: Little Women (1933)
Real name: Luisa-Stephanie Zelinska
Born: August 11, 1912

Parkyakarkus...{17/92}
1708 Vine Street (East)
Near: Collectors Book Store
Category/As: Radio as Comedian
For: Meet Me at Parky's (1945-1947)
Real name: Harry Einstein
Born: 1904 in Boston, MA   Died: 1958, from heart attack

Parrish, Helen...{18/09}
6263 Hollywood Boulevard (North)
Near: Equitible Building
Category/As: Motion Pictures as Actress
For: Our Gang (1927)
Born: March 12, 1922 in Columbus, GA   Died: 1959, from long illness

Parsons, Louella...{28/05}
6302 Hollywood Boulevard (South)
Near: New York Pizza Express
Category/As: Radio as Gossip Reporter
For: Hollywood Hotel (1931) CBS
Real name: Louella Oettinger
Born: August 6, 1893 in Freport, IL
Died: 1972, from arteriosclerosis and buried in Culver City, CA

Parsons, Louella O. ...{31/31}
6418 Hollywood Boulevard (South)
Near: Hollywood Discount Center
Category/As: Motion Pictures as Columnist
For: Hollywood Hotel (1937)

Parton, Dolly...{35/16}
6712 Hollywood Boulevard (South)
Near: Egyptian Theater
Category/As: Recording as Singer
For: 9 to 5
Dedicated on June 14, 1984
Born: January 19, 1946

Pasternak, Joe...{26/75}
1549 Vine Street (West)
Near: TAV Celebrity Center
Category/As: Motion Pictures as Producer
For: Please Don't Eat the Daisies (1960)
Dedicated on April 19, 1984
Born: September 19, 1901 in Hungary
Died: 1991, from Parkinson's disease
Studio: MGM

Paul, Les & Mary Ford...{26/70}
1549 Vine Street (West)
Near: TAV Celebrity Center
Category/As: Recording as Musicians
For: How High the Moon
Real Names: Lester William Polfus, Colleen Summers
Born: Les, June 9, 1915 in Pasadena, CA ,
          Mary, July 7, 1924 in Waukesha, WI
Died: 1977 (Mary)

Paxinou, Katrina...{27/87}
1645 Vine Street (West)
Near: Hollywood Vine Building
Category/As: Motion Pictures as Actress
For: For Whom the Bell Tolls (1943)
Real name: Katrinas Constantopoulous
Born: 1901 in Piraeus, Greece   Died: 1973, from cancer
Studio: Paramount   Awards: Oscar

Payne, John...{20/54}
6125 Hollywood Boulevard (North)
Near: Pep Boys
Category/As: Motion Pictures as Actor
For: Springtime in the Rockies (1942)
Born: May 23, 1912 in Roanoke, VA   Died: 1989, from heart failure
Studio: 20th Century
Related to Anne Shirley, Gloria De Haven (spouses)

Payne, John...{09/06}
6687 Hollywood Boulevard (North)
Near: Me & Me
Category/As: Television as Actor
For: The Restless Gun (1957-1958)
Studio: NBC

Pearce, Al...{28/45}
6330 Hollywood Boulevard (South)
Near: Tacosy Marsicos
Category/As: Radio as Actor
For: Al Pierce & His Gang (1933)
Real name: same or unknown

Pearl, Jack...{24/14}
1680 Vine Street (East)
Near: Taft Building
Category/As: Radio as Comedian
For: The Jack Pearl Show (1933) as Peter Pfeiffer
Real name: Jack Pearlman
Born: 1894 in NY   Died: 1982
Studio: NBC

Pearson, Drew...{10/23}
6623 Hollywood Boulevard (North)
Near: Mona Lisa Tops
Category/As: Radio as Newscaster
For: Calling America (1939)
Real name: Andrew Pearson
Born: December 13, 1897 in Evanston, IL   Died: 1969
Studio: Mutual System

Peary, Harold...{27/70}
1637 Vine Street (West)
Near: Early World Restaurant
Category/As: Radio as Actor
For: The Great Gildersleeve (1941) as Throckmorton P. Gildersleeve

Real name: same or unknown
Born: July 25, 1908 in San Leandro, CA   Died: 1985, from heart attack
Studio: NBC

Peary, Harold...{16/37}
1719 Vine Street (West)
Near: parking lot
Category/As: Television as Actor
For: The Great Gildersleeve (1950)

Peck, Gregory...{21/03}
6100 Hollywood Boulevard (South)
Near: Chevron Gas Station
Category/As: Motion Pictures as Actor
For: To Kill a Mockingbird (1962)
Real name: Eldred Gregory Peck
Born: April 5, 1916 in La Jolla, CA
Awards: Oscar

Peerce, Jan...{16/92}
1749 Vine Street (West)
Near: parking lot
Category/As: Recording as Opera Singer
For: Vesti La Giubba
Real name: Jacob Perelmuth
Born: June 3, 1904 in NY   Died: 1984, from pneumonia
Studio: NBC

Penner, Joe...{17/23}
1750 Vine Street (East)
Near: Capitol Record Bldg
Category/As: Radio as Comedian
For: Joe Penner Show (1936-1940)
Real name: Jozsef Pinter
Born: November 11, 1904 in Hungary
Died: 1941, from heart attack and buried in Glendale, CA
Studio: CBS

Peppard, George...{09/21}
6675 Hollywood Boulevard (North)
Near: Vogue Theater (closed)
Category/As: Motion Pictures as Actor
For: The Carpetbaggers (1964)
Dedicated on July 17, 1985
Real name: same or unknown
Born: October 1, 1928 in Detroit, MI

Perkins, Anthony...{06/19}
6821 Hollywood Boulevard (North)
Near: Hollywood Hambruger
Category/As: Motion Pictures as Actor
For: Psycho (1960)
Born: April 4, 1932 in New York   Died: 1992 from A.I.D.S.
Studio: Paramount

Perreau, Gigi...{22/51}
6200 Hollywood Boulevard (South)
Near: parking lot
Category/As: Television as Actress
For: Betty Hutton Show (1959) CBS
Real name: Ghislaine Elizabeth Marie Theresa Perreau-Saussine
Born: February 6, 1941 in Los Angeles, CA
Related to Jeanine Perreau (sister(, Peter Miles (brother)

Perrin, Jack...{16/97}
1749 Vine Street (West)
Near: parking lot
Category/As: Motion Pictures as Acror
For: Blind Husbands (1919)
Real name: same or unknown
Born: Three Rivers, MI

Peters, Bernadette...{35/14}
6706 Hollywood Boulevard (South)
Near: burned out
Category/As: Live Theater as Actress

For: Sunday in the Park with George (1984)
Dedicated on April 23, 1987
Real name: Bernadette Lazzaro
Born: 1948

Peters, Brock...{38/59}
7024 Hollywood Boulevard (South)
Near: Roosevelt Hotel parking
Category: Live Theater
Dedicated on April 23, 1992
Real name: Brock Fisher
Born: 1927

Peters, House...{20/06}
6161 Hollywood Boulevard (North)
Near: Network Body Shop
Category/As: Motion Pictures as Actor
For: The Great Divide (1915)
Real name: same or unknown
Born: March 28, 1880 in England   Died: 1967

Peters, Susan...{27/15}
1605 Vine Street (West)
Near: Molly Coney Island
Category/As: Motion Pictures as Actress
For: Meet John Doe (1941) MGM
Real name: Suzanne Carnahan
Born: July 3, 1921 in Spokane, WA
Died: October 23, 1952, from kidney infection
Related to Richard Quine (spouse)

Petrova, Olga...{33/28}
6562 Hollywood Boulevard (South)
Near: Hollywood Toys Inc.
Category/As: Motion Pictures as Actress
For: Daughter of Destiny (1918)
Real name: Muriel Harding
Born: February 19, 1886 in Great Britain   Died: 1977

Phillips, Dorothy...{29/10}
6358 Hollywood Boulevard (South)
Near: Glad's Discount Mini-Mall
Category/As: Motion Pictures as Actress
For: The Man Who Shot Liberty Valance (1962)
Real name: Dorothy Strible
Born: December 23, 1892   Died: 1980

Pickford, Jack...{26/38}
1501 Vine Street (West)
Near: Shopping Center
Category/As: Motion Pictures as Actor
For: Tom Sawyer (1917)
Real name: Jack Smith
Born: August 18, 1896 in Toronto, Canada
Died: 1933, from multiple neuritis and buried in Glendale, CA
Related to Mary Pickford (sister)

Pickford, Mary...{23/46}
6282 Hollywood Boulevard (South)
Near: Original Coney Island
Category/As: Motion Pictures as Actress
For:
Real name: Gladys Mary Smith
Born: April 8, 1892 in Toronto, Canada
Died: 1979, from cerebral hemorrhage and buried in Glendale, CA
Studio: United Artists   Awards: Oscar
Related to Douglas Fairbanks, Owen Moore, Buddy Rogers (spouses),
            Jack Pickford (brother)
Note: Co-founder or United Artists

Pidgeon, Walter...{31/27}
6410 Hollywood Boulevard (South)
Near: F.W. Woolworth
Category/As: Motion Pictures as Actor
For: How Green Was My Valley? (1941)

Born: September 23, 1897 in New Brunswick, Canada
Died: September 25, 1984, from stroke after fall
Studio: MGM

Pierce, Webb...{24/90}
1600 Vine Street (East)
Near: DMV
Category/As: Recording as Singer
For: Slowly
Real name: same or unknown
Born: August 8, 1926   Died: 1981, from cancer

Pinza, Enzio...{27/16}
1605 Vine Street (West)
Near: Molly Coney Island
Category/As: Recording as Opera Singer
Real name: Fortunato Pinza
Born: May 18, 1892 in Italy   Died: 1957, from stroke

Pioneers, Sons of the...{06/16}
6841 Hollywood Boulevard (North)
Near: Pose with Stars
Category/As: Recording as Vocal gGoup
For: Cool Water

Pitts, ZaSu...{33/18}
6556 Hollywood Boulevard (South)
Near: Hollywood Jewelry Exchange
Category/As: Motion Pictures as Actress
For: Life With Father (1947)
Real name: Eliza Susan Pitts
Born: January 3, 1898 in Parsons, KS
Died: 1963, from cancer and buried in Culver City, CA

Pollard, Snub...{13/41}
6415 Hollywood Boulevard (North)
Near: Diamalaye
Category/As: Motion Pictures as Comedian
For: A Pocketful of Miracles (1961)
Real name: Harold Fraser
Born: April 2, 1886 in Australia
Died: 1962 and buried in Los Angeles, CA

Pons, Lily...{38/16}
7000 Hollywood Boulevard (South)
Near: Roosevelt Hotel
Category/As: Recording as Opera Singer
Real name: Alice Josephine Pons
Born: April 12, 1904 in France   Died: 1976, from cancer

Potter, H.C. ...{10/07}
6633 Hollywood Boulevard (North)
Near: Fame of Hollywood Cafe
Category/As: Motion Pictures as Director
For: The Farmer's Daughter (1947)
Real name: Henry C. Potter
Born: November 13, 1904 in New York   Died: 1977

Powell, David...{27/85}
1645 Vine Street (West)
Near: Hollywood Vine Building
Category/As: Motion Pictures as Actor
Real name: same or unknown
Died: 1925

Powell, Dick...{05/44}
6925 Hollywood Boulevard (North)
Near: Mann's Chinese Theater
Category/As: Motion Pictures as Actor
For: 42nd Street (1933)
Real name: same or unknown
Born: November 14, 1904 in Mountain View, AR
Died: 1963, from cancer and buried in Glendale, CA
Related to Joan Blondell, June Allyson (spouses)

Powell, Dick...{25/44}
1560 Vine Street (East)
Near: parking lot
Category/As: Radio as Actor
For: Richard Diamond, Private Detective (1949)
Studio: NBC

Powell, Dick...{08/07}
6743 Hollywood Boulevard (North)
Near: B. Dalton Book
Category/As: Television as Host
For: Co-Founder of Four Star Television

Powell, Eleanor...{26/69}
1549 Vine Street (West)
Near: TAV Celebrity Center
Category/As: Motion Pictures as Actress
For: Born to Dance (1936) MGM
Dedicated on February 15, 1984
Born: November 21, 1912 in Springfield, MA
Died: February, 1982, from cancer and buried in Hollywood, CA

Powell, Jane...{37/28}
6818 Hollywood Boulevard (South)
Near: vacant
Category/As: Motion Pictures as Actress
For: Seven Brides for Seven Brothers (1954) MGM
Real name: Suzanne Burce
Born: April 1, 1929 in Portland, OR

Powell, William...{24/36}
1636 Vine Street (East)
Near: vacant
Category/As: Motion Pictures as Actor
For: The Thin Man (1934) MGM
Real name: same or unknown
Born: July 29, 1892 in Pittsburg, PA
Died: 1984, from natural causes and ashes scattered
Related to Carole Lombard (spouse)

Power, Tyrone...{08/01}
6743 Hollywood Boulevard (North)
Near: B. Dalton Book
Category/As: Motion Pictures as Actor
For: The Sun Also Rises (1957)
Real name: Tyrone Edmund Power
Born: May 5, 1913 in Cincinnati, OH
Died: November 15, 1985, from heart attack and buried in Hollywood, CA
Studio: 20th Century
Related to Tyrone Power, Jr.

Powers, Mala...{29/16}
6360 Hollywood Boulevard (South)
Near: Africa Princess International
Category/As: Television as Actress
For: Hazel (1965)
Real name: Mary Ellen Powers
Born: December 29, 1931

Powers, Stefanie...{36/63}
6776 Hollywood Boulevard (South)
Near: McDonald's
Category/As: Television as Actress
For: Hart to Hart (19__)as Mrs. Hart
Dedicated on November 25, 1992
Real name: Stefanie Zofia Federkiewicz
Born: In Hollywood, CA

Prado, Perez...{26/50}
1541 Vine Street (West)
Near: TAV Celebrity Center
Category/As: Recording as Pianist
For: Cherry Pink and Apple Blossom White
Born: December 11, in Matangas, Cuba

Preminger, Otto...{33/78}
6624 Hollywood Boulevard (South)
Near: The Gallery
Category/As: Motion Pictures as Director
For: Porgy & Bess (1959)
Real name: same or unknown
Born: December 5, 1906 in Vienna, Austria   Died: 1986, from cancer
Related to Hope Bryse (spouse)

Presley, Elvis...{07/14}
6777 Hollywood Boulevard (North)
Near: Hollywood First National Building
Category/As: Recording as Singer
For: You Ain't Nothin' But a Hound Dog
Real name: Elvis Aaron Presley
Born: January 8, 1935 in Tupelo, MS
Died: August 16, 1977, from cardiac arrhythmia and buried in Memphis, TN
Related to Priscilla Presley (spouse)

Prevost, Marie...{19/13}
6211 Hollywood Boulevard (North)
Near: Capitol Records annex office
Category/As: Motion Pictures as Actress
For: Kiss Me Again (1925)
Real name: Marie Bickford Dunn
Born: November 8, 1898 in Canada   Died: 1937, from alcoholism

Price, Vincent...{19/23}
6207 Hollywood Boulevard (North)
Near: parking lot
Category/As: Motion Pictures as Actor
For: The Fly (1958)
Real name: same or unknown
Born: May 27, 1911 in St. Louis, MO

Price, Vincent...{12/39}
6501 Hollywood Boulevard (North)
Near: burned out
Category/As: Television as Actor
For: The Chevy Mystery Show (1960)

Primrose, William...{06/53}
6801 Hollywood Boulevard (North)
Near: vacant
Category/As: Recording as Violinist
Real name: same or unknown
Born: August 23, 1904 in Scotland   Died: 1956

Pringle, Aileen {08/29}
6723 Hollywood Boulevard (North)
Near: GiGi Boutique
Category/As: Motion Pictures as Actress
For: Jane Eyre (1933)
Real name: Aileen Bisbee
Born: July 23, 1895 in San Francisco, CA   Died: 1989

Pryor, Richard...{31/62}
6440 Hollywood Boulevard (South)
Near: Playmates
Category/As: Motion Pictures as Actor
For: See No Evil, Hear No Evil (19__)
Dedicated on May 20, 1993
Related to Rain Pryor (daughter)

Puente, Tito...{05/20}
6935 Hollywood Boulevard (North)
Near: Mann's Chinese parking
Category: Recording
Dedicated on August 14, 1990
Real name: same or unknown

Putnam, George...{30/11}
6378 Hollywood Boulevard (South)
Near: burned out
Category/As: Television as Newscaster

For: KTTV-TV (L.A.)
Dedicated on April 21, 1982

Quinn, Anthony...{18/18}
6251 Hollywood Boulevard (North)
Near: Dos Burritos
Category/As: Motion Pictures as Actor
For: Viva Zapata (1952)
Real name: same or unknown
Born: April 21, 1915 in Chihuahua, Mexico
Awards: Oscar

Raft, George...{22/05}
6150 Hollywood Boulevard (South)
Near: Network Body Shop
Category/As: Motion Pictures as Actor
For: Scarface, Shame of the Nation (1932)
Real name: George Rauft
Born: September 26, 1895 in New York, NY
Died: 1980, from leukemia and buried in Los Angeles, CA

Raft, George...{25/52}
1550 Vine Street (East)
Near: parking lot
Category/As: Television as Actor
For: I'm the Law (1952)

Rainier, Luise...{28/07}
6304 Hollywood Boulevard (South)
Near: 7 Tourist and Travel
Category/As: Motion Pictures as Actress
For: The Good Earth (1937)
Real name: same or unknown
Born: January 12, 1912 in Vienna
Studio: MGM   Awards: Oscar

Raines, Ella...{04/45}
7021 Hollywood Boulevard (North)
Near: Hollywood Galaxy
Category/As: Motion Pictures as Actress
For: Hail the Conquering Hero (1947)
Real name: Ella Wallace Raubles
Born: August 5, 1921 in Snoqualmie Falls, WA
Died: 1988, from throat cancer
Studio: Universal

Raines, Ella...{33/42}
6602 Hollywood Boulevard (South)
Near: J.J. Newberry
Category/As: Television as Actress
For: Janet Dean, R.N. (1957)

Rains, Claude...{31/01}
6400 Hollywood Boulevard (South)
Near: Pizza Deli
Category/As: Motion Pictures as Actor
For: Mr. Smith Goes to Washington (1939)
Real name: William Rains
Born: November 10, 1889 in Sandwich, NH
Died: 1967, from intestinal hemorrhage
Studio: Warner Brothers

Raitt, John...{21/40}
6126 Hollywood Boulevard (South)
Near: Henry Fonda Theater
Category: Live Theater
For: The Pajama Game (1957)
Dedicated on January 24, 1992
Real name: same or unknown
Born: 1921

Ralston, Esther...{34/27}
6664 Hollywood Boulevard (South)
Near: Supply Sergeant
Category/As: Motion Pictures as Actress
For: Tin Pan Alley (1940) as Nora Bayes
Born: September 17, 1902 in Bar Harbor, ME

Ralston, Vera...{17/21}
1750 Vine Street (East)
Near: Capitol Record Building
Category/As: Motion Pictures as Actress
For: Ice Capades (1941)
Real name: Vera Hruba
Born: July 12, 1921 in Prague, Czecholovakia
Studio: Republic
Related to Herbert J. Yates (spouse)

Rambeau, Marjorie...{28/52}
6336 Hollywood Boulevard (South)
Near: Alberts Hosery
Category/As: Motion Pictures as Actress
For: Tugboat Annie Sails Again (1941)
Real name: same or unknown
Born: July 15, 1889   Died: 1970

Rathbone, Basil...{11/25}
6551 Hollywood Boulevard (North)
Near: Bruce Fashion
Category/As: Motion Pictures as Actor
For: Sherlock Holmes (1939)
Real name: Philip St. John Basil Rathbone
Born: June 13, 1892 in Johannesburg, South Africa
Died: 1967, from heart attack and buried in Hartsdale, NY
Studio: Universal

Rathbone, Basil...{28/19}
6310 Hollywood Boulevard (South)
Near: Olympic Electronics
Category/As: Radio as Actor
For: Sherlock Holmes (1939-1946) NBC

Rathbone, Basil...{05/39}
6925 Hollywood Boulevard (North)
Near: Mann's Chinese Theater
Category/As: Television as Actor
For: David Copperfield (1935) as Dr. Murdstone

Ratoff, Gregory...{21/11}
6100 Hollywood Boulevard (South)
Near: Chevron Gas Station
Category/As: Motion Pictures as Actor
For: All About Eve (1950)
Real name: same or unknown
Born: April 20, 1897 in Petrograd, Russia   Died: 1950
Studio: Fox

Rawlinson, Herbert...{22/17}
6150 Hollywood Boulevard (South)
Near: Network Body Shop
Category/As: Motion Pictures as Actor
For: Playthings of Destiny (1921)
Real name: same or unknown
Born: October 13, 1885   Died: 1953

Rawls, Lou...{05/04}
6935 Hollywood Boulevard (North)
Near: Casablanca Tours
Category/As: Recording as Singer
Dedicated on December 15, 1982
Real name: same or unknown
Born: December 1, 1936

Ray, Charles...{14/46}
6357 Hollywood Boulevard (North)
Near: Star Fashion
Category/As: Motion Pictures as Actor
For: The Old Swimming Hole (1920)
Real name: same or unknown
Born: March 15, 1891 in Jacksonville, FL
Died: 1943, from aninfected tooth and buried in Glendale, CA

Ray, Johnnie...{19/03}
6211 Hollywood Boulevard (North)
Near: Capitol Records annex office
Category/As: Recording as Singer
For: Cry
Real name: John Ray
Born: January 10, 1927 in Dallas, OR   Died: 1990, from liver failure

Raye, Martha...{18/26}
6251 Hollywood Boulevard (North)
Near: parking lot
Category/As: Motion Pictures as Actress
For: Four Jills in a Jeep (1944)
Real name: Margaret Theresa Yvonne Reed
Born: August 27, 1916 in Butte, MT

Raye, Martha...{11/29}
6547 Hollywood Boulevard (North)
Near: Outfitters Wigs
Category/As: Television as Actress
For: The Martha Raye Show (1954-1956)

Raymond, Gene...{04/62}
7003 Hollywood Boulevard (North)
Near: Haagen Dazs
Category/As: Motion Pictures as Actor
For: Flying Down to Rio (1933)
Real name: Guion Raymond
Born: April 13, 1908   Died: 1965
Related to Jeanette MacDonald (spouse)

Raymond, Gene...{17/101}
1704 Vine Street (East)
Near: Krisseli's Center
Category/As: Television as Host
For: Fireside Theater (1953)

Reagan, Ronald...{30/12}
6378 Hollywood Boulevard (South)
Near: burned out
Category/As: Television as Actor
For: Death Valley Days (1962)
Real name: Ronald Wilson Reagan
Born: February 6, 1911 in Tampico, IL
Related to Jane Wyman (spouse)

Reddy, Helen...{17/22}
1750 Vine Street (East)
Near: Capitol Record Bldg
Category/As: Recording as Singer
For: I Am Woman
Real name: same or unknown
Born: October 25, 1941 in Australia
Awards: Grammy

Reed, Donna...{24/78}
1612 Vine Street (East)
Near: Hollywood Collateral
Category/As: Motion Pictures as Actress
For: It's A Wonderful Life (1947) as Mary Bailey

Real name: Donna Belle Mullenger
Born: January 27, 1921 in Dennison, IA
Died: 1986, from pancreatic cancer and buried in Los Angeles, CA

Reeves, George...{08/45}
6709 Hollywood Boulevard (North)
Near: American Leather Shop
Category/As: Television as Actor
For: The Adventures of Superman (1951) as Clark Kent/Superman
Real name: George Besselo
Born: April 6, 1914 in IA
Died: 1959, from suicide (gunshot) and buried in Glendale, CA

Reid, Wallace...{10/31}
6617 Hollywood Boulevard (North)
Near: Hollywood Fashion Place
Category/As: Motion Pictures as Director
For: The Birth of a Nation (1915)
Real name: William Wallace Reid
Born: April 15, 1891 in St. Louis, MO
Died: January 18, 1923, from drug addiction and buried in Glendale, CA

Reiner, Carl...{13/35}
6421 Hollywood Boulevard (North)
Near: Four M Shoes
Category/As: Television as Writer
For: The Dick Van Dyke Show (1961)
Real name: same or unknown
Born: March 29, 1922 in Bronx, NY
Studio: CBS   Awards: Emmy
Related to Rob Reiner (son)

Reis, Irving...{37/90}
6914 Hollywood Boulevard (South)
Near: Hamburger Hamlet
Category/As: Motion Pictures as Director
For: The Bachelor & the Bobby Soxer (1963)
Real name: same or unknown
Born: May 7, 1906 in New York, NY   Died: 1953
Studio: RKO

Remick, Lee...{21/16}
6100 Hollywood Boulevard (South)
Near: Chevron Gas Station
Category/As: Motion Pictures as Actress
For: The Days of Wine and Roses (1963)
Dedicated on April 29, 1991
Real name: same or unknown
Born: 1936   Died: 1991, from lung cancer

Renaldo, Duncan...{24/06}
1680 Vine Street (East)
Near: Taft Building
Category/As: Television as Actor
For: The Cisco Kid (1951-1956) as Cisco Kid
Real name: Renault Renaldo Duncan
Born: April 23, 1904   Died: September 3, 1980, from cancer
Studio: ZIV-TV

Rene, Henri...{24/81}
1610 Vine Street (East)
Near: Vine Street Bar & Grill
Category/As: Recording as Arranger
Born: December 29, 1906 in New York, NY

Rennahan, Ray...{37/101}
6916 Hollywood Boulevard (South)
Near: Gulliver's Travel
Category/As: Motion Pictures as Cinematographer
For: Gone With The Wind (1939)
Born: May 1, 1896 in Las Vegas, NV   Died: 1980

Renoir, Jean...{22/53}
6200 Hollywood Boulevard (South)
Near: parking lot

Category/As: Motion Pictures as Director
For: Madame Bouvary (1934)
Real name: same or unknown
Born: September 15, 1894 in Paris, France
Died: 1979, from Parkinson's disease
Awards: Oscar

Reynolds, Burt...{37/53}
6838 Hollywood Boulevard (South)
Near: El Capitan
Category/As: Motion Pictures as Actor
For: Smokey & the Bandit (1977)
Real name: Burton Leon Reynolds
Born: February 11, 1936 in Waycross, VA
Related to Loni Anderson (spouse)

Reynolds, Debbie...{34/11}
6656 Hollywood Boulevard (South)
Near: Ritz Theater
Category/As: Motion Pictures as Actress
For: Susan Slept Here (1954)
Real name: Mary Frances Reynolds
Born: April 1, 1932 in El Paso, TX
Studio: MGM
Related to Eddie Fisher (spouse)

Reynolds, Marjorie...{26/42}
1501 Vine Street (West)
Near: West Sunset Offices
Category/As: Television as Actress
For: The Life of Riley (1953-1958) as Peg Riley
Real name: Marjorie Goodspeed
Born: August 1, 1921 in ID

Reynolds, Quentin...{18/60}
6225 Hollywood Boulevard (North)
Near: vacant
Category/As: Radio as Narrator
For: Naked Africa (1959)
Died: 1965

Rice, Grantland...{24/48}
1630 Vine Street (East)
Near: parking lot
Category/As: Radio as Sportscaster
For: Grantland Rice Sportslights
Real name: same or uknown
Born: November 1, 1880 in TN   Died: 1954

Rich, Irene...{18/63}
6225 Hollywood Boulevard (North)
Near: vacant
Category/As: Motion Pictures as Actress
For: Joan of Arc (1948)
Real name: Irene Luther
Born: October 13, 1891 in Buffalo, NY   Died: 1988, from heart failure

Rich, Irene...{22/07}
6150 Hollywood Boulevard (South)
Near: Network Body Shop
Category/As: Radio as Host
For: Dear John (1933) NBC

Riddle, Nelson...{36/08}
6724 Hollywood Boulevard (South)
Near: Scientology
Category/As: Recording as Conductor
For: The Great Gatsby
Real name: same or unknown
Born: June 1, 1921   Died: 1985, from kidney failure

Riggs, Tommy & Betty Lou...{22/29}
6162 Hollywood Boulevard (South)
Near: Hastings Hotel
Category/As: Radio as Ventriloquist

For: Tommy Riggs and Betty Lou (1938)
Born: October 21, 1908 in PA   Died: 1967

Rin-Tin-Tin...{27/41}
1627 Vine Street (West)
Near: parking lot
Category/As: Motion Pictures as Dog
For: Where the North Begins (1925)
Born: 1916   Died: 1932

Ripley, Robert...{31/05}
6400 1/2 Hollywood Boulevard (South)
Near: Georgio Cassini
Category/As: Radio as Author
For: Believe It or Not (1930) NBC
Born: December 25, 1893   Died: 1949

Ritter, John...{10/12}
6631 Hollywood Boulevard (North)
Near: Hollywood Book City
Category/As: Television as Actor
For: Three's Company (1977) as Jack Tripper
Dedicated on September 28, 1983
Real name: Jonathan Ritter
Born: September 17, 1948 in Burbank, CA
Studio: ABC   Awards: Emmy
Related to Tex Ritter (father)

Ritter, Tex...{10/11}
6631 Hollywood Boulevard (North)
Near: Hollywood Book City
Category/As: Recording as Singer
For: High Noon
Real name: Maurice Woodward Ritter
Born: January 12, 1905 in Texas   Died: January 2, 1973, from heart attack
Related to John Ritter (son)

Ritz Brothers, The...{36/39}
6756 Hollywood Boulevard (South)
Near: The Dome
Category/As: Motion Pictures as Comedy Team
For: The Goldwyn Follies (1938)
Dedicated on November 17, 1987
Real names: Al, Jimmy and Harry Ritz
Born: Al, August 27, 1901; Jimmy, October 23, 1904;
           Harry, May 28, 1907 in Newark, NJ
Died: Al, 1965; Jimmy, 1986; Harry, 1986

Rivers, Joan...{38/46}
7024 Hollywood Boulevard (South)
Near: Roosevelt Hotel parking
Category/As: Television as Comedienne
For: Joan Rivers Show (19__)
Dedicated on July 26, 1989
Real name: Joan Sandra Molinsky
Born: June 8, 1933

Roach, Hal...{24/17}
1654 Vine Street (East)
Near: Wig Shop
Category/As: Motion Pictures as Pioneer
For: Founder Hal Roach Studios (1919)
Born: January 14, 1892 in Elmira, NY
Died: November, 1992
Studio: Hal Roach   Awards: Oscar

Robbins, Gale...{32/17}
6508 Hollywood Boulevard (South)
Near: Fox Theater (closed)
Category/As: Television as Actress
For: Double Jeopardy (1955)
Real name: same or unknown
Born: May 7, 1924   Died: 1980, from lung cancer

Robbins, Harold...{08/10}
6743 Hollywood Boulevard (North)

Near: B. Dalton Book Store
Category/As: Motion Pictures as Author
For: The Carpetbaggers (1964)
Real name: Francis Kane
Born: May 21, 1916 in NY

Robbins, Marty...{34/31}
6666 Hollywood Boulevard (South)
Near: vacant
Category/As: Recording as Singer
For: El Paso
Real name: Martin David Robinson
Born: September 26, 1925   Died: 1982

Roberts, Theodore...{22/33}
6162 Hollywood Boulevard (South)
Near: Hastings Hotel
Category/As: Motion Pictures as Actor
For: The Ten Commandments (1923)
Born: October 2, 1861 in San Francisco, IL
Died: 1928, from flu attack

Robertson, Cliff...{06/64}
6801 Hollywood Boulevard (North)
Near: vacant
Category/As: Motion Pictures as Actor
For: PT-109 (1963)
Dedicated on December 17, 1986
Real name: Clifford Parker Robertson III
Born: September 9, 1925 in La Jolla, CA
Awards: Oscar, Emmy

Robertson, Dale...{32/01}
6500 Hollywood Boulevard (South)
Near: Nikki's
Category/As: Television as Actor
For: Tales of Wells Fargo (1957-1960) NBC
Real name: Dayle Robertson
Born: July 14, 1923

Robeson, Paul...{34/16}
6658 Hollywood Boulevard (South)
Near: In-Step Shoes
Category/As: Motion Pictures as Actor
For: Showboat (1936)
Real name: same or unknown
Born: April 9, 1898
Died: 1976, from vascular disorder and buried in Hartsdale, NY

Robinson, Edward G. ...{18/48}
6233 Hollywood Boulevard (North)
Near: Pantages Theater
Category/As: Motion Pictures as Actor
For: Little Caesar (1931) as Caesar Enrico Bandello
Real name: Emmanuel Goldenberg
Born: December 12, 1893 in Bucharest, Rumania
Died: January 26, 1973, from cancer and buried in Ridgewood, NY
Studio: Warner Brothers   Awards: Oscar

Robinson, Smokey...{25/79}
1500 Vine Street (East)
Near: Home Savings
Category/As: Recording as Singer
For: Tears of a Clown
Dedicated on February 22, 1983
Real name: same or unknown
Born: February 19, 1940 in Detroit, MI

Robson, Mark...{17/66}
1724 Vine Street (East)
Near: parking lot
Category/As: Motion Pictures as Director
For: Von Ryan's Express (1965)
Born: December 4, 1913 in Montreal Canada
Died: 1978, from heart attack

Rochester...{12/25}
6513 Hollywood Boulevard (North)
Near: burned out
Category/As: Radio as Actor
For: The Jack Benny Program (1938-1964) NBC
Real name: Eddie Anderson
Born: September 18, 1905
Died: 1977, from heart attack and buried in Los Angeles, CA

Roddenberry, Gene...{09/11}
6683 Hollywood Boulevard (North)
Near: Lazar Shoes
Category/As: Television as Producer
For: Star Trek (1966)
Dedicated on September 4, 1985
Real name: same or unknown
Born: August 19, 1921 in El Paso, TX   Died: 1991, from blood clot

Rogers, Buddy...{20/46}
6141 Hollywood Boulevard (North)
Near: Mid-Towing
Category/As: Motion Pictures as Actor
For: Wings (1927)
Real name: Charles Rogers
Born: August 13, 1904 in Olathe, KS   Died: 1979
Related to Ginger Rogers, Mary Pickford (spouses)

Rogers, Ginger...{36/60}
6776 Hollywood Boulevard (South)
Near: McDonald's
Category/As: Motion Pictures as Actress
For: Kitty Foyle (1940)
Real name: Virginia Katherine McMath
Born: July 16, 1911 in Independence, MO
Studio: RKO   Awards: Oscar
Related to Lew Ayres, Jacques Bergerac, William Marshall,
        Buddy Rogers (spouses)

Rogers, Kenny...{34/30}
6666 Hollywood Boulevard (South)
Near: vacant
Category/As: Recording as Singer
For: Lucille
Real name: same or unknown
Born: August 21, 1938 in Texas

Rogers, Roy...(17/31)
1750 Vine Street (East)
Near: Capitol Record Building
Category/As: Motion Pictures as Actor
For: The Yellow Rose of Texas (1944)
Real name: Leonard Slye
Born: November 5, 1912 in Cincinnati, OH
Studio: Republic
Related to Dale Evans (spouse)

Rogers, Roy...{16/56}
1735 Vine Street (West)
Near: Palace
Category/As: Radio as Singer
For: The Roy Rogers Show (1944-1955)
Studio: Mutual

Rogers, Roy...{24/65}
1628 Vine Street (East)
Near: Brown Derby ruins
Category/As: Television as Actor
For: The Roy Rogers Show (1951-1956) NBC

Rogers, Will...{13/63}
6401 Hollywood Boulevard (North)
Near: Community Check Cashing
Category/As: Motion Pictures as Actor
For: Judge Priest (1934)

Real name: William Penn Adair Rogers
Born: November 4, 1879 in Cologan, OK
Died: 1935, from airplane crash and buried in Claremore, OK

Rogers, Will...{33/54}
6608 Hollywood Boulevard (South)
Near: Frederick's of Hollywood
Category/As: Radio as Humorist on NBC
For: The Gulf Show (1933-1935)

Roland, Gilbert...{36/12}
6730 Hollywood Boulevard (South)
Near: parking lot
Category/As: Motion Pictures as Actor
For: She Done Him Wrong (1933)
Real name: Luis Antonio Damaso de Alanso
Born: December 11, 1905 in Chihuahua, Mexico
Related to Constance Bennett (spouse)

Roland, Ruth...{23/18}
6256 Hollywood Boulevard (South)
Near: vacant lot
Category/As: Motion Pictures as Actress
For: The Masked Woman (1920)
Real name: same or unknown
Born: August 26, 1892 in San Francisco, CA
Died: 1937, from cancer and buried in Glendale, CA

Roman, Ruth...{34/41}
6672 Hollywood Boulevard (South)
Near: National Stereo
Category/As: Television as Actress
For: The Long Hot Summer (1965)
Born: December 22, 1924 in Boston, MA
Studio: RKO

Romero, Cesar...{10/35}
6615 Hollywood Boulevard (North)
Near: China King
Category/As: Motion Pictures as Actor
For: Viva Cisco Kid (1940)
Real name: same or unknown
Born: February 15, 1907 in New York, NY
Studio: Fox

Romero, Cesar...{16/31}
1719 Vine Street (West)
Near: parking lot
Category/As: Television as Actor
For: Batman (1965) as Joker
Real name: same or unknown
Born: February 15, 1907 in New York, NY

Rooney, Mickey...{17/77}
1718 Vine Street (East)
Near: Sun Palace Restaurant
Category/As: Motion Pictures as Actor
For: Andy Hardy Comes Home (19__) as Andy Hardy
Real name: Joe Yule, Jr.
Born: September 23, 1920 in Brooklyn, NY
Studio: MGM   Awards: Oscar, Emmy
Related to Ava Gardner, Martha Vickers (spouse)

Rooney, Mickey...{30/10}
6378 Hollywood Boulevard (South)
Near: burned out building
Category: Radio as Actor

Rooney, Mickey...{11/33}
6541 Hollywood Boulevard (North)
Near: Janes House
Category/As: Television as Actor
For: The Mickey Rooney Show (1954)

Rose, David...{32/25}
6512 Hollywood Boulevard (South)
Near: Roma Fashions
Category/As: Recording as Composer
For: Bonanza Theme Song
Real name: same or unknown
Born: June 24, 1910   Died: 1990, from heart disease

Ross, Diana...{35/20}
6712 Hollywood Boulevard (South)
Near: Egyptian Theater
Category/As: Recording as Singer
For: Baby Love
Dedicated on May 6, 1982
Real name: same or unknown
Born: March 26, 1944

Ross, Lanny...{07/02}
6777 Hollywood Boulevard (North)
Near: Hollywood First National Bldg
Category/As: Radio as Singer
For: The Packard Hour (1937) CBS
Real name: Lancelot Patrick Ross
Born: 1906   Died: 1988, from stroke

Rossen, Robert...{06/05}
6845 Hollywood Boulevard (North)
Near: Starline Tours & Gifts
Category/As: Motion Pictures as Director
For: All The King's Men (1949)
Real name: Robert Rosen
Born: March 16, 1908   Died: 1966

Roth, Lillian...{28/47}
6332 Hollywood Boulevard (South)
Near: Photo City
Category/As: Motion Pictures as Actress
For: Animal Crackers (1930)
Real name: Lillian Rutstein
Born: December 13, 1910   Died: 1980

Rowland, Henry...{28/44}
6330 Hollywood Boulevard (South)
Near: Tacosy Mariscos
Category/As: Television as Actor
For: Television Playhouse (1969)
Real name: same or unknown
Born: 1914   Died: 1984

Rowland, Richard...{26/72}
1549 Vine Street (West)
Near: TAV Celebrity Center
Category/As: Motion Pictures as Pioneer
For: Founder of Metro Film Corp. (1914)
Born: 1947

Rubens, Alma...{31/17}
6408 Hollywood Boulevard (South)
Near: Christian Science Reading
Category/As: Motion Pictures as Actress
For: Intolerance (1916)
Real name: Alma Smith
Born: February 8, 1897   Died: 1931, from pneumonia

Rubinstein, Artur...{16/64}
1735 Vine Street (West)
Near: Palace
Category/As: Recording as Pianist
For: NBC Symphony Orchestra
Real name: same or unknown
Born: January 28, 1886 in Lodz, Poland   Died: 1982, from natural causes

Rudie, Evelyn...{37/02}
6800 Hollywood Boulevard (South)
Near: Souvenirs of Hollywood

Category/As: Television as Actress
For: Eloise (1956) as Eloise
Real name: Evelyn R. Bernauer
Born: March 28, in Los Angeles, CA

Ruggles, Charles...{23/26}
6724 Hollywood Boulevard (South)
Near: parking lot
Category/As: Motion Pictures as Actor
For: Charilie's Aunt (1930)
Real name: same or unknown
Born: February 8, 1886 in Los Angeles, CA
Died: 1970, from cancer and buried in Glendale, CA
Studio: Mack Sennett
Related to Wesley Ruggles (brother)

Ruggles, Charles...{14/40}
6359 Hollywood Boulevard (North)
Near: vacant
Category/As: Radio as Announcer
For: The Charlie Ruggles Show (1944)

Ruggles, Charlie...{24/46}
1630 Vine Street (East)
Near: parking lot
Category/As: Television as Actor
For: The Bullwinkle Show (1961)

Ruggles, Wesley...{31/41}
6424 Hollywood Boulevard (South)
Near: Mr. Burkes Shoes
Category/As: Motion Pictures as Director
For: I'm No Angel (1933)
Real name: same or unknown
Born: June 11, 1889   Died: 1972, from stroke and buried in Glendale, CA
Studio: Mack Sennett
Related to: Charles Ruggles (brother)

Russell, Gail...{05/13}
6935 Hollywood boulevard (North)
Near: Mann's Chinese parking
Category/As: Motion Pictures as Actress
For: The Uninvited (1944)
Born: September 21, 1924 in Chicago, IL
Died: August 26, 1961, from alcohol abuse and buried in Burbank, CA
Related to Guy Madison (spouse)

Russell, Harold...{36/32}
6752 Hollywood Boulevard (South)
Near: Hollywood Passage
Category/As: Motion Pictures as Actor
For: The Best Years of Our Lives (1946)

Russell, Jane...{37/66}
6840 Hollywood Boulevard (South)
Near: Masonic Temple
Category/As: Motion Pictures as Actress
For: The Outlaw (1946)
Real name: Ernestine Jane Geraldine Russell
Born: June 21, 1921 in Bemidji, MN
Studio: RKO
Related to Bob Waterford, Roger Barrett (spouses)

Russell, Rosalind...{17/91}
1708 Vine Street (East)
Near: Collectors Book Store
Category/As: Motion Pictures as Actress
For: His Girl Friday (1940)
Real name: same or unknown
Born: June 4, 1912 in Waterbury, CN   Died: November 28, 1976, from c
Studio: MGM
Related to Fred Brisson (spouse)

Rutherford, Ann...{37/42}
6834 Hollywood Boulevard (South)

Near: Rocket Hollywood
Category/As: Motion Pictures as Actress
For: Love Finds Andy Hardy (1938) as Polly
Real name: Theresa Ann Rutherford
Born: November 2, 1920 in Toronto, Canada
Related to David May, William Dozier (spouses)

Rutherford, Ann...{15/10}
6331 Hollywood Boulevard (North)
Near: Guaranty Building
Category/As: Television as Panelist
For: Leave It To The Girls (1949)

S

Sabu...{18/21}
6251 Hollywood Boulevard (North)
Near: parking lot
Category/As: Motion Pictures as Actor
For: Elephant Boy (1937)
Real name: Sabu Dastagir
Born: January 27, 1924 in Karapur, India
Died: December 2, 1963, from heart attack
Studio: United Artists

Saint, Eva Marie...{36/14}
6730 Hollywood Boulevard (South)
Near: parking lot
Category/As: Motion Pictures as Actress
For: On the Waterfront (1954)
Born: July 4, 1924 in Newark, NJ

Saint, Eva Marie...{33/76}
6624 Hollywood Boulevard (South)
Near: The Gallery
Category/As: Motion Pictures as Actress
Studio: MGM   Awards: Oscar

Sanders, George...{24/37}
1636 Vine Street (East)
Near: Vacant
Category/As: Motion Pictures as Actor.
For: All About Eve (1950)
Real name: George Sanders, Jr.
Born: July 3, 1906 in St. Petersburg, Russia.
Died: 1972, from suicide (overdose)
Studio: 20th Century   Awards: Oscar
Related to Zsa Zsa Gabor, Benita Hume, Magda Gabor (spouses)

Sanders, George...{04/58}
7005 Hollywood Boulevard (North)
Near: Hollywood Mementos
Category/As: Television as Actor
For: George Sanders Mystery Theater (1958)

Sanderson, Julia...{24/79}
1610 Vine Street (East)
Near: Vine Street Bar & Grill
Category/As: Radio as Singer
For: Let's Be Charming (1943)   NBC
Born: August 20, 1887 in Springfield, MA   Died: 1975
Related to Frank Crumit (spouse)

Sandrich, Mark...{16/32}
1719 Vine Street (West)
Near: parking lot
Category/As: Motion Pictures as Director.
For: Holiday Inn (1942)
Born: August 26, 1900 in New York, NY   Died: 1945
Studio: Paramount   Awards: Oscar

Sands, Tommy...{25/03}
1560 Vine Street (East)
Near: parking lot
Category/As: Recording as Singer
For: Love in a Goldfish Bowl
Born: August 27, 1937 in Chicago, IL

Savalas, Telly...{06/58}
6801 Hollywood Boulevard (North)
Near: Vacant
Category/As: Motion Pictures as Actor
For: The Dirty Dozen (1967)
Dedicated on October 26, 1983
Real name: Aristotle Savalas
Born: January 21, 1924
Awards: Emmy

Schenck, Joseph...{07/42}
6753 Hollywood Boulevard (North)
Near: Vacant
Category/As: Motion Pictures as Producer
For: Co-Founder of 20th Century (1933)
Real name: Joseph M. Schenck
Born: December 25, 1878   Died: 1961
Studio: 20th Century   Awards: Oscar
Related to Norma Talmadge (spouse)

Schertzinger, Victor...{27/20}
1615 Vine Street (West)
Near: Doolittle Theater
Category/As: Motion Pictures as Director
For: The Mikado (1939)
Born: April 8, 1880 in Mahanoy City, PA
Died: 1941, and buried in Glendale, CA

Schifrin, Lalo...{38/37}
7000 Holywood Boulevard (South)
Near: Roosevelt Hotel
Category/As: Recording As Composer
For: Cool Hand Luke (1967)
Dedicated on June 21, 1988
Born: 1932 in Buenos Aires

Schildkraut, Joseph...{36//74}
6780 Hollywood Boulevard (South)
Near: Ripley's Museum
Category/As: Motion Pictures as Actor
For: The Diary of Anne Frank (1959)
Born: March 22, 21895 in Austria
Died: 1964, and buried in Hollywood, CA
Awards: Oscar

Schlatter, George...{38/42}
7024 Hollywood Boulevard (South)
Near: Roosevelt Hotel Parking
Category/As: Television as Producer
For: Laugh-In (19__)
Dedicated on January 31, 1989

Schoedsach, Ernest B. ...{23/36}
6274 Hollywood Boulevard (South)
Near: parking lot
Category/As: Motion Pictures as Director
For: King Kong (1933)
Born: June 8, 1893 in Council Bluffs, IA

Schulberg, B. P. ...{25/84}
1500 Vine Street (East)
Near: Home Savings
Category/As: Motion Pictures as Producer
For: It (1927)
Real name: Ben P. Schulberg
Born: January 19, 1892 in Bridgeport, CN
Died: 1957

Schumann-Heink...{33/108}
6640 Hollywood Boulevard (South)
Near: J. C. Amber
Category/As: Recording as Opera Singer
Real name: Ernestine Rossler
Born: June 15, 1861
Died: 1936, from leukemia and buried in San Diego, CA

Schwarzenegger, Arnold...{36/51}
6764 Hollywood Boulevard (South)
Near: Guiness World of Records
Category/As: Motion Pictures as Actor
For: Terminator (1984)

Scott, Lizabeth...{24/63}
1628 Vine Street (East)
Near: Brown Derby ruins
Category/As: Motion Pictures as Actress
For: I Walk Alone (1947)
Real name: Emma Matzo
Born: September 29, 1922 in Scranton, PA
Studio: Paramount

Scott, Martha...{21/42}
6126 Hollywood Boulevard (South)
Near: Henry Fonda Theater
Category/As: Live Theater as Actress
Dedicated on April 23, 1993

Scott, Randolph...{18/32}
6245 Hollywood Boulevard (North)
Near: Frolic Room
Category/As: Motion Pictures as Actor
For: Ride the High Country (1961)
Real name: George Randolph Crane
Born: January 23, 1903 in Orange County, VA
Died: 1987, from natural causes
Studio: Paramount   Awards: Oscar
Related to Maria duPont (spouse)

Scott, Zachary...{14/56}
6349 Hollywood Boulevard (North)
Near: Hollywood Book & Poster
Category/As: Motion Pictures as Actor
For: Mildred Pierce (1945)
Real name: Zachary Thomson Scott, Jr.
Born: February 24, 1914 in Austin, TX
Died: October 3, 1965, from brain tumor

Scully, Vin...{09/23}
6675 Hollywood Boulevard (North)
Near: Vogue Theater (closed)
Category/As: Radio as Sportscaster
For: Dodger's Announcer (1950)
Dedicated on June 9, 1982
Born: November 29, 1927

Seaton, George...{17/30}
1750 Vine Street (East)
Near: Capitol Record Building
Category/As: Motion Pictures as Screenwriter
For: Miracle on 34th Street (1947)
Born: April 17, 1911 in South Bend, IN
Died: 1979, from cancer
Studio: MGM   Awards: Oscar

Sebastian, Dorothy...{09/54}
6655-3 Hollywood Boulevard (North)
Near: USA Jeans Factory
Category/As: Motion Pictures as Actress
For: many silent films
Born: April 24, 1903 in Birmingham, AL   Died: 1957

Sedaka, Neil...{25/89}
1500 Vine Street (East)

Near: Home Savings
Category/As: Recording as Singer
For: Calendar Girl
Born: March 13, 1939 in Brooklyn, NY

Sedgwick, Edward...{06/63}
6801 Hollywood Boulevard (North)
Near: Vacant
Category/As: Motion Pictures as Director
For: Ma & Pa Kettle on the Farm (1951)
Born: November 7,1892 in TX   Died: 1953

Seeger, Bob and the Silver Bullet Band...{17/08}
1770 Vine Street (East)
Near: parking lot
Category/As: Recording as Musicians
Dedicated on March 13, 1987
Born: in Detroit, MI

Seiter, William...{22/57}
6240 Hollywood Boulevard (South)
Near: West Coast Ensemble
Category/As: Motion Pictures as Director
For: Room Service (1938)
Real name: Will A. Seiter
Born: June 10, 1892 in New York, NY   Died: 1964

Selig, William N. ...{21/33}
6100 Hollywood Boulevard (South)
Near: Chevron Gas Station
Category/As: Motion Pictures as Pioneer
For: Founder of Selig Polyscope
Real name: William Nicholas Selig
Born: March 14, 1864 in Chicago, IL   Died: 1948

Selleck, Tom...{05/51}
6925 Hollywood Boulevard (North)
Near: Mann's Chinese Theater
Category/As: Motion Pictures as Actor
For: Lassiter (1983)
Dedicated on June 4, 1986
Born: January 29, 1945 in Detroit, MI

Selznick, Lewis J. ...{31/25}
6410 Hollywood Boulevard (South)
Near: F. W. Woolworth
Category/As: Motion Pictures as Mogul
For: Founder of Selznick Productions
Born: May 2, 1870   Died: 1933
Related to David O. Selznick (son)

Semon, Larry...{05/05}
6935 Hollywood Boulevard (North)
Near: Casablanca Tours
Category/As: Motion Pictures as Director
For: Spuds (1927)
Born: July 16, 1889 in West Point, MO
Died: 1928, from pneumonia
Studio: Vitagraph

Sennett, Mack...{35/21}
6712 Hollywood Boulevard (South)
Near: Egyptian Theater
Category/As: Motion Pictures as Executive
For: Owner of Mack Sennett Comedies
Real name: Mickall Sinott
Born: January 17, 1880 in Richmon, Ontario
Died: 1960, and buried in Culver City, CA
Studio: Keystone Films   Awards: Oscar

Serkin, Rudolf...{16/91}
1749 Vine Street (West)
Near: parking lot
Category/As: Recording as Musician
Born: May 28, 1903
Died: 1991, from cancer

Serling, Rod...{37/63}
6840 Hollywood Boulevard (South)
Near: Masonic Temple
Category/As: Television as Host
For: Twilight Zone (1959-1964) CBS
Dedicated on October 6, 1988
Born: 1924 in Syracuse, NY
Died: 1975, after heart surgery

Serrurier, Mark (Moviola)...{09/41}
6667 Hollywood Boulevard (North)
Near: Musso & Fran Grill
Category/As: Motion Pictures as Inventor
For: Created "Moviola" editing device
Dedicated on March 24, 1982
Awards: Oscar

Shamroy, Leon...{05/49}
6925 Hollywood Boulevard (North)
Near: Mann's Chinese Theater
Category/As: Motion Pictures as Cinematographer
For: The Robe (1953)
Born: July 16, 1901 in New York   Died: 1974
Awards: Oscar

Shatner, William...{05/53}
6925 Hollywood Boulevard (North)
Near: Mann's Chinese Theater
Category/As: Television as Actor
For: Star Trek (1966) as Captain James T. Kirk
Dedicated on May 19, 1983
Born: March 22, 1931 in Montreal, Canada

Shaw, Artie...{16/01}
1711 vine Street (West)
Near: Vacant
Category/As: Recording as Bandleader
For: Begin the Beguine
Real name: Arthur Isaac Arshawsky
Born: May 23, 1920 in New York, NY
Related to Lana Turner, Ava Gardner (spouses)

Shaw, Robert...{26/98}
1555 Vine Street (West)
Neat: TAV
Category/As: Recording as Conductor
For: Robert Shaw Chorale
Born: April 30, 1916 in Great Britan
Died: 1978, from heart attack

Shearer, Norma...{33/102}
6638 Hollywood Boulevard (South)
Near: Hollywood Gift Connection
Category/As: Motion Pictures as Actress
For: The Divorcee (1930)
Real name: Edith Norma Fisher
Born: August 10, 1900 in Montreal, Canada
Died: 1983, from pneumonia and buried in Glendale, CA
Studio: MGM   Awards: Oscar
Related to Irving Thalberg (spouse)

Shearing, George...{17/90}
1708 Vine Street (East)
Near: Collectors Book Store
Category/As: Radio as Composer
For: Light, Airy and Swinging
Born: August 13, 1919 in England

Sheen, Martin...{25/51}
1550 Vine Street (East)
Near: parking lot
Category/As: Motion Pictures as Actor
For: Apocaalypse Now (1977)
Dedicated on August 25, 1989
Real name: Ramon Estevez
Born: August 3, 1940 Related to/as/ Charlie Sheen (son), Emelio Estevez

Sheldon, Sidney...{08/12}
6739 Hollywood Boulevard (North)
Near: Capitol Rock
Category/As: Television as Author
For: The Bachelor & The Bobby Soxer (1947)
Dedicated on June 9, 1988
Born: 1917

Shepherd, Cybill...{38/25}
7000 Hollywood Boulevard (South)
Near: Roosevelt Hotel
Category/As: Television as Actress
For: Moonlighting (19__)
Dedicated on January 21, 1988

Sheridan, Ann...{38/40}
7000 Hollywood Boulevard (South)
Near: Roosevelt Hotel
Category/As: Motion Pictures as Actress
For: Angels with Dirty Faces (1938)
Real name: Clara Lou Sheridan
Born: February 21, 1915 in Denton, TX
Died: January 21, 1967, from cancer and buried in Los Angeles, CA
Studio: Warner Brothers
Related to George Brent (spouse)

Sherman, Richard & Robert...{37/97}
6914 Hollywood Boulevard (South)
Near: Hamburger Hamlet
Category/As: Motion Pictures as Songwriters
For: Mary Poppins (1964)
Born: 1928, 1925

Sherwood, Bobby...{27/48}
1627 Vine Street (West)
Near: parking Lot
Category/As: Television as Actor
For: The Milton Berle Show (1952)
Born Indianapolis, IN
Died: 1981

Shirley, Anne...{38/34}
7000 Hollywood Boulevard (South)
Near: Roosevelt Hotel
Category/As: Motion Pictures as Actress
For: Anne of Green Gables (1934)
Real name: Dawn Evelyn Paris
Born: April 17, 1918

Shore, Dinah...{16/59}
1749 Vine Street (West)
Near: parking lot
Category/As: Radio as Singer
For: The Dinah Shore Show (1943) NBC
Real name: Frances Rose Shore
Born: March 1, 1917 in Winchester, TN
Related to George Montgomery (spouse)

Shore, Dinah...{05/56}
6925 Hollywood Boulevard (North)
Near: Mann's Chinese Theater
Category/As: Recording as Singer
For: Follow the Boys

Shore, Dinah...{37/94}
6914 Hollywood Boulevard (South)
Near: Hamburger Hamlet
Category/As: Television as Singer
For: The Dinah Shore Chevy Show (1957)

Sidney, George...{15/51}
6305 Hollywood Boulevard (North)
Near: Ventas
Category/As: Motion Pictures as Director
For: Bye Bye Birdie (1963)

Born: October 4, 1916 in NY
Awards: Oscar

Sidney, Sylvia...{18/31}
6245 Hollywood Boulevard (North)
Near: Frolic Room
Category/As: Motion Pictures as Actress
For: Les Miserables (1952)
Real name: Sophia Koskow
Born: August 8, 1910 in NY
Related to Luther Adler (spouse)

Sills, Beverly...{17/20}
1750 Vine Street (East)
Near: Capitol Record Building
Category/As: Recording as Singer
For: Barber of Seville
Real name: Belle Miriam Silverman
Born: May 25, 1929 in NY
Awards: Grammy, Emmy

Sills, Milton...{18/06}
6263 Hollywood Boulevard (North)
Near: Equitible Building
Category/As: Motion Pictures as Actor
For: The Sea Wolf (1930)
Born: January 12, 1882 in Chicago, IL
Died: 1930, from heart disease

Silverheels, Jay...{32/58}
6540 Hollywood Boulevard (South)
Near: Greg Ward Levi
Category/As: Television as Actor
For: The Lone Ranger (1952) ABC
Real name: Harold J. Smith
Born: May 26, 1919 in Ontario, Canada
Died: 1980, from pneumonia and ashes sent to Canada

Simms, Ginny...{31/15}
6408 Hollywood Boulevard (South)
Near: Christian Science Reading
Category/As: Radio as Singer
For: That's Right, You're Wrong
Real name: Virginia Sims
Born: May 25, 1916

Sinatra, Frank...{24/98}
1600 Vine Street (East)
Near: D M V
Category/As: Motion Pictures as Actor
For: From Here to Eternity (1953)
Real name: Francis Alber Sinatra
Born: December 12, 1915 in Hoboken, NJ
Awards: Oscar, Grammy
Related to Ava Gardner, Mia Farrow, Barbara Marx (spouses)

Sinatra, Frank...{27/64}
1637 Vine Street (West)
Near: Plaza Hotel
Category/As: Recording as Singer
For: New York, New York

Sinatra, Frank...{32/59}
6540 Hollywood Boulevard (South)
Near: Greg Ward Levi
Category/As: Television as Singer
For: The Frank Sinatra Show (1950-1952)

Singleton, Penny...{11/27}
6547 Hollywood Boulevard (North)
Near: Outfitters Wigs
Category/As: Motion Pictures as Actress
For: Blondie (1938) Blondie
Real name: Dorothy McNulty
Born: September 15, 1908 in Philadelphia, PA

Singleton, Penny...{06/01}
6845 Hollywood Boulevard (North)
Near: Starline Tours & Gifts
Category/As: Radio as Actress
For: Blondie (1939-1948) Blondie Bumsted

Skelton, Red...{07/34}
6763 Hollywood Boulevard (North)
Near: This Is Hollywood
Category/As: Radio as Comedian
For: The Red Skelton Show (1941)   NBC
Real name: Richard Bernard Skelton
Born: July 18, 1910 in Vincinnes, IN

Skelton, Red...{34/01}
6650 Hollywood Boulevard (South)
Near: Hurricane
Category/As: Television as Actor
For: The Red Skelton Show (1953-1970)   CBS

Sloane, Everett...{23/07}
6254 Hollywood Boulevard (South)
Near: burned out
Category/As Television as Actor
For: Official Detective (1958)
Born: October 1, 1909 in NY
Died: 1965, from suicide (pills)

Small, Edward...{26/01}
1501 Vine Street (West)
Near: Shopping Center
Category/As: Television as Producer
For: Witness for the Prosecution (1958)
Born: February 1, 1891 in NY   Died: 1977

Smith, C. Aubrey...{15/18}
6327 Hollywood Boulevard (North)
Near: Chicken Delight
Category/As: Motion Pictures as Actor
For: The Four Feathers (1939)
Real name: Sir Charles Aubrey Smith
Born: July 21, 1863 in England
Died: 1948, from pneumonia

Smith, Carl...{26/24}
1501 Vine Street (West)
Near: Shopping Center
Category/As: Recording as Singer
For: Kisses Don't Lie
Born: March 15, 1927 in TN

Smith, Jack...{20/24}
6161 Hollywood Boulevard (North)
Near: Network Body Shop
Category/As: Radio as Singer
For: The Jack Smith Show (1941) as Whispering Jack Smith
Born: 1898   Died: 1950, from A.I.D.S.
Studio: CBS

Smith, Jaclyn...{38/47}
7024 Hollywood Boulevard (South)
Near: Roosevelt Hotel Parking
Category/As: Television as Actress
For: Charlie's Angels (1976) ABC
Dedicated on November 6, 1989
Born: TX

Smith, Kate...{35/31}
6718 Hollywood Boulevard (South)
Near: International Electronic
Category/As: Radio as Host
For: The Kate Smith Show (1939)   CBS
Real name: Kathryn Smith
Born: May 1, 1909   Died: 1986, from diabetes

Smith, Kate...{20/10}
6161 Hollywood Boulevard (North)
Near: Network Body Shop
Category/As: Recording as Singer
For: When the Moon Comes Over the Mountain

Smith, Pete...{27/40}
1627 Vine Street (West)
Near: parking lot
Category/As: Motion Pictures as Producer
For: Penny Wisdon (1937)
Real name: Pete Schmidt
Born: September 3, 1892 in NY
Died: 1979, from suicide (jumped)
Awards: Oscar

Smothers Brothers ...{11/18}
6555 Hollywood Boulevard (North)
Near: Legends of Hollywood
Category/As: Television as Hosts
For: The Smothers Brothers Show (1967)   CBS
Dedicated on November 2, 1989
Real name: Thomas Bolyn Smothers III, Dick Smothers

Sothern, Ann...{24/77}
1612 Vine Street (East)
Near: Hollywood Collaterial
Category/As: Motion Pictures as Actress
For: A Letter to Three Wives (1949)
Real name: Harriet Lake
Born: January 22, 1909 in Valley City, ND

Sothern, Ann...{24/38}
1634 Vine Street (East)
Near: Madame Rosinka
Category/As: Television as Actress
For: Private Secretary (1952-1954)

Sousa, John Philip...{25/45}
1550 Vine Street (East)
Near: parking lot
Category/As: Recording as Musician
For: Stars and Stripes Forever
Dedicated on June 14, 1990
Born: 1855
Died: 1932, from heart attack and buried in Washington, DC

Spelling, Aaron...{09/33}
6667 Hollywood Boulevard (North)
Near: Musso & Frank Grill
Category/As: Motion Pictures as Producer
For: Charlie's Angels (1976)
Born: April 22, 1928 in Texas

Spiegel, Arthur...{24/13}
1680 Vine Street (East)
Near: Taft Building
Category/As: Motion Pictures as Executive
For: President of Equitible Motion Pictures
Died: 1916

Spinners, The...{08/28}
6723 Hollywood Boulevard (North)
Near: GiGi Boutique
Category/As: Recording as Singers
For: Could It Be I'm Falling In Love

Spitalny, Phil...{29/20}
6364 Hollywood Boulevard (South)
Near: Shaky Wigs
Category/As: Radio as Orchestra Leader
For: The Hour of Charm (1935-1948) CBS
Born: November 7, 1890
Died: 1970, from cancer

St. John, Adela...{31/39}
6424 Hollywood Boulevard (South)
Near: Mr. Burkes Shoes
Category/As: Motion Pictures as Screenwriter
For: What Price Hollywood? (1932)
Real name: Adelea Rogers St. Johns
Born: May 20 1894   Died: 1988

St. John, Al...{15/42}
6315 Hollywood Boulevard (North)
Near: Cave Theater
Category/As: Motion Pictures as Comedian
For: Various Silent Films
Born: September 10, 1893 in Santa Ana, CA
Died: 1963, from heart attack

Stack, Robert...{04/60}
7005 Hollywood Boulevard (North)
Near: Hollywood Momentos
Category/As: Motion Pictures as Actor
For: Written On The Wind (1956)
Real name: Robert Modini
Born: January 13, 1919 in Los Angeles, CA

Stafford, Hanley...{24/32}
1638 Vine Street (East)
Near: Hollywood Import House
Category/As: Radio as Actor
For: The Baby Snooks Show (1939) Daddy
Born: September 22, 1898 in England   Died: 1968

Stafford, Jo...{16/02}
1711 Vine Street (West)
Near: vacant
Category/As: Radio as Singer
For: Chesterfield Supper Club (1944)
Born: November 12, 1918 in Coalinga, CA
Studio: NBC   Awards, Grammy

Stafford, Jo...{27/50}
1627 Vine Street (West)
Near: parking lot
Category/As: Recording as Singer
For: I'll Never Smile Again

Stafford, Jo...{23/33}
6274 Hollywood Boulevard (South)
Near: parking lot
Category/As: Television as Singer
For: The Jo Stafford Show (1954)

Stahl, John M. ...{33/10}
6546 Hollywood Boulevard (South)
Near: Hollywood Hudson Building
Category/As: Motion Pictures as Director
For: Magnificent Obsession (1935)
Born: January 21, 1886 in New York, NY
Died: 1950, from heart attack
Studio: Tiffany-Stahl

Stallone, Sylvester...{35/22}
6712 Hollywood Boulevard (South)
Near: Egyptian Theater (closed)
Category/As: Motion Pictures as Actor
For: Rocky (1976) as Rocky Balboa
Dedicated on June 14, 1984
Real name: Michael Sylvester Stallone
Born: July 6, 1946 in New York, NY

Stanwyck, Barbara...{16/72}
1749 Vine Street (West)
Near: parking lot
Category/As: Motion Pictures as Actress
For: Double Indemnity (1944)
Real name: Ruby Stevens

Born: July 16, 1907 in Brooklyn, NY
Died: 1990, from heart failure
Studio: RKO   Awards: Oscar, Emmy
Related to Frank Fay, Robert Taylor (spouses)

Starke, Pauline...{20/60}
6125 Hollywood Boulevard (North)
Near: Pep Boys
Category/As: Motion Pictures as Actress
For: Intolerance (1916)
Born: January 10, 1900

Starr, Kay...{17/86}
1718 Vine Street (East)
Near: Sun Palace Restaurant
Category/As: Recording as Singer
For: Rock & Roll Waltz
Real name: Katherine Starks
Born: July 31, 1922 in OK

Staub, Ralph...{17/33}
1750 Vine Street (East)
Near: Capitol Record Building
Category/As: Motion Pictures as Cameraman
For: Screen Snapshots series
Studio: Columbia

Steber, Eleanor...{17/107}
1700 Vine Street (East)
Near: Equitible Building
Category/As: Recording as Opera Singer
Born: July 17, 1916 in Wheeling, WV
Died: 1990, from heart failure

Stein, Jules C. ...{06/27}
6821 Hollywood Boulevard (North)
Near: Hollywood Hamburger
Category/As: Motion Pictures as Executive
For: President of MCA
Born: April 26, 1896
Died: 1981

Steinberg, William...{27/75}
1645 Vine Street (West)
Near: Hollywood Vine Building
Category/As: Recording as Conductor
Real name: Hans Wilhelm Steinberg
Born: August 1, 1899

Steiner, Max...{26/95}
1555 Vine Street (West)
Near: TAV
Category/As: Motion Pictures as Composer
For: Gone With The Wind (1939)
Born: May 10,1888 in Vienna, Austria
Died: 1971
Studio: RKO   Awards: Oscar

Step Brothers, The Four...{38/39}
7000 Hollywood Boulevard (South)
Near: Roosevelt Hotel
Category/As: Live Theater as Dancers
Dedicated on July 14, 1988

Sterling, Ford...{33/58}
6608 Hollywood Boulevard (South)
Near: Frederick's of Hollywood
Category/As: Motion Pictures as Comedian
For: Keystone Kops (19__)
Real name: George F. Stitch
Born: November 3, 1883
Died: 1939, from heart attack
Studio: Keystone

Sterling, Jan...{37/54}
6838 Hollywood Boulevard (South)

Near: El Capitan
Category/As: Motion Pictures as Actress
For: Appointment with Danger (1951)
Real name: Jane Adriance
Born: April 3, 1923
Related to Paul Douglas (spouse)

Sterling, Robert...{16/12}
1711 Vine Street (West)
Near: Vacant
Category/As: Television as Actor
For: Topper (1953-1955) George Kirby
Real name: William Sterling Hart
Born: November 13, 1917 in New Castle, PA

Stern, Bill...{06/23}
6821 Hollywood Boulevard (North)
Near: Hollywood Hamburger
Category/As: Radio as Sportscaster
For: Colgate Sports Newsreel (1938) CBS
Born: July 1, 1907 in New York   Died: 1971

Stern, Isaac...{32/63}
6540 Hollywood Boulevard (South)
Near: Greg Ward Levi
Category/As: Recording as Violinist
For: Fiddler on the Roof
Born: July 21, 1920

Stevens, Connie...{18/27}
6249 Hollywood Boulevard (North)
Near: RTD Customer Service
Category/As: Television as Actress
For: Hawaiian Eye (1959-1963) ABC
Real name: Concetta Ann Ingolia
Born: August 8, 1938 in Brooklyn, NY
Related to Eddie Fisher (spouse)

Stevens, George...{16/04}
1711 Vine Street (West)
Near: Vacant
Category/As: Motion Pictures as Director
For: Giant (1955)
Born: December 18, 1904 in Oakland, CA
Died: 1975, from heart attack
Studio: RKO   Awards: Oscar

Stevens, Mark...{10/02}
6633 Hollywood Boulevard (North)
Near: Fame of Hollywood Cafe
Category/As: Television as Actor
For: Big Town (1954) Steve Wilson
Real name: Richard Stevens
Born: December 13, 1915 in Cleveland, OH

Stevens, Onslow...{14/58}
6349 Hollywood Boulevard (North)
Near: Hollywood Book & Poster
Category/As: Motion Pictures as Actor
For: The Three Musketeers (1935)
Real name: Onlsow Ford Stevenson
Born: March 29, 1902 in Los Angeles, CA
Died: 1977, murdered

Stewart, Anita...{36/06}
6724 Hollywood Boulevard (South)
Near: Scientology
Category/As: Motion Pictures as Actress
For: Niver the Twain Sahll Meet (1925)
Real name: Anita May Stewart
Born: February 7, 1895
Died: May 4, 1961, and buried in Glendale, CA

Stewart, James...{17/113}
1700 Vine Street (East)
Near: Equitible Building

Category/As: Motion Pictures as Actor
For: It's a Wonderful Life (1947)
Real name: James Naitland Stewart
Born: May 20, 1908 in Indiana, PA
Awards: Oscar

Stiller, Mauritz...{16/21}
1713 Vine Street (West)
Near: Dan Dee Shoe Repair
Category/As: Motion Pictures as Director
For: Sir Arne's Treasure (1919)
Real name: Moshe Stiller
Born: July 17, 1883 in Helsinki, Finland
Died: 1928, from pleurisy

Stock, Frederick...{26/76}
1549 Vine Street (West)
Near: TAV Celebrity Center
Category/As: Recording as Musician
Born: November 11, 1872   Died: 1842

Stockwell, Dean...{38/56}
7024 Hollywood Boulevard (South)
Near: Roosevelt Hotel Parking
Category/As: Motion Pictures as Actor
For: The Boy With the Green Hair (1946)
Dedicated on February 29, 1992
Real name: Robert Dean Stockwell
Born: 1938

Stokowski, Leopold...{24/88}
1606 Vine Street (East)
Near: vacant
Category/As: Recording as Conductor
For: Fantasia (1941)
Real name: Leopold Bolesowowicz
Born: April 18, 1882 in England
Died: 1977, from coronary attack
Awards: Oscar

Stoloff, Morris...{35/07}
6702 Hollywood Boulevard (South)
Near: Hollywood Beauty
Category/As: Recording as Conductor
For: The Jolson Story (1946)
Born: 1893   Died: 1980

Stone, Andrew L. ...{07/10}
6777 Hollywood Boulevard (North)
Near: Hollywood First National Building
Category/As: Motion Pictures as Director
For: Cry Terror (1958)
Born: July 16, 1902 in Oakland, CA
Studio: Paramount
Related to Virginia Stone (spouse)

Stone, Cliffie...{26/07}
1501 Vine Street (West)
Near: Shopping Center
Category: Radio
Dedicated on March 1, 1989

Stone, Ezra...{24/39}
1634 Vine Street (East)
Near: Madame Rosinka
Category/As: Radio as Actor
For: The Aldrich Family (1939-1953) as Henry Aldrich
Born: December 2, 1917
Studio: NBC

Stone, Fred...{24/41}
1630 Vine Street (East)
Near: parking lot
Category/As: Motion Pictures as Actor
Born: August 19, 1893 in Denver, CO

Died: 1959, from long illness and buried in Glendale, CA

Stone, George E. ...{37/116}
6922 Hollywood Boulevard (South)
Near: Hollywood Center
Category/As: Motion Pictures as Actor
For: The Front Page (1930)
Real name: George Stein
Born: May 23, 1903 in Poland
Died: 1967, from a stroke

Stone, Lewis...{32/45}
6524 Hollywood Boulevard (South)
Near: Blaxx Clothing
Category/As: Motion Pictures as Actor
For; Love Finds Andy Hardy (1938)
Real name: Louis Shepherd Stone
Born: November 15, 1879
Died: 1953, from a heart attack

Stone, Milburn...{06/55}
6801 Hollywood Boulevard (North)
Near: Vacant
Category/As: Television as Actor
For: Gunsmoke (1955-1975) Doc
Born: July 5, 1904 in KS
Died: 1980, from heart attack
Stuido: CBS   Awards: Emmy

Stooges, The Three...{25/09}
1560 Vine Street (East)
Near: parking lot
Category/As: Motion Pictures as Comedians
For: Over 250 movies
Dedicated on August 30, 1983
Real name: Larry Fine, Moses Howard, Jerome Howard
Born: Moe Howard, Brooklyn, NY, June 19, 1897: Larry Fine,
Philadelphia, PA
Died: 1975, 1975, 1952

Storey, Edith...{26/34}
1501 Vine Street (West)
Near: Shopping Center
Category/As: Motion Pictures as Actress
Born: March 18, 1892

Storm, Gale...{24/03}
1680 Vine Street (East)
Near: Taft Building
Category/As: Radio as Actress
For: My Little Margie (19__)
Real name: Josephone Owaissa Cottle
Born: April 5, 1922 in Bloomington, TX
Studio: RKO

Storm, Gale...{26/28}
1501 Vine Street (West)
Near: Shopping Center
Category/As: Recording as Singer
For: I Hear You Knocking

Storm, Gale...{20/68}
6125 Hollywood Boulevard (North)
Near: Pep Boys
Category/As: Television as Actress
For: My Little Margie (1952) Margie

Stout, Bill...{25/53}
1550 Vine Street (East)
Near: parking lot
Category/As: Television
Dedicated on February 3, 1988
Born: 1927   Died: 1989, from cardiac attack

Strasberg, Lee...{07/39}
6757 Hollywood Boulevard (North)
Near: Vacant
Category/As: Motion Pictures as Acting Teacher
For: Lee Strasberg Institute of the Theater
Real name: Israel Strasberg
Born: November 17, 1901 in Austria
Died,: 1982, from heart attack

Stravinsky, Igor...{28/61}
6340 Hollywood Boulevard (South)
Near: (closed) Mr. Submarine
Category/As: Radio as Conductor
Born: June 17, 1882   Died: 1971

Streisand, Barbra...{05/36}
6925 Hollywood Boulevard (North)
Near: Mann's Chinese Theater
Category/As: Motion Pictures as Actress
For: Funny Girl (1968)
Dedicated on December 16, 1976
Real name: Barbara Streisand
Born: April 24, 1942 in Brooklyn, NY

Strongheart...{17/43}
1750 Vine Street (East)
Near: Capitol Record Building
Category/As: Motion Pictures as Dog
For: The Silent Call (1921)
Real name: Etzel van Oeringen
Born: Germany

Sturges, John...{12/29}
6511 Hollywood Boulevard (North)
Near: Hollywood High Fashion Shoes
Category/As: Motion Pictures as Director
For: The Magnificent Seven (1960)
Born: January 3, 1911 in Oak Park, IL

Sturges, Preston...{27/05}
1601 Vine Street (West)
Near: Parking Lot
Category/As: Motion Pictures as Screenwriter
For: The Great McGinty (1940)
Real name: Edmond P. Biden
Born: August 29, 1898 in Chicago, IL
Died: 1959, from heart attack and buried in Hartsdale, NY
Studio: Paramount   Awards: Oscar

Sullavan, Margaret...{16/73}
1749 Vine Street (West)
Near: parking lot
Category/As: Motion Pictures as Actress
For: So Red the Rose (1935)
Real name: Margaret Brooke Sullavan
Born: May 19, 1911 in Norfolk, VA
Died: 1960, from suicide (pills)
Related to Henry Fonda (spouse)

Sullivan, Barry...{22/23}
6160 Hollywood Boulevard (South)
Near: Raji
Category/As: Motion Pictures as Actor
For: The Bad and the Beautiful (1952)
Real name: Patrick Barry
Born: August 29, 1912

Sullivan, Barry...{25/88}
1500 Vine Street (East)
Near: Home Savings
Category/As: Television as Actor
For: Harbormaster (1957)

Sullivan, Ed...{20/90}
6125 Hollywood Boulevard (North)

Near: Pep Boys
Category/As: Television as Host
For: The Ed Sullivan Show (1948-1971)
Born: September 28, 1902 in New York, NY
Died: 1974, from cancer and buried in Hartsdale, CA

Sumac, Yma...{13/01}
6445 Hollywood Boulevard (North(
Near: Best Tomy #21
Category/As: Recording as Singer
Real name: Emperatriz Chavarri Yma Sumac
Born: September 10, 1927 in Peru

Summer, Donna...{38/57}
7024 Hollywood Boulevard (South)
Near: Roosevelt Hotel Parking
Category/As: Recording as Singer
For: Various Disco Era Recordings
Dedicated on March 18, 1992
Real name: La Donna Andrea Gaines

Summerville, Slim...{13/51}
6411-A Hollywood Boulevard (North)
Near: Hollywood Boots
Category/As: Motion Pictures as Actor
For: The Front Page (1931)
Real name: George J. Summerville
Born: July 10, 1892 in Albuquerque, NM
Died: 1946, from stroke

Swain, Mack...{25/76}
1500 Vine Street (East)
Near: Home Savings
Category/As: Motion Pictures as Actor
For: The Gold Rush (1925)
Born: February 16, 1876 in Salt Lake City, UT
Died: 1935

Swanson, Gloria...{36/30}
6752 Hollywood Boulevard (South)
Near: Hollywood Passage
Category/As: Motion Pictures as Actress
For: Sunset Boulevard (1950) as Norma Desmond
Real name: Josephone Swenson
Born: March 27, 1897 in Chicago, IL
Died: 1983: from heart surgery
Related to Wallace Beery (spouse)

Swanson, Gloria...{15/58}
6301 Hollywood Boulevard (North)
Near: vacant
Category/As: Television as Actress
For: The Gloria Swanson Hour (1948)

Swarthout, Gladys...{23/63}
6290 Hollywood Boulevard (South)
Near: Holly Vine Shoppe
Category/As: Recording as Singer
For: Give Us This Night (1937)
Born: December 25, 1904 Died: 1969

Sweet, Blanche...{16/82}
1749 Vine Street (West)
Near: parking lot
Category/As: Motion Pictures as Actress
For: Anna Christie (1923)
Real name: Daphne Wayne
Born: June 18, 1895 in Chicago, IL
Died: 1986, from stroke

Swit, Loretta...{22/56}
6240 Hollywood Boulevard (South)
Near: West Coast Ensemble
Category/As: Television as Actress
For: M.A.S.H. (1973)   CBS

Dedicated on September 1, 1989
Born: 1947

Szigeti, Joseph...{33/40}
6602 Hollywood Boulevard (South)
Near: J.J. Newberry
Category/As: Recording as Violinist
Born: September 5, 1892   Died: 1973

T

Takei, George...{09/13}
6681 Hollywood Boulevard (North)
Near: Dynamite Boutique
Category/As: Television as Actor
For: Star Trek (1966)
Dedicated on October 39, 1986
Born: Los Angeles, CA

Taliaferro, Mabel...{35/35}
6720 Hollywood Boulevard (South)
Near: Hollywood 21 Market
Category/As: Motion Pictures as Actress
For: Cinderella (1911)

Talmadge, Constance...{28/01}
6302 Hollywood Boulevard (South)
Near: New York Pizza Express
Category/As: Motion Pictures as Actress
For: Intolerance (1916)
Born: April 19, 1899 in Brooklyn, NY
Died: November 12, 1973, from pneumonia
        and buried in Hollywood, CA
Studio: First National
Related to Norma Talmadge (sister)

Talmadge, Norma...{25/74}
1500 Vine Street (East)
Near: Home Savings
Category/As: Motion Pictures as Actress
For: Camille (1927)
Born: May 26, 1893 in Niagra Falls, NY
Died: 1957, from pneumonia and buried in Hollywood, CA
Related to Constance Talmage (sister);
        Joseph M Schneck, George Jessel (spouse)

Tamiroff, Akim...{24/42}
1630 Vine Street (East)
Near: Parking Lot
Category/As: Motion Pictures as Actor
For: For Whom the Bell Tolls (1943)
Born: October 29, 1899 in Baku, Russia   Died: 1972

Tandy, Jessica...{23/60}
6290 Hollywood Boulevard (South)
Near: Holly Vine Shoppe
Category/As: Motion Pictures as Actress
For: Driving Miss Daisy (1990)
Born: June 7, 1909 in England

Taurog, Norman...{24/87}
1606 Vine Street (East)
Near: vacant
Category/As: Motion Pictures as Director
For: Boy's Town (1938)
Born: February 23, 1899 in Chicago, IL   Died: 1981
Awards: Oscar

Taylor, Elizabeth...{28/51}
6336 Hollywood Boulevard (South)

Near: Alberts Hosery
Category/As: Motion Pictures as Actress
For: Who's Afraid of Virginia Woolfe? (1966)
Real name: Elizabeth Rosemond
Born: February 27, 1932 in North London, England
Studio: MGM   Awards: Oscar
Related to Richard Burton, Mickey Hilton,
        Eddie Fisher, Mike Todd (spouses)

Taylor, Estelle...{24/67}
1628 Vine Street (East)
Near: Brown Derby ruins
Category/As: Motion Pictures as Actress
For: The Ten Commandments (1923)
Real name: Estelle Boylan
Born: May 20, 1899 in Wilmington, DE
Died: 1958, from cancer
Related to Jack Dempsey (spouse)

Taylor, Kent...{27/81}
1645 Vine Street (West)
Near: Hollywood Vine Building
Category/As: Motion Pictures as Actor
For: Payment on Demand (1951)
Real name: Louis Weiss
Born: May 11, 1907
Died: 1987, from heart operation

Taylor, Kent...{37/26}
6818 Hollywood Boulevard (South)
Near: vacant
Category/As: Television as Actor
For: Boston Blackie (1951-1953)

Taylor, Rip...{33/83}
6626 Hollywood Boulevard (South)
Near: Wig Outfitters
Category/As: Live Theater as Actor
Dedicated on October 15, 1992

Taylor, Robert...{25/66}
1500 Vine Street (East)
Near: Parking Lot
Category/As: Motion Pictures as Actor
For: Bataan (1943)
Real name: Spangler Arlington Brugh
Born: August 5, 1911 in NE
Died: 1969, from lung cancer and buried in Glendale, CA
Studio: MGM
Related to Barbara Stanwyck (spouse)

Taylor, Ruth Ashton...{25/05}
1560 Vine Street (East)
Near: Parking Lot
Category/As: Television
Dedicated on December 13, 1990

Tebaldi, Renata...{33/88}
6628 Hollywood Boulevard (South)
Near: Asian Collection
Category/As: Recording as Opera Singer
Born: February 1, 1922

Temple, Shirley...{25/62}
1550 Vine Street (East)
Near: Parking Lot
Category/As: Motion Pictures as Actress
For: Heidi (1937)
Born: April 23, 1928 in Santa Monica, CA
Awards: Oscar
Related to John Agar (spouse)

Templeton, Alex...{17/42}
1750 Vine Street (East)
Near: Capitol Record Building

Category/As: Radio as Host
For: Alec Templeton Time (1939)
Born: July 4, 1910 in Wales   Died: 1963

Terry, Alice...{33/86}
6628 Hollywood Boulevard (South)
Near: Asian Collection
Category/As: Motion Pictures as Actress
For: The Prisoner of Zenda (1922)
Real name: Alice Frances Taafe
Born: July 24, 1899 in Vincennes, IN   Died: 1987
Related to/as: Rex Ingram (spouse)

Thalberg, Irving...{38/14}
7000 Hollywood Boulevard (South)
Near: Roosevelt Hotel
Category/As: Motion Pictures as Executive
For: Production Manager Universal
Real name: Irving Grant Thalberg
Born: 1899 in New York, NY
Died: 1936, from pneumonia and buried in Glendale, Ca
Studio: Universal   Awards: Oscar
Related to Norma Shearer (spouse)

Thaxter, Phyllis...{11/58}
6531 Hollywood Boulevard (North)
Near: Timing Collection
Category/As: Motion Pictures as Acress
For: Thirty Seconds Over Tokyo (1944)
Real name: Phyllis St. Fexlis Thaxter
Born: November 20 1921 in Portland, ME

Thebom, Blanche...{27/96}
1645 Vine Street (West)
Near: Hollywood Vine Building
Category/As: Recording as Opera Singer
Born: September 19, 1918

Thomas, Bob...{06/08}
6845 Hollywood Boulevard (North)
Near: Starline Tours & Gifts
Category/As: Motion Pictures
Dedicated on December 1, 1988

Thomas, Danny...{05/54}
6925 Hollywood Boulevard (North)
Near: Mann;s Chinese Theater
Category/As: Television as Actor
For: Make Room for Daddy (1960-1965)
Real name: Muzyad Yakhoob
Born: January 6, 1914 in Deerfield, MI
Died: 1991, from heart attack
Studio: CBS Awards: Emmy
Related to Marlo Thomas (daughter)

Thomas, Jay...{20/21}
6161 Hollywood Boulevard (North)
Near: Network Body Shop
Category/As: Radio as Host
For: Host KPWR, Los Angeles, Ca
Dedicated on June 1, 1989

Thomas, John Charles...{05/23}
6935 Hollywood Boulevard (North)
Near: Mann's Chinese Parking
Category/As: Recording as Opera Singer
Born: September 6, 1891
Died: 1960, from cancer

Thomas, Lowell...{13/18}
6433 Hollywood Boulevard (North)
Near: Pacific Theater

Category/As: Motion Pictues as Announcer
For: Movietone News
Born: April 6, 1892 in OH
Died: 1981, from heart attack

Thomas, Lowell...{17/15}
1750 Vine Street (East)
Near: Capitol Record Building
Category/As: Radio as Host
For: Headline Hunters (1929)

Thomas, Marlo...{37/73}
6904 Hollywood Boulevard (South)
Near: Hollywood Tourist & Gifts
Category/As: Television as Actress
For: That Girl (1966-1970) ABC
Dedicated on December 18, 1992
Real name: Margaret Julie Thomas
Born: 1944
Related to Danny Thomas (father)

Thompson, Bill...{04/25}
7021 Hollywood Boulevard (North)
Near: Hollywood Galaxy
Category/As: Radio as Actor
For: Fibber McGee & Molly (1938)
Born: July 8, 1913   Died: 1971

Thomson, Fred...{37/68}
6840 Hollywood Boulevard (South)
Near: Masonic Temple
Category/As: Motion Pictures as Actor
Born: February 26, 1890
Died: 1928, from gall stone surgery

Thorpe, Richard...{20/96}
6125 Hollywood Boulevard (North)
Near: Pep Boys
Category/As: Motion Pictures as Director
For: Jailhouse Rock (1957)
Real name: Rollo Smolt Thorpe
Born: February 24, 1896 in Hutchinson, KS   Died: 1991
Studio: MGM

Tibbett, Lawrence...{15/22}
6325 Hollywood Boulevard (North)
Near: Dr. Pachman Optometrist
Category/As: Recording as Singer
For: Love Song (1932)
Born: November 16, 1896 in Bakersfield, CA
Died: 1960, from head injury surgery and buried in Glendale, CA

Tierney, Gene...{20/52}
6125 Hollywood Boulevard (North)
Near: Pep Boys
Category/As: Motion Pictures as Actress
For: Laura (1944)
Real name: Gene Eliza Taylor Tierney
Born: November 20, 1920 in Brooklyn, NY
Died: 1991, from emphysema
Studio: 20th Century
Related to Oleg Cassini (spouse)

Tobin, Genevieve...{20/72}
6125 Hollywood Boulevard (North)
Near: Pep Boys
Category/As: Motion Pictures as Actress
For: One Hour With You (1932)
Born: November 29, 1901

Todd, Thelma...{23/19}
6262 Hollywood Boulevard (South)

Near: vacant Lot
Category/As: Motion Pictures as Actress
For: Horse Feathers (1932)
Born: July 29, 1905 in Lawrence, MA
Died: 1935, murdered

Tone, Franchot...{33/26}
6560 Hollywood Boulevard (South)
Near: Fame Fashion Chest Jewel
Category/As: Motion Pictures as Actor
For: In Harms Way (1964)
Real name: Stanislas Pascal Franchot Tone
Born: February 27, 1906 in Niagra Falls, NY
Died: 1968, from lung cancer
Studio: MGM
Related to Joan Crawford (spouse)

Toomey, Regis...{04/39}
7021 Hollywood Boulevard (North)
Near: Hollywood Galaxy
Category/As: Motion Pictures as Actor
For: Guys and Dolls (1955)
Born: August 13, 1902   Died: 1991

Torme, Mel...{26/61}
1541 Vine Street (West)
Near: TAV Celebrity Center
Category/As: Recording as Singer
For: Lulu's Back In Town
Dedicated on June 18, 1981
Born: September 13, 1925 in Chicago, IL

Torrence, David...{33/32}
6562 Hollywood Boulevard (South)
Near: Hollywood Toys Inc.
Category/As: Motion Pictures as Actor
For: Sherlock Holmes (1922)
Born: April 23, 1880 in Scotland   Died: 1951

Torrence, Ernest...{06/68}
6801 Hollywood Boulevard (North)
Near: vacant
Category/As: Motion Pictures as Actor
For: King Of Kings (1927)
Born: June 26, 1878 in Scotland
Died: 1933, from gall stone surgery

Toscanini, Arturo...{28/53}
6336 Hollywood Boulevard (South)
Near: Alberts Hosery
Category/As: Radio as Conductor
For: NBC Symphony Orchestra leader (1937-1954)
Born: March 25, 1867   Died: 1957, from stroke

Toscanini, Arturo...{08/27}
6723 Hollywood Boulevard (North)
Near: GiGi Boutique
Category/As: Recording as Conductor
Born: March 25, 1867 in Parma, Italy

Tourneur, Maurice...{18/34}
6243 Hollywood Boulevard (North)
Near: Ticketmaster
Category/As: Motion Pictures as Director
For: Treasure Island (1920)
Real name: Maurice Thomas
Born: February 2, 1876 in Paris, France   Died: 1961
Studio: Associated Producers

Tracy, Lee...{24/34}
1638 Vine Street (East)
Near: Hollywood Import House

Category/As: Motion Pictures as Actor
For: Dinner at Eight (1933)
Real name: William Lee Tracy
Born: April 14, 1898 in Atlanta, GA
Died: 1968, from liver cancer

Tracy, Spencer...{37/22}
6814 Hollywood Boulevard (South)
Near: Greco's Pizza
Category/As: Motion Pictures as Actor
For: Boy's Town (1938)
Real name: Spencer Bonaventure Tracy
Born: April 5, 1900 in Milwaukee, WI
Died: June 11, 1967, from Heart attack and buried in Glendale, CA
Studio: MGM   Awards: Oscar

Traubel, Helen...{31/35}
6420 Hollywood Boulevard (South)
Near: Hilla of Hollywood
Category/As: Recording as Opera Singer
Born: June 20, 1899
Died: 1972, from heart attack and buried in Los Angeles, CA

Travolta, John...{05/59}
6925 Hollywood Boulevard (North)
Near: Mann's Chinese Theater
Category/As: Motion Pictures as Actor
For: Grease (1978)
Dedicated on June 5, 1985
Born: February 18, 1954 in Englewood, NJ

Treacher, Arthur...{23/40}
6274 Hollywood Boulevard (South)
Near: parking Lot
Category/As: Motion Pictures as Actor
For: Mary Poppins (1964)
Real name: Arthue Veary
Born: July 23, 1894 in London, England
Died: 1975, from heart ailment

Trevor, Claire...{05/19}
6935 Hollywood Boulevard (North)
Near: Mann's Chinese parking
Category/As: Motion Pictures as Actress
For: Key Largo (1948)
Real name: Claire Wemlinger
Born: March 8, 1909 in New York, NY
Studio: Fox   Awards: Oscar

Trimble, Laurence...{28/54}
6338 Hollywood Boulevard (South)
Near: El Golfo de Fonseca
Category/ As: Motion Pictures as Director
For: White Fang (1925)
Born: April 1, 1885   Died: 1954

Truex, Ernest...{08/31}
6721 Hollywood Boulevard (North)
Near: vacant
Category/As: Television as Actor
For: Mr. Peepers (1952-1955) as Mr. Remington
Born: September 19, 1890 in Kansas City, MO
Died: 1973, from heart attack and buried in Flushing, NY

Tubb, Ernest...{16/85}
1749 Vine Street (West)
Near: parking lot
Category/As: Recording as Singer
For: Walkin' the Floor Over You
Born: February 9, 1914 in Texas
Died: 1984 from emphysema

Tucker, Forrest...{14/07}
5385 Hollywood Boulevard (North)
Near: Security Pacific Bank
Category/As: Motion Pictures as Actor
For: Sands of Iwo Jima (1949)
Dedicated on August 21, 1986
Born: February 12, 1919 in Plainsfield, IN
Died: 1986, from throat cancer and buried in Los Angeles, CA

Tucker, Sophie...{15/29}
6321 Hollywood Boulevard (North)
Near: Vine Theater
Category/As: Motion Pictures as Singer
For: Honky Tonk (1929)
Real name: Sonia Abuza
Born: January 13, 1884 in Russia
Died: 1966, from kidney aidment

Tully, Thomas L. ...{20/70}
6125 Hollywood Boulevard (North)
Near: Pep Boys
Category/As: Motion Pictures as Actor
For: The Caine Mutiny (1954)
Born: August 21, 1896 in Durango, CO
Died: 1982 from long illness

Tuna, Charlie...{25/13}
1560 Vine Street (East)
Near: Parking Lot
Category/As: Radio as Announcer
Dedicated on January 10, 1990

Tune, Tommy...{16/115}
1779 Vine Street (West)
Category: Live Theater
Near: Capezio Dance
Dedicated on August 12, 1993

Turner, Lana...{18/37}
6233 Hollywood Boulevard (North)
Near: Pantages Theater
Category/As: Motion Pictures as Actress
For: Peyton Place (1957)
Real name: Julia Jean Mildred Frances Turner
Born: February 8, 1920 in Wallace, ID
Studio: Warner Brothers
Related to Artie Shaw, Lex Barker (spouses)

Turner, Tina...{17/14}
1750 Vine Street (East)
Near: Capitol Record Building
Category/As: Recording as Singer
For: Proud Mary
Dedicated on August 28, 1986
Real name: Anna Mae Bullock
Born: November 25, 1941 in Texas
Related to Ike Turner (spouse)

Turpin, Ben...{27/86}
1645 Vine Street (West)
Near: Hollywood Vine Building
Category/As: Motion Pictures as Comedian
For: Million Dollar Legs (1932)
Real name: Bernard Turpin
Born: September 17, 1874 in New Orleans, LA
Died: 1940, from heart desease and buried in Glendale, CA
Studio: Mack Sennett

Tuttle, Lurene...{17/11}
1770 Vine Street (East)
Near: parking lot
Category/As: Radio as Actress

For: The Red Skelton Show (1944)
Born: August 29, 1906   Died: 1986

Tuttle, Lurene...{04/55}
7009 Hollywood Boulevard (North)
Near: Fame & Fortune
Category/As: Television as Actress
For: Life With Father (1953-1955) CBS

Twelvetrees, Helen...{18/10}
6263 Hollywood Boulevard (North)
Near: Equitible Building
Category/As: Motion Pictures as Actress
For: The Painted Desert (1931)
Real name: Helen Jurgens
Born: December 25, 1907 in Brooklyn, NY
Died: 1958, from suicide

V

Vague, Vera...{17/70}
1724 Vine Street (East)
Near: parking lot
Category/As: Motion Pictures as Actress
For: Mrs. Wiggs of the Cabbage Patch (1942)
Real name: Barbara Jo Allan
Born: September 2, 1905 in New York, NY   Died: 1974

Vague, Vera...{27/67}
1637 Vine Street (West)
Near: Early World Restaurant
Category/As: Radio as Actress
For: The Pepsodent Show (1934)

Valens, Ritchie...{08/22}
6727 Hollywood Boulevard
Near: Artesian Patio
Category/As: Recording as Singer
For: Various Pop Recordings
Dedicated on May 11, 1990
Real name: same or unknown
Died: 1959, in an airplane crash

Valenti, Jack...{38/05}
7000 Hollywood Boulevard (South)
Near: Roosevelt Hotel
Category: Motion Pictures
For: President of Motion Picture Association of America
Dedicated on November 1, 1988
Born: 1921 in Texas

Valentino, Rudolph...{22/31}
6162 Hollywood Boulevard (South)
Near: Hastings Hotel
Category/As: Motion Pictures as Actor
For: The Sheik (1921)
Real name: Rodolofo Alfonzo Raffaelo Pierre Gugliemi
                di Valentina d'Antongulla
Born: May 6, 1895 in Taranto, Italy
Died: 1926, from ruptured appendix and buried in Hollywood, CA
Related to Natacha Rambova (spouse)

Vallee, Rudy...{24/47}
1630 Vine Street (East)
Near: parking lot
Category/As: Radio as Singer
For: The Fleishcman Hour (1929-1944) NBC
Real name: Hubert Prior Vallee
Born: July 28, 1901 in Island Point, VT   Died: 1986, from heart attack

Related to Jane Greer (spouse)

Valli, Virginia...{20/56}
6125 Hollywood Boulevard (North)
Near: Pep Boys
Category/As: Motion Pictures as Actress
For: A Lady of Quality (1924)
Real name: Virginia McSweeney
Born: June 12, 1898 in Chicago, IL
Died: September 24, 1968 from stroke and buried in Palm Springs, CA
Related to Charles Farrell (spouse)

Van Dyke, Dick...{04/44}
7021 Hollywood Boulevard (North)
Near: Hollywood Galaxy
Category/As: Television as Actor
For: The Dick Van Dyke Show (1961-1966) CBS as Rob Petrie
Dedicated on February 25, 1993

Van Dyke, W.S....{20/42}
6141 Hollywood Boulevard (North)
Near: Mid-Town Towing
Category/As: Motion Pictures as Director
For: The Thin Man (1934)
Real name: Woodbridge Strong Van Dyke II
Born: 1887 in San Diego, CA
Died: 1944, from after a short illness and buried in Glendale, CA
Studio: MGM

Van Fleet, Jo...{38/22}
7000 Hollywood Boulevard (South)
Near: Roosevelt Hotel
Category/As: Motion Pictures as Actress
For: East of Eden (1955)
Real name: same or unknown
Born: December 30, 1919

Van Patten, Dick...{26/73}
1549 Vine Street (West)
Near: TAV Celebrity Center
Category/As: Television as Actor
For: Eight is Enough (1977)
Dedicated on November 20, 1985
Born: December 9, 1928

Vance, Vivian...{38/53}
7024 Hollywood Boulevard (South)
Near: Roosevelt Hotel parking
Category/As: Television as Actress
For: I Love Lucy (1951-1957) CBS as Ethel Mertz
Dedicated on February 14, 1991
Real name: same or unknown
Born: 1903   Died: 1979, from cancer

Vaughan, Sarah...{37/45}
6834 Hollywood Boulevard (South)
Near: Rocket Hollywood
Category/As: Recording as Singer
Dedicated on July 31, 1985
Real name: same or unknown
Born: March 27, 1924 in Newark, NJ   Died: 1990 from lung cancer
Awards: Emmy

Vaughan, Sarah...{17/59}
1724 Vine Street (East)
Near: parking lot
Category/As: Recording as Singer
For: Copacabana

Velez, Lupe...{05/31}
6925 Hollywood Boulevard (North)
Near: Mann's Chinese Theater

Category/As: Motion Pictures as Actress
For: Mexican Spitfire (1940)
Real name: Guadalupe Velez de Vallalobos
Born: July 18, 1908   Died: 1944, from suicide (pills)
Related to Johnny Weismuller (spouse)

Venable, Evelyn...{25/46}
1550 Vine Street (East)
Near: parking lot
Category/As: Motion Pictures as Actress
For: Mrs. Wiggs of the Cabbage Patch (1934)
Real name: same or unknown
Born: October 18, 1913 in Cincinnati, OH

Vera, Billy...{17/03}
1770 Vine Street (East)
Near: parking lot
Category: Recording
Dedicated on February 16, 1988

Verdugo, Elena...{16/17}
1711 Vine Street (West)
Near: closed restaurant
Category/As: Television as Actress
For: Marcus Welby M.D. (1969) as Connseulo Lopez
Born: April 20, 1926 in Hollywood , CA

Vernon, Bobbie...{06/54}
6801 Hollywood Boulevard (North)
Near: vacant office building
Category/As: Motion Pictures as Comedian
For: various Mack Sennett movies
Real name: Silvion Jardins
Born: March 9, 1897 in Chicago, IL
Died: 1939, from a heart attack and buried in Glendale, CA

Vidor, Charles...{34/47}
6674 Hollywood Boulevard (South)
Near: Explosion
Category/As: Motion Pictures as Director
For: A Farewell to Arms (1957)
Born: July 27, 1900 in Budapest, Hungary
Died: 1959, from a heart attack and buried in Los Angeles, CA

Vidor, King...{08/09}
6743 Hollywood Boulevard (North)
Near: B. Dalton Book Store
Category/As: Motion Pictures as Director
For: War and Peace (1956)
Real name: King Wallace Vidor
Born: February 8, 1894 in Galveston, TX
Died: 1982, from a heart ailment
Awards: Oscar

Vincent, Gene...{16/88}
1749 Vine Street (West)
Near: parking lot
Category/As: Recording as Singer
For: Be-Bop-Alula
Real name: Vincent Craddock
Born: February 11, 1935 in VA   Died: 1971

Vinson, Helen...{25/36}
1560 Vine Street (East)
Near: parking lot
Category/As: Motion Pictures as Actress
For: I'm a Fugitive from a Chain Gang (1932)
Real name: Helen Rulfs
Born: September 17, 1907 in TX

Vinton, Bobby...{37/95}
6914 Hollywood Boulevard (South)
Near: Hamburger Hamlet

Category/As: Recording as Singer
For: Roses Are Red
Born: April 16, 1935

von Sternberg, Josef...{13/64}
6401 Hollywood Boulevard (North)
Category/As: Motion Pictures as Director
For: Shanghai Express (1932)
Real name: Jonas Jo Sternberg
Born: May 20, 1894 in Vienna, Austria
Died: 1969, from a heart attack

Von Stroheim, Erich...{37/32}
6822 Hollywood Boulevard (South)
Near: Starline Tours & Gifts
Category/As: Motion Pictures as Director
For: The Wedding March (1928)
Real name: Hans Erich Maria Stroheim von Nordenwall
Born: September 22, 1885 in Vienna, Austria
Died: May 12, 1957 from cancer

Von Zell, Harry...{12/15}
6521 Hollywood Boulevard (North)
Category/As: Radio as Announcer
For: Burns & Allen Show (1950-1958)
Real name: same or unknown
Born: July 11, 1906 in Indianapolis, IN
Died: 1981, from cancer

Wagner, Lindsay...{07/21}
6767 Hollywood Boulevard (North)
Near: Hollywood Wax Museum
Category/As: Motion Pictures as Actress
Dedicated on December 12, 1984
Real name: same or unknown
Born: June 22, 1949 in Los Angeles, CA
Awards: Emmy

Wagner, Roger...{04/64}
7003 Hollywood Boulevard (North)
Near: Haagen Dazs
Category/As: Recording as Singer
Real name: same or unknown

Wakely, Jimmy...{24/11}
1680 Vine Street (East)
Near: Taft Building
Category/As: Recording as Singer
For: Slippin' Around
Born: February 15, 1914 in Mineola, AZ
Died: 1982, from heart failure

Walker, Clint...{26/12}
1501 Vine Street (West)
Near: Shopping Center
Category/As: Television as Actor
For: Cheyene (1955) as Cheyene Bodie
Real name: Norman Walker
Born: May 30, 1927 in IL

Walker, Robert...{16/18}
1711 Vine Street (West)
Near: vacant
Category/As: Motion Pictures as Actor
For: Bataan (1943)
Real name: Robert Hudson Walker
Born: October 13, 1918 in Salt Lake City, UT
Died: August 28, 1951, from respiratory failure
Studio: MGM

Related to Jennifer Jones, Barbara Ford (spouses)

Wallace, Mike...{18/03}
6263 Hollywood boulevard (North)
Near: Equitible Building
Category/As: Television as Interviewer
For: 60 Minutes (1968)
Real name: Myron Leon Wallace
Born: May 9, 1918 in Brookline, MA
Studio: CBS   Awards: Emmy

Wallace, Richard...{25/16}
1560 Vine Street (East)
Near: parking lot
Category/As: Motion Pictures as Director
For: The Young in Heart (1938)
Born: August 26, 1894 in Sacramento, CA   Died: 1951

Wallington, James...{34/21}
6660 Hollywood Boulevard (South)
Near: Rock Center
Category/As: Radio as Announcer
For: Voice of America (1966-1972)
Born: 1907   Died: 1972

Walsh, Raoul...{20/44}
6141 Hollywood Boulevard (North)
Near: Mid-Town Towing
Category/As: Motion Pictures as Director
For: High Sierra (1941)
Born: March 11, 1887 in New York, NY
Died: 1981, from heart attack

Walter, Bruno...{37/76}
6904 Hollywood Boulevard (South)
Near: Hollywood Tourist & Gifts
Category/As: Recording as Conductor
Real name: Bruno Schlesinger
Born: September 15, 1876   Died: 1962

Walters, Charles...{31/07}
6402 Hollywood Boulevard (South)
Near: The Spot
Category/As: Motion Pictures as Director
For: Easter Parade (1948)
Born: November 17, 1911 in Pasadena, CA
Died: 1982, from lung cancer

*Walthall, Henry B. *...{19/25}
6207 Hollywood Boulevard (North)
Near: parking lot
Category/As: Motion Pictures as Actor
For: The Birth of a Nation (1915)
Real name: same or unknown
Born: March 16, 1878 in Columbia, AL
Died: 1936, from chronic illness

Waring, Fred...{33/22}
6558 Hollywood Boulevard (South)
Near: Body Image
Category/As: Radio as Conductor
For: The Fred Waring Show (1945-1950) NBC
Born: June 9, 1900   Died: 1984, from stroke

Waring, Fred...{28/03}
6302 Hollywood Boulevard (South)
Near: New York Pizza Express
Category/As: Recording as Conductor

Waring, Fred...{16/90}
1749 Vine Street (West)
Near: parking lot
Category/As: Television as Conductor
For: The Chevy Show (1956)

Warner, H.B. ...{33/36}
6602 Hollywood Boulevard (South)
Near: J.J. Newberry
Category/As: Motion Pictures as Actor
For: The King of Kings (1927)
Real name: Henry Byron Warner Lickford
Born: October 26, 1876   Died: 1958

Warner, Harry...{13/11}
6439 Hollywood Boulevard (North)
Near: Schtromberg Jewelers
Category/As: Motion Pictures as Pioneer
For: Co-founder of Warner Brothers
Real name: same or unknown
Born: December 12, 1881 in Kraznashiltz, Poland
Died: 1958, from cerebral occlusion

Warner, Jack...{11/31}
6541 Hollywood Boulevard (North)
Near: Janes House
Category/As: Motion Pictures as Pioneer
For: Co-founder of Warner Brothers
Real name: Jack L. Warner
Born: August 2, 1892 in London, Ontario   Died: 1978

Warner, Sam...{19/27}
6207 Hollywood Boulevard (North)
Near: parking lot
Category/As: Motion Pictures as Producer
For: Co-founder of Warner Brothers
Real name: same or unknown
Born: August 10, 1888 in Baltimore, MD   Died: 1927, from pneumonia

Warrick, Ruth...{09/04}
6689 Hollywood Boulevard (North)
Near: Sub City
Category/As: Motion Pictures as Actress
For: Citizen Kane (1941)
Real name: same or unknown
Born: June 29, 1915 in St. Louis, MO

Warwick, Dionne...{37/103}
6920 Hollywood Boulevard (South)
Near: Pro Electronics
Category/As: Recording as Singer
For: Do You Know The Way To San Jose?
Dedicated on December 12, 1985
Real name: Marie Dionne Warwick
Born: December 12, 1941

Waterman, Willard...{27/17}
1605 Vine Street (West)
Near: Molly Coney Island
Category/As: Radio as Actor
For: Those Websters (1945) NBC
Real name: same or unknown

Wayne, John...{26/64}
1541 Vine Street (West)
Near: TAV Celebrity Center
Category/As: Motion Pictures as Actor
For: True Grit (1969)
Real name: Marion Michael Morrison
Born: May 26, 1907 in Winterset, IA
Died: June 11, 1979, from lung cancer and buried in Newport Beach, CA
Awards: Oscar

Weaver, Dennis...{37/119}
6922 Hollywood Boulevard (South)
Near: Hollywood Center
Category/As: Television as Actor
For: Gunsmoke (1955-1975) CBS
Dedicated on September 9, 1986
Born: June 4, 1924

Webb, Clifton...{37/64}
6840 Hollywood Boulevard (South)
Near: Masonic Temple
Category/As: Motion Pictures as Actor
For: Cheaper by the Dozen (1950)
Real name: Webb Parmalee Hollenbeck
Born: November 19, 1891 in Indianapolis, IN
Died: 1966, from heart attack and buried in Hollywood, CA
Studio: Fox

Webb, Jack...{38/70}
7040 Hollywood Boulevard (South)
Near: Hollywood Liquor Store
Category/As: Radio as Actor
For: Dragnet (1949-1956) NBC
Born: April 2, 1920 in Santa Monica, CA
Died: 1982, from heart attack and buried in Los Angeles, CA
Related to Julie London (spouse)

Webb, Jack...{23/43}
6274 Hollywood Boulevard (South)
Near: parking lot
Category/As: Television as Actor
For: Dragnet (1952)
Studio: NBC

Webber, Sir Andrew Lloyd...{18/46}
6233 Hollywood Boulevard (North)
Category: Live Theater
For: Joseph and His Coat of Many Colors (1993)
Dedicated on February 26, 1993

Weber, Lois...{32/31}
6518 Hollywood Boulevard (South)
Near: New World Jewelry
Category/As: Motion Pictures as Producer
For: The Angel of Broadway (1927)

Weems, Ted...{24/07}
1680 Vine Street (East)
Near: Taft Building
Category/As: Recording as Bandleader
Real name: same or unknown
Born: September 26, 1901 in PA   Died: 1963, from emphysema

Weintraub, Jerry...{05/10}
6935 Hollywood Boulevard (North)
Near: Mann's Chinese Parking
Category/As: Motion Pictures as Producer
For: Oh, God! (1977)
Dedicated on April 24, 1984
Real name: same or unknown
Born: September 26, 1937

Weismuller, Johnny...{11/45}
6541 Hollywood Boulevard (North)
Near: Janes House
Category/As: Television as Actor
For: Tarzan the Ape Man (1932)
Born: June 2, 1904 in Chicago, IL   Died: 1984, from heart disease
Related to: Lupe Velez (spouse)

Welk, Lawrence...{10/37}
6613 1/2 Hollywood Boulevard (North)
Near: L.A. Roxx
Category/As: Recording as Bandleader
Born: March 11, 1903 in Strasburg, ND   Died: 1992

Welk, Lawrence...{27/09}
1601 Vine Street (West)
Near: parking lot
Category/As: Television as Bandleader
For: The Lawrence Welk Show (1955-1970) ABC

Welles, Orson...{24/92}
1600 Vine Street (East)
Near: DMV
Category/As: Motion Pictures as Actor
For: Citizen Kane (1941)
Real name: George Orson Welles
Born: May 6, 1915 in Kenosha, WI   Died: 1985, from heart attack
Studio: RKO   Awards: Oscar
Related to Rita Hayworth, Virginia Nicholson (spouses)

Welles, Orson...{33/16}
6554 Hollywood Boulevard (South)
Near: Prestige Jewelry
Category/As: Radio as Director
For: The War of the Worlds (October 30, 1938) CBS

Wellman, William...{20/58}
6125 Hollywood Boulevard (North)
Near: Pep Boys
Category/As: Motion Pictures as Director
For: The High and the Mighty (1954)
Real name: William Augustus Wellman
Born: February 29, 1896 in Brookline, MA   Died: 1975, from leukemia
Awards: Oscar

Welsh, Bill...{29/19}
6362 Hollywood Boulevard (South)
Near: Palmer Building
Category/As: Television as Announcer
For: KTTV-TV Director of Sports and Special Events
Born: In Greely, CO

West, Mae...{25/14}
1560 Vine Street (East)
Near: parking lot
Category/As: Motion Pictures as Actress
For: She Done Him Wrong (1932)
Real name: same or unknown
Born: August 7, 1892 in Brooklyn, NY
Died: November 23, 1980, from stroke and buried in Brooklyn, NY

Weston, Paul...{26/58}
1541 Vine Street (West)
Near: TAV Celebrity Center
Category/As: Recording as Composer
Real name: P. Wetstein
Born: March 12, 1912 in Springfield, MA

White, Alice...{26/16}
1501 Vine Street (West)
Near: Shopping Center
Category/As: Motion Pictures as Actress
For: Hot Stuff (1929)
Real name: Alva White
Born: August 28, 1907 in Patterson, NJ   Died: 1983, from stroke

White, Betty...{08/03}
6743 Hollywood Boulevard (North)
Near: B. Dalton Book Store
Category/As: Television as Actress
For: The Golden Girls as Rose
Real name: same or unknown
Born: Janaury 17, 1924 in Oak Park, IL
Awards: Emmy
Related to Allen Ludden (spouse)

White, Jack...{29/22}
6364 Hollywood Boulevard (South)
Near: Shaky Wigs
Category/As: Motion Pictures as Actor
For: Sign of the Cross (1932 & 1944)
Real name: J. Irving White
Died: 1949

White, Jules...{26/96}
1555 Vine Street (West)
Near: TAV
Category/As: Motion Pictures as Director
For: The Three Stooges (1945)
Real name: same or unknown
Born: In Budapest, Hungary   Died: From Alzheimer's disease

White, Pearl...{37/56}
6838 Hollywood Boulevard (South)
Near: El Capitan Theater
Category/As: Motion Pictures as Actress
For: The Perils of Pauline (1914)
Real name: same or unknown
Born: March 4, 1889 in Greenridge, MO   Died: 1938, from liver ailment

White, Snow...{37/85}
6912 Hollywood Boulevard (South)
Near: Harley Davidson Shop
Category/As: Motion Pictures as Animated Character
For: Snow White & the Seven Dwarfs (1937)
Dedicated on June 28, 1987
Born: 1937

Whiteman, Paul...{27/06}
1601 Vine Street (West)
Near: parking lot
Category/As: Radio as Orchestra Leader
For: Paul Whiteman Presents (1943) NBC
Born: March 28, 1991 in Denver, CO
Died: 1967, from heart attack

Whiteman, Paul...{20/04}
6161 Hollywood Boulevard (North)
Near: Network Body Shop
Category/As: Recording as Bandleader
For: Whispering

Whiting, Barbara...{13/07}
6443 Hollywood Boulevard (North)
Near: Fast Break Shoes
Category/As: Television as Actress
For: Those Whiting Girls (1955) CBS
Real name: same or unknown
Born: May 19, 1931 in Los Angeles, CA

Whiting, Margaret...{10/21}
6623 Hollywood Boulevard (North)
Near: Mona Lisa Tops
Category/As: Recording as Singer
For: Come Rain or Come Shine
Real name: same or unknown
Born: July 22, 1926 in Detroit, MI

Whitman, Slim...{16/11}
1711 Vine Street (West)
Near: vacant
Category/As: Recording as Singer
For: China Doll
Real name: Otis Whitman, Jr.
Born: January 20, 1924 in Tampa, FL

Whitmore, James...{10/43}
6611 1/2 Hollywood Boulevard (North)
Near: Je Taime Boutique
Category/As: Television as Actor
For: The Law & Mr. Jones (1960) Abraham Lincoln
Real name: same or unknown
Born: October 1, 1921 in White Plains, NY

Whittinghill, Dick...{30/25}
6384 Hollywood Boulevard (South)
Near: Popeye Chicken
Category/As: Radio as Disc Jockey
For: KMPC Radio DJ

Real name: same or unknown

Widmark, Richard...{37/04}
6800 Hollywood Boulevard (South)
Near: Souvenirs of Hollywood
Category/As: Motion Pictures as Actor
For: The Bedford Incident (1965)
Real name: same or unknown
Born: December 26, 1914 in Sunrise, MN

Wilcoxon, Henry...{23/12}
6256 Hollywood Boulevard (South)
Near: vacant lot
Category/As: Motion Pictures as Actor
For: Cleopatra (1934)
Real name: same or unknown
Born: September 8, 1905   Died: 1984, from heart failure

Wilde, Cornel...{27/63}
1637 Vine Street (West)
Near: Plaza Hotel
Category/As: Motion Pictures as Director
For: Lancelot & Guinevere (1962)
Real name: Cornelius Louis Wilde
Born: October 13, 1915 in New York, NY
Died: 1989, from leukemia
Studio: 20th Century
Related to Jean Wallace (spouse)

Wilder, Billy...{16/77}
1749 Vine Street (West)
Near: parking lot
Category/As: Motion Pictures as Director
For: Sunset Boulevard (1950)
Real name: Samuel Wilder
Born: June 22, 1906 in Vienna, Austria
Awards: Oscar

Wilkerson-Kassel, Tichi...{38/45}
7024 Hollywood Boulevard (South)
Near: Roosevelt Hotel parking structure
Category/As: Motion Pictures as Executive
For: Hollywood Reporter Newspaper
Dedicated on July 13, 1989

William, Warren...{26/88}
1555 Vine Street (West)
Near: TAV
Category/As: Motion Pictures as Actor
For: Cleopatra (1934)
Real name: Warren William Krech
Born: December 2, 1895 in MN   Died: 1948, from blood disease

Williams, Andy...{09/31}
6669 Hollywood Boulevard (North)
Near: Asia Imports
Category/As: Recording as Singer
For: Moon River
Dedicated on November 3, 1982
Real name: Howard Williams
Born: December 3, 1928 in Wall Lake, IA
Awards: Emmy

Williams, Bill...{20/22}
6161 Hollywood Boulevard (North)
Near: Network Body Shop
Category/As: Television as Actor
For: The Adventures of Kit Carson (1951)
Real name: William Katt
Born: 1916

Williams, Billy Dee...{26/31}
1501 Vine Street (West)
Near: Shopping Center
Category/As: Motion Pictures as Actor

For: Lady Sings the Blues (1972)
Dedicated on March 27, 1985
Born: April 6, 1937 in NY

Williams, Earle...{16/94}
1749 Vine Street (West)
Near: parking lot
Category/As: Motion Pictures as Actor
For: Say It With Diamonds (1927)
Real name: same or unknown
Born: February 28, 1880 in Sacramento, CA
Died: 1927, from pneumonia and buried in Glendale, CA

Williams, Ester...{25/28}
1560 Vine Street (East)
Near: parking lot
Category/As: Motion Pictures as Actress
For: Bathing Beauty (1944)
Born: August 8, 1923 in Los Angeles, CA
Studio: MGM
Related to Fernando Lamas, Ben Gage (spouses)

Williams, Hank...{31/02}
6400 Hollywood Boulevard (South)
Near: Pizza Deli
Category/As: Recording as Singer
For: Lovesick Blues
Real name: Hiram Williams
Born: September 17, 1923   Died: 1953, from heart attack
Related to: Hank Williams, Jr. (son)

Williams, Joe...{32/16}
6508 Hollywood Boulevard (South)
Near: Fox Theater (closed)
Category/As: Recording as Singer
For: Alright, Okay, You Win
Dedicated on June 13, 1983
Real name: Joseph Goreed
Born: December 12, 1918

Williams, Kathleen...{38/68}
7038 Hollywood Boulevard (South)
Near: Andrea's Pizza
Category/As: Motion Pictures as Actress
For: The Adventures of Kathleen (1913)
Born: May 31, 1888

Williams, Paul...{05/06}
6935 Hollywood Boulevard (North)
Near: Mann's Chinese Parking
Category/As: Recording as Songwriter
For: Rainy Days and Mondays
Dedicated on August 10, 1983
Real name: same or unknown
Born: September 19, 1940

Williams, Robin...{05/57}
6925 Hollywood Boulevard (North)
Near: Mann's Chinese Theater
Category/As: Motion Pictures as Actor
For: Good Morning, Viet Nam (19__)
Dedicated on December 12, 1990
Real name: same or unknown

Williams, Roger...{26/56}
1541 Vine Street (West)
Near: TAV Celebrity Center
Category/As: Recording as Composer
For: Born Free
Real name: Louis Weertz
Born: October 1, 1926 in Omaha, NE

Williams, Tex...{31/23}
6410 Hollywood Boulevard (South)
Near: F.W. Woolworth

Category/As: Radio as Singer
Real name: Sol Williams
Born: August 23, 1917   Died: 1985, from cancer

Willock, Dave...{29/12}
6358 Hollywood Boulevard (South)
Near: Glad's Discount Mini-Mall
Category/As: Television as Actor
For: Boots and Saddles (1957)
Real name: same or unknown
Born: 1909   Died: 1990, from stroke

Wills, Chill...{05/41}
6925 Hollywood Boulevard (North)
Near: Mann's Chinese Theater
Category/As: Motion Pictures as Actor
For: The Alamo (1960)
Real name: same or unknown
Born: July 18, 1903 in Texas   Died: 1978

Willson, Meredith...{13/47}
6411-A Hollywood Boulevard (North)
Near: Hollywood Boots
Category/As: Radio as Lyricist
For: The Big Show (1950) NBC
Real name: Robert Meredith Reiniger
Born: May 18, 1902 in Mason City, IA   Died: 1984, from heart failure

Wilson, Carey...{15/60}
6301 Hollywood Boulevard (North)
Near: vacant
Category/As: Motion Pictures as Writer
For: Mutiny on the Bounty (1935)
Real name: same or unknown
Born: May 10, 1889 in Philadelphia, PA

Wilson, Don...{25/70}
1500 Vine Street (East)
Near: parking lot
Category/As: Radio as Announcer
For: The Jack Benny Show (1934-1967)
Real name: same or unknown
Born: September 1, 1900   Died: 1982, from stroke

Wilson, Lois...{05/21}
6935 Hollywood Boulevard (North)
Near: Mann's Chinese Parking
Category/As: Motion Pictures as Actress
For: Bright Eyes (1934)
Real name: same or unknown
Born: June 28, 1894 in Pittsburg, PA   Died: 1983, from pneumonia

Wilson, Marie...{10/57}
6601 Hollywood Boulevard (North)
Near: Station Market
Category/As: Motion Pictures as Actress
For: My Friend Irma (1949) as Irma
Real name: Katherine Elizabeth Wilson
Born: Decmeber 30, 1918 in Anaheim, CA
Died: 1972, from cancer and buried in Los Angeles, CA

Wilson, Marie...{15/54}
6301 Hollywood Boulevard (North)
Near: vacant
Category/As: Radio as Actress
For: My Friend Irma (1947-1954) CBS

Wilson, Marie...{07/28}
6765 Hollywood Boulevard (North)
Near: Runkel's Jewelers
Category/As: Television as Actress
For: My Friend Irma (1952-1954)

Wilson, Nancy...{11/34}
6541 Hollywood Boulevard (North)

Near: Janes House
Category/As: Recording as Singer
Dedicated on October 1, 1990
Real name: same or unknown

Winchell, Paul...{15/07}
6331 Hollywood Boulevard (North)
Near: Guaranty Building
Category/As: Television as Ventriloquist
For: Paul Winchell/Jerry Mahoney Show (1950)
Real name: same or unknown
Born: December 21, 1924 in NY

Winchell, Walter...{35/27}
6714 Hollywood Boulevard (South)
Near: Numero Uno Pizza
Category/As: Radio as Commentator
For: Walter Winchell's Journal (1932-1952) NBC
Real name: Walter Winechel
Born: April 7, 1897   Died: 1972

Winchell, Walter...{27/74}
1645 Vine Street (West)
Near: Hollywood Vine Building
CategoryAs: Television as Narrator
For: The Untouchables (1952-1955) ABC

Windsor, Claire...{04/33}
7021 Hollywood Boulevard (North)
Near: Hollywood Galaxy
Category/As: Motion Pictures as Actress
For: Rich Men's Wives (1922)
Real name: Clara Viola Cronk
Born: April 14, 1897   Died: 1972, from heart attack

Windsor, Marie...{26/93}
1555 Vine Street (West)
Near: TAV
Category/As: Motion Pictures as Actress
For: The Narrow Margin (1951)
Dedicated on January 19, 1983
Real name: Emily Marie Bertelson
Born: December 11, 1922 in VT

Wing, Toby...{11/09}
6561 Hollywood Boulevard (North)
Near: Hollywood Stars
Category/As: Motion Pictures as Actress
For: 42nd Street (1933)
Real name: Martha Virginia Wing
Born: July 14, 1913 in Richmond, VA
Studio: Warner Brothers

Winkler, Henry...{18/38}
6233 Hollywood Boulevard (North)
Near: Pantages Theater
Category/As: Television as Actor
For: Happy Days (1974) ABC as Arthur Fonzarelli (Fonzie)
Dedicated on March 24, 1981
Born: October 30, 1945 in New York, NY

Winninger, Charles...{15/03}
6331 Hollywood Boulevard (North)
Near: Guarantey Building
Category/As: Radio as Actor
For: Show Boat (1932-1937) ABC as Captain Henry
Real name: Karl Winninger
Born: May 26, 1884 in Athens, WI   Died: 1969

Winterhalter, Hugo...{24/99}
1600 Vine Street (East)
Near: DMV
Category/As: Recording as Conductor
For: Fandango
Real name: same or unknown

Born: August 15, 1909 in PA

Winters, Jonathan...{23/57}
6290 Hollywood Boulevard (South)
Near: Holly Vine Shoppe
Category/As: Television as Actor
For: The Wacky World of Jonathan Winters (1972)
Real name: same or unknown
Born: November 11, 1925 in Dayton, OH

Winters, Shelly...{17/40}
1750 Vine Street (East)
Near: Capitol Record Bldg
Category/As: Motion Pictures as Actress
For: The Diary of Anne Frank (1959)
Real name: Shirley Schrift
Born: August 18, 1922 in St. Louis, MO
Awards: Oscar

Wise, Robert...{28/57}
6338 Hollywood Boulevard (South)
Near: vacant
Category/As: Motion Pictures as Director
For: West Side Story (1961)
Born: September 10, 1914 in Winchester, IN

Withers, Jane...{20/64}
6125 Hollywood Boulevard (North)
Near: Pep Boys
Category/As: Motion Pictures as Actress
For: Bright Eyes (1934)
Real name: same or unknown
Born: April 12, 1926 in Atlanta, GA

Wolper, David...{25/93}
1500 Vine Street (East)
Near: Home Savings
Category/As: Television as Producer
For: Judgement (series) (1974-1975)
Born: January 11, 1928 in NY
Studio: ABC   Awards: Emmy

Wong, Anna May...{17/105}
1700 Vine Street (East)
Near: Equitible Building
Category/As: Motion Pictures as Actress
For: Portrait in Black (1960)
Real name: Wong Lui Tsong
Born: January 3, 1907 in Los Angeles, CA
Died: 1961, from heart attack and buried in Los Angeles, CA

Wood, Natale...{38/19}
7000 Hollywood Boulevard (South)
Near: Roosevelt Hotel
Category/As: Motion Pictures as Actress
For: Splendor in the Grass (1961)
Dedicated on February 1, 1987
Real name: Natasha Gurdin
Born: July 20, 1938 in San Francisco, CA
Died: November 29, 1981, from drowning and buried in Los Angeles, CA
Studio: Warner Brothers
Related to Robert Wagner (spouse)

Wood, Sam...{35/29}
6718 Hollywood Boulevard (South)
Near: international Electronic
Category/As: Motion Pictures as Director
For: Goodbye, Mr. Chips (1939)
Born: July 18, 1883 in Philadelphia, PA
Died: 1949, from heart attack and buried in Glendale, CA

Woodpecker, Woody...{38/50}
7024 Hollywood Boulevard (South)
Category/As: Motion Pictures as Animated Character
Dedicated on September 13, 1990

Woods, Donald...{23/17}
6256 Hollywood Boulevard (South)
Near: vacant lot
Category/As: Television as Actor
For: Tammy (1965)
Real name: Ralph L. Zink

Woodward, Joanne...{06/67}
6801 Hollywood Boulevard (North)
Near: vacant
Category/As: Motion Pictures as Actress
For: Three Faces of Eve (1957)
Real name: same or unknown
Born: February 27, 1930 in Thomasville, GA
Studio: Fox   Awards: Oscar
Related to Paul Newman (spouse)

Woolley, Monty...{33/02}
6542 Hollywood Boulevard (South)
Near: Consumer's Discount
Category/As: Motion Pictures as Actor
For: The Man Who Came to Dinner (1941)
Real name: Edgar Montillion Wooley
Born: August 17, 1888 in New York, NY
Died: May 6, 1963, from heart ailment
Studio: MGM

Wray, Fay...{14/54}
6349 Hollywood Boulevard (North)
Near: Hollywood Book & Poster
Category/As: Motion Pictures as Actress
For: King Kong (1933)
Real name: Vina Fay Wray
Born: September 15, 1907 in Canada

Wright, Teresa...{24/09}
1680 Vine Street (East)
Near: Taft Building
Category/As: Motion Pictures as Actor
For: Mrs. Miniver (1942)
Real name: Muriel Teresa Wright
Born: October 27, 1918 in Maplewood, NJ
Studio: RKO   Awards: Oscar

Wright, Teresa...{13/57}
6405 Hollywood Boulevard (North)
Near: Greco's Pizza
Category/As: Television as Actress

Wyatt, Jane...{29/08}
6352 Hollywood Boulevard (South)
Near: vacant
Category/As: Television as Actress
For: Father Knows Best (19__) CBS
Born: August 12, 1912

Wyler, William...{16/55}
1735 Vine Street (West)
Category/As: Motion Pictures as Director
For: Ben Hur (1959)
Real name: same or unknown
Born: July 1, 1902 in Germany   Died: 1981, and buried in Glendale, CA
Awards: Oscar

Wyman, Jane...{10/51}
6607 Hollywood Boulevard (North)
Near: vacant
Category/As: Motion Pictures as Actress
For: Johnny Belinda (1948)
Real name: Sarah Jane Fulks
Born: January 4, 1914 in St. Joseph, MO
Awards: Oscar
Related to Ronald Reagan (spouse)

Wyman, Jane...{24/66}
1628 Vine Street (East)

Near: Brown Derby ruins
Category/As: Television as Actress
For: Falcon Crest (1981)
Awards: Oscar

Wynn, Ed...{26/66}
1541 Vine Street (West)
Near: TAV Celebrity Center
Category/As: Motion Pictures as Actor
For: Mary Poppins
Real name: Isaiah Edwin Leopold
Born: November 9, 1886 in Philadelphia, PA
Died: 1966, from cancer and buried in Glendale, CA
Related to Keenan Wynn (son)

Wynn, Ed...{15/06}
6331 Hollywood Boulevard (North)
Near: Guaranty Building
Category/As: Radio as Actor
For: The Fire Chief of Texaco (1932)

Wynn, Ed...{31/45}
6426 Hollywood Boulevard (South)
Near: Hollywood Discount Center
Category/As: Television as Actor
For: The Ed Wynn Show (1949-1950) CBS

Wynn, Keenan...{26/22}
1501 Vine Street (West)
Near: Shopping Center
Category/As: Television as Actor
For: Dallas (1979)
Real name: Francis Keenan Wynn
Born: July 27, 1916 in New York, NY
Died: 1986, from cancer and buried in Glendale, CA
Related to Ed Wynn (father)

Young, Alan...{05/33}
6925 Hollywood Boulevard (North)
Near: Mann's Chinese Theater
Category/As: Radio as Actor
For: The Alan Young Show (1949) ABC
Real name: Angus Young
Born: November 19, 1919 in Great Britain

Young, Carelton...{08/19}
6733 Hollywood Boulevard (North)
Near: Artesian Patio
Category/As: Radio as Actor
For: The Adventures of Ellery Queen (1939) CBS
Real name: same or unknown
Born: May 26, 1907   Died: 1971

Young, Clara Kimball...{12/27}
6513 Hollywood Boulevard (North)
Near: Burned Out
Category/As: Motion Pictures as Actress
For: Beau Brummel (1913)
Real name: same or unknown
Born: 1891 in Chicago, IL   Died: 1960

Young, Gig...{06/06}
6845 Hollywood Boulevard (North)
Near: Starline Tours & Gifts
Category/As: Television as Actor
For: The Rogues (1964) as Tony Fleming
Real name: Byron Ellsworth Barr
Born: November 4, 1913 in St. Cloud, MN
Died: October 18, 1978, from suicide (gunshot)

Awards: Oscar
Related to Elizabeth Montogmery (spouse)

Young, Loretta...{21/17}
6100 Hollywood Boulevard (South)
Near: Chevron Gas Station
Category/As: Motion Pictures as Actress
For: The Farmer's Daughter (1947)
Real name: Gretchen Belzer
Born: January 6, 1912 in Salt Lake City, UT
Studio: 20th Century Fox   Awards: Oscar

Young, Loretta...{20/50}
Near: Mid-Town Towing
Category/As: Television as Actress
For: The Loretta Young Show (1953-1960)

Young, Robert...{05/03}
6935 Hollywood Boulevard (North)
Near: Casablanca Tours
Category/As: Motion Pictures as Actor
For: The Enchanted Cottage (1945)
Real name: same or unknown
Born: February 22, 1907 in Chicago, IL
Studio: MGM
Related to Betty Henderson (spouse)

Young, Robert...{24/69}
1616 Vine Street (East)
Near: Juice Fountain
Category/As: Radio as Actor
For: Father Knows Best (1949-1954) NBC

Young, Robert...{29/14}
6358 Hollywood Boulevard (South)
Near: Glad's Discount Mini-Mall
Category/As: Television as Actor
For: Marcus Welby (1969-1976) ABC

Young, Roland...{12/13}
6523 Hollywood Boulevard (North)
Near: Maya Shoes
Category/As: Motion Pictures as Actor
For: Topper (1937) as Cosmo Topper
Real name: same or unknown
Born: November 11, 1887 in London, England   Died: 1952

Young, Roland...{15/37}
6315 Hollywood Boulevard (North)
Near: Cave Theater
Category/As: Television as Actor
For: William and Mary (1942)

Young, Victor...{14/28}
6371 Hollywood Boulevard (North)
Near: Antenna of Hollywood
Category/As: Recording as Songwriter
For: Around the World in 80 Days (1956)
Real name: same or unknown
Born: August 8, 1900 in Chicago, IL   Died: 1956

Zabach, Florian...{32/15}
6508 Hollywood Boulevard (South)
Near: Fox Theater (closed)
Category/As: Television as Composer
For: Club Embassy (1952)
Born: August 15, 1921

Zanuck, Darryl...{28/50}
6336 Hollywood Boulevard (South)
Near: Alberts Hosery
Category/As: Motion Pictures as Producer
For: The Grapes of Wrath (1940)
Real name: Darryl F. Zanuck
Born: September 5, 1902 in Wahoo, NE
Died: 1979 and buried in Los Angeles, CA
Related to Richard D. Zanuck (son)

Zanuck, Richard D. ...{05/45}
6925 Hollywood Boulevard (North)
Near: Mann's Chinese Theater
Category/As: Motion Pictures as Executive
For: President of 20th Century Fox (1969)
Real name: same or unknown
Born: December 13, 1934
Studio: 20th Century Fox   Awards: Oscar
Related to Darryl F. Zanuck (father)

Zinnemann, Fred...{10/13}
6631 Hollywood Boulevard (North)
Near: Hollywood Book City
Category/As: Motion Pictures as Director
For: From Here to Eternity (1953)
Real name: same or unknown
Born: April 29, 1907 in Vienna, Austria
Studio: MGM   Awards: Oscar

Zukor, Adolph...{27/31}
1615 Vine Street (West)
Near: Doolittle Theater
Category/As: Motion Pictures as Executive
For: Queen Elizabeth (1912)
Born: January 7, 1873 in Ricse, Hungary   Died: 1976
Awards: Oscar

The following twenty-nine people in the new Labrea Gateway extension are included here, although not completely detailed at this time.

Pearl Bailey	7080	RE
The Beatles	7051	RE
Irving Berlin	7095	RE
Lloyd Bridges	7065	TV
Sam Cooke	7051	RE
The Dead End Kids	7080	MP
Frances Dee	7080	MP
George Fisher	7072	RA
John Garfield	7065	MP
Dan Haggerty	7070	TV
Signe Hasso	7080	MP
Jerry Herman	7095	LT
Pedro Infante	7083	RE
Katy Jurado	7065	MP
Clevon Little	7080	MP
Frankie Lymon	7083	RE
Mako	7095	MP
Spanky McFarland	7095	MP
Terry Moore	7076	MP
Paul Newman	7060	MP
The Nicholas Brothers	7083	MP
Sidney Poitier	7065	MP
Jon Provost	7080	TV
Mamie Van Doren	7057	MP
Vera-Ellen	7083	MP
Richard Webb	7059	TV
Stevie Wonder	7060	RE
Efrem Zimbalist, Jr.	7095	TV

☆ ☆ ☆ ☆ ☆ ☆ ☆ ☆ ☆ ☆ ☆ ☆ ☆ ☆ ☆ ☆ ☆ ☆ ☆

LATE ADDITIONS

Placido Domingo	RE	7000	{38/62}	Aug 30, 1993
Richard Mulligan	TV	6777	{07/xx}	Sep 30, 1993
Joel Silver	MP	6925	{05/xx}	Oct 7, 1993

☆ ☆ ☆ ☆ ☆ ☆ ☆ ☆ ☆ ☆ ☆ ☆ ☆ ☆ ☆ ☆ ☆ ☆ ☆

Order Form

Exposure Unlimited

3087 30th Street
Grandville, MI 49418
616-532-1404

☆☆

SOLD TO:

_____
_____
_____
_____

SHIP TO:

_____
_____
_____
_____

Customer ID _____
Invoice # _____
Date _____ / _____ / _____

YOUR #	OUR #	SALES REP	FOB	SHIP VIA	TERMS	TAX ID
	Book	Mail Order		UPS	CWO	None

QTY	LEVEL	ITEM ID	DESCRIPTION	RATE	T	PRICE	TOTAL
	1	WOFD	Walk of Fame Directory		CWO		
	*	FWOF	Fun with The Walk of Fame	9.95	CWO		
	*	HHO	Hollywood, A Historical Overview	19.95	CWO		
	*	BB	Beyond the Boulevard	12.95	CWO		
	*	HSH	Hollywood Studio Histories	24.95	CWO		

All orders shipped UPS Grand Rapids, MI
All orders prepaid shipping
Make checks payable to Exposure Unlimited
Sorry, No COD's
* Soon to be released. Write for details.

WOFD
Pricing Schedule:
1 = $9.95
3 = $9.35
6 = $8.50
12 = $7.95
48 = $7.50

SUBTOTAL	
TAX	N/A
SHIPPING	
MISC	
BAL DUE	

Here's your opportunity to purchase additional copies.
Great Gifts for friends, family and associates.
Orders normally shipped within seven working days.

Caution

Please be careful showing this Directory to friends, relatives and associates. Lending this book out is even more dangerous!

Everyone wants one; you may lose your only copy.

One sure fire-method to protect your valuable ***First Edition of the Hollywood Walk of Fame Directory*** is to purchase several copies as souvenirs and gifts.

Please return to the store where you got this issue and be prepared when you get home. ☆

Michael H. Kwas

Let Us Hear From You

If you are a movie or television fan, we would like to hear from you with any questions or comments (a SASE is *not* required for a reply).

As you read through this book you will notice some areas where information has been omitted. This is where the data is incomplete or unavailable at this time.

The spaces filled with "same or unknown" are also incomplete for several reasons, one of which is that the information was unable to be verified prior to publication.

Unfortunately, you will also find errors. At times, our sources may have been incorrect or early recordkeeping was sloppy at best and conflicting information is very common.

In any of the above cases, if you have documented data to offer to complete or correct these errors or omissions, please forward any information available along with your name and address to:

The Hollywood Connection
3087 - 30th Street
Grandville, MI 49418

This is a continously changing memorial to the entertainment industry, as is the industry itself, and will it be updated annually. Availability is through the **Hollywood Chamber of Commerce**, most souvenir shops in Hollywood, many major airport gift shops, the *Orchid Suites Hotel* (1753 North Orchid) , *the Hollywood Celebrity Hotel* (1775 Orchid), and assorted bookstores across America, and by Mail Order from :

Exposure Unlimited
3087 30th Street   Suite 124
Grandville, MI 49418

New information will be added with each issue so collect them in sequence for future comparisons.

There are many people who seem neglected. If you feel someone deserving of recognition has been excluded, let us know. ☆